Managing Web Usage in the Workplace: A Social, Ethical and Legal Perspective

Murugan Anandarajan
Drexel University, USA

Claire A. Simmers
St. Joseph's University, USA

IRM Press
Publisher of innovative scholarly and professional
information technology titles in the cyberage

Hershey • London • Melbourne • Singapore • Beijing

Acquisitions Editor:	Mehdi Khosrow-Pour
Managing Editor:	Jan Travers
Development Editor:	Michele Rossi
Copy Editor:	Beth Arneson
Typesetter:	LeAnn Whitcomb
Cover Design:	Tedi Wingard
Printed at:	Integrated Book Technology

Published in the United States of America by
> IRM Press (an imprint of Idea Group Inc.)
> 701 E. Chocolate Avenue, Suite 200
> Hershey PA 17033-1240
> Tel: 717-533-8845
> Fax: 717-533-8661
> E-mail: cust@idea-group.com
> Web site: http://www.idea-group.com

and in the United Kingdom by
> IRM Press (an imprint of Idea Group Inc.)
> 3 Henrietta Street
> Covent Garden
> London WC2E 8LU
> Tel: 44 20 7240 0856
> Fax: 44 20 7379 3313
> Web site: http://www.eurospan.co.uk

Library of Congress Cataloging-in-Publication Data

Managing web usage in the workplace : a social, ethical, and legal perspective / [edited by] Murugan Anandarajan, Claire Simmers.
   p. cm.
  Originally published: Hershey, PA : Idea Group Pub. : Information Science Pub., c2002.
  Includes bibliographical references and index.
  ISBN 1-931777-72-1 (paper)
   1. Business enterprises--Computer networks. 2. Computer networks--Law and legislation. 3. Electronic commerce--Management. 4. Internet industry--Management. 5. World Wide Web. I. Anandarajan, Murugan, 1961- II. Simmers, Claire, 1950-

  HD30.37 .M358 2003
  004.67'8--dc21

                                                                      2003040627

eISBN 1-59140-003-1

Previously published in a hard cover version by Idea Group Publishing.

British Cataloguing in Publication Data
A Cataloguing in Publication record for this book is available from the British Library.

New Releases from IRM Press

Managing Web Usage in the Workplace: A Social, Ethical and Legal Perspective

Table of Contents

Shane Meakim, J. D. Edwards, USA

Dedication

We dedicate this book to Magid Igbaria, our friend and mentor, who inspires us, by his example, to strive for knowledge and work ethic.

Preface

The ubiquitous nature of the Internet is dramatically revolutionizing the manner in which organizations and individuals share information. Developed out of necessity during the cold war, the Internet was created as a means to help governmental institutions and collegiate institutions send documents and research materials electronically (Williams et al., 1999). Over 30 years it has grown slowly and painstakingly; though vast quantities of information existed on this "network of networks," it was so scattered and disorganized that finding anything taxed even the most computer literate devotees. The developments that made the Internet a "25-year overnight success" were the creation of HTML (Hypertext Markup Language) and the development of server/browser software to view the interconnected documents. It is this layer of the Internet architecture, the Web, which has become synonymous with the Internet. Users access information on the Web, or "the Net," by simply pointing and clicking on key words or images linking individual or organizational home pages. New business and personal applications are being developed on a daily basis, and the number of people using the Internet ("users") is increasing exponentially with each passing day. At the end of 2000, there were an estimated 407.1 million people "surfing the Web" (Nua Internet Surveys, 2000) world wide; United States users comprised almost 153.84 million, or over 55 percent of the US population.

The Internet is having a dramatic impact on the scope of business applications and has become the foundation for the world's new information infrastructure. Technological advancements and the promise of cost reductions have set the stage for the emergence of the World Wide Web as a vehicle for electronic commerce (e-commerce). Conservative estimates forecast that Internet generated revenue will reach approximately US $300 to $360 billion by the year 2002 (Hoffman et al., 1999; Hinde, 1998). Consumers worldwide use the Web to acquire information, find and compare products, and purchase these products. The Web is a conduit for transactions between businesses and consumers as well as between businesses and other businesses. It has allowed business to compete and thrive, succeed or perish in an environment that is free of geographic limitations (Kannan et al., 1998). Ninety million people utilize it to exchange information or transact business around the world (Hof et al., 1998), linking directly to suppliers, factories, distributors, as well as customers.

The business explosion on the Net has made Internet usage a significant activity in firms and most organizations are grappling with the many complex issues triggered by this explosion (Judge, 1998; McWilliams & Stepanek, 1998). A recent survey of 300 United States corporations found that, despite recognition of the importance of the Web, the majority of companies were unclear about their Web business strategies and few companies had definitive plans for the formulation of such strategies (Melymuka, 2000). The development of business models, systems to benchmark progress, and strategic plans is critical for the success of organizations attempting to utilize the Web as an effective business tool (Jutla et al., 1999; Rao et al., 1998). Many business analysts and academics feel that this is the start of a continuing paradigm shift in the way organizations conduct business (Palmer & Griffith, 1998; Clark, 1997); the business of doing business is changed. Information intensive industries like financial services, entertainment, health care, education, and government are particularly good candidates for this business model transformation. The Internet has the potential to boost the rate of innovation by increasing the speed at which ideas spread among businesses and across countries. Worldwide business-to-business e-commerce is estimated to rise to $3.5 trillion in 2003 from just over $1 trillion in 2001 (Mandel & Hof, 2001).

The millions of businesses around the globe increasingly use the Internet as a tool for e-commerce, marketing, supply chain management, remote site connectivity, and customer support. Users are able to:

- Circulate product and company information at an increasing rate and range.
- Communicate instantly around the globe, sharing information with partners, suppliers, customers, and other stakeholders.
- Lower the costs of providing information and services.
- Leverage the power of electronic commerce and multimedia applications in the competitive marketplace.

However, the Web is more than a commercial exchange channel; it provides access to the world's biggest playground. Just as the Internet transforms business activities, it changes personal lives as it is integrated into a myriad of facets in everyday life (Cappel et al., 1996). Individual users take advantage of the many social and commercial opportunities, utilizing the Web to keep in touch via e-mail, to meet people in chat rooms, to shop online, to play games, and to find movie listings and sports scores. So why should employers be concerned about personal Web usage? Many employers are coming to the painful realization that the boundaries between personal and work Web usage are increasingly fuzzy and work time versus personal time is not as clearly delineated as it was 10 years ago. A study conducted in a manufacturing firm found that in a typical 8-hour working day, over 250,000 Internet sites were accessed by a workforce of 386 employees. Of particular concern was the discovery that approximately 90% of the accessed sites were non-work-related (LaPlante, 1997). This rapid growth and increasing importance of the Internet represents a significant development and is prompting a growing interest in understanding and managing Internet usage at work (Cronin, 1996). The cost of ignoring this phenomenon can be enormous. In addition to the problem of productivity loss, Web surfing can also clog networks, resulting in slower access for legitimate business users. Possibly even more significant, the Internet opens up companies to confidential information leaks and litigation on offensive material. Understanding and solving such problems have increasingly become a major priority for today's companies.

Many organizations attempt to address these issues through the formation of numerous guidelines and policies regarding Internet usage. A recent survey on employee misuse of the Internet at work found that over 84% of the companies surveyed had some form of Internet access policy in place (Saratoga Institute, 2000). Yet that same survey found that those policies have met with limited success in effectively managing employee Internet usage behavior: "More than 60 percent of companies have disciplined–and more than 30 percent have terminated–employees for inappropriate use of the Internet." One of the main reasons many of these policies fail to achieve their intended results is that they fail to adequately understand the nature of the problem. Akin to a doctor treating the symptoms, but not the illness itself, the majority of the companies focus only on the legal aspect of usage behaviors, and while this is a significant aspect, it is but one dimension. The social and ethical aspects of the issues surrounding the Internet are just as significant and failing to take into account the multidimensional nature of the Web reduces the effectiveness of policies. The business world is not alone in its confusion regarding the Internet. Understanding the complex variables which frame ethical business practices, consumer usage, business applications, and social dimensions of the Web, is an important issue which researchers in the field of information systems, as well as management, marketing, psychology, sociology and a host of other academic disciplines have only recently begun to address (Chatterjee & Sambammurthy, 1999).

The World Wide Web has rapidly become an integral part of society. Applications are taking years and sometimes months to develop and disseminate rather than the decades it took for other technologies in the past. To achieve 50 million users it took radio 38 years, for television 13 years and for the Internet 4 years. The accelerated pace of change means that the legal, social and ethical frameworks governing and guiding Internet usage lag behind the usage. The Web site Napster.com is a popular current example. Utilizing the Web, Napster software allowed users to download copyrighted material without charge. The Web site became as controversial as it was popular. Downloading music was acceptable socially, of questionable legality and yet it was unethical by most standards to take the "product" of an artist's labor without compensation. Yet, millions of users frequented the site. To further complicate the issue, what are the implications for organizations when the downloading from Napster occurs during work time or with company owned computers?

This example also illustrates the problem of relying strictly on governmental laws and guidelines. As is the Napster case, many times no applicable law exists. As a result of the complexity of the Web and the explosion of Web sites and commercial applications, governmental legislation and legal precedence trail behind usage. Thus, ethical guidelines and self-governance are even more important. The world is now faced with a new "cyber-frontier" which demands a similar obligation of both individuals and organizations, and furthermore the legal, ethical, and social issues of Internet usage are global issues. While early Web usage was primarily focused in the United States, it is now a worldwide phenomenon. In 2000 about 49% of the Internet population is non-English speaking; by 2003, 75% of the Web population is expected to be non-English speaking (Global Reach, 2000). In 1999, the United States accounted for 62% of worldwide e-commerce spending while, in 2003, 56% of e-commerce transactions are expected to be conducted outside of the United States ("As the Net," 2000). In terms of US dollars, global e-commerce is forecasted to be worth $6.9 trillion annually by 2004, with online buyers in North America accounting for $3.4 trillion annually (WITSA, 2000).

Openness is the most critical property of the Internet. Although Internet usage and microcomputer usage employ similar technological media (i.e., microcomputers), the pervasive nature of the Web opens up the boundaries of an organization. Microcomputer usage, on the other hand, is a more closed system, with usage usually physically and socially confined within the organization. With the Internet, information can flow more freely between the organization and the environment, thus enlarging the sets of people who interact, raising ethical questions about usage and content, and increasing organizational liability for the misuse of information. Thus, the benefits of Internet connectivity are coupled with risks.

In this volume, we have collected papers that address a variety of social, legal, and ethical issues on Internet usage worldwide. The central theme is how do organizations identify and manage a balance between the benefits and risks of the Internet across individuals, organizations, and societies. Gaining an understanding of the factors that lead to Internet usage aids in setting the boundaries of appropriate Internet behaviors. Once we increase our understanding of the consequences of Internet usage, we can be better prepared to build upon our knowledge of positive consequences and avoid negative consequences. Finally, we need to ask how systems and policies help organizations align individual usage with business priorities to manage the social, ethical, and legal aspects of the Internet, not just in the United States, but also in other parts of the world.

Section I: Antecedent Factors Leading to Individual Internet Usage

The antecedent factors leading to individual Internet usage are examined in Section I. The first chapter, *"Understanding Senior Executives' Use of Information Technology and the Internet"* by Guus Pijpers, begins from the position that senior executives have not committed themselves to information technologies, and that the management of the benefits and risks of the Internet depend, in large part, on senior management leadership. The author proposes interventions to facilitate senior executive adoption and acceptance of a new IT tool, an information system or the Internet. In chapter 2, *"Predictors of Internet Usage for Work Tasks,"* Lyndal Stiller-Hughes and Ivan Robertson discuss both person and situation factors which are associated with higher Internet usage as well as positive impact on individual work outcomes. They argue that the implementation of the Internet into the workplace is analogous to other forms of organizational change where the key component of successful change is understanding the social nature of the workplace. Chapter 3, *"Factors Influencing Web Access Behavior in the Workplace: A Structural Equation Approach"* by Murugan Anandarajan and Claire Simmers, examines the antecedent and motivational factors impacting accessing work-related Web sites and personal Web sites in the work environment. The findings indicate that perceived ethical beliefs is a key intervening variable linking antecedent variables with Web usage. In chapter 4, Uzoamaka Anakwe discusses *"Internet Usage in Sub-Saharan Africa,"* specifically citing examples from Nigeria, Ghana, and Kenya. She provides background information on Internet usage in these countries and the factors that influence Internet usage. The dominant issues relating to the role of the government and nongovernmental organizations in facilitating Internet usage in these countries are examined.

The last two papers in Section I examine how organizations manage Internet issues from external users of their systems, specifically e-commerce customers. In chapter 5, *"E-commerce System: An Examination of User Experiences of the E-commerce Site With the Standard User Interface,"* Shin-Ping Liu and Dennis Tucker investigate how an individual's perceptions of the e-commerce standard navigation system would influence the individual's decision to accept these e-commerce sites for online shopping purposes. In chapter 6, *"Factors Affecting Behavioral Intentions to Adopt Electronic Shopping on the World Wide Web: A Structural Equation Modeling Approach,"* Bay Arinze and Christopher Ruth show that factors such as perceived usefulness, intrinsic motivation and perceived information privacy play a significant role in influencing Web shoppers' behavior.

Section II: Consequences of Internet Usage

The consequences of Internet usage are the focus of the second section of this book. The first of the four chapters in this section is entitled *"Organizational Impacts and Social Shaping of Web Management Practice."* In this chapter, Kristin Eschenfelder describes the results of a multi-case study exploring the problems of post-implementation management of Web information systems. The author argues that organizations must identify parties responsible for the maintenance of content and provide incentives to them for maintaining Web systems. Chapter 8, entitled *"Internet Gambling in the Workplace,"* by Mark Griffiths outlines the major issues surrounding gambling in the workplace (including types of gambling at work and implications for employers) before going on to examine the issues raised by how the Internet facilitates gambling. In chapter 9, *"Internet User Satisfaction, Job Satisfaction, and Internet Background: An Exploratory Study,"* Claire Simmers and Murugan Anandarajan examine the relationship among Internet user satisfaction, job satisfaction, and users' Internet background. They report that Internet user satisfaction and job satisfaction are positively related and that self-training is a key variable in both user satisfaction and job satisfaction. Chapter 10, *"The Measurement of Telecommuting Performance"* by Magid Igbaria, Patrick Devine and Eunyoung Cheon, presents a new approach to measuring telecommuting activities.

Section III: Development of Internet and System Policies

Section III is concerned with the development of Internet and system policies. The first chapter in this section, *"Classifying Web Usage Behavior in the Workplace: An Artificial Neural Network Approach"* by Murugan Anandarajan, proposes the use of a behavior-based AI system to classify employee Web usage behavior. Two artificial neural networks incorporating genetic algorithm techniques are developed. The output of this intelligent system can be extremely beneficial to managers in designing effective Internet security programs. In chapter 12, *"Managing Large Modules–E-mail or Web Sites,"* Elayne Coakes and Dianne Willis address issues concerning the suitability of particular media as mass communication tools in a higher education setting in the United Kingdom. It looks first at the use of e-mail as a communication method for managing two large modules. The paper then goes on to examine the use of a Web site to provide a mass communication method more suited to the needs of both the staff and the students. In chapter 13, *"Managing E-business: Security Issues and Solutions,"* authors Keng Siau and Shane Meakim investigate the need for information security and privacy and the role that organizations have in managing the legal risks through security measures such as PKI and passwords. In chapter 14, *"Reducing Legal, Financial, and Operational Risks,"* Claire Simmers and Adam Bosnian explore how Web and e-mail usage can be aligned with business priorities by Internet policy management which integrates an enterprise-wide written Internet/E-mail usage policy, filtering/monitoring software, and enforcement. This is followed by chapter 15, *"Universal Site Accessibility: Barrier Free For All"* by Beth Archibald Tang, who discusses the importance of educating Web designers about the different regulations and industry standards, as well as helping Web designers understand how accessibility translates into good business, such as improved communication with clients and customers. In chapter 16, *"An Accounting Framework for Identifying Internet Abuse"* Asokan Anandarajan proposes the use of an activity-based costing system for budgeting the costs associated with Internet usage. The costs thus budgeted can then be compared to actual costs to arrive at a variance for better control policies.

The last two chapters focus on sociotechnical systems issues. In Chapter 17, *"Web Management and Usage: A Critical Social Perspective,"* Steve Clarke critically reviews both technology-based and human-centered approaches to information systems, followed by an examination of the Internet from a social theoretical perspective. He concludes that Web management should be examined within a social framework. In chapter 18, entitled *"Fuzzy Boundaries, Strange Negotiations: Problems of Space, Place and Identity in Cyberspace,"* Andrew Wenn raises our awareness of how technology and humans interact and how the richness and complexity of social interactions are enhanced in e-mail usage.

References

Anonymous, As the net goes global, U.S. e-commerce dominance slips. (2000). *CTO FirstMover*, September, S16-S17.

Cappel, J. and Myerscough, M. (1996). World Wide Web uses for electronic commerce: Toward a classification scheme. Paper presented at the *Association for Information Systems 1996 Americas Conference*, Pheonix, Arizona.

Chatterjee, D. and Sambammurthy, V. (1999). Business implications of Web technology: An insight into usage of the World Wide Web by US companies. *Electronic Markets*, 9, (2).

Clark, B. (1997). Welcome to my parlor...market. *Manage*, Winter, 11-25.

Global Reach. (2000). *Global Internet Statistics* (by Language). Available on the World Wide Web at: http://www.glreach.com/globstats. Accessed May 5, 2001.

Hinde, S. (1998). Privacy and security–The drivers for growth in e-commerce. *Computers and Security*, 17, 475-478.

Hoffman, D., Novak, T. and Peralta, M. (1999). Building consumer trust online. *Communications of the ACM*, April, 42(4), 80-85.

Internet Usage Statistics. (2000). *NUA Internet Surveys*, November. Available on the World Wide Web at: http://www.nua.net/surveys.

Jutla, D., Bodorik, P. and Wang, Y. (1999). Developing Internet e-commerce benchmarks. *Information Systems*, 24(6), 475-493.

Kannan, P., Chang, A. and Whinston, A. (1998). Marketing information on the I-Way. *Communications of the ACM*, March, 4(13), 35-43.

Melymuka, K. (2000). Survey finds companies lack e-commerce blueprint. *ComputerWorld*, April 17, 38.

Nua Internet Services. (2000). *Internet Usage Statistics* November. Available on the World Wide Web at: http://www.nua.net/surveys.

Palmer, J. and Griffith, D. (1998). An emerging model of Web site design for marketing. *Communications of the ACM*, March, 41(3), 45-51.

Rao, H., Salam, A. and DosSantos, B. (1998). Marketing and the Internet. *Communications of the ACM*, March, 41(3), 32-34.

Saratoga Institute. (2000). *Survey on Internet Misuse in the Workplace*, January 11. David Greenfield.

Williams, B., Sawyer, S. and Hutchinson, S. (1999). *Using Information Technology*, Third Edition. Richard D. Irwin, Inc., 307-353.

World Information Technology and Services Alliance–International Survey of e-Commerce. (2000). *How Ready are World Markets for Electronic Commerce?* Available on the World Wide Web at: http://www.witsa.org/paper/ EcomSurv.pdf/. Accessed May 5, 2000.

SECTION I:
Antecedent Factors Leading to Individual Internet Usage

Chapter I

Understanding Senior Executives' Use of Information Technology and the Internet

Guus G. M. Pijpers
Philips Electronics, The Netherlands

The Internet and information technology (IT) have received considerable attention from senior executives, yet they still have not committed themselves fully to these technologies. Consequently, they are not reaping the full benefits. Recent studies investigated the factors that influence senior executives' use of IT and the Internet. Surprisingly, only a few factors had a significant influence on usage, directly or indirectly. A better understanding of these factors can facilitate the design of interventions that address the adoption and acceptance of a new IT tool, an information system or the Internet. This chapter proposes a limited number of interventions aimed at improving usage. The Internet will change the way information is being gathered, evaluated, and communicated. This also applies for senior executives and their main constituencies. Now is the time for senior executives to hone their Internet skills so that they can receive the right information in the right way, leading to enhanced decision-making.

INTRODUCTION

Senior executives are constantly being told that information technology is the key to the success of the business, yet the so-called IT productivity paradox leads managers to believe that investments in IT are reaching unprecedented levels with no commensurate increase in productivity. However, to measure whether investments in any technology deliver value, we must assume the technology is being adopted and used. Furthermore, few organizations derive full value from their IT investments, either because people have not learned how to use technology well enough or because managers have not yet learned how to manage its benefits (Orlikowski, 2000). One reason for the poor return on IT investments in the perception of the senior executive could be their lack of personal involvement and low level of use of IT and its applications. A number of senior executives still have not committed themselves to IT and consequently have not been able to experience the benefits at first hand. As a result their attitudes and behavior remain unchanged.

One might argue that senior executives need not to be involved with IT use in an organization, but rather with its deployment. Others consistently advocate that the use of the technology rather than technology itself should be evaluated, and innovative use of IT should be rewarded (Orlikowski, 2000). It could be argued that senior executives do not warrant special attention when investigating the acceptance and use of IT, especially because they form only a small percentage of the total user population. However, recent studies showed these individuals should be treated differently (Ghorab, 1997; Igbaria & Iivari, 1995; Seeley and Targett, 1999). Most notably their willingness to adopt and use IT, their role model, the confidentiality and integrity of their information, and their external orientation differentiate their work and, hence, the IT tools for their tasks.

The few research projects targeting senior executives reported that the main obstacle to executives using IT was the lack of IT literacy. Other arguments mentioned were that executives felt intimidated by the computer—that it would require too much time for them to learn and that they would be embarrassed about taking courses to attain IT literacy. Many senior executives argue that the real reason they do not use IT is that they do not see a connection between what IT does and their tasks as executives. The same reasoning might be valid for using the Internet for their daily work, although compelling evidence is not yet available. Most senior executives, now in their late 40s or 50s, had scant if any contact with IT during their college years. At the same time, during their careers they have attained positions with no involvement or experience of IT.

Recent developments in managerial IT tools (e.g., balanced scorecards, management cockpits, Internet-based business intelligence systems) put senior executives more in the driver's seat with respect to business information and the business environment. Peers and subordinates both inside and outside the company are doing so too because information gathering, processing and dissemination turning more readily to IT with tools based on Internet technologies. To communicate and to inform and be informed are key activities of senior executives, for which these new Web-based tools are very much suited. Moreover, compared to most existing management information systems which are considered closed, the Internet is an open system using commonly accepted standards to connect individuals and organizations worldwide to one another. The rapid penetration of the Internet both in companies and in home life gives promising ground for organizations to develop new business and products. However, to make effective use of the Internet, senior executives must accept it, learn how to interact directly with aspects of the hardware and software, and adapt the Internet and corresponding tools to their task requirements.

From the above we can see that the perceptions and attitudes of senior executives influence their behavior regarding the use of information technology, including the Internet. Senior executives might have not used this new technology because it has not provided the information they need for their own tasks, as is the case until now with many IT tools specifically aimed at the senior executive level. Therefore, it is important to understand the factors affecting both IT and Internet acceptance and use by senior executives. If usage is to improve, first and foremost the factors actually influencing the acceptance of IT in general and the Internet in particular must be identified. Next, it would enable responsible management to design organizational interventions that would increase user acceptance and usage of new and existing systems, including the Internet. As a result, senior executives will have access to better information leading in turn to more effective decision-making in their jobs. Moreover, individual and organizational performance would improve, leading to a more competitive position in today's global economy.

This chapter will answer the following practical question:

What are the major factors influencing senior executives' use of IT and in particular the Internet?

Building upon existing research (Pijpers, 2001) and the few studies to date that address the behavioral and attitudinal factors influencing Internet usage (e.g., Anandarajan et al., 2000; Chuan-Chuan Lin & Lu, 2000; Chueng et al., 2000; Lederer et al., 2000; Moon & Kim, 2001; Teo et al., 1998; Teo et al., 1999) this chapter will, in addition to the above question, investigate from a theoretical and practical point of view:

- whether senior executives are a very diverse group and whether they are significantly different from other Internet users;
- which factors influence use;
- which organizational and individual interventions would enable the key determinants of Internet usage to be manipulated.

The level of analysis is at the individual level, i.e., the senior executive. While the term senior executive is not unambiguously described in literature, for this chapter a senior executive is defined as "an executive who is concerned with the strategic direction of their organization's business" (Seeley & Targett, 1997) and:

- is in a position to influence significantly the strategic decision-making processes;
- has substantial control and authority over how resources are deployed;
- is in a position to influence the strategic direction of the business;
- may have other senior managers reporting to him or her.

This is in line with Fisher's (1995) definition of a senior executive: those people who are only three hierarchical steps removed from the post of chief executive officer on the organizational chart.

Finally, it should be born in mind that all study findings described here assume that the IT tool or the Internet is being used by the subjects under review. Yet the possible interventions given at the end of the chapter will most likely also apply to reluctant or anxious senior executives, who have not yet experienced the huge amount of information on literally any subject readily available on the Internet.

The remainder of this chapter is organized as follows. The next section begins with the term senior executive, followed by a discussion of the managerial IT tools used to date. The next section introduces the factors influencing use, as they were found in previous studies. The organizational and individual interventions aimed at improving usage are described in the next section. The peers of the senior executive are also reviewed before the future of IT and the Internet for senior executives is discussed. Also, a discussion of the potential avenues of future research is given. Finally, the chapter ends with some thoughts about the use of information, information technology, and the Internet.

SENIOR EXECUTIVES

The primary task of senior executives is to manage and control their business. As Mintzberg (1994) indicates,

"In almost every serious study of managerial work the formal information–in other words, information capable of being processed in a computer–does not play a dominant role. Oral information–much of it too early or too 'soft' to formalize, such as gossip and hearsay–and even nonverbal information forms a critical part of every serious managerial job."

Davenport (1994) argues as one of his "information facts of life" that "managers prefer to get information from people rather than computers; people add value to raw information by interpreting it and adding context". A recent study of Kotter (1999) confirmed that general managers spend most of their time with others in short, disjointed conversations, skillfully asking a lot of questions.

There is a continuing trend in organizations away from hierarchical, command-and-control structures toward networks of empowered, autonomous teams working around the globe. People are working from their home, cars, and offices, leading to the emergence of virtual offices and a highly mobile workforce. Thus, managers are faced with the dilemma of managing people who work outside the local sphere of control, while at the same time managing productivity improvements. Physical resources and processes are no longer managed directly by managers but indirectly with information representing these processes, activities, and resources. And the larger the business unit that a manager oversees, the more dependent he becomes on information to manage. Finally, human communication and collaborative activities require that employees and managers operate remotely using state-of-the-art information technology. A decade ago, PCs were sufficient for the manager's task, as they were usually confined within the organization.

This closed system changed with the introduction of an executive information system (EIS), because these systems are able to provide information on the organization's environment. The EIS, a dedicated system supporting tasks, was introduced to senior executives at the beginning of the '80s. An EIS is a computer-based information system designed to provide senior executives and, in many cases, middle- and lower-level managers access to information relevant to their management activities (Leidner et al., 1999). It might be argued that other IT tools or managerial tools with an IT component will increasingly win favor among senior management. A stand-alone EIS is rare nowadays but it forms part of integrated application software aimed at business and information functions in the organization. Furthermore, the proliferation of the Internet intensifies IT acceptance and usage issues for organizations and end users by creating an interactive, open system with direct contact between organizations and their constituencies.

SENIOR EXECUTIVES AND INFORMATION TECHNOLOGY TOOLS

The value of information technology for senior executives often depends on the perspective taken by academics and practitioners alike. On the one hand, many researchers argue that senior executives will become active users of IT and the ubiquitous Internet (e.g., Applegate et al., 1996), whereas others posit, that due to the nature of the executives' tasks use of IT will remain limited (e.g., Mintzberg, 1994). Senior executives have little time to play around with new technologies because time is probably their most precious resource. There appears to be a reluctance by senior executives to use the Internet. The ingenuity of some senior executives in not using any information technology demonstrates their mastery in dealing with problems. However, even when a senior executive is not required to use a given technology for his information needs, it is intuitively interesting to observe his or her perceptions on the technology in question. Furthermore, in the near future every senior executive will use IT tools without the luxury of dedicated staff to answer all his questions. These managerial IT tools will then be used in a more mandatory way because it will be the only source of information and method of communication for the senior executive. Moreover, developments in technologies like the Internet and PC office packages appear to imply that certain information can only be unlocked using this technology. It is highly likely that the Internet will play a major role in both the technologies used as well as the philosophy of sharing information within the organization and between the organization and its stakeholders.

As various researchers found, senior executives constitute a separate category in IT acceptance and use (Boone, 1993; Holtham & Murphy, 1994; Kanter, 1995; Nord & Nord, 1995; O'Brien & Wilde, 1996; Pijpers, 2001; Seeley & Targett, 1997, 1999). The question arises as to whether the findings of these studies generally apply to the World Wide Web and Internet, because the studies were not aimed at this technology. To my knowledge, no previous study to date has exclusively targeted the combination of senior executives and their usage of the Internet. Although compelling evidence other than obtained from the studies mentioned and studies aimed at the use of the Internet in general is not available, it is assumed that the attitude and behavior of senior executives regarding the Internet is similar to any other IT tool. This does not mean that there are no differences in the way senior executives use the Internet compared to other users, or that their systems based on Internet technologies are not different compared to end-user systems, on the contrary.

Regarding using information technology and the Internet, senior executives differ in a number of ways with respect to other people in an organization. First, they are appointed for their vision, style, and personality and hence are unlikely to be highly influenced by peers or subordinates. Any mandate imposed on them about using IT for their job is doomed to fail. Second, once they use an information system or IT tool, it is likely that the influence of peers and superiors will diminish to nonsignificance over time with increasing experience. Finally, it is also highly likely that senior executives are not required by superiors or subordinates to use IT and are obliged to decide themselves how they will use IT. The effect of social environment on senior executive perceptions and use of IT is therefore very low. As a result, there need to be other incentives for the senior executive to start using IT and the Internet to its full extent.

The majority of studies of senior executives focus on their use of systems dedicated for their tasks, mainly to provide them support for their decision roles. These roles are, however, only a subset of all the tasks and responsibilities a senior executive has to perform. These responsibilities can be divided in two groups, each supported by different methods and procedures. First, most senior executives have staff that helps them in day-to-day operations. Apart from secretarial employees, specialists in finance, legislation, or other areas are available. All these employees normally have dedicated systems to support their work, e.g., financial systems or customer database systems. Second, some senior executive tasks are well supported by generic tools, such as word processing packages, e-mail systems, and spreadsheet software. Most organizations set one standard for the whole company so as to make communication and exchange of information as easy as possible.

These generic systems do not warrant special attention for senior executives, although implementation and actual use of these systems is much harder to accomplish for this user population. The often-referred notion that executives attempt to hide their basic computer illiteracy by claiming they do not have the skills to learn all new IT applications no longer rings true in the light of the adequacy of the readily available, easy-to-use tools and the supporting organization nowadays. Nor does the dedicated staff of the senior executive require special attention, because part of their work is adopting and using information systems and applications to do their job. These users typically have a very low learning curve with respect to new technologies, mainly because they are intrinsically rewarded by using new applications to obtain the information they need. The Internet has put them more in control, and sometimes in command, of new developments within their departments.

Many new IT tools for the senior executive, many of which are successors to EIS software, are rapidly being developed. Most of the new software uses a Web interface as well as an interface design closely resembling the way executives work (e.g., cockpit-like arrangements of instrument panels and displays with information on the senior executive's PC screens). Internally, however, these systems still have the four key aspects of the "old" executive information system functionality, identified by among others Bajwa et al. (1998): (1) communication, (2) coordination, (3) control, and (4) planning. New systems such as business intelligence systems, data warehousing, and so on, build upon the EIS concept. The main difference with the older managerial IT systems is that new software often targets middle and lower management levels of an organization. With the decentralization and empowering trend in most organizations this scarcely comes as a surprise.

As mentioned, a number of studies investigating the acceptance factors for Internet usage are available. They do not specifically target senior executives, which is unsurprising given the fact that they were not among the first to embrace Internet. Moreover, senior executives often view the Internet as a source of entertainment rather that directly related to work (Teo et al., 1999), although this view is changing rapidly as e-business initiatives multiply. However, in the area of executive information systems, robust findings regarding senior executives' use are available to be applied and translated to the Internet environment. The next section describes these findings that are then put in perspective with regard to Internet use by the senior executive and his peers.

FACTORS INFLUENCING SENIOR EXECUTIVES' USE

Recent research (Pijpers, 2001) indicates that we are gaining an understanding of the key factors and relationships likely to influence IT use by senior executives. Pijpers used a well-established model of IT usage behavior, the technology acceptance model (TAM; Davis, 1989; Davis et al., 1989).

However, most TAM-based research to date has primarily focused on the core model instead of the key external factors directly and indirectly affecting the intermediate and dependent variables. These external variables represent the levers through which desired actions may be exercised. Building upon TAM, a theoretical research model was developed to investigate a large number of external factors that are possible antecedents of managerial beliefs, attitude, and use of IT.

A cross-sectional field survey was conducted to investigate the theoretical research model. Structural equation modeling (Hair et al., 1998) was used to analyze questionnaire data from 87 senior executives drawn from 21 different multinational, European-based companies. The results showed significant support for external factors, mostly of an individual nature, in the categories demographics, managerial and IT knowledge, personality of the manager, company characteristics, and characteristics of the IT resource. The study of Pijpers (2001) has corroborated the core TAM model as a foundation for understanding managerial usage behavior with IT, although beliefs and attitude do not fully mediate the influence of the external factors. This study further presents empirical evidence to suggest a limited number of antecedents, under managerial control influencing beliefs, attitude, and use. A better understanding of the various factors that may impede or increase effective utilization of IT can facilitate the design of organizational or managerial interventions that address these issues. The next sections will elaborate in detail on these findings. Where applicable, the impact of the key factors and relationships related to Internet usage by senior executives will be highlighted.

Although one might expect a number of organizational and environmental factors, such as IT maturity, task characteristics, or competitor behavior, to influence use of IT and the Internet, Pijpers' study demonstrated that they have no significance for this particular user group. Compared to studies investigating factors that significantly impact the use of the Web or the Internet, factors such as information quality, response time, and cognitive absorption (Agarwal & Karahanna, 2000; Chuan-Chuan Lin & Lu, 2000) are not relevant with respect to senior executives' acceptance. The main reason is the lack of compelling evidence in literature to date. As was found in Pijpers' study (2001), three categories of factors and relationships can be identified influencing beliefs about IT and the Internet.

The first category consists of the factors accessibility and implementation process, which are in fact prerequisites for effective use of an IT tool. Accessibility is understood to mean access to a PC with an the Internet connection, and indicates in this respect that user beliefs about Internet are influenced. The implementation process refers to the strategy used to effectively incorporate the information system in the activities of the senior executive. The presence of a senior executive as sponsor also acts as a tremendous boost and encourages the use of an IT tool, whether it is a dedicated system, a generic application, or tools like the Internet. It may be concluded that senior executives' involvement in the implementation of IT is necessary but not sufficient by itself to secure full use of all the capabilities of the IT tool. To rephrase it regarding the Internet, if tools are created to provide information to senior executives using Web-based technologies, these executives should be involved in both development as well as final implementation phase. Otherwise, if they are imposed it is highly unlikely that these systems will be optimally used.

In conclusion, senior executives (1) need to have physical access to the Internet or to any system that they are supposed to use and (2) should be actively involved in the development and implementation phases of dedicated Web-based systems.

The second category consists of four uncontrollable factors--age, education, professional experience, and cognitive style. Uncontrollable means that they cannot be easily manipulated; age or professional managerial experience are good examples. Cognitive style is innate and therefore hard to influence, whereas education is completed long before the senior executive has achieved his present position.

Age is an interesting factor because it has a strong negative effect on technology beliefs. This means that younger executives perceive an IT tool to be more useful and easier to use in their work environments than older counterparts. In light of the fact that the average senior executive received no IT training at school, bringing senior management up to scratch on IT use is a prerequisite to breaking the circle of computer anxiety. Learning IT skills is not just something younger executives do; it is simply that older managers generally have limited or no opportunity to gain from their investment in learning new technologies and skills. However, executives often have a long enough career in front of them before retirement to be able to reap the benefits of their new skills. The above suggests that older senior executives have less positive technology beliefs and need more time to familiarize themselves with its information potential.

The educational level of senior executives is directly and positively linked to technology beliefs and use, suggesting that level of education is a good indicator of a manager's ability to learn new information technologies. One might conclude that better educated persons develop positive opinions about IT and its use and have a greater ability to learn in a novel situation. The length of tenure in a managerial position, i.e., professional experience, is positively related to technology beliefs but negatively to IT use. This suggests that experienced managers see the benefits of IT and, hence, the Internet, although they clearly do not make use of those benefits.

Cognitive style can be noted as the characteristic processes individuals exhibit in the acquisition, analysis, evaluation, and interpretation of data used in decision-making (Igbaria and Parasuraman, 1989). Findings show that senior executives who are more analytical, rational, and sequential have a more positive attitude towards technology than other executives do. However, some studies suggest that an analytical/directive style may be incompatible with the demands of many top executives (Elam & Leidner, 1995). As regards the Internet that has a long technical history, analytically adept senior executives are likely to have favorable attitudes toward the Internet.

In conclusion, older senior executives need more time to gain knowledge concerning IT and the Internet. Better-educated senior executives are more suited to deal with new technologies such as the Internet. Senior executives with greater managerial experience also think positively about technology, including the Internet, but do not act accordingly. Analytically oriented executives hold favorable attitudes toward technology, resulting in extended use.

Finally, the third category of factors influencing IT use consists of three controllable factors: computer self-efficacy, perceived fun/enjoyment, and organizational support. Controllable factors means that one can influence or even manipulate factors as part of a goal or objective to improve knowledge, change perceptions or increase use.

Computer self-efficacy is defined as the individual's perception of his or her ability to use computers in the accomplishment of a task. It is not concerned with what an individual has accomplished in the past, but rather with judgments of what could be achieved in the future. Nor is it concerned with simple skills, but with judgments of the ability to apply those skills to broader tasks (Compeau & Higgins, 1995). Because successful and increased use and, as a result, improved performance are often the objectives of all IT tools, one should concentrate on users who are confident of their ability to use computers, information technology, or Internet. Computer self-efficacy is the determined to have a positive relationship with technology beliefs.

Perceived fun/enjoyment refers to the extent to which the activity of using the computer is perceived to be enjoyable in its own right. When senior executives have great fun using a system, they like both the ease of use and the utility of the system. Perceived fun/enjoyment positively influences beliefs and attitude about the technology as well as actual usage. Therefore, this factor plays a pivotal role in the adoption and use of any information technology, whether it is an IT tool, information system, or the Internet. A number of studies have found that perceived fun or equivalent factors such as perceived playfulness, perceived enjoyment, or playfulness influence Internet usage (Atkinson and Kydd, 1997; Moon and Kim, 2001; Teo et al., 1999) and are important in predicting and explaining Internet usage. All the studies, however, did not distinguish between user populations, while some investigated only students.

Organizational support consists of both technical support and management support. Technical support is defined as the availability of development, assistance, and specialized instruction, guidance, coaching, and consultation in using microcomputer applications, whereas management support means management encouragement and sufficient allocation of resources. In the context of technology acceptance and usage in the workplace, evidence indicates that providing support staff is a key organizational response to help senior executives overcome barriers and hurdles to technology use. Recent research on the antecedents of Internet usage confirmed the importance of supporting mechanisms (Anandarajan et al., 2000; Cheung et al., 2000). Organizational support is able to ensure sufficient resource allocations and act as change agents to create a more conducive environment for information system success. Organizational support directly affects actual use. Several researchers (e.g., Kanter, 1995) have consistently advocated that most people need proper support: a qualified adviser–a mentor, friend, spouse, or peer. One could argue that support is only helpful during initial usage of the technology and its importance declines with continued use. However, as practice shows, new releases of software packages or new ways of using existing software tools make it necessary to have help at first hand to ensure the best use of IT.

In conclusion, the role of the three controllable factors is important because they are the only ways to manipulate effective use of an IT tool. Three controllable factors--two individual ones, computer self-efficacy and perceived fun/enjoyment, and one organizational factor, organizational support--have an indirect or direct effect on technology use. Controllable means one can intervene with appropriate measures to steer use in the desired direction. The next section elaborates on the practical application that gives guidance when organizations want to influence or improve senior executives' use of IT, including the Internet.

ORGANIZATIONAL AND INDIVIDUAL INTERVENTIONS

The Internet is increasingly permeating all aspects of organizational life and individual executives from a wide variety of backgrounds, with different experiences and personalities, need to use these technologies for organizational work. This leads to a number of implications: (1) responsible management can provide appropriate training and other situational experiences or they can specifically target individuals for IT implementation through recruitment, development, and selection, and (2) management can proactively influence beliefs, attitude, and use through appropriate actions on the external factors that directly or indirectly impact IT use. In both cases interventions can substantially influence use of information technologies. This in turn will lead to better information, improved decision-making, greater worker productivity, or other benefits. Although a great deal more can be said about the relationship between more and longer use compared to effective use, the following sections assume that IT tools, including the Internet, that are better utilized will result in efficiency and effectiveness gains.

As was found and explained in the previous sections, three controllable factors can be manipulated. However, they differ in the way they affect the use of IT and the Internet. First, organizational support is under the full control of the company in that as a rule more support yields more and better use. This means that qualified IT personnel are available to the end user so that problems can be resolved by providing relatively easy access to expertise. Furthermore, top management proactively encourages IT use and allocates sufficient resources for the support function.

Second, perceived fun/enjoyment is an interesting construct as it theoretically represents an intrinsic motivator for system use or, as Webster and Martocchio (1992) contend, a motivational characteristic of individuals (the trait of perceived fun/enjoyment). These traits can be situation-specific or general thus the individual may perceive that it is fun to work with a specific IT tool, e.g., the Internet or the World Wide Web, or may enjoy interacting with computers. As a result, it is important to understand that senior executives have different individual attitudes towards perceived fun/enjoyment, yet it is assumed that overall attitudes to IT are more relevant than any liking for a specific computer system. As demonstrated by Davis et al. (1992), if potential users perceive IT usage as intrinsically increasing their utilities (e.g., if such usage provides them enjoyment or social status among their peers), they will be motivated to use it appropriately.

Third, computer self-efficacy has been treated as a unidimensional construct in literature, although recently Marakas et al. (1998) argued that insufficient attention has been paid to the multileveled, multifaceted nature of the computer self-efficacy construct. An important finding in their study highlights the difference between general and task-specific levels of computer self-efficacy. Task-specific computer self-efficacy refers to an individual's perception of efficacy in performing specific computer-related tasks within the domain of general computing, whereas general computer self-efficacy refers to an individual's judgment of efficacy across multiple computer application domains (Marakas et al., 1998). When it comes to the Internet, an individual's perception or ability to use it refers to their general computer self-efficacy. It is important to understand that executives do not acquire computer self-efficacy overnight, but need to develop IT skills and perception continuously.

In sum, of the three factors influencing use, organizational support is the easiest to effect, whereas computer self-efficacy requires continuous attention by top management before uneasy and ambivalent opinions about IT change for the better. A few potential interventions will be described in the next section. These merely serve as a starting point, yet at the same time highlight the importance of the interventions.

Organizational support has a direct effect on usage and is the easiest to effect. Moreover, support employees can indeed help increase computer self-efficacy among senior executives by explaining and demonstrating the fun element of IT tools. Support staff should focus on encouraging anxious individuals to use IT. The reverse training mechanism, whereby young knowledge workers in effect train senior, usually older, colleagues is a good example of an organizational support intervention. This solution helps executives overcome barriers and hurdles to IT use. Some organizations employ a reverse mentoring approach, similar to the qualified adviser mentioned earlier with one-to-one sessions. It should be intensely personal and the advisers should be preferably company insiders. Rogers (1995) argues that managers learn best from peers, who act as change agents. These interventions can also deal with the limited time most senior executives have available and, at the same time, the speed and capacity with which they familiarize themselves with new ideas or situations. Of course, the reverse training and the reverse mentoring approaches must fit the corporate culture and organizational structure (Coutu, 2000).

Apart from providing staff, special attention could be given to the fun factor of IT and the Internet. For this intervention, the Internet and its huge amount of fun information is a good starting point. By combining this with business information, e.g., daily or weekly e-mail newsletters with interesting links, the role of IT in the specific area of the senior executive could be given the right focus. Another intervention method is to give various managerial levels access to the latest real-time business information through the company's intranet via an easy to use Web-based interface.

Recent developments in business intelligence can provide senior executives with information and IT tools to satisfy their information needs for decision-making.

A final intervention is aimed at the perception level of senior executives who are increasingly concerned about understanding the value of information and information technology. To change their mind-sets they need to improve their self-confidence and IT literacy before they positively embrace IT. Venkatesh and Davis (1996) have already noted that millions of dollars have been wasted on systems that are rejected, often attributed to usability issues, while a key part of the problem could well be the users, who do not possess a good, positive computer self-efficacy belief. It should be kept in mind that computer self-efficacy is not about basic IT tasks, but refers to the ability to apply IT skills to broader tasks (Compeau & Higgins, 1995). To reinforce computer self-efficacy, Torkzadeh et al. (1999) emphasized the importance of continuous improvement programs so that executives do not fall so far behind they cannot catch up. Measures to improve senior executives' self-efficacy would be instrumental in this respect, e.g., top management could urge every senior executive to use available information systems, promulgating they support its use with enough resources in time, money, and personnel. Marakas et al. (1998) argue that any manipulation or intervention aimed at changing computer self-efficacy should be directed at changes within the person rather than between persons, as a number of other factors also influence the degree of change in computer self-efficacy, e.g., level effects, variability, and controllability.

To summarize, many senior executives are subject to time and interest constraints when it comes to using IT tools and the Internet. Having to perform a series of keystrokes to receive information they need is often regarded as a task they would prefer to do without. However, once familiar with the practicalities of a particular IT tool, they rarely question whether the task involved is being done effectively. A periodical review of how management uses IT for their information needs would appear to be a useful way of gauging whether executives are conversant and comfortable with IT.

PEERS OF THE SENIOR EXECUTIVE

The question arises as to whether literate senior executives will and do proactively influence their environment. According to the social exchange Theory (SET), Kelley and Thibaut (1978) argue that human behavior is the product of a rational cost-benefit analysis. When confronted with a behavior-related decision, individuals assess the various costs and benefits associated with different possible courses of action and then choose the most beneficial behavior based on expected costs and individual outcomes. With respect to the Internet, senior executives will act only when they perceive the expected rewards, e.g., increased and better information for their decision-making, are greater than the costs of action, e.g., putting valuable time into learning about the Internet and its practical applications. SET asserts that in a typical social exchange each party decides on a course of action based on expected benefits. As a prerequisite, there should be a willingness to invest in the relationships that underpin the social exchange. This is precisely the main goal of the reverse mentoring approach described earlier. Both individuals, who preferably have no hierarchical relationship, will influence the cost-reward outcome of the other. There will be increased rewards once both individuals recognize they can learn and benefit from one another, either by gaining insight into the executive's working area or the nice things you can do with the information technology and the Internet.

WILL THE FUTURE BE BETTER TOMORROW?

Senior executives need to muster the courage to face the reality that they will not have access to the information they need to complete managerial tasks unless they use IT and the Internet properly. Moreover, senior executives' attitudes toward information and information technology are still seen as the barometer of the company's information culture. Senior executives do not have to be IT-literate or IT-experienced, but IT-oriented and IT-savvy. They have to be conversant and comfortable with IT (Earl & Feeney, 2000). New tools based on Internet technologies are used to access information the senior executive needs to know how to use. His mind-set, behaviors, and practices regarding information technology can lead to increased credibility among his staff (Marchand, 2000). In addition to investing in and deploying IT, the senior executive must also encourage employees to embrace the right behaviors and values for working with information (Marchand et al., 2000). The behavior of senior executives sends strong messages to the rest of the organization and creates the culture of what constitutes acceptable behavior, whether dealing with either IT or other areas. So if they believe in using IT and the Internet, they should practice what they preach. If top executives do not embrace the Internet, how can they expect other people to embrace it?

What is particularly interesting about the way senior executives use IT is that they are indifferent to the fact they are using a computer as long as they receive the information they want. Executives want to accomplish something, do something meaningful. Irrespective of whether it is a car navigation system, CD player, or microwave oven, the computer inside need not to be seen. The computer disappears into the tool, serving valuable functions but remaining invisible, although it does not hurt for executives to understand IT. And computers ought to be invisible, automatic, and useful–not just in the car, but in the home, at schools and in the office (Norman, 1993, 2000). But the more the computer or IT tool is invisible for the executive, the more he will question the quality of the information received. As a result, executives are beginning to understand what the real added value of IT is: delivering the right information with the right information technology in the right way so he can make better decisions.

Several avenues for future research emerge in this area. First, an avenue worth investigation is social pressure, the influence of peers in the IT acceptance process. Several recent studies showed the importance of the social environment in the Internet environment (Anandarajan et al., 2000; Cheung et al., 2000). Marginson et al. (2000) also confirmed the importance of the executive's social environment. Social pressure, an indicator of the influence of the social environment, is key to understanding a person's decisions, which are influenced by other people's attitude or opinion. New managerial tools, promoted as successors of the "old" executive systems, are likely to be based on collaborative teamworking and, as a consequence, social norms of peers and possibly subordinates are becoming influential for actual use (Karahanna and Limayem, 2000).

Second, another perspective that should be investigated is the individual and organizational interventions aimed at helping the senior executive become sufficiently IT literate for his job. Taking use seriously requires managers to dedicate resources to help users build effective use habits and to have resources available over time to support not just the evolving technology but also people's evolving use (Orlikowski, 2000). Further, experimental research is needed to design interventions to successfully manipulate the key controllable interventions to foster favorable perceptions and eventually create better acceptance and increased usage. Introducing new executive systems or Internet-based tools should receive balanced support in emphasizing ease of use, functionality, and user enjoyability.

Finally, to date most research and empirical studies target the Internet in general. An interesting line of research is to apply acceptance and usage theories to specific Web sites, most likely those aimed at the senior executive level. Also, applications specifically developed for senior executives and using Web-based technologies, at least for the user interface, are a promising ground for research. As a result, additional insights may well be obtained, the possibly leading to more effective use of the Internet for senior executives.

FINAL THOUGHTS

Trends in society and business organizations indicate the emergence of different perspectives on how we deal with information, on the one hand, and the facilitating role of information technology, on the other. In the new economy, senior executives must begin thinking about how people use information, not how they use IT tools or Internet. In other words, the new the open-network economy is much more people-focused and how information is used rather than on IT. Having the right managerial IT tools in place is necessary, but not sufficient for good information and information use. Too many managers still believe that once the right technology is in place, appropriate information use will follow. The ability of an organization to deal with a changing environment depends on the flexibility and dedication of their top managers in leveraging information and IT for improved business performance. As a result, it is not IT investments that are key but how IT is used by every employee from the top to the bottom of a company. Also, if the company is becoming more dependent on sharing and using information and knowledge, senior executives should pay particular attention to the cultural values and behaviors associated with information and IT use in their company. Changing a company's information culture requires altering behavior, attitudes, and incentives that relate to information (Davenport, 1994).

It has long been recognized that information adds value to a business. In today's business world, organizations use information to gain a competitive advantage (Marchand, 2000). Business imperatives, such as growth and continuous innovation, require senior executives to use available IT tools to obtain timely and accurate information. If senior executives use a computer or an information system, they want information to help them make the right decision at that particular moment. Moreover, providing executives with analysis capability to look at new and unusual information should take precedence over providing more accurate, timely, and reliable versions of currently available information. But the paradox emerges that executives will not use such an analysis tool or the Internet in this respect until it becomes an essential part of the management process, but this will not happen unless executives commit adequate time to the process of developing and using the right IT tools.

Executives must use IT and the Internet so that they can serve the needs of the members of their organization: Above all this involves communicating with one another. New technologies such as the Internet can serve this goal. Moreover, the computer is invisible within the Internet. Even the PC, primarily used to date to access the Internet, is being rapidly replaced with information appliances with dedicated functions. Interestingly enough, the PC was the front end of the executive information system investigated in earlier research. Gershenfeld (1999) and Norman (1999) argue that the PC is perhaps the most frustrating technology ever produced in that it is not task-specific. They advocate that any IT tool should be designed in such a way that it fits the task it is supposed to support. Perhaps this explains why most executives are quick to take to new gadgets such as mobile phones, PDAs, and electronic organizers, all of which have dedicated functions. Gradually, new task-specific tools, using intelligent interfaces alongside the tried and trusted keyboard and mouse, will fully connect the executive to his organizational infrastructure. Finally, it is worth noting that although the Internet may only be one of many communications channels, it undoubtedly has been the driver behind the change in attitudes by many executives to the opportunities IT offers. The Internet is ubiquitous, has no switch to turn it off, is easy to use, is designed to be always active, and is likely to be used by every senior executive in the near future to manage geographically dispersed employees. Any intervention or support either by support staff or personal secretary then becomes superfluous, because there are a range of carrots and sticks to help persuade even reluctant executives to use IT actively. After all, valuable IT tools are still just tools: New technologies or even the Internet alone will not change the attitude and behavior of the senior executive.

CONCLUSION

This chapter contributed to existing research by providing the factors that influence senior executives' use of IT and the Internet. A better understanding of the factors that may impede or increase effective utilization of IT can facilitate the design of programs or interventions addressing issues regarding the introduction of a new IT tool, information system or the Internet. Based on a number of studies addressing the issue of IT usage by senior executives, three factors were identified that can be manipulated using the right interventions. It has been shown that these factors play a significant role in the use of any tool targeted at the individual senior managerial level, whether it is a dedicated application such as the Internet, a software package, or a Web-based system for the senior executive. It is time for senior executives to hone their Internet skills. In the not too distant future, the employees of the company will work any time, any place, anywhere, with any device. The senior executive had better be prepared.

REFERENCES

Agarwal, R. and Karahanna, E. (2000). Time flies when you're having fun: Cognitive absorption and beliefs about information technology usage. *MIS Quarterly*, 24(4), 665-694.

Anandarajan, M., Simmers, C. and Igbaria, M. (2000). An exploratory investigation of the antecedents and impact of Internet usage: An individual perspective. *Behaviour & Information Technology*, 19(1), 69-85.

Applegate, L. M., Farlan, F. W. and McKenney, J. L. (1996). *Corporate Information Systems Management: Text and Cases*. Homewood: Irwin Book.

Atkinson, M. and Kydd, C. (1997). Individual characteristics associated with World Wide Web use: An empirical study of playfulness and motivation. *The Data Base for Advances in Information Systems*, 28(2), 53-62.

Bajwa, D. S., Rai, A. and Ramaprasad, A. (1998). The structural context of executive information system adoption. *Information Resources Management Journal*, 11(3), 28-38.

Boone, M. E. (1993). *Leadership and the Computer: Top Executives Reveal How They Personally Use Computers to Communicate, Coach, Convince and Compete*. Rocklin: Prima Publishing.

Cheung, W., Chang, M. K. and Lai, V. S. (2000). Prediction of Internet and World Wide Web usage at work: A test of an extended Triandis model. *Decision Support Systems*, 30(1), 83-100.

Chuan-Chuan Lin, J. and Lu, H. (2000). Towards an understanding of the behavioral intention to use a Web site. *International Journal of Information Management*, 20(3), 197-208.

Compeau, D. R. and Higgins, C. A. (1995). Computer self-efficacy: Development of a measure and initial test. *MIS Quarterly*, 19(2), 189-211.

Coutu, D. L. (2000). Too old to learn? *Harvard Business Review*, November-December, 37-52.

Davenport, T. H. (1994). Saving IT's soul: Human-centered information management. *Harvard Business Review*, March-April, 119-131.

Davis, F. D. (1989). Perceived usefulness, perceived ease of use and user acceptance of information technology. *MIS Quarterly*, 13(5), 319-339.

Davis, F. D., Bagozzi, R. P. and Warshaw, P. R. (1989). User acceptance of computer technology: A comparison of two theoretical models. *Management Science*, 35(8), 982-1003.

Davis, F. D., Bagozzi, R. P. and Warshaw, P. R. (1992). Extrinsic and intrinsic motivation to use computers in the workplace. *Journal of Applied Social Psychology*, 22(14), 1111-1132.

Earl, M. and Feeny, D. (2000). How to be a CEO for the information age. *Sloan Management Review*, 41(2), 11-23.

Elam, J. J. and Leidner, D. G. (1995). EIS adoption, use, and impact: the executive perspective. *Decision Support Systems*, 14(2), 89-103.

Fisher, R. (1995). Managers and executive information systems: Examining linkages among individual characteristics, attitudes, computer use and intentions. *Psychological Reports*, 77(3), 1171-1184.

Gershenfeld, N. A. (1999). *When Things Start to Think*. London: Hodder and Stoughton.

Ghorab, K. E. (1997). The impact of technology acceptance considerations on system usage, and adopted level of technological sophistication: An empirical investigation. *International Journal of Information Management*, 17(4), 249-259.

Hair, J. F., Anderson, R. E., Tatham, R. L. and Black, W. C. (1998). *Multivariate Data Analysis with Readings*. Upper Saddle River, NJ: Prentice-Hall.

Holtham, C. and Murphy, C. (1994). Executive information systems and senior management: Principles and practice. *Journal of Decision Systems*, 3(4), 259-276.

Igbaria, M. and Iivari, J. (1995). The effects of self-efficacy on computer usage. *OMEGA International Journal of Management Science*, 23(6), 587-605.

Igbaria, M. and Parasuraman, S. (1989). A path analytic study of individual characteristics, computer anxiety and attitudes toward microcomputers. *Journal of Management*, 15(3), 373-388.

Kanter, J. (1995). Computer-information literacy for senior management. *Information Strategy: The Executive's Journal*, 11(3), 6-12.

Karahanna, E. and Limayem, M. (2000). E-mail and v-mail usage: Generalizing across technologies. *Journal of Organizational Computing and Electronic Commerce*, 10(1), 49-66.

Kelley, H. H. and Thibaut, J. W. (1978). *Interpersonal Relations: A Theory of Interdependence*. New York, John Wiley & Sons.

Kotter, J. P. (1999). *What Leaders Really Do*. Boston, MA: Harvard Business School Press.

Lederer, A. L., Maupin, D. J., Sena, M. P. and Zhuang, Y. (2000). The technology acceptance model and the World Wide Web. *Decision Support Systems*, 29(3), 269-282.

Leidner, D. E., Carlsson, S. A., Elam, J. J. and Corrales, M. (1999). Mexican and Swedish managers' perceptions of the impact of EIS on organizational intelligence, decision making and structure. *Decision Sciences*, 30(3), 633-658.

Marakas, G. M., Yi, M. Y. and Johnson, R. D. (1998). The multilevel and multifaceted character of computer self-efficacy: Toward clarification of the construct and an integrative framework for research. *Information System Research*, 9(2), 126-163.

Marchand, D. A. (Ed.). (2000). *Competing with Information-A Manager's Guide to Creating Business Value with Information Content*. London: John Wiley & Sons.

Marchand, D. A., Kettinger, W. D. and Rollins, J. D. (2000). Information orientation: People, technology and the bottom line. *Sloan Management Review*, 41(4), 69-80.

Marginson, D., King, M. and McAuley, L. (2000). Executives' use of information technology: Comparison of electronic mail and an accounting information system. *Journal of Information Technology*, 15(2), 149-164.

Mintzberg, H. (1994). Rounding out the managers job. *Sloan Management Review*, Fall, 11-26.

Moon, J. W. and Kim, Y. G. (2001). Extending the TAM for a World Wide Web context. *Information & Management*, 38(4), 217-230.

Nord, J. H. and Nord, G. D. (1995). Executive information systems: A study and comparative analysis. *Information & Management*, 29(2), 95-106.

Norman, D. A. (1993). *Things That Make Us Smart*. Reading, MA: Perseus Book.

Norman, D. A. (1999). *The Invisible Computer: Why Good Products Can Fail, the Personal Computer Is So Complex and Information Appliances Are the Solution*. Boston, MA: MIT Press.

Norman, D. A. (2000). The invisible computer. In Marchand, D.A., Davenport, T. H. and Dickson, T. (Eds.), *Mastering Information Management*. London: Prentice-Hall.

O'Brien, G. J. and Wilde, W. D. (1996). Australian managers' perceptions, attitudes and use of information technology. *Information & Software Technology*, 38(12), 783-789.

Orlikowski, W. J. (2000). Managing use not technology: a view from the trenches, In Marchand, D. A., Davenport, T. H. and Dickson, T. (Eds.), *Mastering Information Management*. London: Prentice-Hall.

Pijpers, A. G. M. (2001). *Senior Executives' Use of Information Technology*. Doctoral dissertation, Eindhoven University of Technology. Available on the World Wide Web at: http://www.guuspijpers.com.

Rogers, E. M. (1995). *Diffusion of Innovation*. New York: The Free Press.

Seeley, M. E. and Targett, D. (1997). A senior executive end-user framework. *Information Systems Journal*, 7(4), 289-308.

Seeley, M. E. and Targett, D. (1999). Patterns of senior executives' personal use of computers. *Information & Management*, 35(6), 315-330.

Teo, T. S. H., Lim, V. K. H. and Lai, R.Y.C. (1999). Intrinsic and extrinsic motivation in Internet usage. *OMEGA International Journal of Management Science*, 27(1), 25-37.

Teo, T. S. H., Tan, M. and Buk, W. K. (1998). A contingency model of Internet adoption in Singapore. *International Journal of Electronic Commerce*, 2(2), 95-118.

Torkzadeh, R., Pflughoeft, K. and Hall, L. (1999). Computer self-efficacy, training effectiveness and user attitudes: An empirical study. *Behaviour & Information Technology*, 18(4), 299-309.

Venkatesh, V. and Davis, F. D. (1996). A model of the antecedents of perceived ease of use: Development and test. *Decision Sciences*, 27(3), 451-481.

Webster, J. and Martocchio, J. J. (1992). Microcomputer playfulness: Development of a measure with workplace implications. *MIS Quarterly*, 16(2), 201-226.

Chapter II

Predictors of Internet Usage for Work Tasks

Lyndal Stiller-Hughes and Ivan T. Robertson
University of Manchester Institute of Science and Technology, UK

INTRODUCTION

Introducing and capitalizing on the Internet for business gain is engulfing modern day business thought. Yet little is available to guide the decisions of organizational leaders on issues around workforce usage. This chapter begins to close the gap by presenting the findings of a new empirical study, which specifically targets the factors associated with Internet usage for work tasks. A framework is presented to help organizations manage the usage of the Internet. It contains both person and situation factors which are associated with higher Internet usage. This work is based on the view that implementation of the Internet into the workplace is analogous to other forms of organizational change, in that people form a key success criteria.

BACKGROUND

Internet Usage: An Employee Perspective

Discussions within organizations on the Internet invariably focus on the technology and business processes. Rarely are the actions and contributory roles of employees considered. Outside of specific Internet programs, the question of whether and for what purpose employees are using the Internet is scarcely raised. Discussions around use of the Internet for business tend to be within the highly technical models of business-to-business electronic commerce (e-commerce), where transactions between organizations occur in purely online terms. This bounded view of the Internet means that the numerous transactions conducted by employees who have access to the Internet are not being considered. Employees are consumers of the Internet within the context of a work environment. Considering the Internet from an employee perspective provides valuable information such as the amount of wasted time in using the Internet for personal reasons and more importantly the benefits which are being reaped through its use for work tasks.

When referring to the Internet, this paper gives attention to use of the World Wide Web (WWW), a network of sites using technology which allows for the ready transfer of text, sound and images. *Web usage* is the particular focus of the chapter and is defined as accessing and navigating through Web sites to locate information, interact with other organizations or make transactions. Examples of such use are recruitment officers downloading updated aptitude tests, and marketing managers in manufacturing organizations accessing the Web to conduct market research and to identify revenue-generating possibilities. The range of possibilities is enormous. The empirical findings presented later in the chapter demonstrate that they are less influenced by the nature of the task compared to the initiative of the individual and encouragement of the environment.

The Internet as a Form of Organizational Change

Exploiting the Internet to gain competitive advantage requires more than just compelling technology. It is people who ultimately exploit the change for competitive advantage. History has shown that technology can not be the sole answer to commercial success. Even in what are sometimes described as the parallel events of the industrial revolution, success relied on the output of workers along with the new machines (Coyle, 1999).

Prominent models of change all include a strong orientation towards the importance of people. Models emerging from the 1980s, such as the total quality management program, and the 1990s, such as business process reengineering, place motivation, responsibility and skills of people as critical to success. An analysis of 100 companies attempting to transform themselves highlights eight lessons for organizations. Each lesson for successful change involves actions of people, whether they be the instigators of the change or the recipients (Kotter, 1998).

MODELS AND FACTORS TO GUIDE INTERNET UNDERSTANDING

Considering the Internet as another form of change opens up a range of literature to help managers understand its use. Reciprocal determinism and the technology acceptance model (TAM) are particularly relevant.

Reciprocal Determinism

The interaction between the person and situation has long been a basis from which to understand behavior within organizations. The person, situation and behavior represent the three cornerstones within the model. The interaction between each cornerstone is called reciprocal determinism under the social cognitive theory. That is, there is a mutual action between these factors, for example, people play an active role in choosing how they will behave, while at the same time being influenced by environmental forces (Pervin & John, 1997). Within the context of this paper, using the Web for work tasks is the behavior of interest. The situation is the work environment including infrastructures, work practices, culture, work colleagues and leaders. The person is each individual who has access to the Internet including aspects relating to them such as their skills, attitudes, experiences and personality. In order to manage use of the Web within an organization, managers need to be aware of key aspects of both the individual as well as the environment.

Technology Acceptance Model

Since little has been investigated with regards to the Internet, it is important to consider the findings from prior information technology (IT) research. The technology acceptance model (TAM) has successfully been applied to other information technologies such as word processing (Davis, Bagozzi & Warshaw, 1989), electronic mail (Davis, 1989) and spreadsheets (Al-Gahtani & King, 1999). Central to the TAM is the role of an individual's beliefs about technology. Under TAM, the main belief is called perceived usefulness and is defined as the "prospective user's subjective probability that using a specific application system will increase his or her job performance within an organizational context." (Davis et al., 1989, p. 985). External variables, such as training, influence actual technology usage indirectly via the individual's beliefs, along with their attitudes and intentions to use the technology.

To date, the authors are aware of only two studies which focus exclusively on understanding the factors related to Internet usage in the workplace

(Anandarajan, Simmers & Igbaria, 2000; Simmers & Anandarajan, 1999). Both studies used the TAM as a basis for the research models. A general finding from both was that there is only marginal support for the TAM when considering the Internet and secondly that person factors appear to be more strongly related to Internet usage than organization factors.

The first study (Anandarajan et al., 2000) found important relationships among person factors with attitudes/beliefs and Internet usage. For example, an individual's imaginative use of the Internet was associated with perceptions of usefulness and job satisfaction. In a more in-depth study, Simmers and Anandarajan (1999) found that length of experience with the Internet and participation in Internet training exerted a greater influence on Internet usage (time and frequency) than did beliefs such as perceived usefulness or perceived ease of use.

Although relevant to the topic of this chapter, both these studies were based on US data alone. It is generally recognized that the US is championing all manner of Internet usage, with 45% of its population online. Data from another English-speaking country, such as the UK, where the level of Internet usage is considered to be in the "middle" (26% of the population), will perhaps be more relevant to global organizations (Wall, 2000). The new empirical research presented below meets this need. It builds on the model of reciprocal determinism and the TAM to select a range of person and situation factors from prior Internet, microcomputer and organizational studies (see Figure 1).

Figure 1: Person and Situation Factors Selected From Prior Research

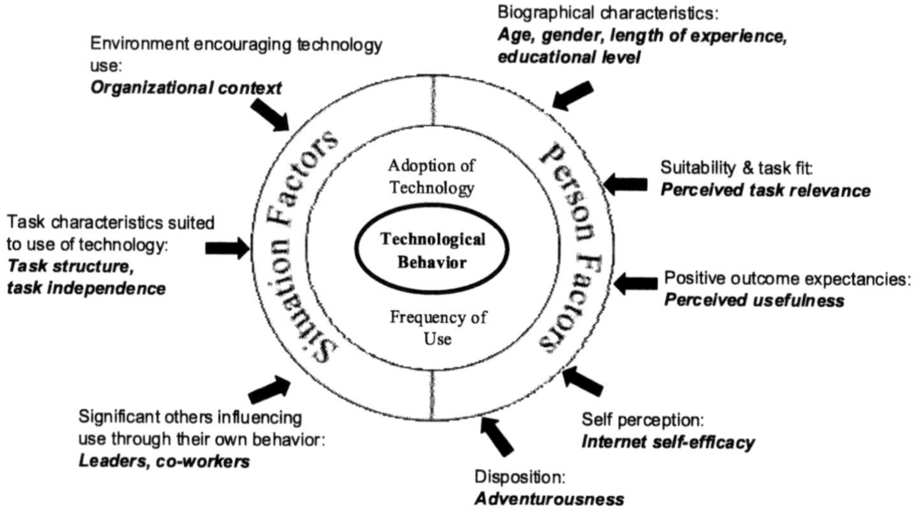

RESEARCH QUESTIONS

The goal of this new empirical study was to identify, from a selection of factors (see Figure 1), those which are significantly related to increased use of the Internet for work tasks. Specifically, the study sought to answer (a) which person factors relate to increased Internet usage, (b) which situation factors relate to increased Internet usage, and (c) which set of factors has the strongest relationship with increased Internet usage.

THE RESEARCH STUDY

In addition to answering the research questions concerned with amount of Internet usage for work tasks, the impact on work outcomes was also investigated. Volume of Internet use is not necessarily an indicator of "quality" use. High achievement organizations are interested in performance and productivity levels which impact on overall work outcomes. Data were gathered in two parts: a qualitative study and broader field survey.

Qualitative Study

Interviews were conducted to explore factors influencing Internet usage in the workplace and thus support the research model. Fifteen participants (six female, nine males) participated in the semi-structured interviews. Each was a recognized Internet "expert" in their respective organizations, which included a global business consulting firm, a UK-based airline and an Internet design company. An "expert" was defined as someone who had depth of knowledge and/or had worked extensively in the area of the Internet. Table 1 presents a summary of the person and situation factors raised. The overall result showed a substantial overlap with the factors extracted from the literature, as presented in Figure 1. An additional biographical characteristic was added: job level, as it was suggested that higher job level rather than age may be associated with lower levels of Internet usage. For example, those at more senior job levels may have less time and inclination to use the Internet.

Main Field Survey

Method: Sample

Questionnaires were used to gather data from 277 UK-based working adults from a broad spectrum of organizations and industries. A prerequisite for participation was having access to the Internet for work tasks. Participants ranged in age between 18 and 69 years ($m = 33.96$, $sd = 8.97$). The vast

Table 1: Summary Data from Qualitative Study

Factor Group	Factor/Theme	f
Person	Capability & skill	4
	Positive view towards Internet	9
	Comfort with using Internet	5
	Job level/work position	2
	Age (younger age)	5
	Prior experience with the Internet	3
	Exploring personality	6
	Risk taking personality	3
	Gender (males use Internet more)	2
Situation	Aligned with organization strategy	2
	Leadership behavior & role models	9
	Supervisor encouragement	3
	Culture of Internet acceptance	7
	Incentives	5
	Provision of training	6
	Provision of assistance/support	3
	Use by colleagues	3
	Characteristics of the job/task	6
	Processes for new way of working	2
	Internal marketing of Internet	3
	Convenient access	8

majority of the participants had undergone higher level education, with 113 (40.8%) participants attaining a bachelor's degree and 121 (43.7%) participants attaining postgraduate or doctorate level degrees. The participants were from a variety of functions and 21 organizations including: business consulting (33.9%), manufacturing (9.4%), wholesale trade (4.7%), IT services (14.4%), self-employed (1.5%), HR consulting (15.2%), government (1.8%) and university education (19.1%). The sample represented a wide range of employment levels including (a) junior employees (49.5%), (b) managers and lecturers (34.6%) and (c) executives and professors (15.9%).

Procedure

A key contact was established in each organization who "sponsored" the questionnaire and determined the most appropriate method of distribution. The questionnaire was available in both paper and electronic (Excel 97) formats. The latter utilizing "drop-down" lists to lessen the skill level required by participants. Clarity and ease were tested in a pilot study with nine participants. Three out of the 21 organizations requested the paper version ($n = 59$, 21%). An overall response rate of 38% was achieved for the questionnaires.

Measures

The questionnaire contained 77 self-reported items. The majority were fixed form measures using a 7-point Likert-type scale for the responses (1 = strongly disagree; 7 = strongly agree). Written responses were sought for the items relating to biographical characteristics. The instructions emphasized two main points: (a) use of the word "Internet" referred to use of Web sites in the World Wide Web and (b) responses were to reflect use of the Internet for work tasks only, not personal use. The scales were developed a priori from the literature and are described below (see also Figure 1).

Biographical characteristics: Age, gender, educational level and job level of the participants were gathered along with their length of experience in using the Internet generally and for work in particular.

Perceived task relevance: This scale refers to the extent an individual sees the Internet as meeting a job need. A four-item scale was developed taking guidance from previous works (Leonard-Barton & Deschamps, 1988; Yetton, Sharma & Souton, 1999). The items included statements such as "I do not need to use the Internet to do my job."

Perceived usefulness: This scale refers to a belief that using the Internet will increase job performance. The five-item scale consisted of four items developed by Davis (1989) with the words "electronic mail" being replaced with "Internet," for example "Using the Internet enables me to accomplish some tasks more quickly." A fifth item was added to account for an emphasis on value in the workplace: "Use of the Internet adds value to some of my work tasks."

Internet self-efficacy: This scale refers to a person's perceived self-ability to use the Internet. It consisted of five items adapted from previous computer self-efficacy scales (Compeau and Higgins, 1995; Hollenbeck & Brief, 1987). The items included statements such as "I am confident in using the Internet to complete work tasks" and "I need a lot of support to complete tasks using the Internet."

Adventurousness: This scale refers to an openness to act upon new experiences and contained eight items from the NEO-PI-R developed by Costa and McCrae (Goldberg, 1999). Adventurousness measures are a sub-scale of the openness to experience personality factor, which refers to the curiosity, imaginativeness and open-mindedness of an individual (Costa & McCrae, 1992). The items included statements such as "I prefer variety to routine."

Organizational context: This scale refers to the extent that the organizational environment encourages Internet usage. A nine-item scale was developed utilizing outcomes from the qualitative study and an existing scale called organizational support (Simmers & Anandarajan, 1999). The items included statements such as "The organization has provided opportunities for me to learn how to use the Internet for work."

Task structure: This scale refers to the extent that there is a set procedure for conducting the job itself. Unstructured tasks are characterized by a variety of issues which require new types of information and new ways to analyze them (Goodhue, 1995). A four-item scale was constructed based on an instrument used by Anandarajan et al. (2000) and included statements such as "There is a clearly known way to do the major types of work that I normally encounter."

Task independence: This scale measures the extent to which completion of tasks requires coordination with other people or departments. Tasks where an individual can work without information from others are "independent" (Goodhue, 1995). Five items were taken from a scale used by Sharma and Yetton (2001). The words "on the Internet" were added to each item to provide context, for example, "My tasks on the Internet can be performed fairly independently from other people."

Leader influence: This scale refers to the extent that organizational leaders and immediate supervisors encourage Internet usage through their own behavior. A four-item scale included statements such as "I have benefited from watching my immediate supervisor/manager using the Internet."

Coworker influence: The scale of coworker influence refers to the extent that work colleagues encourage Internet usage through their behavior. A four-item scale included statements such as "I have benefited from observing my colleagues using the Internet."

Behavioral measures: Amount or duration of Internet usage was the main dependent variable for the study. Hours of Internet usage was captured for "yesterday," in a "typical day" and in a "typical week." A five-item scale called work enhancement was used in the study to measure the impact of Internet usage on job performance. The work enhancement items included statements such as "Using the Internet enables me to produce work of a higher quality."

Results

Table 2 presents descriptive statistics for each of the study variables. Scales were created by computing the mean of all items in the scale, with items being reversed as necessary. As shown in Table 2, the scale reliabilities were at an acceptable level being near or above 0.7. An alpha level of 0.5 was set to test for levels of significance. Statistical power was calculated using a two-tailed test and was found to be greater than .99 for effect sizes of 9% ($r = .30$) of the variance (Cohen, 1977). The three items (yesterday; in a typical day; in a typical week) measuring hours of Internet usage were summed and transformed, by calculating their square root, in order to minimise error and account for a high level of skewness. The result was the main dependent measure used within the analyses (skewness = 0.676, $m = 2.2$, $sd = 1.3$).

Table 2: Sample Number, Mean, Standard Deviation and Alpha Reliabilities of Study Variables

	N	M	SD	α
Person measures				
Age	276	33.96	8.97	-
Length of time since first use	277	5.68	0.74	-
Length of time since first work use	277	5.26	1.04	-
Length of time since regular use	277	4.47	1.58	-
Internet self-efficacy	247	5.95	0.91	.83
Perceived task relevance	269	4.75	1.28	.71
Perceived usefulness	236	5.57	0.82	.87
Adventurousness	267	5.66	0.78	.81
Situation measures				
Organizational context	258	4.99	0.83	.73
Leader influence	267	4.17	1.18	.69
Co-worker influence	269	5.38	1.04	.70
Task structure	271	4.06	1.22	.71
Task independence	244	5.43	0.85	.72
Behavior measures				
Hours yesterday	276	0.85	1.22	-
Hours per typical day	277	1.02	1.42	-
Hours per typical week	277	5.00	5.6	-
Work enhancement	247	5.40	0.85	.70

Relationship Between Factors and Internet Usage

Biographical characteristics: The only biographical characteristic to have a significant relationship with amount of Internet usage was length of experience. A Pearson correlation between hours of Internet use and length of experience was significant for length of time since first Internet use ($r^2 = .04, p < .001$), first Internet use for work ($r^2 = .11, p < .0001$), or first regularly using the Internet for work ($r^2 = .24, p < .0001$). The latter accounted for the greatest variance.

No relationship was found between age and number of hours in which the Internet was used for work ($r = -.07$). The number of hours of Internet usage by males ($m = 2.35, sd = 1.32$) was not significantly different from females ($m = $ as 2.14, $sd = 1.36$) ($t = 1.27, df = 274, p = .466$). The means of each education level were not found to be significantly different, $f(4, 269) = .552, p = .698$, ns; (a) high school certificate ($m = 2.09, sd = 1.18$), (b) college diploma ($m = 2.38, sd = 1.87$), (c) bachelor's degree ($m = 2.36, sd = 1.53$), (d) postgraduate/master's qualification ($m = 2.22, sd = 0.94$), and (e) doctorate degree ($m = 2.24, sd = 1.35$). Finally, analyses of the differences between job level and duration of Internet usage were also found to be nonsignificant ($f[2,272] = 1.96, p = .142$).

Internet beliefs and disposition: Pearson correlational analyses for the scales relating to Internet beliefs and disposition were all highly significant ($p < .0001$). Higher levels of Internet self-efficacy, perceived usefulness and perceived task relevance were each associated with greater hours of Internet usage for work tasks. Pearson correlation results showed that each factor accounted for at least 10% of the variance in duration of Internet usage; (a) Internet self-efficacy ($r^2 = .10$), (b) perceived task relevance ($r^2 = .23$), and (c) perceived usefulness ($r^2 = 12$). The literature suggested that participants' adventurousness would be positively related to duration of Internet usage. The correlational results showed that there was a significant positive relationship between these two variables ($r^2 = .05, p < .0001$).

Organizational context: The organizational factor accounting for the greatest variance on duration of Internet usage was organizational context ($r^2 = .18$). The Pearson correlation was .42 ($p < .0001$). Increases in aspects of the work environment supporting Internet usage were associated with increases in hours of Internet usage.

Leader and coworker influence: Both leader influence and coworker influence were positively related to the duration of Internet use for work purposes. The strongest relationship was for leader influence ($r^2 = .09, p < .0001$), with co-worker influence ($r^2 = .03$) being significant at the .05 probability level.

Task structure and task independence: The results of Pearson correlations showed that there were no discernable relationships with duration of Internet usage for either of the variables: task structure ($r^2 = 8.1$), task independence ($r^2 = 6.4$).

Factors Most Strongly Related to Internet Usage

The third research question centered around the set of factors which has the strongest association with levels of Internet usage for work tasks. A stepwise multiple regression was performed between each independent measure and duration of Internet use. Only three variables were identified as contributing significantly to variance in duration of Internet usage: (a) length of time since first using the Internet for work, (b) perceived task relevance, and (c) organizational context. Together these accounted for 27% of the variance in Internet behavior. Table 3 presents the results from the stepwise regression with all significant independent measures on duration of Internet usage.

Mediation by Internet Beliefs

Post-hoc exploration of the data was conducted to understand whether it supported the TAM model. According to this model, the influence of external variables is fully mediated by an individual's Internet beliefs. A linear regression was performed with the three Internet beliefs as the mediator for the situation variables. A regression analysis was conducted with duration of Internet usage as the dependent variable, situation factors (organizational context, leader influence, coworker influence) as the independent variables, and the Internet beliefs (Internet self-efficacy, perceived task relevance, perceived usefulness) as the mediating variables.

Table 3: Stepwise Regression of Situation and Person Variables on Duration of Internet Usage

Variable	β	t	r^2	F
Predictor Model				23.41****
Perceived task relevance	.31	4.47****	.20	
Organizational context	.24	3.52***	.25	
Length of time since first regular work use	.16	2.39*	.27	

Note.   *p < .05   **p < .01   ***p < .001   ****p < .0001
Standardized regression weights and adjusted r^2 are shown.

Table 4 presents the findings from the separate regression analysis conducted for each situation factor. The figures in the table refer to the final outcome for the situation factors after the effect of Internet beliefs has been entered into the analysis. After any mediating influence of the Internet beliefs had occurred, organizational context, leader influence and coworker influence continued to have a direct relationship with duration of Internet usage.

Relationship Between Duration of Internet Use and Work Enhancement

A post-hoc analysis was conducted to help understand the relationship between Internet usage and impact on work outcomes. A Pearson correlation showed that there was a significant positive relationship ($r^2 = .09, p < .0001$) between amount of Internet usage and work enhancement.

IMPLICATIONS

The research findings provide new and relevant information for organizations seeking to increase employee use of the Internet and the benefits gained from it. In particular, a set of factors were identified which can form the basis of managerial interventions (see Figure 2). Just as people are central to the success of other forms of organizational change such as total quality management and business process reengineering, people appear to be key to successful employment of Internet technology. On a cautionary note, it should be recognized that the data provide relationships between factors and Internet usage, but does not establish causal or antecedent links. The study demonstrated unequivocally that employees are using the Internet for work purposes and, more importantly, that higher levels of Internet usage for work tasks are associated with higher levels of enhancement to that work, such as higher quality and being able to do more in a day. A large number of people from many types of occupations are using the Internet, suggesting that the Internet

Table 4: Linear Regression Analysis With Internet Self-Efficacy, Perceived Task Relevance and Perceived Usefulness as Mediators

Situation variable	β	t	r^2	F
Organizational context	.22	3.32	.27	20.17***
Leader influence	.16	2.56	.25	18.70*
Co-worker influence	.05	0.78	.22	16.35

Note. *p < .05   **p < .01   ***p < .001   ****p < .0001

Figure 2: Framework of Factors Related to Increased Internet Usage

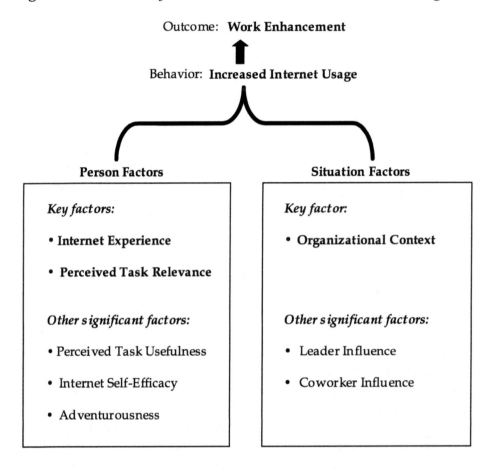

is not a "special" tool in the domain of a few, but a tool which can be employed across a broad spectrum of tasks.

Figure 2 presents the person and situation factors which relate to increased Internet usage and resultant work enhancement. The factors with the strongest relationship are emboldened.

Strongest Associations with Internet Usage

Factors showing the strongest relationship with amount of Internet usage were perceived task relevance, organizational context and length of experience. This mix of person and situation factors reinforces the view that both sets of factors need to be considered by managers when seeking to influence behavior. Perceived task relevance and organizational context have not previously been studied for Internet behavior and provide new insights for managers. Each factor is discussed below with examples to be considered within the unique circumstances of an organization.

Perceived Task Relevance

Perceived task relevance builds on the idea of an individual assessing the characteristics of the Internet and the characteristics of their work task to determine the degree of fit and thus relevance. This is a type of task-technology fit which has been shown within microcomputing studies to be a precursor to beliefs about the technology (Goodhue & Thompson, 1995), such as perceived poor fit being associated with negative attitudes. Quite obviously the design of the technology plays a key part in the perception of relevance. Yet in terms of the Internet, the design of Web sites is often outside of the scope of organizations, especially when encouraging employees to use the full array of existing WWW sites. At an organizational level, portal technology could be introduced to ease access to the most "relevant" work sites. A portal is a combination of technologies which creates a personalized user interface across the Internet and other organizational information systems. However, as demonstrated in the research, individuals will use the Internet more if they "perceive" it to be relevant. Providing the technology alone may not be the answer.

The emphasis for managers is to encourage a *perception* of relevance for the individual. This is more than "sanctioning" the Internet to be relevant and requires it being linked to an individual's unique tasks. Many vehicles exist to help build a view of relevance, such as providing tailored training, "expert" coaching, focused communications and perhaps making it a topic for work performance evaluations. Perceived task relevance cannot be established through mass campaigns, only through taking an individual perspective.

Organizational Context

Organizational context refers to the extent that the organizational environment encourages Internet usage. It represents the myriad of cues, such as access to the Internet, provision of training and reward for Internet behavior, from which an individual perceives a general positive or negative view towards Internet usage, therefore establishing a perception of the credibility for the work tool.

Organizational context was the only situation factor which showed a particularly strong relationship with amount of Internet usage. This indicates that in considering Internet behavior the pervasive environment is more important than any single aspect of it. Cues in the environment, partly reflected through the organizational culture, must be understood by managers. The attitudes, behaviors and approaches of immediate managers/supervisors become paramount to set a context of Internet encouragement and credibility. Managers can employ incentive schemes and formal communications as well as publicly encouraging, endorsing and recognizing employee use of the Internet.

Length of Experience

The length of time since first using the Internet, the length of time since first using the Internet for work tasks, and the length of time since beginning to use the Internet *regularly* for work tasks were all highly related to current levels of Internet usage for work. Unlike previous consumer/marketing research where the effects of experience were found to plateau over time (Hammond, McWilliam & Narholz Diaz, 1997), the present study found a continual increase regardless of whether experience started this month or more than two years ago.

The most interesting finding was that even though the study was only interested in use of the Internet for work tasks, experience elsewhere in using the Internet was associated with differences in levels of usage. Organizations may benefit from assisting employees in gaining access to the Internet for home use. Perhaps increased level of experience aided the extraction and comprehension of relevant information (Titus & Everett, 1995) and increased adeptness in accessing sites. The findings however showed that the strongest relationship was found for the "length of time since beginning to use the Internet regularly for work tasks." Greatest value may occur when organizations encourage regular use of the Internet for work-related activities, such as encouraging employee use of e-mail and providing mandatory training through the Internet.

Other Factors Associated With Internet Usage

In addition to the three factors showing the strongest association with Internet usage, other significant person and situation factors need to be considered.

Internet Beliefs

Two Internet beliefs (perceived usefulness and Internet self-efficacy) were found to positively relate with amount of Internet usage, suggesting that managers must focus on the way interventions act upon the beliefs of employees. For example, rather than providing lecture-based training, behavioral modeling training might be more influential in terms of Internet self-efficacy, as is the case with computer self-efficacy (Gist, Schwoerer & Rosen, 1989). Internet self-efficacy is a person's self-perception about his or her own ability to cope with the Internet. Self-efficacy has been related to adoption of high-technology products (Hill, Smith & Mann, 1986) and innovations (Burkhardt & Brass, 1990), and the strength of the present finding suggests that Internet self-efficacy may be a better predictor of Internet usage than other measures of self-perception such as perceived ease of use (Davis, 1989). Perceived usefulness refers to the extent that using the Internet is seen to be advantageous. Whereas perceived task relevance shows that the individual assesses suitability in using the Internet for a task, perceived usefulness shows that the individual expects a positive outcome from using it. The present study supports the view that adoption of technology is influenced by an evaluation of both factors (Yetton et al., 1999).

Disposition

Disposition or the general personality of a person has not been well studied in terms of the Internet nor microcomputer usage, yet the present study shows that it plays a significant role. Adventurousness was the personality trait measured and refers to an openness to action, such as a willingness to try new things (Costa & McCrae, 1992). Although an organization has no control over the personality of its existing personnel, it can seek to capitalize on those unique characteristics of the workforce when seeking organizational change. For example, a short survey could quickly ascertain those who have high levels of adventurousness. Perhaps these individuals could be offered the opportunity to have early access to the Internet, be coaches to others, and be advocates of the change.

Leader and Coworker Influence

The behaviors of leaders and coworkers were found to positively relate to Internet usage. Leader behavior showed a stronger relationship with Internet usage than coworker behavior, possibly as leaders are more influential in the environment through their ability to influence distribution of rewards. The relative infancy of the Internet in UK organizations also may mean that individuals look to their leaders for guidance in the expected behavior. The role of coworker behavior should not be ignored. Again eliciting the active support of early adopters within work teams may speed the take-up of the Internet by all.

A key feature of the study was that the scale *leader influence* was composed of items solely around the *behavior* of leaders, not what they said. Observation and modeling the behaviors of others are key vehicles for the diffusion of innovations (Bandura, 1977). Managers need to make their Internet behavior observable to their employees, such as through e-mailing hyperlinks to relevant sites.

Factors of Little Significance

The *biographical characteristics* of age, gender, job level and educational level of the employees did not show a significant relationship with amount of Internet usage. Although differences in age and gender have been shown to exist in acceptance of computers (e.g., Harrison & Rainer, 1992; Dawes & Smith, 1985), the present study supports the view that the profile of Internet users is becoming close to the profile of the general population and therefore is not a predictor of Internet behavior.

Unexpectedly the *characteristics* of the task itself were not found to be linked with Internet usage. One explanation may simply be that the task variables investigated (task structure, task independence) may not be relevant to usage of the Internet for work purposes. This view supports an exploratory finding by Anandarajan et al. (2000). An alternative explanation could be that investigating use of the WWW, rather than specific Internet applications, was too broad to allow associations between usage and task characteristic to take effect.

FUTURE TRENDS AND CONCLUSIONS

Workplace use of the Internet is still at an early stage. More research and rigor in the area will provide a foundation for more sophisticated employment of the Internet's potential. The research study showed that theoretical models other than those traditionally associated with microcomputers are worthy for understanding the Internet. Social psychology offers much insight, especially through the model of reciprocal determinism. Although the TAM has been used in numerous microcomputer studies, the findings in the present study along with the work of Simmers and Anandarajan (1999) suggest that modifications to the TAM are required in order to account for Internet behavior.

Quite clearly employees with access to the Internet are already using it for work purposes. The decision for organizations is around whether or not to optimize its use. This chapter has provided much needed information on the factors which are associated with Internet usage. As the Internet becomes an increasingly indispensable part of work, it is important for all managers to take note of both individual and organizational factors related to Internet usage. Higher levels of Internet usage are associated with positive work outcomes.

As organizations seek the ultimate goal of embedding the Internet within work practices, the findings from the present study indicate that focus should be placed on (a) creating opportunities to increase the amount of regular Internet experiences for work, (b) supporting an organizational context where the Internet is seen to be a credible business tool, and (c) encouraging employees to perceive the relevance of the Internet for their unique set of work tasks. Exploitation of the Internet by business will not occur haphazardly, but requires the concerted effort of management on these key factors.

REFERENCES

Al-Gahtani, S. S. and King, M. (1999). Attitudes, satisfaction and usage: Factors contributing to each in the acceptance of information technology. *Behaviour & Information Technology*, 18(4), 277-297.

Anandarajan, M., Simmers, C. and Igbaria, M. (2000). An exploratory investigation of the antecedents and impact of Internet usage: An individual perspective. *Behaviour & Information Technology*, 19(1), 69-85.

Bandura, A. (1977). *Social Learning Theory*. Englewood Cliffs, NJ: Prentice-Hall.

Burkhardt, M. E. and Brass, D. J. (1990). Changing patterns or patterns of change: The effects of a change in technology on social network structure and power. *Administrative Science*, March, 35(1), 104-127.

Cohen, J. (1977). *Statistical Power Analysis for the Behavioral Sciences*. New York: Academic Press.

Compeau, D. R. and Higgins, C. A. (1995). Computer self-efficacy: Development of a measure and initial test. *MIS Quarterly*, June, 189-211.

Costa, P. J. and McCrae, R. R. (1992). *NEO-PI-R: Revised NEO Personality Inventory (NEO-PI-R)*. Odessa, FL: Psychological Assessment Resources.

Coyle, D. (1999). *The Weightless World*. Oxford, UK: Capstone Publishing Limited.

Davis, F. D. (1989). Perceived usefulness, perceived ease of use, and user acceptance of information technology. *MIS Quarterly*, 13, 319-340.

Davis, F. D., Bagozzi, R. P. and Warshaw, P. R. (1989). User acceptance of computer technology: A comparison of two theoretical models. *Management Science*, 35(8), 982-1003.

Dawes, R. M. and Smith, T. L. (1985). Attitude and opinion measurement. In Lindzey, G. and Aronson, E. (Eds.), *Handbook of Social Psychology* (3rd ed.) 509-566. New York: Random House.

Gist, M. E., Schwoerer, C. E. and Rosen, B. (1989). Effects of alternative training methods on self-efficacy and performance in computer software training. *Journal of Applied Psychology*, 74(6), 884-891.

Goldberg, L. R. (1999). *International Personality Item Pool*. Available on the World Wide Web at: http://ipip.ori.org/ipip/neoprelim.

Goodhue, D. L. (1995). Understanding user evaluations of information systems. *Management Science*, 41(12), 1827-1844.

Goodhue, D. L. and Thompson, R. L. (1995). Task-technology fit and individual performance. *MIS Quarterly*, June, 213-236.

Hammond, K., McWilliam, G. and Narholz Diaz, A. (1997, October). *Fun and Work on the Web: Differences in Attitudes Between Novices and Experienced Users* (Working paper No. 97-803). London: London Business School, Centre for Marketing.

Harrison, A. W. and Rainer, R. K. (1992). The influence of individual differences on skill in end-user computing. *Journal of Management Information Systems*, 9(1), 93-11.

Hill, T., Smith, N. D. and Mann, M. F. (1986). Communicating innovations: Convincing computer phobics to adopt innovative technologies. In Lutz, R. J. (Ed.), *Advances in Consumer Research*, 13, 419-422. Provo, USA: Association for Consumer Research.

Hollenbeck, J. R. and Brief, A. P. (1987). The effects of individual differences and goal origin on goal setting and performance. *Organizational Behavior and Human Decision Processes*, 40, 392-414.

Kotter, J. P. (1998). Leading change: Why transformation efforts fail. In *Harvard Business Review on Change*. Boston, MA: Harvard Business School Publishing.

Leonard-Barton, D. and Deschamps, I. (1988). Managerial influence in the implementation of new technology. *Management Science*, 34(10), 1252-1265.

Pervin, L. A. and John, O. J. (1997). *Personality: Theory and Research* (7th Ed.). New York: John Wiley & Sons.

Schein, E. H. (1997). *Organizational Culture and Leadership* (2nd ed.). San Francisco, USA: Jossey-Bass Inc.

Sharma, R. and Yetton, P. (2001). The contingent effects of implementation process and task interdependence on successful IS implementation: A meta-analysis. In *Proceddings of the Ninth European Conference on Information Systems*, Bled, Slovenia.

Simmers, C. and Anandarajan, M. (1999). Internet usage in the work environment: An extension of the technology acceptance model. Paper presented at the meeting of the *Academy of Management Conference*, Chicago, August.

Titus, P. and Everett, P. (1995). The consumer retail search process: A conceptual model and research agenda. *Journal of the Academy of Marketing Science*, 23(2), 106-119.

Wall, M. (2000). The wired divide. *The Sunday Times (UK): Culture*, Section 8, April 23, 47-48.

Yetton, P., Sharma, R. and Souton, G. (1999). Successful IS innovation: The contingent contributions of innovation characteristics and implementation process. *Journal of Information Technology*, 14, 53-68.

Chapter III

Factors Influencing Web Access Behavior in the Workplace: A Structural Equation Approach

Murugan Anandarajan
Drexel University, USA

Claire A. Simmers
Saint Joseph's University, USA

As more and more organizations provide employees access to the Web, the level of abuse is on the rise. Structured equation modeling was used to examine the antecedent and perceptual factors impacting accessing work-related Web sites and personal-related Web sites in the work environment. The results indicate that management support, experience and perceived ethical beliefs have a significant negative influence, while self-training and perceived enjoyment had a positive influence on personal-related Web access. Internet experience, formal training, and all the perceptual factors influenced work-related Web site access. The findings of the study contribute to an expanding understanding of the factors promoting Web usage and have important implications for the management of information systems.

INTRODUCTION

The ubiquitous nature of the Internet is dramatically revolutionizing the manner in which organizations and individuals alike are sharing information. The Internet, designed and developed out of cold war fear in the early 1970s, grew slowly and painstakingly as an electronic forum for academic and scientific researchers. Vast quantities of information were scattered about the network but finding this information taxed even those computer literate devotees. The development that made the Internet a "25 year overnight success" was the creation of HTML (Hypertext Markup Language) and the server/browser software to view the interconnected documents that became the World Wide Web or the Web. It is this layer of the Internet architecture, the Web, which has become synonymous with the Internet.[1] Users access information on the Web, simply by pointing and clicking on key words or images that have links to individual or organizational home pages. This simplicity has resulted in the rapid growth of Web users. According to the US Department of Commerce there were over 60 million Web users in 1998, and this number is expected to increase by at least 20% every month.

In addition to being a channel for commercial exchange, the Web also provides access to the world's biggest playground. For instance, a study conducted in a manufacturing firm found that in a typical 8-hour working day, over 250,000 Web sites were accessed by a workforce of 386 employees. Of particular concern to the organization was the discovery that approximately 90% of the accessed sites were non-work-related (LaPlante, 1997). The cost of ignoring this phenomenon can be enormous. According to the Gartner group, non-work-related Web surfing activities cost organizations approximately $8 million in 1997. In addition to this obvious problem of loss of productivity, Web surfing can also clog networks, resulting in slower access for legitimate business users. Such problems have prompted organizations to show a growing interest in understanding and managing Web access behavior in the workplace (Cronin, 1996; Judge, 1998; McWilliams & Stepanek, 1998).

To date most information systems (IS) research has focused on understanding the factors that promote the use of microcomputer technologies. For instance voice mail and word processing (Adams, Nelson, & Todd, 1992), e-mail and graphics (Davis, 1989; Davis, Bagozzi, & Warshaw, 1989), spreadsheets (Mathieson, 1991), database systems (Szajna, 1996), and group support systems (Chin & Gopal, 1995). However the generalizability of these findings to the Web is questionable. This is because many of these findings related to microcomputer-based technologies, where the social context of the technology is limited to the confines of the organization. The ubiquitous nature of the Web, however, substantially expands the boundaries an organization shares with the environment (Vadapalli & Ramamurthy 1998). Teo and King (1997) further highlight this point when they state that the "factors which influence the adoption of inter-organizational systems are not necessarily the same as those influencing the adoption of the Internet" (p.56). Thus, from an organizational anthropological perspective the Web can be classified as an open system.

The current study attempts to break new ground by examining Web access behavior (or Web usage, we use the terms interchangeably) in the workplace. We assess the importance of antecedent (management support, experience, formal training and self-training) and perceptual factors (perceived enjoyment, perceived usefulness, perceived ethical beliefs and social pressure) which influence an individual to access various Web sites.

HYPOTHESES DEVELOPMENT

The theoretical basis for this study stems from the technology acceptance model (TAM), a behavioral model frequently used for understanding various types of IS usage. The TAM posits that an individual's technology usage behavior is influenced by intentions to use the technology, which in turn are based on attitudes toward the technology. Attitudes are based on potential users' perceptual beliefs regarding the technology. The TAM is derived from the Theory of Reasoned Action (TRA), the theory of individual attitudes, intentions, and actions based on work of behavioral psychologists who use an expectations-based model for examining individual behavior (Ajzen, 1991; Ajzen & Fishbein, 1980; Fishbein & Ajzen, 1975).

The research model examined in this study is illustrated in Figure 1. The model hypothesizes that Web site access behavior is a function of four perceptual factors, namely usefulness, enjoyment, ethical beliefs and social pressure. Additionally, it is proposed that the antecedent variables (management support, experience, and formal/self-training) have a direct influence on access. It is further proposed that the perceptual factors mediate the effects of the antecedent factors on Web usage. The network of relationships illustrated in the model and the rationale for the proposed linkages are explained in the ensuing section.

Figure 1: Research Model

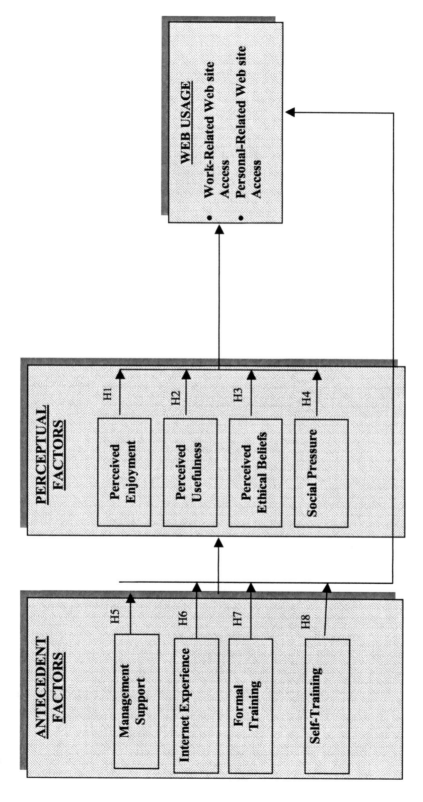

Web Usage

In the study of personal computing acceptance, researchers have identi-fied user satisfaction and system usage as the most generally affirmed measures of acceptance (DeLone & McLean, 1992; Montazemi, 1988; Raymond, 1990; Straub, Limayem, & Karahanna, 1995). However, system usage has been the primary indicator of technology acceptance (Adams et al., 1992; Davis, 1989; Straub et al., 1995; Szajna, 1996; Thompson, Higgins, & Howell, 1991). System usage is a good surrogate for gauging the effective deployment of IS resources in the organization and is a necessary condi-tion for ensuring productivity payoffs (Davis, 1989; Mathieson, 1991; Taylor & Todd, 1995). Since the focus of this study is to understand the factors promoting Web site usage, types of Web sites accessed at work were utilized as the dependent variables. Additionally, it is important to note that Web access relates to usage in its entirety rather than to a specific tool (such as a browser or Web service provider), thus enhancing user comparability across firms.

Perceptual Factors

The innovation diffusion suggests that individual usage decisions are a function of perceptual factors. These include intrinsic factors, which pertain to the performance of an activity because of the activity itself, apart from any performance consequences. This study examines two such factors, namely, perceived enjoyment and perceived ethical beliefs. Extrinsic perceptual factors involve performance of an activity because of expected results, distinctive from the activity itself. Perceived usefulness and social pressure are examples of extrinsic motivation.

Perceived enjoyment represents a type of intellectual enjoyment and is defined as an individual's tendency to interact spontaneously, inventively, and imaginatively with the artifact. Empirical research indicates that the general characteristic of enjoyment/fun relates positively to creativity and to exploratory behavior when interacting with technology (Webster, 1992). Research further indicates that individuals who perceive any activity involv-ing use of microcomputers as inherently enjoyable, apart from any anticipated improvement in performance, are likely to use it more extensively than others (Davis, 1992; Malone, 1981; Webster, 1989). Jordan (1996) examined enjoyment in terms of the hedonic benefits and feeling associated with the use of artifacts for entertainment purposes and found a strong correlation between enjoyment and artifact usage. Popular literature report that users find the Web provided them with excitement as well as satisfaction. Thus, it is hypoth-esized that:

H1: Perceived enjoyment is directly related to Web site access behavior.

Perceived usefulness is defined as "the degree to which a person believes that using a particular system would enhance his or her job" p.320 (Davis et al., 1989, p.320). The importance of perceived usefulness as a motivating factor derives from the TRA and TAM models, which propose that perceived usefulness affects usage due to reinforcement values of outcomes. The Web offers many such utilitarian benefits including rapid information access, identifying opportunities, and research development among others (Teo, Tan, & Buk, 1998). Adams et al. (1992) and Davis (1989) reported that user acceptance of computer systems was driven to a large extent by perceived usefulness. In addition, Davis (1989) found that perceived usefulness exhibited a stronger and more consistent relationship with usage than did other variables reported in the literature including various attitudes, satisfaction and perceptions measures. Other studies by Davis et al. (1992), Robey (1979), and Thompson et al. (1994) suggested that perceived usefulness was a major contributor to information system usage. More recently Teo et al. (1999) found that perceived usefulness had a significant influence in Internet usage. This leads us to propose the following hypothesis:

H2: Perceived usefulness is directly related to Web site access behavior.

Perceived ethical beliefs can be defined as the degree to which a person has a favorable or unfavorable evaluation of the behavior in question. Ethical behavior has been a subject of many studies. Several authors such as Bommer et al. (1987), Hegarty and Sims (1979), and Trevino and Webster (1992) among others suggest that a person's decision to act ethically or unethically is determined by antecedent variables such as training and education (Rest, 1979) management Thus the following hypothesis is proposed:

H3: Ethical belief is directly related to Web site access behavior.

Social pressure refers to a person's perception of the social urgency put on him or her to perform the behavior in question (Ajzen & Fishbein, 1980). The social movement literature suggests that people take account of others when making decisions about participation in an activity. Thus, if there is a subset of a group that uses the Web, the acceptance by this subset becomes a critical mass influencing the usage of others. In the context of this study, social pressure refers to an individual's perceptions of behavior about using the Web. Individuals may use the Web for work-related purposes because of pressure from those in the work environment to use the Web. Such pressure can force individuals to disengage from self-limiting behavior such as surfing (Asch, 1951; Veiga, 1991). Therefore we propose that:

H4: Social pressure is directly related to Web site access behavior.

Antecedent Factors

Management support refers to management endorsements of technology usage. It typically ensures sufficient resource allocations and reinforces the importance of adopting new work behaviors. It is associated with greater system success and lack of such support is considered a critical barrier to the effective utilization of information technology (Cerveny & Sanders, 1986; Gist, Schwoerer, & Rosen, 1989). Igbaria et al. (1997) found that management support has a direct effect on perceived usefulness in computer acceptance in small businesses. Research also suggested that management support was positively related to enjoyment (Trevino & Webster, 1992) and was also closely associated with greater system usage. Since the ubiquitous nature of the Web permits employees' easy access to various non-work-related Web sites, management would have to trust their employees to surf the Web for work-related purposes only. Management support thus would be of vital importance in motivating appropriate behavior (Fornell & Larcker, 1981; Igbaria, Parasuraman, & Baroudi, 1996). Hence we suggest that:

H5: Management support has a direct and indirect effect on Web site access behavior.

Web experience is defined as a user's knowledge or expertise in performing tasks on the Web. Experience in performing a task is an important factor contributing to behavior (Ajzen & Fishbein, 1980). It is positively related to perceived usefulness (Igbaria, 1993; Taylor & Todd, 1995), enjoyment (Webster, 1992) as well as system usage (DeLone, 1988; Igbaria, Pavri, & Huff, 1989). Recent findings by Hammond et al. (1998), suggest that experienced users appear to have enduring involvement with the Web than novice users. Thus, having Web experience could promote positive attitudes towards the Web, which in turn will lead to increased Web usage. Therefore it is hypothesized that:

H6: Web experience has a direct and indirect effect on Web site access behavior.

Web formal/self-training refers to structured instruction on the use of the Web, focusing on efforts to transfer knowledge (Nelson & Cheney, 1987). The TAM proposes that antecedent factors, such as training, will affect behavior through the effect on beliefs. The use of information technology depends on the technology itself and the level of training of the individual using it (Nelson, 1990). In a Web environment with its extensive boundaries, employees have to be trusted to ensure that the Web is used only for work-related and not for personal-related purposes. Thus, it's important that the organization provides its employees with formal training as to increase confidence in user perceptions about the benefits of the system so that they would use the Web to boost their productivity. Prior research on end-user training reported that training promoted greater understanding and more favorable attitudes. Training was found to have a positive impact on perceived usefulness (Igbaria, 1995; Lee, 1986; Raymond, 1988). There has been some support for a direct link between training and technology usage (Amoroso & Cheney, 1991; Nelson & Cheney, 1987). Lack of training, on the other hand, could result in employees exhibiting hedonic behavior, using the Web for pleasure purposes. Thus, it hypothesized that:

H7: Web formal training has a direct and indirect effect on Web site access behavior.

H8: Web self-training has a direct and indirect effect on Web site access behavior.

METHODOLOGY

Sample and Procedure

Data for this study were collected using a questionnaire survey sent to alumni of a major university in the northeastern United States during 1998. Because of the exploratory nature of research in Web usage, it was viewed as important to obtain a cross section of responses in the sample rather than to focus on a particular industry or business. Participation in the study was voluntary and people were assured that their individual responses would be treated as confidential.

Questionnaires were sent to 3,000 alumni who were randomly selected from the university's alumni database. Reminders were mailed two weeks later. In total 505 responses were received, yielding a response rate of about 17%. Of the 445 usable responses, only 334 had Web access at work. The lower than average level of response (average response rate for this type of survey is about 20%) can be attributed the length of the questionnaire. To evaluate non-response bias, comparisons between respondent and non-respondent individuals and between early responses and late responses were made on the basis of two objective measures (age and gender). No statistically significant differences were found, strengthening confidence in the representativeness of the sample.

Table 1 summarizes the characteristics of the sample. Men comprised 63.5% (212) of the sample and women 36.5% (122). Their ages ranged from 21 to 70, with an average of 40.50 years (S.D. = 11.31). The majority of the respondents had a graduate or professional degree (51.5%); the remaining had either a bachelor's degree (24.6%) or some graduate/professional study (18.3 %).

Table 1: Respondent Profiles (n=334)

Age		Gender	
Below 26	8.2%	Male	63.5%
26-30	12.8%	Female	36.5%
31-35	18.6%		
36-40	13.1%		
41-45	12.8%		
46-50	13.7%		
51-55	8.8%		
56-60	7.5%		
61 and above	4.5%		

Types of Business

Services	20.1%
Manufacturing	16.2%
Financial/Insurance	14.1%
Education	11.7%
Government	10.8%
Wholesale/Retail	2.1%
Self-employed	3.3%
Other	21.7%

Organizational Position

Top-level manager	17.1%
Middle-level manager	19.8%
Lower-level manager	9.0%
Professional	38.9%
Administrative support and other	15.2%

Web users came from a range of businesses, including services (20.1%), manufacturing (16.2%), finance/insurance/real estate (14.1%), education (11.7%), government (10.8%), self-employed (3.3%), and wholesale or retail trade (2.1%). Forty-one percent of the respondents worked in companies with fewer than 500 employees and 59% worked in companies with more than 500 employees. The length of time employed in the company ranged from 1 to 38 years, with an average of 8.7 years (S.D. = 8.19). Top-level manager was reported as the respondent's position for 17.1% of the sample, middle-level manager by 19.8%, lower-level manager by 9.0%, professional by 38.9% and administrative support and other by 15.2%. Hence the sample represented those for whom use of the Web was likely to be voluntary rather than mandatory (Hiltz & Johnson, 1989). The length of time in the present position ranged from 1 to 35 years, with an average of 5.86 years (S.D.= 6.13), with

61.8% of the respondents reporting tenure in current position of 5 years or less. The overwhelming majority (84.4%) reported their companies as having a Web site and three quarters reported using the Web outside of work.

Operationalization of Theoretical Constructs

Web usage at work was assessed through the following indicators: accessing work-related sites and personal-related Web sites.

Web site access measures were created for this study and suggested by Cronin (1995). Individuals were asked to indicate how likely they were to access seven different types of Web pages while at work, on a scale ranging from 1 (very unlikely) to 5 (very likely). The first factor (work-related Web sites) consisted of three Web sites: competitors, suppliers, and customers. The second factor (personal-related Web sites) consisted of four Web sites: arts and entertainment, travel and leisure, living/consumer, and sports/news.

Perceived enjoyment was an extension of work on microcomputer playfulness and our measure was based on the scale developed by Webster and Martocchio (Webster, 1992; Webster & Martocchio, 1995). Individuals were asked to characterize themselves when using the Internet by indicating their level of agreement on 5-point scales ranging from 1 (strongly disagree) to 5 (strongly agree), on four adjectives: spontaneous, imaginative, flexible, and creative.

Perceived usefulness was constructed from a five-item scale adapted from prior research (Davis, 1989; Davis et al., 1989; Igbaria, 1990), with appropriate modifications to make them specifically relevant to the Internet. Individuals were asked to indicate the extent of agreement or disagreement with five statements concerning the Internet on a 5-point Likert-type scale ranging from 1 (strongly disagree) to 5 (strongly agree). The measure included items such as "Using the Internet would increase my productivity on the job" and "Using the Internet would enhance my effectiveness in the job."

Perceived ethical beliefs were operationalized with a three-item scale developed for this study. Individuals were asked to indicate the extent of agreement or disagreement with three statements concerning the Internet on a 5-point Likert-type scale ranging from 1 (strongly disagree) to 5 (strongly agree). The measure included items such as "I feel that using the Internet for personal searches is acceptable," "In my company, it seems that accessing the Internet for personal searches is tolerated" and "I feel my company should block access to Internet sites which are deemed inappropriate for business."

Social pressure was operationalized by a single-item question modified by substituting "Internet" for "microcomputer" (Igbaria et al., 1996). Individuals indicated their agreement or disagreement with the following statement: "At my workplace, most people who are important to me think I should be regularly using the Internet." The response options were anchored in a 5-point scale, ranging from 1 (strongly disagree) to 5 (strongly agree).

Management support was measured by assessing general support, which included encouragement by top management and allocation of adequate resources. Individuals were asked to indicate the extent of agreement or disagreement with three statements concerning organizational support on a 5-point scale ranging from 1 (strongly disagree) to 5 (strongly agree). Examples of items included: "Management has provided the necessary help and resources to get me used to the Internet quickly" and "I am always supported and encouraged by my boss to use the Internet in my job."

Web experience was assessed by three items asking respondents to indicate the extent of their experience with accessing the Internet, using Internet search engines, and downloading files from the Internet on a 5-point scale from 1 (none) to 5 (very extensive). The mean was used as a measure of general Internet experience.

Internet formal/self-training was assessed by asking respondents to indicate the extent of training they had received from four different sources: vendors or outside consultants, in-house company courses, fellow workers, and self-training. The measures were on a 5-point scale ranging from 1 (very little) to 5 (very extensive). A principal components factor analysis (with varimax rotation) yielded two factors. The mean of the first three was used as a measure of Web formal training. Web self-training was a single-item measure.

Data Analysis

The hypothesized relationships in this study were tested using structured equation modeling. This is a second-generation multivariate technique that facilitates testing of the psychometric properties of the scales used to measure a variable, as well as estimation of the parameters of a structural model, i.e., the strength and direction of the relationships among the model variables (Fornell, 1982; Lohmoller, 1989; Wold, 1982).

The path coefficient of an exogenous variable delineates the direct effect of that variable on the endogenous variable. An indirect effect represents the effect of a particular variable (antecedent factor) on the third variable (Web access behavior) through its effects on a second mediating variable (perceptual factor). It is the product of the path coefficients along an indirect route from cause to effect via arrows in the headed direction only. When more than one indirect path exists, the total indirect effect is their sum. The sum of the direct and indirect effect reflects the total effect of the variable on the endogenous variable (Alwin & Hauser, 1975; Ross, 1975).

The use of latent variables requires a two-stage analysis (Anderson & Gerbing, 1988). The first stage includes the assessment of the measurement model and the evaluation of the construct independence, while the second stage provides verification for the structural model. Such an assessment empirically discriminates the theoretical constructs and validates the operational measures of the constructs through confirmatory factor analysis.

There should be at least three manifest variables as indicants of each latent variable, thereby reducing the biasing effects of random and systematic errors (Williams & Hazer, 1986; Williams & Podsakoff, 1989). Eight of the ten constructs met this constraint, while social pressure and self-training had only one indicator. The factor loadings between latent constructs to its manifest constructs (l) were greater than .61, meeting the criteria suggested by Nunnally (1978). Further, consistent with the recommendations of Fornell and Larcker (1981), communality estimates i.e., the square of the factor loadings were greater than 30% of the variance of the manifest constructs. Table 2 shows the factor loadings and reliability indices.

To assess discriminant validity of the measures, i.e., the degree to which items differentiate among constructs or measure distinct concepts, we examined the correlations between the measures of potentially overlapping constructs (Grant, 1989). The items comprising an instrument that measured the constructs correlate more highly with each other than with items measuring other constructs in the model, indicating the measure had adequate discriminant validity. In addition, the correlations between the residuals of the manifest constructs were below .04, thus indicating that each of the blocks of the measurement model was defined correctly and that each block as designed was a separate construct. The correlations are presented in Table 3. To examine the inner blocks of the measurement model the squared mean correlations (SMC) were measured. SMC represent the percent of variance in the endogenous constructs that is accounted for by the predictors in the measurement model.

Results

Several statistics were used to assess the model's goodness of fit. The goodness of fit indices for this model included $x^2/df = 2.09$; goodness of fit index (GFI) = 0. 82; root mean square error of approximation (RMSEA) = 0.05; comparative fit index (CFI) = 0.92. All measures were within the

Table 2: Reliability of Measures

	Estimate λ	Composite Reliability	Average Variance Extracted
Management Support		0.79	0.56
MS 1	0.71		
MS 2	0.80		
MS 3	0.73		
Internet Experience		0.85	0.68
IE 1	0.71		
IE 2	0.82		
IE 3	0.94		
Internet Formal Training		0.60	0.54
IT 1	0.76		
IT 2	0.77		
IT 3	0.68		
Percieved Enjoyment		0.69	0.51
PP 1	0.61		
PP 2	0.66		
PP 3	0.71		
PP 4	0.86		
Perceived Usefulness		0.91	0.81
PU 1	0.95		
PU 2	0.94		
PU 3	0.87		
PU 4	0.89		
PU 5	0.86		
Perceived Ethical Beliefs		0.68	0.55
EB 1	0.69		
EB 2	0.72		
EB 3	0.81		
Personal-Related Web Sites		0.86	0.63
PE 1	0.83		
PE 2	0.82		
PE 3	0.86		
PE 4	0.67		
Work-Related Web Sites		0.71	0.53
PR 1	0.68		
PR 2	0.81		
PR 3	0.71		

Table 3: Construct Correlations (n= 334)

Latent Constructs	Correlations									
	1	2	3	4	5	6	7	8	9	10
1 Management Support	0.75									
2 Internet Experience	0.48	0.82								
3 Internet Formal Training	0.44	0.21	0.74							
4 Internet Self Training	0.23	0.64	0.02	1.00						
5 Perceived Usefulness	0.42	0.38	0.14	0.01	0.90					
6 Perceived Enjoyment	0.46	0.45	0.15	0.21	0.22	0.71				
7 Perceived Ethical Beliefs	0.24	0.41	0.23	0.36	0.19	0.23	0.74			
8 Social Pressure	0.65	0.27	0.28	0.15	0.26	0.31	0.15	1.00		
9 Work-related Web Sites	0.24	0.21	0.18	0.22	0.27	0.27	0.06	0.27	0.73	
10 Personal-related Web Sites	0.15	0.35	0.13	0.20	0.12	0.33	0.59	0.09	0.12	0.80

The diagonals represent the square root of the average variance extracted

The absolute values of correlation >.10 are significant at .05 or lower

Figure 2: Structural Model

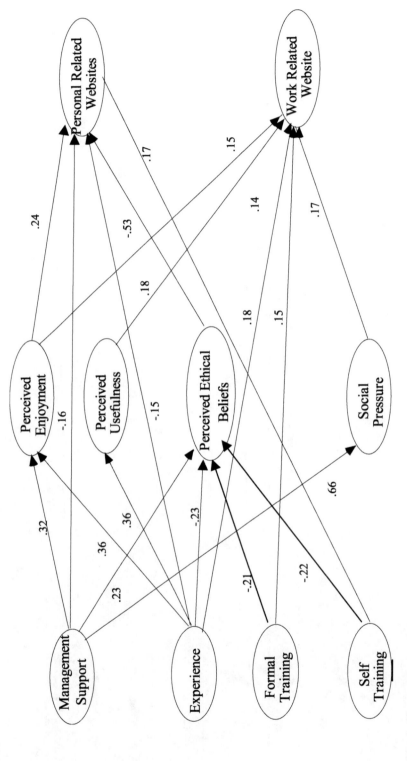

Only significant paths are shown
* p<0.05
** p<.01
***p<.001

acceptable levels as recommended by Bentler (1990) and Bagozzi and Youjae (1988), thus indicating acceptable model fit.

The results of the multivariate test of the structural model are presented in Table 4 and illustrated in Figure 2. Hypothesis (H1) was supported with perceived enjoyment having significant direct effects on accessing work-related Web sites: $\beta = .15$, $p < .05$; and personal Web sites: $\beta = .24$, $p < .001$. Perceived usefulness has a significant direct effect on only on work-related Web sites ($\beta = .18$, $p < .05$), thus only providing partial support for (H2). Hypothesis (H3) was supported with ethical beliefs having a strong negative influence on personal Web sites ($\beta = -.53$, $p < .001$) and positive influence on work-related Web sites ($\beta = .14$, $p < .05$). Partial support was also obtained for hypothesis (H4), where social pressure had a significant direct effect on work-related Web sites ($\beta = .17$, $p < .05$).

Partial support was obtained for hypothesis (H5), where management support had a direct negative effect on personal-related Web access ($\beta = -.16$, $p < .05$). It should be noted that management support had a significant indirect effect on accessing work-related Web sites mainly through social pressure. In terms of Web experience, hypothesis (H6) was partially supported, with only work-related Web sites ($\gamma = .18$, $p < .05$).

Contrary to hypothesis (H7), Web formal training had only significant direct effect on work-related Web sites and no mediating effect through the perceptual constructs. Self-training had a direct effect on time personal Web sites ($\gamma = .17$, $p < .05$), showing partial support for hypothesis (H8). Web self-training had a strong indirect effect on accessing personal Web sites through the perceptual factors.

In summary, the tests of the structural model show that management support, experience and perceived ethical beliefs had a significant negative influence, while self-training and perceived enjoyment had a positive influence on personal-related Web access. Internet experience, formal training, and all the perceptual factors influenced work-related Web site access.

DISCUSSION AND IMPLICATIONS

Anecdotal evidence shows us that as more and more companies provide Web access to their employees the level of abuse is on the rise as well. Accessing personal-related Web sites during work hours has serious repercussions including loss of productivity and clogged networks among others. This study breaks new ground in research on information system usage by examining the effect of both antecedent and perceptual variables on Web usage in the work environment. We extend the theoretical perspectives and empirical findings of research from use of microcomputers to Web usage. We argue that the research findings of IS usage cannot be applied to the Internet, since these systems are open in terms of boundaries and social context in contrast to microcomputer-based systems, which are typically closed in nature. We propose and test a structural model examining the role of various antecedent and perceptual factors, which could promote the access of specific types of Web sites.

Prior studies have foreshadowed the increasing importance of perceptual factors in promoting usage of information technology and our results reinforce the importance of these factors in stimulating Web usage (Igbaria et al., 1989; Webster, 1992). The potential for enjoyment and the heightened social pressures and ethical beliefs for usage are more fully realized in work-related Web site access. Further, the findings reiterate the importance of perceived usefulness in promoting usage. However, contrary to prior research on microcomputer usage (Adams et al., 1992; Davis, 1989; Igbaria et al., 1997; Judge, 1998) and to our expectations, perceived usefulness did not play as critical of a mediating role in Web usage as in microcomputer usage. This is shown by a lack of significant effects on accessing work-related and personal-related Web sites. It is possible that Web users already have strong positive beliefs about the usefulness of information technology gained from previous experiences with microcomputers. Successfully adopting one level of information technology may predispose one to believe in the ease of use and usefulness of additional information technology. In addition, the results also indicate that low levels of management support, formal training and ethical beliefs as well as high levels of self-training and perceived enjoyment can lead individuals to engage in self-limiting behavior such as surfing the Web for non-work-related activities.

The results indicate partial support for the proposed linkages among the model variables and provide interesting insights into the paths through which the antecedent variables influence Web usage. The findings indicate that perceived ethical beliefs is a key intervening variable linking antecedent variables with Web usage. In addition, social pressure links management support with accessing work-related Web sites. As predicted by the technology acceptance model, the impact of Web experience and formal training is direct, with support for a mediated route.

The findings of the present study contribute to a better theoretical understanding of the factors promoting Web usage. It should be noted, however, that the model variables explained 22% of the variation in accessing work-related Web sites and 42% of the variation in accessing personal-related

Web sites. The fact that much of the variance remains unexplained points to the need for additional research. It should also be noted that research into the antecedents, usage, and the impact of the Web is in its infancy. Additionally, the relatively low response rate (17%) calls into question generalizability of the findings, thus requiring additional research to see if similar results are obtained with other samples. A few possible extensions of this work include examining additional work environments, both in the United States and globally, and conducting experiments. Also, it is possible that the variables have interactive effects with motivating factors and eventually usage. Finally, while cross-sectional studies, such as the present one, are useful for identifying patterns of relationships among relevant variables, longitudinal research design is essential to confirm causal linkages. The strengths of the findings would also be enhanced by the use of both subjective and objective measures of usage, as common method variance contributing to the results cannot be ruled out.

Based on the findings of this study, formal training programs aimed at managing Web usage are important to channel learning into more structured and sanctioned programs (Cronin, 1996). Additionally as Levin (1989) points out, ethical behavior is the product of training, thus indicating that such training programs should include an element of ethical usage of the Web. Our results suggest that enjoyment is an important motivator of both accessing work-related as well as personal Web sites. The direct impact of social pressure on work-related Web site access and its role as a mediator (between management support and work-related access) suggest that individuals are responsive to management support and that decisions to use the Web are consistent with collective action theories (Oliver & Marwell, 1985). Web usage is a social event that organizations can manage both directly through policies and software controls, but also through organizational culture. Nevertheless, it is important to remember that Web connectivity is not equivalent to using the Web to gain competitive advantage. Much still needs to be done by both academics and practitioners to discover how to make this leap.

ENDNOTE

[1] The term Internet in this study refers to Web usage.

REFERENCES

Adams, D. A., Nelson, R. R. and Todd, P. A. (1992). Perceived usefulness, ease of use and usage of information technology: A replication. *MIS*

Quarterly, 16, 227-247.

Ajzen, I. (1991). The theory of planned behavior. *Organizational Behavior and Human Decision Processes*, 50, 179-211.

Ajzen, I. and Fishbein, M. (1980). *Understanding Attitudes and Predicting Behavior*. Englewood Cliffs: Prentice-Hall.

Alwin, D. E. and Hauser, R. M. (1975). Decomposition of effects in path analysis. *American Sociological Review*, 40, 37-47.

Amoroso, D. L. and Cheney, P. H. (1991). Testing a causal model of end-user application effectiveness. *Journal of Management Information Systems*, 8(1), 63-89.

Anderson, J. and Gerbing, D. (1988). Structural equation modeling and practice: A review and recommendation of a two step approach. *Psychological Bulletin*, 103, 411-423.

Asch, S. E. (1951). *Effects of Group Pressure on the Modification and Distortion of Judgments*. Pittsburgh, PA: Carnegie Institute of Technology Press.

Bagozzi, P. R. and Youjae, Y. (1988). On the evaluation of structural equation models. *Journal of the Academy of Marketing Science*, 16(1), 74-94.

Bentler, P. (1990). Comparative fit indexes in structural models. *Psychological Bulletin*, 107, 238-246.

Bommer, M., Gratto, C., Gravander, J. and Tuttle, M. (1987). A behavioral model of ethical and unethical decision making. *Journal of Business Ethics*, May, 265-280.

Cerveny, R. P. and Sanders, G. L. (1986). Implementation and structural variables. *Information & Management*, 11, 191-198.

Chin, W. and Gopal, A. (1995). Adoption intention in GSS: Relative importance of beliefs. *DATA BASE*, 26(2-3), 42-63.

Cronin, M. (1995). *Doing More Business on the Internet*. Van Nostrand Reinhold: ITP Inc.

Cronin, M. J. (1996). *The Internet as a Competitive Business Resource*. Boston: Harvard Business School Press.

Davis, F. D. (1989). Perceived usefulness, perceived ease of use and user acceptance of information technology. *MIS Quarterly*, 13, 983-1003.

Davis, F. D. (1992). Extrinsic and intrinsic motivation to use computers in the workplace. *Journal of Applied Social Psychology*, 22, 1111-1132.

Davis, F. D., Bagozzi, R. P. and Warshaw, P. R. (1989). User acceptance of computer technology: A comparison of two theoretical models. *Management Science*, 35, 982-1003.

DeLone, W. H. (1988). Determinants of success for computer usage in small business. *MIS Quarterly*, 12(1), 51-61.

DeLone, W. H. and McLean, E. R. (1992). Information systems success: The quest for the dependent variable. *Information Systems Research*, 3(1), 60-95.

Fishbein, M. and Ajzen, I. (1975). *Belief Attitude Intentions and Behavior: An Introduction to Theory and Research*. Boston, MA: Addison-Wesley.

Fornell, C. R. (1982). *A Second Generation of Multivariate Analysis Methods: Volume I and II*. New York: Praeger Special Studies.

Fornell, C. R. and Larcker, D. F. (1981). Structural equation models with unobservable variables and measurement error. *Journal of Marketing Research*, 18, 39-50.

Gist, M. E., Schwoerer, C. E. and Rosen, B. (1989). Effects of alternative training methods on self efficacy and performance in computer software training. *Journal of Applied Psychology*, 74(6), 884-891.

Grant, R. A. (1989). Building and testing causal models of an information technology's impact. Paper presented at the *Proceedings of the Tenth International Conference on Information Systems*, Boston, MA.

Hammond, K., G., M. and Diaz, N. A. (1998). Fun and work on the Web: Differences in attitudes between novices and experienced users. *Advances in Consumer Research*, 25, 372-378.

Hegarty, W. H. and Sims, H. (1979). Organizational philosophy, policies and objectives related to unethical decision behavior: A laboratory experiment. *Journal of Applied Psychology*, 64, 332-338.

Hiltz, S. R. and Johnson, K. (1989). Measuring acceptance of computer-mediated communication systems. *Journal of American Society for Information Science*, 40(6), 386-397.

Igbaria, M. (1990). End-user computing effectiveness: A structural equation model. *International Journal of Management Science*, 18(6), 637-652.

Igbaria, M. (1993). User acceptance of microcomputer technology: An empirical test. *International Journal of Management Science*, 21(1), 73-90.

Igbaria, M. (1995). Testing the determinants of microcomputer usage via a structural equation model. *Journal of Management Information Systems*, 11(4), 87-105.

Igbaria, M., Parasuraman, S. and Baroudi, J. (1996). A motivational model of microcomputer usage. *Journal of Management Information Systems*, 13(1), 127-143.

Igbaria, M., Pavri, F. and Huff, S. (1989). Microcomputer application: An empirical look at usage. *Information and Management*, 16(4), 187-196.

Igbaria, M., Zinatelli, N., Cragg, P. and Cavaye, A. L. (1997). Personal computing acceptance factors in small firms: A structural equation model. *MIS Quarterly*, 21(3), 279-300.

Jordan, P. W. (1996). *Dipleasure and How to Avoid it*. London: Taylor and Francis.

Judge, P. C. (1998). How safe is the Net? *Business Week*, June 22, 148-152.

LaPlante, A. (1997). Start small, think infinite. *Computerworld*, 24-30.

Lee, D. S. (1986). Usage pattern and sources of assistance to personal computer users. *MIS Quarterly*, 10(4), 313-325.

Levin, M. (1989). Ethics courses: Useless. *New York Times*, November 25.

Lohmoller, J. B. (1989). Latent variable path modeling with partial least squares. Physica Heidelberg. *Cognitive Science*, 4, 333-369.

Malone, T. W. (1981). Toward a theory of intrinsically motivating instruction. *Cognitive Science*, 4, 333-369.

Mathieson, K. (1991). Predicting user intentions: Comparing the technology acceptance model with the theory of planned behavior. *Information Systems Research*, 3(3), 173-191.

McWilliams, G. and Stepanek, M. (1998). Taming the info monster. *Business Week*, June 22, 170-172.

Montazemi, A. R. (1988). Factors affecting information satisfaction in the context of the small business environment. *MIS Quarterly*, 12(2), 239-256.

Nelson, R. (1990). Individual adjustment to information-driven technologies: A critical review. *MIS Quarterly*, 14(1), 87-98.

Nelson, R. and Cheney, P. (1987). Training end-users: An exploratory study. *MIS Quarterly*, 11(4), 547-559.

Nunnally, J. C. (1978). *Psychometric Theory*. (2nd ed.). New York, NY: McGraw-Hill.

Oliver, P. and Marwell, G. (1985). A theory of the critical mass. Interdependence, group hetergeneity and the production of collective action. *AJS*, 91(3), 522-556.

Raymond, L. (1988). The impact of computer training on the attitudes and usage behavior of small business managers. *Journal of Small Business Management*, 26(3), 8-13.

Raymond, L. (1990). Organizational context and IS success. *Journal of Management Information Systems*, 6(4), 5-20.

Rest, J. R. (1979). *Development in Judging Moral Issues*. Minneapolis, MN: University of Minnesota Press.

Robey, D. (1979). User attitudes and management information systems use.

Academy of Management Journal, 22, 527-538.

Ross, D. R. (1975). Direct, indirect and spurious effects: Comment on causal analysis of inter-organizational relations. *Administrative Science Quarterly*, 20, 295-297.

Straub, D., Limayem, M. and Karahanna, E. E. (1995). Measuring system usage: Implications for IS theory testing. *Management Science*, 41(8), 1328-1342.

Szajna, B. (1996). Empirical evaluation of the revised technology acceptance model. *Management Science*, 42(1), 85-92.

Taylor, S. and Todd, P. (1995b). Assessing IT usage: The role of prior experience. *MIS Quarterly*, 19(4), 561-570.

Teo, S. H. T., Tan, M. and Buk, W. K. (1998). A contingency model of Internet adoption in Singapore. *International Journal of Electronic Commerce*, 2(2), 95-118.

Teo, T. S. H., Lim, V.K.G. and Lai, R. Y. C. (1999). Intrinsic and extrinsic motivation in Internet usage. *Omega*, 27, 25-37.

Teo, T. S. H. and King, W. (1997). Integration between business planning and information systems planning: An evolutionary-contingency perspective. *Journal of Mangement Information Systems*, 14(1), 185-214.

Thompson, R. L., Higgins, C. A. and Howell, J. M. (1991). Personal computing: Toward a conceptual model of utilization. *MIS Quarterly*, 15, 125-143.

Thompson, R. L., Higgins, C. A. and Howell, J. M. (1994). Influence of experience on personal computer utilization: Testing a conceptual model. *JMIS*, 11(1), 167-187.

Trevino, K. L. and Webster, J. (1992). Flow in computer-mediated communication: Electronic mail and voice mail evaluation and impacts. *Communication Research*, 19(5), 539-573.

Vadapalli, A. and Ramamurthy, K. (1998). Business use of the Internet: An analytical framework and exploratory case study. *International Journal of Electronic Commerce*, 2(2), 71-94.

Veiga, J. F. (1991). The frequency of self-limiting behavior in groups: A measure and explanation. *Human Relations*, 44(8), 877-895.

Webster, J. (1989). *Playfulness and Computers at Work*. Unpublished Unpublished PhD dissertation, New York University, New York.

Webster, J. (1992). Microcomputer playfulness: Development of a measure of workplace implications. *MIS Quarterly*, 16(2), 201-226.

Webster, J. and Martocchio, J. J. (1995). The differential effects of software training previews on training outcomes. *Journal of Management*, 21, 757-787.

Williams, L. and Hazer, J. (1986). Antecedents and consequences of satisfaction and commitment in turnover models: A reanalysis using latent variable structural equation methods. *Journal of Applied Psychology*, 71, 219-231.

Williams, L. and Podsakoff. (1989). *Longitudinal Field Methods for Studying Reciprocal Relationships in Organizational Behavior Research: Toward Improved Causal Analysis*. (Vol. 11). Greenwich, CT.: JAI Press.

Wold, H. (1982). *Soft Modeling-The Basic Design and Some Extensions*. Amsterdam.

Chapter IV

Internet Usage in Sub-Saharan Africa

Uzoamaka P. Anakwe
Pace University, USA

INTERNET USAGE IN SUB-SAHARA AFRICA

Using the Internet in the developed part of the world has become a necessity or a matter of choice. However, for the majority in countries of Sub-Saharan Africa, Internet usage is still an illusion since Africa has remained the least Internet-connected region in the world (Lishan, 1997). Such "digital divide" between the developed and developing countries has raised interests and concerns from different parties, ranging from indigenes and governments of these countries to international organizations or agencies. Since such a gap impedes development and progress in these countries, as well as limits the potential of a truly global and competitive e-economy, the need to understand the dynamics of Internet usage in these countries becomes relevant.

This chapter discusses Internet usage in Sub-Saharan Africa, citing examples from Nigeria, Ghana, and Kenya. The factors that influence Internet usage in these countries are presented, followed by two general propositions. Furthermore, organizational implications and suggested guidelines for connectivity are discussed, as well as future trends, followed by a conclusion.

BACKGROUND

Internet usage has grown substantially since its inception in 1969. It is predicted that there will be over 700 million users by 2001 and in over five years 900 million electronic devices could be connected to the Internet (Brown, 2000). Despite the significant growth of the Internet on a global scale over the past few years, the poorer regions of the world such as Sub-Saharan Africa have relatively slow growth. Almost half of the world's online users live in US and Canada (136 million) and more people use the Internet in Sweden (3.5 million) than in Africa (2.5 million) (Moeller, 2000).

There is growing concern that as technology becomes an increasingly important part of the global economy, Sub-Saharan Africa, which has nearly 10% of the world's population but just 0.1% of Internet connections, will be left behind (Brown, 2000). For instance, by 1996 only 11 African countries had Internet access, but by September 2000, 53 of the 54 countries had Internet connections at least in their capital cities. Although this indicates over 480% increase in Internet usage from 1996, this increase is confined mainly to the capital cities (Jensen, 2000; Fraser, Hamish, & McGrath, 2000; Fadeyi, 2000). Also, 70 to 80% of the population who reside in the rural areas of Africa have no access to the Internet (Ukwe, 1999). Subsequently, bridging the technology divide between the developed and developing countries such as Sub-Saharan Africa is attracting a lot of attention from various parties (e.g., individuals, governments, organizations, and international agencies). A synthesis of these interests and concerns reveals the following:

- Strong desire for countries of Sub-Saharan Africa to benefit from the versatility and immeasurable capabilities of the Internet.
- Acknowledgement of the enormous challenges and constraints [e.g., lack of adequate infrastructure, restrictive decisions and inappropriate policies vis-à-vis global telecommunications trend; lack of competition, especially in international service (Ugwoke, 2000a)] that limit increasing Internet usage in countries of Sub-Saharan Africa.
- Suggestions and initiatives to alleviate challenges on increasing Internet usage.

Hence, Internet usage in developing countries of Sub-Saharan Africa is plagued by a lack of awareness, accessibility, and bottlenecks to feasibility.

FACTORS THAT INFLUENCE INTERNET USAGE IN SUB-SAHARA AFRICA

Internet usage in Sub-Saharan Africa has been influenced by two sets of factors: those that limit Internet usage and those that promote Internet usage. In summary, Internet usage has been limited by complex socio-economic, political, and infrastructural problems. Such impediments have triggered interests from various parties who promote Internet usage in Sub-Saharan Africa. These include: governments of these countries (e.g., Nigeria, Ghana, and Kenya), foreign governments (e.g., United States and UK), international agencies (e.g., World Bank, United Nations, UNESCO), and nongovernmental organizations (e.g., local businesses, multinational companies and/or their affiliates, and volunteer organizations). This section will focus on the contribution of these groups to Internet usage in the countries of Sub-Saharan Africa.

Governments (National and Others)

Any government of any nation that wants to grow wealthier has to have the basics right—managing the economy well, keeping the markets open, establishing the rule of law, creating a good climate for investment.

(President Clinton, Vanguard, August 28, 2000)

The above excerpt from President Clinton's speech in his visit to Nigeria highlights the significant role of the government in conducting the affairs of any country. However, the extent of government involvement varies with respect to the type of government, the level of development, and the sophistication of the particular society. Most developed countries have a democratic or mixed system of government, developed market economy, established and functional legal system, and developed human capital. Developing countries of Sub-Saharan Africa were dominated by totalitarian, socialist or unstable systems of government, fledgling market economy stifled by political instability, poorly enforceable legal system, and scarce human capital. Since the 1980s, many of the countries have been transitioning into a democratic mode of government, leaning towards market economic systems. These countries are cognizant of the need for functional legal systems and the development of human capital, especially since the more democratic governments with developed markets and/or mixed economies have experienced more success in advancing the needs of their people and achieving progress in all aspects of development. The governments of countries of Sub-Saharan Africa are capable of increasing the use of the Internet in their respective countries. Many of these governments are intrigued by the potential of the Internet to contribute to the economic development of their countries and overall well-being of their people. The governments have initiated regulations, policies and practices, and programs to revamp and strengthen their telecommunication sector with particular interest in facilitating increasing use of the Internet. The case of Nigeria is presented. Additional insights are provided with Ghana and Kenya.

Nigeria has been backward in promoting initiatives to increase Internet usage with its history of political instability and military regimes with totalitarian forms of government. However, its transition to a democratic form of government since 1999 has contributed to recent positive developments in many sectors of the economy including telecommunication. Consistent with most of the world, Nigeria recognizes the Internet as one of the most pervasive information technology advances in recent years. For instance, the president of the Nigerian communications commission (NCC)–the national regulator of Communication–stated that the "Internet will replace nearly all the vehicles for business transaction, commercial activities, learning processes, and will change the way the world economy functions" (Ugwoke, 2000b, p.1008209u3122). He emphasized the commitment of his commission to providing solutions to barriers that limit maximizing the potential benefits of the Internet. Such conviction is reflective of the government's stance and motivation to increase Internet usage in Nigeria.

The government is pursuing an aggressive agenda geared towards alleviating the impediments restricting greater Internet access and usage. It has undertaken massive privatization of the telecommunication sector designed to address the inadequate infrastructure and communication monopolies. The government in conjunction with the NCC has vowed to give private companies "unhindered access to Nigeria's telecommunications market" (Ogunbiyi & O'Brien, 2000, p. 39) by enacting policies, rules and regulations that promote active participation of businesses and other parties in the telecommunication sector; encouraging the bringing of ideas to the market through tax incentives and deepening of financial markets; and nurturing a knowledgeable workforce through on-the-job training initiatives. For example, greater access to the Internet is predicted with the latest approval of the NCC to allow business centers to offer telephony and related services (Muoka, 2000). Through government directives, the national telecommunications operator–Nitel–has established a national Internet backbone and has established a relationship with Global One in the US to provide the necessary link for Internet service. The government has authorized independent licenses to companies such as Motorphone, Omnes and Trend Communications to establish Internet and voice services. Also, the government intends to increase privatization of other industries.

The NCC collaborates with nonprofit academic-based organizations such as the Nigerian Internet Society that is devoted to advancing increasing use of the Internet and other technologies. It has welcomed input from these organizations in developing a national communications strategy. It participates and sponsors summits/workshops or conferences geared towards sharing ideas, increasing awareness and suggesting progressive practices and policies towards the Internet. Recently, the NCC hosted the AFRINET 2000, Internet summit exhibition, in Nigeria. The summit affirmed the urgency and need for African countries to address critical issues (e.g., education, commerce, and social life) relating to Internet development and usage. The summit concluded with specific recommendations encompassing: affordable and sustainable Internet service, building the information superhighway, human resource and gender issues, funding, policy and regulation (www.ncc.gov.ng/update.htm and www.ncc.gov.ng/summit%20_report.htm).

Ghana is among the few countries of Sub-Saharan Africa that has maintained a more stable political environment. The government has initiated economic reforms, which have contributed to investor interests and confidence. Ghana's Internet market is described as one of the largest in Africa. The government has played an active role in restructuring the communications sector, liberalizing the telecoms and value-added services (Jensen, 1999). For instance, the government, through the Ministry of Transport and Communications, addressed the stagnant growth in Internet and related services by initiating major reforms in the telecommunications sector. These reforms included the establishment of a centralized regulatory body, the National Communications Authority (NCA), responsible for regulating the telecommunications sector. The government combined the restructuring and privatization of aspects of the telecommunications sector and sought collaboration and/or involvement of foreign investors, such as the Malaysian consortium and a consortium led by the Ghana National Petroleum Corporation (GNPC) with the African Communications Group and Western Wireless, a US company based in Cambridge, Massachusetts. GNCP and Gilat, an Israeli company, have exclusive 20-year licenses to deploy a V-SAT-based telephone network around the country (http://www2.sn.apc.org/africa/countdet.CFM?countries_ISO_Code=GH).

Ghana's Internet connectivity and growth are attributed to the collaboration of several organizations including the Ministry of Transport and Communications of Ghana, Ghana Telecom, British Telecom, Network Communications Systems, and Pipex International (Tevie, Quaynor, & Bulley, 1996).

Kenya's Internet service is among the largest in Africa, with full Internet services established in 1995. In contrast to Nigeria and Ghana, collaboration between Kenya's government and nongovernmental organizations dedicated to promoting Internet usage has been weak. Rather, many private and nongovernmental organizations (NGOs) sought and established Internet access on their own. For example, the UN Department of Humanitarian Affairs, Urban Mission Support Group, United Bible Societies and east African Internet Association sought Internet access through their own independent initiatives. Multinational corporations, international organizations and NGOs are the main Internet users in Kenya. They make up more than 50% of all subscribers, with government and educational institutions making up less than 5% of all subscribers.

The government's restrictive regulatory policies and the high cost of international lines stunted the growth of the Internet initially. However, the future for the Internet market is promising as the government recently passed the Kenyan Communication Bill, which will establish the Kenya Communication Commission and ultimately lead to the privatization of its monopoly organization, the Kenya Posts and Telegraphs (Jensen, 1999). Internet users in Kenya are between 30,000 and 50,000, with an estimated monthly growth of 300 (Mweu, 2000).

International Agencies and Other Governments

International agencies have been instrumental towards increasing Internet access to countries in developing economies such as Sub-Saharan Africa. For instance, the World Bank in association with Softbank, the Japanese Internet group is setting up $500 million investment fund aimed at encouraging start-up digital technology ventures in about 100 developing countries by investing in a range of different Internet projects. James Wolfensohn, the president of the World Bank, vowed to take the lead in the effort to close the digital divide between developed and developing countries (O'Kane, 2000).

The United Nations and member nations such as the US are advocating greater involvement by developed countries to bridge the digital divide. The United States Agency for International Development (USAID), which focused on health and education for developing nations, has included promoting Internet access to developing nations of Africa (Myers, 1998). The United States government, through former US Vice President Al Gore, initiated the

Leland Initiative program to offer Internet assistance packages to some African countries. This program was executed through the USAID (Quaynor, 1996). Prime Minister Tony Blair of Britain initiated an ambitious partnership with the world's top information technology (IT) companies to provide resources (e.g., pledges of equipment, staff, software licenses, goods and services) for training teachers and ultimately the children (Atkinson, 2000). The Norwegian and Danish governments have been noted to provide financial and technical support to several African countries to help them purchase the necessary equipment and establish links for accessibility (Chepesiuk 1998).

Local Businesses and Multinational Corporations and/or Affiliates

Local businesses and multinational corporations or their affiliates are contributing to increasing Internet usage in Sub-Saharan Africa. These businesses, which include banks, oil companies, advertising firms, small- and medium-sized technology based companies, are responding to the global trends in information technology. For instance, 100% of the Association of Advertising Practitioners of Nigeria (AAPN) agencies have computerized all their operations and 40-50% of the agencies have various levels of access on the Internet (Amuzu, 1998). The brewery and cigarette industry invested 20% of their total revenue in 1998 into infrastructural development (Amuzu, 1998). Local companies, such as INLAKS computers, partner with multinational companies such as Unisys and QAD Inc., both of the USA, and DataStream and Liebert, to maintain competitive edge in the high-profile end of the IT business. In October 1999, INLAKS Computers acquired a Java-based product that enabled it to interface with the Internet. This development enable electronic and Internet banking (Aihe, 2000). Phone calls through the Internet are becoming popular across Nigerian cities. Nitel is also embarking in Internet telephony, which allows calls by anybody connected to the Internet. The banks have always kept up with technological advances and have been described as "pockets of sophistication" in Africa. For example, the executive director of one the new generation banks–Diamond Bank Limited– discussed his bank's introduction of "FLEXCUBE," designed to operate as a fully automated system. However, he acknowledged that the system was more automated than the environment, and there were provisions to modify or adjust the system and provide the customers with the infrastructure to operate in the system. His bank is committed to providing "versatile product"–e-banking in addition to Internet banking because ideally the Internet banking will be able to address the remote needs (Vanguard, Sept. 11, 2000).

Competition among the banks and among information technology companies striving to provide high-quality and latest technology to the banking industry are increasing Internet usage. For example, recent products such as "MoneyNet" and "CashFast," Internet-based international money transfer systems, offered by BT limited, a Lagos-based information technology company in partnership with Dello Sc Associates Inc. of the United States. Furthermore the BT Limited in partnership with STM Wireless Inc. of the US "has the best and latest V-SAT technology which some banks in the country have started adopting" (Vanguard, 2000). Gemcard Nigeria Limited recently introduced an electronic payment system (SmartPay) that has been adopted by some banks. It allows payment and transactions through the Internet (Akinmutimi, 2000). More electronic banking products are being developed for the Nigerian and global financial markets by BT and its foreign associates.

PROPOSITIONS

Internet usage, application and progression for countries of Sub-Saharan Africa seem to follow similar patterns. The examples of Nigeria, Ghana, and Kenya reveal that they all acknowledge and affirm the potential of the Internet in advancing their people's needs and their countries' progress. The governments of the various countries have professed their commitment to facilitate Internet usage in their respective countries. They all welcome the participation of volunteer nongovernmental organizations and outside organizations in promoting Internet usage. Ghana and Kenya and more recently Nigeria provide examples of the importance of collaboration between the government agencies, especially the regulatory bodies, and private and/or nongovernmental organizations in fostering Internet usage in their respective countries. Presently, the participation of multinational companies, international agencies, and professional organizations in the three countries and other countries of Sub-Saharan Africa has contributed to the continuous increase in Internet usage in these countries. For example, Internet users in Ghana increased from 4,500 in January 1998 to 20,000 in July 2000. The more stable governments of Ghana and Kenya that are pursuing privatization programs and an aggressive telecommunications agenda have achieved more advancement. However, the extent of advancement seems to be influenced by the government's policies and commitment to the telecommunications sector. Two propositions seem obvious:

Proposition 1:

Regions of Sub-Saharan Africa in which the governments express commitment to increasing Internet usage through policies and practices that are favorable to providing an active telecommunications sector will experience an increase in the use of the Internet.

Nongovernmental organizations in Sub-Saharan Africa have been instrumental towards increasing Internet usage. These organizations create increasing awareness of the necessity and the benefits of Internet usage. They organize workshops, seminars, and conferences in which the use of the Internet is localized to the African regions. These organizations focus on the issues relating to Africa as well as highlight the urgency of the need to get connected. Furthermore, they recommend policies, practices, and initiatives that will increase Internet use in their respective countries and the African region. An example of these workshops the AFRINET 2000. Hence, **Proposition 2**:

> The presence of nongovernmental organizations devoted to increasing Internet use in a particular country in Sub-Saharan Africa fosters awareness and contributes to the countries' adoption of initiatives to increase Internet usage.

IMPLICATIONS FOR CONNECTIVITY

For organizations operating or wishing to operate in countries of Sub-Saharan Africa, it is important to develop a local responsive communication strategy. Although there are commonalities among the countries of Sub-Saharan Africa with respect to the impediments or constraints and anticipated benefits, high government involvement, and commitment to increasing Internet usage, each of the countries is at a slightly different stage of Internet usage development.

The local responsiveness communication strategies should be developed for the following areas:

Connectivity: Connectivity has attracted the most attention of all the factors that will ensure Internet usage in developing countries of Sub-Saharan Africa. As presented earlier, 53 countries have achieved some level of Internet connectivity in their capital cities. However, these countries differ in many aspects, such as the extent of connectivity to the majority, the extent of government's involvement, and the presence of foreign investors, private companies and nongovernmental agencies, as well as international agencies. For instance, the federal government of Nigeria included e-commerce in its economic policy for 1999-2003, in which it expressed desire to promote the development of payment systems to foster the growth of e-commerce. Within one year of Nigeria's professed commitment to increasing Internet connectivity and usage, it has made unprecedented progress in almost all areas. Here are some examples:

The World of IT Limited Inc. in the UK in 1997 has reported an investment of $1 billion to boost the Nigerian e-commerce market (African News Service, July 17, 2000).

NetSat Express Inc., US, a leader in providing end-to-end satellite-based Internet solutions around the world has been awarded a three-year contract by Microtec, an Internet service provider start-up company based in Nigeria. NetStat will provide the Microtec customers with various benefits including satellite-based Internet connectivity (PR Newswire, August 2, 2000).

Nigerian companies are continually contracting with foreign companies to provide their much needed services, ranging from providing the infrastructure to facilitate connectivity from subscribers to providing engineering and integration skills among the various components. Recent examples include collaboration of three major International players (Global One, Westcon, and Logical) to provide Nitel with the infrastructure, installation and configuration work of a special equipment (the 3Com Total Control), accounting services and related services at three different locations (African News Service, May 15, 2000).

The Nigerian government is courting foreign investors and promising an enabling environment for local and foreign investors, especially in the e-commerce/IT-related areas. For example, the government gave special thanks to Hewlett Packard, which in collaboration with Management Information Systems (MIS) Limited of Nigeria organized an elaborate financial services summit. The government promised protection to Hewlett Packard and other companies who invest in Nigeria and help develop the local expertise (Ogbulie, 2000).

The nongovernmental organizations in collaboration with the NCC are sponsoring exhibitions, summits, and workshops designed to increase awareness, attract investors, and promote progressive policies and practices that will enable Internet connectivity and usage. For example, about 110 companies from across the globe participated in an annual "Computer, Telecommunications and Office Equipment Exhibition" held in May 2000 under the theme "e-Business: Laying the foundation of a digital economy." The chief executive of the Nigerian Communications Commission reemphasized his agency's commitment to "improving the network by creating an environment where services will not be a problem to anybody" (Xinhua News Agency, May 3, 2000).

Standard Trust Bank is financing an IT project with N500 million (about $5 million). This project is expected to increase IT awareness and usage across Nigeria. This will involve the provision of PCs, laptops, and servers.

Other companies involved with this project include Compaq, HP, Dell, IBM, Epson, and Microsoft (Africa News Service, July 9, 2000).

Human capital development: Local expertise in the IT field is extremely lacking. However, local companies in the various countries have acknowledged their lack of expertise and have sought out foreign partners to provide the needed expertise. These countries should pursue the development of human capital aggressively. International agencies and other volunteer organizations have emphasized education and training of the people in these countries.

Although, the various governments and groups acknowledge and emphasize the need to develop local expertise, connectivity and delivering services seem to have become more pressing priorities. For managers of organizations operating in these countries, the provision of training to local employees becomes paramount.

SUGGESTED GUIDELINES FOR CONNECTIVITY

1. Connectivity should be approached on a country-by-country basis. Gather information on the countries of interest through some of these Web sites: http://www.africapolicy.org/inet.htm (APIC Africa on the Internet page) and http://www.bellanet.org/partners/aisi/nici (Economic Commission for Africa National Information and Communications Infrastructure). Also, the embassies or consulates of the respective countries are good sources of information. Although, all the countries acclaim the overwhelming benefits of the Internet as well as note similar challenges and complaints, the dynamics of the political, socio-economic, and cultural factors make them distinct. The political and socioeconomic factors in most of the countries are quite volatile and unplanned. Moreover, the governments of the various countries play a very powerful and dominant role in running the affairs of the countries. This is usually encumbered with local ways of doing things. Networking, connections, understanding of the local politics, and mentalities of how things work in these countries differ and can be very stifling and tasking for a nonlocal. The above reasons lead to the second guideline.

2. Find a local partner. Having a local partner is very critical. However, the company or organization should be very cautious. The local partners should be required to invest their own money; else they will not have long-term stakes in the success of the venture (Maddy, 2000). Moreover,

the local partner should be politically savvy and understand the workings of the business. For Sub-Saharan African countries, especially Nigeria, many local companies are seeking partners that can provide them with the technical expertise and financial resources. The local partners can provide the marketing expertise to the local economy.

3. Patience and financial resources are very important. As Maddy (2000) stated, "A new venture in the third world needs a patient and visionary investor with deep pockets who is willing to ride out the bumps that inevitably appear in the road" (p. 67). This advice applies to connectivity or any business venture with Sub-Saharan Africa. This has become more real with the continuous changes in policies and practices in these countries. Although the policies towards the Internet and connectivity are positive, they have not been tested and could be changed indiscriminately. Moreover, the Internet market still faces numerous challenges, which could translate into higher costs of operation.

4. Develop short-term-to-long-term contractual arrangements and seek out consortiums or other alliances with other multinational corporations who have more experience operating in these countries. Also, because of the infrastructural challenges and other constraints associated with connectivity in these countries, alliances will enable risk sharing and better resource utilization.

5. Participate in the workshops, seminars, and exhibitions sponsored by the governments and/or their telecommunications sector as well as nongovernmental volunteer organizations and local companies who have made Internet awareness and usage their main mandate. An example of this strategy was the summit organized by Hewlett Packard and Management Information Systems of Nigeria, which drew favorable comments from the government towards Hewlett Packard.

FUTURE TRENDS

There has been substantial increase in the level of Internet-related activities in countries of Sub-Saharan Africa. A case in point is Nigeria, in which the overwhelming capabilities of the Internet seem to be driving numerous initiatives that will increase Internet usage and enable the country to reap the benefits in all domains of the economy. Different sectors are seeking out overseas sponsors and donors. For instance, the senior and middle management staff of public and private radio stations in Nigeria will be benefiting from a one-month training workshop organized by Voice of Nigeria and Deutsche Welle Radio of Germany. The training will include the use and application of modern broadcast equipment, including the use of the Internet (Africa News Service, February 20, 2001). Some local companies from countries of Sub-Saharan Africa are already reaping the benefits of connectivity through e-commerce. Examples include: East Africa's Lonrho Hotels (www.kenyaweb.com), and the Naushad Trading Company of Mombasa, Kenya (www.ntclimited.com), which attributes its company's growth from $10,000 to $2 million in just a few years to its use of the World Wide Web. There are many opportunities that have not been explored. For example, the e-commerce initiatives, except for the banking and oil industries, in Nigeria are still at the developmental stage. The future holds great promise in this direction.

The emphasis towards more privatization by governments such as Nigeria is fostering more innovation. Knight (2000) expressed the need for Nigeria to leapfrog traditional phone technology and implement technology infrastructure that can meet current and future world standards. Presently, local companies in partnerships with multinational companies or multinationals and their affiliates are developing alternatives such as digital wireless technology to bypass the inadequate infrastructure. Multinational companies from the UK, Germany, and the US are expanding their operations in Nigeria. Hence, on an operational level, many local businesses and multinational corporations/affiliates use the Internet in the daily functioning of their business.

Some of the countries are increasing accessibility to their general population, including the poor and those in rural communities, through kiosks and cybercafes and adding PCs with Internet access to community phone-shops, schools, police stations and clinics. These alternative avenues that are more characteristics of these countries are worthy of further study.

SOCIAL, LEGAL & ETHICAL PERSPECTIVES

Attitude towards the Internet seems favorable and positive in most of the countries of Sub-Saharan Africa. The government and nongovernmental organizations have written and spoken favorably of the Internet. Internet access and experience have been realized by people from different levels of the society–poor, middle-income, and rich–as a result of the use of avenues that do not require ownership of a PC. As a result, such experience, although limited, is widespread. Generally, the fascination of being able to communicate with anybody, anytime, and in almost any part of the world is widely shared. The advantages of e-mail to poor countries or developing countries are evident because it is cheap, and hardware and software requirements are simple (Fraser & McGrath, 2000).

As the countries of Sub-Saharan Africa transition through the development stage with increasing Internet usage, the legal perspective of Internet usage will gain more attention. Presently, Nii Narku Quaynor, a renowned African IT expert and executive director of Network Computer Systems (NCS) in Ghana, has called for formulation of cyber-related laws to guide the relationship between the information technology sector and other sectors of the economy and also to protect the interests of both IT service providers and users (Xinhua News Agency, January 13, 2001). The banks that are reputably the more advanced in Internet usage in Africa are raising concerns about the use of the Internet and other cyberspace, to commit fraud and to evade the law. The legal perspective of Web usage will be very challenging for the developing countries of Sub-Saharan Africa because presently most of the countries have poorly enforceable legal systems. This is an area for future study and theory development.

Most large industrial companies in developing countries, including those of Sub-Saharan Africa, have Internet access and the trend is filtering down to smaller companies (Awde, 1999). The subject of ethics has always posed a great challenge for international business and related activities. Similarly, the ethical perspective associated with Internet usage, in particular, poses an even greater challenge. These challenges will range from workplace-related issues, such as using the e-mail for personal business, to defrauding the organizations. For these countries where accessibility could be only through the workplace, companies need to provide policies, guidelines and consequences of using e-mail on company time. The ethical perspective of Internet usage in these countries will mirror those of the developed world to some degree. Presently, companies in developed countries struggle with ways to curb employee use of the Internet for personal use on company time, as this affects productivity. However, for developing countries, the monitoring and shadowing mechanisms utilized by developed countries will not attract much controversy, as is the case in the developed countries.

CONCLUSION

The "digital divide" between developed and developing countries, especially those of Sub-Saharan Africa, has generated worldwide interest. This chapter provides background information on Internet usage and factors that nfluence Internet usuage in these countries. Dominant issues relating to the role of the government and nongovernmental organizations in facilitating

Internet usage in these countries culminate into two general propositions. Local responsive communications strategy is advocated for organizations operating or wish to operate in the telecommunications sector of these countries along with suggested guidelines. From all indicators, progress in the Internet connectivity and accessibility to countries of Sub-Saharan Africa is eminent as discussed in Future trends. Likewise, new challenges in the area of Cyber crime and cyber law will become of increasing interest. This chapter has presented a capsulated account of Internet usage in Sub-Saharan Africa, with greater emphasis on Nigeria. The telecommunications sector in these countries is experiencing unprecedented and continual changes. The area is ripe for more comprehensive documentation and theory development.

REFERENCES

Africa News Service. (2001). *Gana To Open Von/Deutsche Welle Workshop.* February 20.

Africa News Service. (2001). *Standard Trust Bank Finances IT Project With N500million.* July 9.

Africa News Service. (2000). *N400b Boots for E-Commerce in Nigeria.* July 17.

Africa News Service. (2000). *Microtec Computer System Nigeria Ltd.* Subscribes to NetSat Express'.

Africa News Service. (2000). Logical plays a part in connecting Nigerians to the Internet. May 15.

Afrinet2000. (2000). Available on the World Wide Web at: http://www.ncc.gov.ng/update.htm.

Akinmutimi, T. (2000). "SmartPay" card holders assured of protection. *The Guardian Online.* Available on the World Wide Web at: http://ngrguardiannews.com. Accessed November 7, 2000.

Amuzu, C. (1998). Beverage industry accounted for 60% billings in 1998. *Vanguard.* Available on the World Wide Web at: http://www.vanguardngr.com/va/042000/b517400.htm. Accessed April 17.

Atkinson, M. (2000). G8 summit: Jamboree is over, so now we want results. *The Guardian,* July 24.

Brown, M. M. (2000). Commentary: The Internet and development. *Choices,* June 4, 9(2).

Chepesiuk, R. (1998). *Bringing the Internet to the Developing World.* American Libraries.

Fadeyi, E. (2000). Poor usage in the Africa worries UNESCO. *The Guardian Online.* Available on the World Wide Web at: http://www.ngrguardiannews.com.

Fraser, H. S. F and McGarth, D. (2000). Information technology and telemedicine in Sub-Saharan Africa. *British Medical Journal.* 321, 456-457.

Impact ISP service and hardware package first-ever contract for news Service Signals NetSat Express' evolution as application service provider. *PR Newswire.* August 2.

Information and Communication Infrastructure in Africa. (2000). Available on the World Wide Web at: http://www2.sn.apc.org/africa/countdet.CFM?countries_ISO_Code=GH.

Jensen, M. (1999). Internet is the driver. *Telecommunications,* 33(10), 185-189.

Jensen, M. (2000). *African Internet Status.* Available on the World Wide Web at: http://www3.wn.apc.org/africa/afstat.htm.

Knight, P. (2000). Digital cellular mobile in Nigeria: A fresh start. *Vanguard.* Available on the World Wide Web at: http://www.vanguardngr.com/va/032000/hT429030.htm.

Lishan, A. (1997). Content and the web for African development. *Journal of Information Science.* 23(1), 91-98.

Maddy, M. (2000). Dream deferred–The story of a high-tech entrepreneur in a low-tech world. *Harvard Business Review.* May-June, 57-69.

Moeller, S. (2000). Wiring up the powerless. *Christian Science Monitor,* 11.

Muoka, R. (2000). Choose mobile system that suites your economy. *Vanguard.* Available on the World Wide Web at: August http://www.vanguardngr.com/WK108200/H1208000.htm. Accessed August 2000.

Mweu, F. 2000. The African Internet and telecom summit, Banjui. *The Gambia.* Available on the World Wide Web at: http://www.itu.int/africainternet2000/countryreports/ken_e.htm.

Myers, J. (1998). Human rights and development: Using advanced technology to promote human rights in sub-Saharan Africa. Case western. *Journal of International Law,* 30(2-3), 343-371.

Ogbulie, N. (2000). Federal government assures Hewlett Packard on protection. *Africa News Service.* AN: CX124U2733.

Ogunbiyi, C. and O'Brien, D. (2000). Nigeria thinks big. *African Business.* 260, 39-42.

O'Kane, G. (2000). World bank to boost Internet in Africa. *African Business,* March 30.

Quaynor, N. (1996). Intelsat earth station launched. *Network Startup Resource Center.* Available on the World Wide Web at: http://www.nsrc.org.

Summit Report. (2000). Available on the World Wide Web at: http://www.ncc.gov.ng/summit%20_report.htm.

Tevie, W., Quaynor, N. and Bulley A. (1996). *Development of the Internet in Ghana*. Available on the World Wide Web at: http://www.chg.ru/inet96/g6/g6_4.htm.

Ugwoke, F. (2000). NCC laments Africa's poor Internet status. *Africa News Service*, July 27, 100809u3122.

Ugwoke, F. (2000). *Nigeria: Others Tasked on Internet Development*, 1008209u3122. Available on the World Wide Web at: http://www.allafrica.com.

Ukwe, C. N. (1999). *Application of the Internet in Knowledge Sharing: Case Study of Global Environment Facility International Waters Learning Exchange and Resource Network Project*, 1-19. Available on the World Wide Web at: http://www.isocnig.org.ng/ConferencePapers/Paper15.htm.

Vanguard. (2000). Afribank, standard trust flex muscle over money transfer, March 27.

Vanguard. (2000). *The Clinton Visit: Nigeria's Economy Needs Diversification*, August 28. Available on the World Wide Web at: http://www.vanguardngr.com/28082000/nn328080.htm.

Vanguard. (2000). Computerized banking services in vernacular underway, September 11. Available on the World Wide Web at: http://www.vanguardngr.com/11092000/bv1611090.htm.

Xinhua News Agency. (2001). African IT calls on establishing cyber-related laws. AN: CX2001013H9351. January 13.

Chapter V

E-commerce System: An Examination of User Experiences of the E-commerce Site with the Standard User Interface

Shin-Ping Liu,
University of North Texas, USA

Dennis Tucker
Transfinity Corporation, USA

E-commerce offers speed, convenience, and often cost-effectiveness for today's busy shopper, but most e-commerce sites are still too hard to use. The problem with e-commerce sites is the controls and organization are different for each site. The question is that "Do e-commerce users need a standard navigation system to make e-commerce sites easy to use?" This research investigates how an individual's perceptions of key beliefs surrounding the use of the e-commerce site with the standard navigation system would influence the individual's decision to accept these e-commerce sites for online shopping purposes. This study applies the technology acceptance model (TAM), identifying components of usefulness, ease of use, and richness that predict user attitude toward the usage of the standard navigation system. The research uses a Web-based survey and is tested by TAM with path analysis. There are 129 subjects in the pretest samples. The study could identify features of the standard navigation system that might contribute to its usefulness, ease of use, and richness. The study would determine whether the standard navigation system would increase the usability of e-commerce or not. It could thus provide implications about usefulness, ease of use, and richness for e-commerce developers and practitioners.

INTRODUCTION

Electronic commerce (e-commerce) offers speed, convenience, and often cost-effectiveness for today's busy shoppers, but most e-commerce sites are still too hard to use (ZDInternet.inc, 1999). Zona Research (1999) found that 62% of online shoppers had given up at least once while looking for products, and 42% had turned to traditional channels to make their purchases. These statistics are astounding. What are the most important features that affect the users' emotions while browsing e-commerce sites (Ahuja, 2000)? Why is the Web too hard to use (ZDInternet.inc, 1999)? What do e-commerce customers want? Books are always printed with the table of contents in front, the index in back, and sequential page numbers in the middle (Shirky, Webber, Newcomer, & Jaworski, 1999). Why should e-commerce sites be any different (Shirky et al., 1999)?

The future of economic competitiveness for most enterprises relies on entrance and active participation in the e-commerce market (Vestal, 1999). E-commerce is changing how businesses market their products, and how they serve their customers and business partners. However, about a third of the time, users fail when they try to purchase products on an e-commerce site (Nielsen & Norman, 2000). In reality, what happens is not just that the user fails, but that the site fails and does not sell a thing. Is "lost-in-hyperspace" primarily a psychological or an engineering problem (McKnight, Dillion, & Richardson, 1991; Theng, 1997; Theng & Thimbleby, 1998)? In other words, is "lost-in-hyperspace" a problem for users, or is it a symptom of poor design, which itself may be a psychological problem for authors of e-commerce sites (Theng & Thimbleby, 1998)?

Current e-commerce sites make it hard to predict what will happen if a link is being followed. Users may get different information than they expect, a new window may open, a download starts, or the destination object is unavailable. Questions arise as to the usability of e-commerce. How long does it take for customers to do typical tasks at an e-commerce site? What percentages of potential customers are leaving the site and why? (Forrester Research suggests it may be as high as 40%.) E-commerce sites are losing money because customers get frustrated and give up trying to use these sites (Forrester Research, 1998). When customers cannot find what they looking for, whether it is a product, a security policy or the order page, they just give up.

The problem with e-commerce sites is that the controls and organization are different for each site. There is no standard way of building the navigation or organization of the site (Nielsen, 1998a). Most sites do not have a standard navigation system and they are confusing to navigate, like mazes (Nielsen, 1998b; ZDInternet.inc, 1999; Hobart, 1995; Gehrke & Turban, 1998). This research investigates how an individual's perceptions of key beliefs and technological issues surrounding the use of an e-commerce site with a standard navigation system would influence the individual's decision to accept the site for online shopping purposes.

BACKGROUND: INTERDISCIPLINARY APPROACH TO E-COMMERCE USABILITY

We took an interdisciplinary approach to the study of e-commerce usability by integrating three disciplines–human-computer interaction, cognitive psychology, and software engineering–as shown in Figure 1. Human computer interaction (HCI) is typically grounded in empirical data from usability studies (Theng & Thimbleby, 1998). Cognitive psychology is typically grounded in models of human behavior and performance (Theng & Thimbleby, 1998). Software engineering is typically grounded in sound engineering practice, such as formal specifications (Theng & Thimbleby, 1998). Academic research often promotes a discipline-specific agenda without seeing the wider picture. This study is concerned with how the concepts, values, methods and procedures from these disciplines can be integrated into the usability of e-commerce research.

TECHNOLOGY ACCEPTANCE MODEL (TAM)

To study user acceptance of e-commerce sites from an interdisciplinary perspective, we adopted the technology acceptance model (TAM) used by Davis (1989) to explain the usage of information technology. Several researchers have validated TAM using different applications including e-mail, voice mail, word processing, microcomputers, automated teller, spreadsheet, calculator, and Web pages development software, among others. (Thompson,

Figure 1: An Interdisciplinary Approach to the Usability of E-commerce: Integrating the Disciplines of Human-Computer Interaction, Software Engineering and Cognitive Psychology into the Usability of E-commerce Research

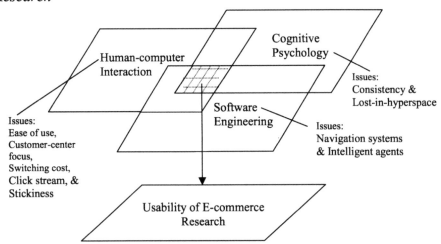

1998; Chau, 1996; Hendrickson & Collins, 1996; Szajna, 1996; Fulk, Schmitz, & Ryu, 1995; Igbaria, Guimaraes, & Davis, 1995; Bagozzi, Davis & Warshaw, 1992; Adams, Nelson, & Todd, 1992; Davis, Bagozzi, & Warshaw, 1989). Other researchers have recommended TAM for the investigation of Web user behavior (Shaw, Gardner, & Thomas, 1997). TAM provides a foundation for research on why users accept or reject information technology and how to increase user acceptance by judicious choice of system design features (Davis, 1993).

Davis' proposed TAM (1993) is shown in Figure 2. A prospective user's overall attitude toward using a given system is hypothesized to be a major determinant of whether the user actually uses it or not. The perception of the stimuli creates cognitive beliefs, which initiate an affective response. The affective response has an influence on consumer behavior. Attitude is determined by cognitive beliefs.

Attitude toward using, in turn, is a function of two beliefs: perceived usefulness and perceived ease of use. Perceived ease of use has a causal effect on perceived usefulness. System design features directly influence perceived usefulness and perceived ease of use. System design features have an indirect effect on attitude toward using and actual usage behavior through their direct effect on perceived usefulness and perceived ease of use (Davis, 1993). Our research model (see Figure 3) has been adopted from two previous studies by Davis (1993) and Fulk et al. (1995).

Figure 2: Technology Acceptance Model by Davis (1993)

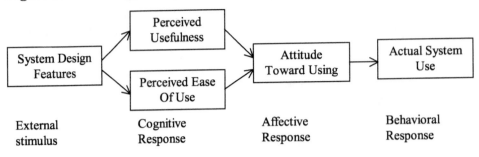

Figure 3: The Adopted Technology Acceptance Model (TAM) With the Standard Navigation System

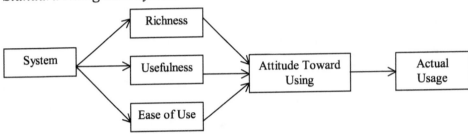

Working definitions of the constructs in the model–perceived useful-ness, perceived ease of use, perceived richness, attitude toward using, and actual system usage–are as follows:

1. *Perceived Usefulness*: The degree to which a person believes that a particular information system would enhance his or her job performance by reducing the time to accomplish a task or providing timely informa-tion (Davis, 1989; Lederer, Maupin, Sena, & Zhuang, 1999).

2. *Perceived Ease of Use*: The degree to which a person believes that using a particular system would be free of effort (Davis, 1989).

3. *Perceived Richness*: The extent of the information-carrying capacity of a system that it can transmit nonverbal cues, convey a sense of personalness, provide timely feedback, and transmit rich and varied language (Fulk et al., 1995).

4. *Attitude Toward Using*: The degree of evaluative affect that an individual associates with using the target system in his or her job; i.e., the user's evaluation of the desirability of employing a particular information systems application (Davis, 1993; Lederer et al. 1999).

5. *Actual System Usage*: TAM's main dependent variable is the actual usage of the system. It has typically been a self-reported measure of time or frequency of employing the application (Lederer et al. 1999).

METHODOLOGY

A Web-based survey study with two specific research objectives was conducted. The first objective was to explore the current usability problems of e-commerce and employ an artificial intelligence user interface agent to create a standard user interface for increasing the usability of e-commerce. The second objective was to examine the user acceptance of the e-commerce site with the standard navigation system. The study employed the technology acceptance model (TAM), identifying components of usefulness, ease of use, and richness that predict user attitude toward the usage of the standard navigation system. The study was designed to identify features of the standard navigation system that might contribute to its usefulness, ease of use, and richness. The study would shed light on whether the standard navigation system increases the usability of e-commerce or not. It could thus provide implications about usefulness, ease of use, and richness for e-commerce developers and practitioners.

Hypotheses

TAM explains the causal links among system, beliefs, attitudes, and actual computer adoption behavior (Davis, 1989). The purpose of TAM is to explain and predict user acceptance of information systems from measures taken after a brief period of interaction with the system. Thus, the statistical significance of the proposed TAM relationships, represented in the following seven hypotheses, was assessed using the t-statistic corresponding to each estimated parameter. The hypotheses for this study are as follows:

H1: *Attitude toward using will have a significant positive effect on actual standard navigation usage.*

H2: *Perceived usefulness will have a significant positive effect on attitude toward using, controlling for perceived ease of use and perceived richness.*

H3: *Perceived ease of use will have a significant positive effect on attitude toward using, controlling for perceived usefulness and perceived richness.*

H4: *Perceived richness will have a significant positive effect on attitude toward using, controlling for perceived usefulness and perceived ease of use.*

H5: Perceived ease of use will have a significant positive effect on perceived usefulness, controlling for system and perceived richness.

H6: Perceived richness will have a significant positive effect on perceived usefulness, controlling for system and perceived ease of use.

H7: System will have a significant positive effect on perceived ease of use, perceived usefulness, and perceived richness.

Furthermore, we postulated two more hypotheses to test whether the causal relationships implicitly hypothesized to be indirect have no significant direct effect or not. Hierarchical regression and associated F-tests of the significance of the increase in R^2 due to the additional variables were used for these hypotheses.

H8: Perceived usefulness, perceived ease of use, perceived richness and system will not have significant direct effects on actual standard navigation usage, controlling for attitude toward using.

H9: System will not have a significant direct effect on attitude toward using, controlling for perceived usefulness, perceived ease of use, and perceived richness.

In addition to testing for the significance of the hypothesized relationships, we also analyzed the data to estimate the magnitudes of the causal parameters. The estimates are the standardized regression coefficients, expressed as both point and confidence interval estimates.

Research Variables

There are six measured variables in this study (see Table 1). Variable 1 is the dummy variable for identifying the existence of the system design features. Variable 2 is a latent construct that is assessed via the questions by directly asking participants about their perceived usefulness of the e-commerce site with the standard navigation system. Variable 3 is a latent construct that is assessed via the questions by directly asking participants about their perceived ease of use of the standard navigation system. Variable 4 is a latent construct that is assessed by directly asking participants about their perceived richness of the standard navigation system. Variable 5 is a latent construct that is assessed by directly asking participants about their attitude toward using of the standard navigation system. Variable 6 is a latent construct that is assessed by directly asking participants about their behavioral expectations about their future actual use of the e-commerce site with the standard navigation system.

Empirical testing has demonstrated that questions about behavioral expectations provide an effective means of estimating future behavior (Davis, 1989; Sheppard, Hartwick, & Warshaw, 1988). Exposure to an e-commerce

Table 1: Research Variables Measured in this Study

Variable	Variables (Latent Constructs)	Type of variables
1.	System design features	Independent
2.	Perceived usefulness	Independent, dependent, mediating
3.	Perceived ease of use	Independent, dependent, mediating
4.	Perceived richness	Independent, dependent, mediating
5.	Attitude toward using	Independent, dependent, mediating
6.	Actual standard navigation usage	Dependent

site with the standard navigation system on the instrument is important, because research has shown that asking users for their perceptions concerning an interface with which they have not had interactive experience, is not an effective method of assessing usability.

Instrument

The Web-based survey instrument contains instructions asking respondents to compare an e-commerce site without a standard navigation system to the same site with the standard navigation system. Altogether the instrument contains 37 items, including six demographic questions.

Web Sites and Standard Navigation System

We evaluated 102 e-commerce sites that had been recognized as most popular with consumers by several independent polling organizations for several design criteria that may affect customer experience. From this evaluation of the 102 sites, we identified and compiled 42 different features commonly used to assist customers who browse e-commerce sites. Some of the most frequently used such features include contact information, privacy statement, company information, customer service/help, search engine, shopping cart, and security statement.

Based on the list of features identified from the 102 e-commerce sites, we constructed a standard user interface that allows users to navigate the site using the interface. The idea behind the standard user interface is that all e-commerce sites should have some type of standard navigation to improve usability and functionality. Unfortunately most e-commerce sites lack such standard navigational systems (Allum, 1998; Booker, 1997; Bort, 1999; Hoffman, 1996).

Based on the findings from the study of the 102 e-commerce sites, we developed a menu bar, as shown in Figure 4, as the standard navigation system to be used by study participants.

Then we selected three sites from the list of 102 e-commerce sites to be used in our study. We used the following criteria in the selection process:

- The site must have been included in the evaluation and study of 102 e-commerce sites.
- The site must be of reasonable size, but not too big.
- The site must not have an overwhelming number of HTML errors.
- The site received a low evaluation from this study.
- The site is not too sophisticated or complicated to be compatible with the proof of concept standard navigation server. In this case "proof of concept" means a computer program that works in a controlled environment to prove that an idea can work.

For each e-commerce site, we created two versions of the site–one with the standard navigation system and another without. Figure 5 compares the two versions of one of the sites used in the study.

Figure 4: The Standard Navigation in Action.

Figure 5: An E-commerce Site Without the Standard Navigation Systems (Left) and With the Standard Navigation Systems (Right)

RESULTS AND DATA ANALYSIS

Subjects

A letter that solicits participation in the study was sent out via e-mail to students and faculty members listed on several mailing lists at a major university. All together a total of 2,946 potential participants were contacted.

The invitation letter explains the nature of the study and states that a randomly selected set of individuals receives the questionnaire. To encourage participation in the study, we offered a raffle in which the winner of a random drawing from the pool of all participants gets a $100 gift certificate. Participants were also promised a copy of the results, if they like.

Data Collection

Respondents filled out and submitted the survey online. Data were automatically sent to the author's e-mail account and saved as a text file in the Web server. The text file from the Web server was imported to SPSS for statistical analysis. All statistical data were analyzed for two-tailed significance at a 0.1 alpha level.

Data Analysis

The survey produced 129 usable responses out of 2,946 students and faculty members for a 4.4% response rate. All duplicate responses and those responses that had too many missing values were removed. This response rate may be low in comparison to conventional paper-based postal surveys. However, the total number of subjects suffices for the analysis described below. While "System" is a dummy variable taking on value 0 for an e-commerce site without the standard navigation system and 1 for an e-commerce site with the standard navigation system, "Usage" refers to intensity of the actual standard navigation usage, "Attitude" refers to attitude toward using, "Usefulness" refers to perceived usefulness, "Ease of use" refers to perceived ease of use, and "Richness" refers to perceived richness. Ordinary least-squares (OLS) regression was used to test this structural equation model. Details of the study including demographics, descriptive statistics, construct reliability, construct validity, hypotheses testing, and results follow.

Demographics

Of the 129 participants, there were more female (68%, n=88) than male (32%, n=41) participants. The education level of the pretest study sample is primarily at the undergraduate and graduate level, with 27% (n=35) attending or having attended undergraduate school at the bachelor level; 43% (n=55) attending or having attended graduate school at the master's level; and 29% (n=37) attending or having attended graduate school at the doctoral level. All of the pretest study samples (N=129) are under the age of 65, with 3% (n=4) under the age of 20; 32% (n=41) between the ages of 20 and 29; 25% (n=32) between the ages of 30 and 39; 22% (n=28) between the ages of 40 and 49; 18% (n=23) between the ages of 50 and 65. Respondents have an average age of 37.3 and an average degree of master's level. This indicates that the subjects are somewhat older and more experienced than Internet users in the general population.

The sample included various majors. The three highest percentage of majors are: 17% library and information science master's degree (n=22), 14% information science doctoral degree (n=18), and 6% history (n=8). The sample included different races: 67% White (n=87), 4% Black (n=5), 5% Hispanic (n=7), 17% Asian (n=22), 0.8% American Indian (n=1), and 4% others (n=5).

Descriptive Statistics

The descriptive statistics produced with the data include the means and standard deviations for the items of perceived usefulness, perceived ease of use, perceived richness, attitude toward using, and actual standard navigation usage in the study as shown in Table 2. In this study, missing values were filled in with the mean of each item.

Construct Reliability

The validity and reliability measures discussed in this section indicate that the instrument has the potential for use in further adoption studies. Does the questionnaire measure customer satisfaction in a useful way? Using reliability analysis, the extent to which the items in the questionnaire are related to each other can be determined, an overall index of the repeatability or internal consistency of the scale as a whole can be gotten, and the problem items that should be excluded from the scale can be identified. The Cronbach model of reliability was also used in the study. The Cronbach's alpha is a model of internal consistency, based on the average inter-item correlation. Table 3 shows Cronbach's alpha measure of internal consistency for the items of perceived usefulness, perceived ease of use, perceived richness, attitude toward using, and actual standard navigation usage.

Although the reliability scores do not approach the desired standard of 0.95 for scales used in applied settings (Nunnally, 1978), a number of

Table 2: Descriptive Statistics

Items	Mean	Std.
I. Demographics: Questions 1-6		
II. Perceived Usefulness (1 Strongly Agree... 5 Strongly Disagree)		
7. Using the e-commerce site with the standard navigation system improves the quality of the navigation I'm able to do.	2.32	.89
8. Using the e-commerce site with the standard navigation system gives me greater control over my navigation.	2.45	.85
9. The e-commerce site with the standard navigation system enables me to accomplish navigation more quickly.	2.18	.90
10. The e-commerce site with the standard navigation system supports critical aspects of my navigation.	2.56	.99
11. Using the e-commerce site with the standard navigation system increases my consumption.	3.13	.99
12. Using the e-commerce site with the standard navigation system improves my navigation performance.	2.31	.92
13. Using the e-commerce site with the standard navigation system allows me to accomplish more navigation than would otherwise be possible.	2.65	.98
14. Using the e-commerce site with the standard navigation system enhances my effectiveness in navigation.	2.32	.96
15. Using the e-commerce site with the standard navigation system makes it easier to navigate. Overall, I find the e-commerce site with the standard navigation system useful in navigation.	2.22	.95
16. Overall, I find the e-commerce site with the standard navigation system useful in navigation.	2.13	.93
III. Perceived ease of use (1 Strongly Agree... 5 Strongly Disagree)		
17. I find the e-commerce site with the standard navigation system cumbersome to use.	3.62	.99
18. Learning to operate the e-commerce site with the standard navigation system is easy for me.	1.90	.75
19. Interacting with the e-commerce site with the standard navigation system is often frustrating.	3.59	.90
20. I find it easy to get the e-commerce site with the standard navigation system to do what I want it to do.	2.31	.83
21. The e-commerce site with the standard navigation system is rigid and inflexible to interact with.	3.59	.86
22. It is easy for me to remember how to perform navigation using the e-commerce site with the standard navigation system.	2.08	.78
23. Interacting with the e-commerce site with the standard navigation system requires a lot of mental effort.	3.85	.87
24. My interaction with the e-commerce site with the standard navigation system is clear and understandable.	2.13	.82
25. I find it takes a lot of effort to become skillful at using the e-commerce site with the standard navigation system.	3.81	.92
26. Overall, I find the e-commerce site with the standard navigation system easy to use.	2.10	.77
IV. Perceived Richness (1 Expert... 5 None)		
27. What is your experience with e-commerce?	3.12	1.23
28. What is your experience with the computers?	1.80	.60
29. What is your experience with the Internet?	1.83	.68
30. Do you use computers at work?	1.83	.74
V. Attitude toward using (1 Always...5 Never)		
31. Do you feel that the standard navigation system is a good system?	2.29	.93
32. Do you feel that the standard navigation system is beneficial?	2.35	.88
33. Do you feel that the standard navigation system is foolish?	4.04	.95
34. Do you feel that the standard navigation system is effective	2.37	.90
VI. Navigation Usage (1 Always ...5 Never)		
35. Would you frequent an e-commerce site that uses the standard navigation system?	2.88	.98
36. Would you like to use an e-commerce site with the standard navigation system for your online shopping in the future?	2.64	1.05
37. Would you like to recommend an e-commerce site with the standard navigation system to your friends?	2.85	1.02

researchers have indicated that lower reliability scores are acceptable in exploratory research. For example, Bearden, Netemeyer, and Mobley (1993) publish a five-item scale for reliability of attitude measures in marketing such as exemplary (0.80 or better), extensive (0.70-0.79), moderate (0.60-0.69), minimal (less than 0.60), and none (not reported). Moreover, Nunnally (1978), in his often-cited *Psychometric Theory*, states,

> "In the early stages of research on predictor tests or hypothesized measures of a construct, one saves time and energy by working with instruments that have only modest reliability, for which purpose reliabilities of .60 or .50 will suffice." (p. 226)

A review of the alpha coefficients for the instrument of this study shows a range of 0.650 to 0.946 (see Table 3). Given the exploratory nature of the research, the reliability of the constructs is judged acceptable.

Construct Validity

To examine the construct validity of the instrument, factor analysis was performed to test the factor loadings of the items on the five constructs. Factorial validity is concerned with whether the items form distinct constructs. The principle estimation method with varimax rotation of the factor analysis procedure was conducted to verify that the five constructs are valid for this study sample. The extraction method used the principal component analysis. The rotation method was performed by the varimax with Kaiser normalization. Table 4 presents the varimax rotated item loadings for factors based on items of constructs involving the use of e-commerce sites with the standard navigation system. The result is consistent with distinct mostly (shown in boldfaced type in Table 4) except the constructs of attitude toward using and actual standard navigation usage. The items load on distinctly different factors demonstrating factorial validity for constructs. Thus, this study refers to a moderate factorial validity of constructs used in this pretest study's sample.

Table 3: Cronbach's Alpha for Reliability Analysis

Set of Items	Number of Items	Cronbach's Alpha
Perceived Usefulness	10 (Q7-Q16)	0.946
Perceived Ease of Use	10 (Q17-Q26)	0.846
Perceived Richness	4 (Q27-Q30)	0.650
Attitude Toward Using	4 (Q31-Q34)	0.825
Standard Navigation Usage	3 (Q35-Q37)	0.870

Table 4: Factor Analysis of Item Constructs for the Pretest Study

Item Construct and Questions		F1	F2	F3	F4	F5
Perceived Usefulness	Q7	**.779**	.135	.254	.063	.016
	Q8	**.648**	.346	.298	.112	.030
	Q9	**.740**	.411	.134	.052	-.008
	Q10	**.725**	.354	.011	.116	-.023
	Q11	**.566**	.052	.298	-.012	-.125
	Q12	**.835**	.247	.165	.118	.064
	Q13	**.714**	.110	.223	-.056	-.035
	Q14	**.863**	.146	.167	.155	-.030
	Q15	**.849**	.208	.190	.146	.053
	Q16	**.861**	.219	.213	.129	.038
Perceived Ease of Use	Q17	.051	.061	.224	**.720**	-.134
	Q18	.167	.832	.171	**.120**	.075
	Q19	-.011	.071	.044	**.794**	.150
	Q20	.425	.651	.194	**.134**	.038
	Q21	.066	.048	.013	**.654**	.126
	Q22	.338	.650	.091	**.261**	.060
	Q23	.088	.365	-.174	**.628**	.072
	Q24	.304	.678	.199	**.070**	.020
	Q25	.093	.505	.063	**.516**	.083
	Q26	.350	.666	.070	**.070**	.166
Perceived Richness	Q27	-.235	.105	.354	-.283	**.463**
	Q28	.090	.126	.081	-.049	**.848**
	Q29	.002	.061	.071	.042	**.789**
	Q30	-.057	.012	-.111	.207	**.784**
Attitude Toward Using	Q31	.477	.201	**.600**	.205	-.105
	Q32	.544	.307	**.546**	.069	-.127
	Q33	.182	.073	**.171**	.481	-.092
	Q34	.513	.260	**.569**	.157	-.147
Standard Navigation Usage	Q35	.238	.045	**.770**	.066	.159
	Q36	.406	.210	**.771**	.067	-.011
	Q37	.348	.121	**.734**	.120	.080

Hypotheses Testing

The testing of the TAM relationships then uses a multiple regression model and a simple linear regression model to test the mean differences among various conditions. The general regression model is stated as:

$$\hat{Y} = \beta_1 X_1 + \beta_2 X_2 + \beta_3 X_3 + \beta_4 X_4 + \beta_5 X_5 + \ \cdots \ + \beta_n X_n$$

where:

$\acute{Y}$ = predicted dependent variable value

β_i = regression coefficients for independent variable constructs

X_i = represents values for the independent constructs, respectively.

Table 5 represents the correlation coefficient (R) that is a measure of the magnitude of the relationship between a criterion variable and some combination of predictor variables (Gall, Borg, & Gall, 1996). The larger the R, the better the prediction of the criterion variable. Coefficient of determination (R^2) is the amount of variance in the criterion variable that is explained in a multiple regression analysis by a predictor variable or a combination of predictor variables (Gall et al., 1996). Variance inflation factors (VIF) did not exceed 10 for any regression. In fact, all of the following regression analysis was less than two. Hence, multicollinearity was not extensive. The dimension of attitude toward using is most correlated with usefulness (r = 0.709) and navigation usage (r = 0.660). The dimension of navigation usage is most correlated with usefulness (r = 0.596) and attitude toward using (r = 0.660).

The regression analysis is performed on data pooled across the two target systems (n=129), which are the original e-commerce site and the same site but containing the standard navigation system. Table 6 contains the results of OLS regressions applied to the hypothesized equations of the model.

Table 7 contains the unrestricted regressions needed to carry out the hierarchical regression test of the nonsignificance of those causal relationships hypothesized to be nonsignificant.

Figure 6 shows the results of the regression analyses. Most of the hypotheses were confirmed by the data. Attitude toward using (β = 0.50) has a significant effect on actual standard navigation usage. Perceived usefulness (β = 0.55) has a significant and strong effect on attitude toward using and is strongly affected (β = -0.47) by the system. Perceived ease of use (β = 0.23) has a smaller but also significant effect on attitude toward using and a strong

Table 5: Pearson Correlations of the Pretest Study

	System	Usefulness	Ease of Use	Richness	Attitude	Navigation Usage
System	1.000	-0.640**	-0.490**	-0.092*	-0.486**	-0.430**
Usefulness	-0.640**	1.000	0.590**	-0.038	0.709**	0.596**
Ease of Use	0.490**	0.590**	1.000	0.109	0.563**	0.416**
Richness	-0.092	-0.038	0.109	1.000	-0.073	0.138
Attitude	-0.486**	0.709**	0.563**	-0.073	1.000	.660**
Navigation Usage	-0.430**	0.596**	0.416**	0.138	0.660**	1.000

** Correlation is significant at the 0.01 level (2-tailed).

* Correlation is significant at the 0.05 level (2-tailed).

Table 6: TAM Regression Test of the Pretest Study Adapted from Davis' Study (1993)

Dependent Variable	R^2	Independent Variable	b	S.E. (b)	β	t-statistics	Significant Level
EaseofUse	0.240	Constant	2.733	0.113		24.255	0.000
		System	-0.749	0.118	-0.490	-6.327	0.000
Usefulness	0.524	Constant	2.545	0.403		6.317	0.000
		System	-1.227	0.187	-0.467	-6.569	0.000
		EaseOfUse	0.643	0.122	0.374	5.255	0.000
		Richness	-0.160	0.082	-0.121	-1.946	0.054
Richness	0.008	Constant	2.313	0.168		13.745	0.000
		System	-0.183	0.177	-0.092	-1.037	0.302
Attitude	0.541	Constant	0.384	0.247		1.554	0.123
		EaseOfUse	0.376	0.120	0.238	3.117	0.002
		Usefulness	0.520	0.070	0.566	7.449	0.000
		Richness	-0.094	0.075	-0.077	-1.254	0.212
Usage	0.436	Constant	0.920	0.198		4.638	0.000
		Attitude	0.848	0.086	0.660	9.901	0.000
Usage (w/ Usefulness & Richness included)	0.503	Constant	0.083	0.301		0.276	0.783
		Usefulness	0.294	0.106	0.250	2.779	0.006
		Richness	0.278	0.098	0.180	2.830	0.005
		Attitude	0.638	0.115	0.499	5.540	0.000

Table 7: Hierarchical Regression Tests of Indirect Relationships of the Pre-Test Study Adapted from Davis' Study (1993)

Dependent Variable	R^2	Independent Variable	b	S.E. (b)	β	t-statistics	Significant Level
Attitude	0.542	Constant	0.490	0.419		1.168	0.245
		System	-0.061	0.196	-0.025	-0.312	0.755
		EaseOfUse	0.369	0.123	0.234	3.015	0.003
		Usefulness	0.507	0.081	0.552	6.234	0.000
		Richness	-0.096	0.075	-0.080	-1.278	0.204
Usage	0.505	Constant	0.315	0.564		0.559	0.577
		System	-0.083	0.263	-0.027	-0.318	0.751
		EaseOfUse	-0.111	0.170	-0.055	-0.654	0.514
		Usefulness	0.299	0.125	0.254	2.402	0.018
		Richness	0.286	0.101	0.185	2.816	0.006
		Attitude	0.657	0.120	0.513	5.456	0.000

effect ($\beta = 0.37$) on perceived usefulness. Perceived ease of use ($\beta = -0.49$) is significantly influenced by the system, with the standard navigation system being perceived as easier to use than the e-commerce site without the standard navigation system. Perceived richness ($\beta = -0.12$) has a slight but also significant effect on perceived usefulness.

Among the hypothesized direct effects, the system-richness ($\beta = -0.09$)

Figure 6: Adapted Technology Acceptance Model (TAM) Results of the Pretest Study

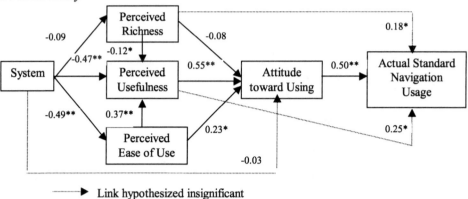

and the richness-attitude($\beta = -0.08$) links are disconfirmed. Hence, the media richness such as the experience in using computers, Internet, and e-commerce is not affected by the system and does not provide perceived impacts on one's attitude toward using. The system and perceived ease of use have no direct effect on actual standard navigation usage, as hypothesized. Counter to expectation, however, perceived usefulness has a direct effect($\beta = 0.25$) on usage. The system does not have a direct effect on attitude toward using($\beta = -0.03$) and actual navigation usage. Unexpectedly, perceived richness($\beta = 0.18$) has a smaller but also significant effect on the actual system usage over and above perceived ease of use.

Table 8 shows the point estimates and confidence intervals for the standardized regression coefficients. The parameters enable one to compute the relative importance of perceived usefulness, perceived ease of use, and perceived richness in influencing actual system usage (Davis, 1993). Perceived usefulness has both a direct effect (0.25) plus an indirect effect via attitude toward using (0.55 x 0.50 = 0.28). Combined, this equals 0.53. Perceived ease of use has an effect on actual standard navigation usage through attitude toward using (0.23 x 0.50 = 0.12); plus an effect through perceived usefulness (0.37 x 0.55 x 0.50 = 0.10). This totals 0.22. Perceived richness has both a direct effect (0.18) plus an indirect effect via attitude toward using (-0.08 x 0.50 = -0.04). This totals 0.16. Comparatively, perceived usefulness is about 2.41 times as important as perceived ease of use in affecting actual system usage. Perceived usefulness is about 3.31 times as important as perceived richness in affecting actual system usage. Perceived ease of use is also about 1.38 times as important as perceived ease of use in affecting actual system usage.

Findings of the Study

The TAM motivational variables of attitude toward using, perceived usefulness, perceived ease of use, and perceived richness mediate the effect of system design features on actual usage. The system characteristics appear to influence behavior through these motivational variables. Just the same as Davis' study (1993), the most striking result is the effect of usefulness on actual navigation usage, both directly and indirectly, through attitude (0.55 x 0.50) + 0.25 = 0.53. However, the fact that perceived usefulness exerts almost the same as attitude toward using does directly influence actual system usage (0.50). In addition, perceived usefulness exerts more than two times as much direct effect on attitude toward using as does perceived ease of use (0.55 vs. 0.23). Perceived usefulness exerts more than six times as much direct effect on attitude toward using as does perceived richness (0.55 vs. 0.08).

Compared to perceived usefulness, perceived ease of use has a direct effect (0.23) on attitude toward using, similar to affecting attitude indirectly via its relatively influence on perceived usefulness (0.37 x 0.55 = 0.20), although inconsistent with Davis' study (1993). The effect of perceived ease of use on actual navigation usage operates through its effect on perceived usefulness, which is 0.37 x (0.25 + 0.55 x 0.50) = 0.19. Comparatively, the effect of perceived ease of use on navigation usage through its direct effect on attitude is only 0.23 x 0.50 = 0.12. The result is similar to Davis' study (1993).

Table 8: TAM Parameter Estimates and 95% Confidence Intervals of the Pretest Study Adapted from Davis' Study (1993)

Causal Link		Point Estimate		95% Confidence Interval	
Independent Variable	Dependent Variable	β	Significance Level	Lower Bound	Upper Bound
System	EaseOfUse	-0.490	0.000	-0.983	-0.515
System	Usefulness	-0.467	0.000	-1.597	-0.858
System	Richness	-0.092	0.302	-0.533	0.166
EaseOfUse	Usefulness	0.374	0.000	0.401	0.885
Richness	Usefulness	-0.121	0.054	-0.322	0.003
System	Attitude	-0.025	0.755	-0.450	0.328
EaseOfUse	Attitude	0.552	0.000	0.346	0.668
Usefulness	Attitude	0.234	0.003	0.127	0.612
Richness	Attitude	-0.080	0.204	-0.246	0.053
Usefulness	Usage	0.250	0.006	0.084	0.503
Richness	Usage	0.180	0.005	0.084	0.473
Attitude	Usage	0.499	0.000	0.410	0.867

Hence, perceived ease of use performs primarily through perceived usefulness, because the usefulness construct may reflect considerations of both the benefit and cost of using the target standard navigation system. Ease of use may be seen as part of the cost of using the system from the user's perspective.

The effect of perceived richness on actual navigation usage performs through its effect on perceived usefulness, which is $-0.12 \times (0.25 + 0.55 \times 0.50) = -0.063$. Comparatively, the effect of perceived richness on system usage through its direct effect on attitude is only $-0.08 \times 0.50 = -0.04$. Another notable result is that perceived richness has a direct effect (0.18) on actual system usage, which is much better than the effect via attitude (-0.04) and usefulness (-0.063). The media richness construct may reflect considerations of computers, Internet, and e-commerce experiences. The more media richness is, the more actual system usage increases.

Another result different from Davis' study is the insignificant direct influence (-0.03) of system characteristics (or system design features) on attitude toward using. This suggests that perceived usefulness, perceived ease of use, and perceived richness may be the beliefs mediating between system and attitude. This tells us that perceived richness may be a good belief to add to the model.

In addition, the previous discussion has emphasized the importance of perceived usefulness, arguing that ease of use performs via this variable. However, perceived richness has a direct effect (0.18) on the actual system usage and it is much better than the effect via usefulness and attitude. Therefore, the result shows that perceived richness is one of the significant intrinsic motives that play an important role in determining usage of computer systems. Thus, the model views the standard navigation usage behavior to be intrinsically motivated, being driven by concern for performance gains more than associated rewards. That is, people use systems in part because users who have more system familiarity or experience enjoy the process of using them per se, not just because they are extrinsically rewarded for the impacts of usage. The result is slightly different from Davis' study (1993).

CONCLUSIONS

Due to the exploratory nature of the study dealing with rapidly changing technological and organizational issues, the study does have several limitations. First, we acknowledge the following limitations with the instrument:

- The instrument only asks respondents to view a demo site, so most respondents may not be able to sense the impact of the standard navigation system across all e-commerce sites on the Web.
- The instrument attempts to measure a number of user attitudes and

perceptions, but it cannot probe deeply into respondents' opinions and feelings.

- The instrument is self-reported via respondents, so it involves the potential problems of honesty, social desirability, or motivation for thoughtful response.
- The sample for the study may be biased as it includes students and faculty members from one university.

The user interface part of the study also has some limitations:

- The study uses sample e-commerce sites that are relatively small and simplistic in design.
- One of the main factors for consideration in choosing these sites is the fact that they are compatible with the proof of concept (In this case "proof of concept" means a computer program that works in a controlled environment to prove that an idea can work) standard navigation server. Compatible, in this sense, means that the standard navigation system is able to communicate with the site's server and process most of the pages on the site.
- The standard navigation server also does not support multilevel redirection, HTTPS, or other types of secure connections.

Despite its limitations primarily due to its exploratory nature, the findings of the study provide valuable insight on the user acceptance of e-commerce Web sites. Many designers believe that the key barrier to user acceptance is the lack of user friendliness and that adding a user-friendly interface to increase usability is the key to success (e.g., Davis, 1993; Branscomb & Thomas, 1985). Yet the current results indicate that, although ease of use is clearly important, the usefulness of the system is even more important by over 2 times. The media richness of system familiarity or experience of users is important as well and should not be overlooked. Users who are familiar with the system may be willing to tolerate a difficult interface in order to access functionality that helps them on their online shopping, while no amount of ease of use can compensate for a system that does not do a useful task. Thus, the intention of this study is to test the behavioral constructs of perceived usefulness, and perceived ease of use, and perceived richness as predictors of usage acceptance of the standard navigation system in e-commerce sites. The results show a strong relationship between users' perceptions of usefulness, ease of use and richness about the standard navigation system. Therefore, e-commerce users apparently need a standard navigation system to make e-commerce sites easy to use. The implication of the findings will contribute to the e-commerce community considerately in the future.

REFERENCES

Adams, D. A., Nelson, R. R. and Todd, P. A. (1992). Perceived usefulness, ease of use, and usage of information technology: A Replication. *MIS Quarterly*, 16(2), 227-247.

Ahuja, J. (2000). *Navigation Systems: An Aid for Increasing the Usability of Web Sites*. Unpublished master's thesis, University of Waterloo, Waterloo, Ontario, Canada. Available on the World Wide Web at: http://pdbeam.uwaterloo.ca/~jahuja/Research.htm. Accessed March 5, 2000.

Allum, M. (1998). *Building Dynamic Menu Bars*. Available on the World Wide Web at: http://webreview.com/wr/pub/98/07/24/coder/index.html. Accessed March 26, 2000.

Bagozzi, R. P., Davis, F. D. and Warshaw, P. R. (1992). Development and test of a theory of technological learning and usage. *Human Relations*, 45(7), 659-686.

Bearden, W. O., Netemeyer, R. G. and Mobley, M. F. (1993). *Handbook of Marketing Scales*: *Multi-Item Measures for Marketing and Consumer Behavior Research*. Newbury Park, CA: Sage.

Booker, E. (1997, July). Defining a strong Web interface usability. *Web Week*. Available on the World Wide Web at: http://www.internetworld.com/print/1997/07/07/undercon/19970707-strong.html. Accessed May 7, 2000.

Bort, J. (1999, December). Navigation: An Art for e-Com Sites. Available on the World Wide Web at: http://www.microtimes.com/201/ecombort201a.html. Accessed April 4, 2000.

Branscomb, L. M. and Thomas, J. C. (1985). Ease of use: A system design challenge. *IBM Systems Journal*, 23, 224-235.

Chau, P. Y. K. (1996). An empirical assessment of a modified technology acceptance model. *Journal of MIS*, 13(2), 185-204.

Davis, F. D. (1989). Perceived usefulness, perceived ease of use, and user acceptance of information technology. *MIS Quarterly*, 13(3), 319-340.

Davis, F. D. (1993). User acceptance of information technology: System characteristics, user perceptions, and behavioral impacts. *International Journal of Man-Machine Studies*, 38, 475–487.

Davis, F. D., Bagozzi, R. P. and Warshaw, P. R. (1989). User acceptance of computer technology: A comparison of two theoretical models. *Management Science*, 35(8), 982-1003.

Duncan, O. D. (1975). *Introduction to Structural Equation Models*. New

York, NY: Academic Press.

Forrester Research, Inc. (1998). *The Forrester Report: Why Web Sites Fail* (p. 10). Available on the World Wide Web at: http://www.forresterresearch.com/. Accessed March 26, 2000.

Fulk, J., Schmitz, J. A. and Ryu, D. (1995). Cognitive elements in the social construction of communication technology. *Management Communication Quarterly*, 8(3), 259-288.

Gehrke, D. and Turban, E. (1998). *Determinants of Successful Website Design: Relative Importance and Recommendations for Effectiveness.* Available on the World Wide Web at: http://www.csulb.edu/~turbanis/CRWEB.htm. Accessed March 25, 2000.

Gall, M. D., Borg, W. R. and Gall, J. P. (1996). *Educational Research: An Introduction.* White Plains, NY: Longman Publishers.

Hendrickson, A. R. and Collins, M. R. (1996). An assessment of structure and causation of IS usage. *The DATA BASE for Advances in Information Systems*, 27(2), 61-67.

Hobart, J. (1995). Principles of good GUI design. *Unix Review*, 13(10), 37-46.

Hoffman, M. (1996). *Enabling Extremely Rapid Navigation in your Web or Document*, March. Available on the World Wide Web at: http://www.pdrinterleaf.com/infoaxcs.htm. Accessed March 3, 2000.

Igbaria, M., Guimaraes, T. and Davis, G. B. (1995). Testing the determinants of Microcomputer usage via a structural equation model. *Journal of Management Information Systems*, 11(4), 87-114.

Lederer A. L., Maupin, D. J., Sena, M. P. and Zhuang, Y. (1999). The technology acceptance model and the World Wide Web. *KIKM Research Paper*, 125.

McKnight, C., Dillon, A. and Richardson, J. (1991). *Hypertext in Context.* Cambridge, UK: University Press.

Nielsen, J. (1998a). *Web Usability: Why and How.* Available on the World Wide Web at: http://www.zdnet.com/devhead/stories/articles/0,4413,2137433,00.html. Accessed March 29, 2000.

Nielsen, J. (1998b). What is "Usability?" Available on the World Wide Web at: http://www.zdnet.com/devhead/stories/articles/0,4413,2137671,00.html. Accessed March 26, 2000.

Nielsen, J. and Norman, D. A. (2000). *Web-Site Usability: Usability on the Web isn't a Luxury*, January. Available on the World Wide Web at: http://www.informationweek.com/773/web.htm. Accessed March 28, 2000.

Nunnally, J. C. (1978). *Psychometric Theory.* New York, NY: McGraw-Hill

Book Co.

Shaw, M. J., Gardner, D. M. and Thomas, H. (1997). Research opportunities in electronic commerce. *Decision Support Systems*, 21, 149-156.

Sheppard, B., Hartwick, J. and Warshaw, P. (1988). The theory of reasoned action: A meta analysis of past research with recommendations for modifications and future research. *Journal of Consumer Research*, 15(3), 325-343.

Shirky, C., Webber, D., Newcomer, J. M. and Jaworski, W. M. (1999). Usability vs. the Web. *Communications of the ACM*, 42(3), 27-32.

Szajna, B. (1996). Empirical evaluation of the revised technology acceptance model. *Management Science*, 42(1), 85-92.

Theng, Y. L. (1997). *Addressing the "Lost in Hyperspace" Problem in Hypertext*. Doctoral dissertation, Middlesex University, London.

Theng, Y. L. and Thimbleby, H. (1998). Addressing design and usability issues in hypertext and on the World Wide Web by re-examining the "lost in hyperspace" problem. *Journal of Universal Computer Science*, 4(11), 839-855.

Thompson, R. (1998). Extending the technology acceptance model with motivation and social factors. *Proceedings of Association for Information Systems Annual Conference*, 757-759.

Vestal, C. (1999). *Electronic Commerce Environments: Corporate Obstacles and Opportunities to Competitiveness*. Master's thesis, Bowie State University.

ZDInternet.inc. (1999). White paper one: Building a great customer experience to develop brand, increase loyalty and grow revenues. *Creative Good*. Available on the World Wide Web at: http://www.creativegood.com/creativegood-whitepaper.pdf. Accessed March 16, 2000.

Zona Research. (1999). *Zona Research's Online Shopping Report*. Available on the World Wide Web at: http://www.zonaresearch.com/info/press/preleases99.htm. Accessed April 4, 2000.

Chapter VI

Factors Affecting Behavioral Intentions to Adopt Electronic Shopping on the World Wide Web: A Structural Equation Modeling Approach

Bay Arinze
Drexel University, USA

Christopher Ruth
Bass Hotels and Resorts, USA

Searching for and purchasing personal goods and services on the Internet, termed hereafter as "Web shopping," has seen tremendous growth over the past 2-3 years. With the advent of the Internet and accompanying technologies such as broader bandwidth modems, more robust browsers and multimedia, growth for Web shopping should explode, sustained only by consumers' perceptions of this new market channel and their subsequent adoption behavior based on these perceptions. Surprisingly, little research has empirically tested an adoption model to this technology to determine critical factors that may influence adoption decisions at the consumer level.

The technology acceptance model (TAM) enjoys a rich base of academic acceptance. This paper uses TAM, while adding technology-specific constructs, developed and validated from prior research. Structural Equation modeling and confirmatory factor analysis were employed to test reliability, validity, and relationships of the constructs. Where prior research exists, comparisons of findings were made.

The results showed that an augmented TAM as described produced measurement and structural models with adequate fits. High construct validities were observed. Three distinct aspects of Internet shopping (browsing, ordering, paying) all revealed good model fits (all superior to TAM alone). In addition, the attitudinal factors of perceived usefulness, intrinsic motivation and perceived information privacy played a significant role in the model. Interestingly, perceived ease of use, system quality and social pressure showed only indirect effects toward usage. Computer experience, age and education showed no effects.

INTRODUCTION

Never before have consumers had more choices in market channels. Today's consumers, in addition to shopping "traditionally" at department or specialty stores, can now shop via phone, fax, catalog, TV, and, of course, the Internet. Of all the shopping mediums mentioned, few have captured the interest of the public more than shopping over the Internet via the World Wide Web (Web shopping).

Much research (both marketing and MIS) has been directed at determining both the motivation for and impact of this new marketing channel. While such studies continue, little empirical research has been done to determine factors that influence the adoption of this shopping medium. This research builds upon prior studies in information technology adoption models to empirically test the influence of certain factors on the adoption of Web shopping systems.

Two unique constructs that may exist, and are proposed, are intrinsic motivation and perceived information privacy. Web shopping is a predominantly voluntary technology. There are few situations, contrary to institutional settings, where a user will feel forced into using the technology. The motivation, therefore, will tend to be more intrinsic than extrinsic. Additionally, the act of shopping involves the exchange of personal information. As such, perceptions of privacy and privacy protection will be more important than uses of technology in institutional settings. This research will introduce a construct to measure the user's perception of information privacy as well as its impact on adoption.

The overall current use of Web shopping contrasts with early predictions. According to the Forrester Research, E-business will account for roughly $1.2 trillion in 2001 and top $6.7 trillion by 2004. The United States will also account for almost half of this trading volume. The Gartner Group also predicts that by 2005, more than 500,000 enterprises will participate in e-markets as buyers or sellers.

These growth rates, while quite significant, will still certainly be dependent, in large part, upon sustained user acceptance of the Web as a shopping medium. As a result, adoption models, well grounded in prior empirical and theoretical IT studies, are needed to explain critical factors that increase or decrease the usage of Web shopping.

Without models that contain relevant and valid constructs, Web shopping adoption cannot be easily explained, predicted, or improved. With a valid model, industry can better develop Web shopping with the appropriate features and benefits and target Web shopping systems to the appropriate audience.

BACKGROUND

From a research perspective, Web shopping is a relatively new subject without much structured definition of terms. In various publications, terms like Internet shopping, virtual shopping, online ordering, and Web shopping, may or may not refer to the same thing. Because of this, it is important to frame the subject of this research, Web shopping.

Alba et al. (1997), while not specifically defining the term, stated three characteristics of what they termed interactive home shopping systems, a surrogate for Web shopping. The first characteristic (as may be evident by the term) is interactivity. Interactivity contains the dimensions of response time and response contingency (Hoffman & Novak, 1996). Response time, ideally, is considered immediate in an electronic medium. In the context of the Internet, however, response time will vary depending upon system capabilities of both buyer and seller.

The second feature considers where shopping occurs. The term "home" is really a surrogate referring to any remote location other than the store. For purposes of this research, we will be even more specific with this term "home" to mean for consumer use, not business use.

The final term, shopping, refers to being able to search, select, and purchase products. The act of shopping may involve one or all of these functions. One may shop by searching only and deciding not to select or purchase. Terms like "online buying" and "online ordering" are more specific forms of shopping that involve a transaction. Shopping can involve a transaction, but does not have to.

Putting these definitions together, interactive home shopping or Web shopping systems are those that allow buyers to interactively search, select, and purchase goods at locations other than physical stores.

With the above definitions and assumptions, this research and the term Web shopping should be generalizeable to most applications that sell goods and services directly to consumers over the Web. These sites must all offer interactive search and ordering functions.

General Marketplace Factors Affecting Acceptance of Web shopping

Before exploring individual consumer factors and how they influence the acceptance of Web shopping, it is also important to examine the macro factors that might lead to acceptance of Web shopping. Only when all motivational factors are fully explained, can individual motivators be explored and explained in full context.

For any commerce application to be accepted, it must offer benefits to the three major players in a transaction, the consumer, the retailer/wholesaler, and the manufacturer. What are the current and future motivations of these groups, which drive development of Web shopping development and use?

Some motivations for consumers are:
- Convenience (Schor, 1989; Cope, 1996).
- Lower prices (Hauser & Wernerfelt, 1990), including tax savings.
- Better product information and better shopping convenience (Burke 1996).
Some motivations for retailers are:
- Operational efficiency, e.g., less inventory (Cope, 1996).
- Ability to exploit customer information and easily adjust the mix of products, pricing and promotions (Phillips et. al., 1997).
Some motivations for manufacturers are:
- To develop or reestablish direct relationships with consumers and thus improve margins (Burke, 1997; Pine et al., 1995).
- To permit targeted marketing and frequency programs as well as "performance-based marketing" (Peterson, 1997).

IT ADOPTION MODEL APPROACHES

We turn to the literature relative to technology adoption. Research that links factors contributing to adoption of information technology can be classified into four theories; new product diffusion models (or Bass models), innovation-diffusion models, theory of reasoned action (TRA), and the technology acceptance model (TAM). TAM was the method chosen for this study.

The Technology Acceptance Model (TAM)

Developed by Davis (1986, 1989), TAM is based on the TRA with two important points of departure. These have to do with constructs and applicability.

While TRA suggests that each adoption model requires that its own distinct belief set be generated, TAM contends that only two primary factors affect behavioral intention to use technology. These factors are ease of use (EOU) and usefulness (U). EOU refers to "the degree to which a prospective user expects the target system to be free of effort," while U refers to the prospective user's subjective probability that using a specific application system will increase his or her job performance" (Davis, 1989).

Second, TAM is proposed only for application in studies dealing with adoption of information technologies. Though never mentioned specifically, Davis (1989) implied that TAM was to be used in organizational settings versus cases of personal use of information technology. This study will be one of the first to test TAM outside the organizational setting.

Modified TAMs

As acceptance for TAM has grown through many of the past studies, so too has a research imperative to improve on it. Some have attempted to capitalize on TAM's validated and reliable scales of EOU and U while augmenting them with other constructs in an attempt to better explain acceptance of certain technologies. Each of these studies has sought to augment TAM based on the subjects tested or the technology used. Some examples of these studies are Igbaria et al. (1996) and Gefen and Straub (1997).

The Literature Gap

To date, no IT acceptance models have dealt empirically with acceptance factors relating to Web shopping at various levels of usage. This research and accompanying model suggest that there are unique features, most notably personal information privacy and intrinsic motivation, in this environment that call out for different constructs and approaches, while building upon others.

Few studies have investigated the more voluntary nature of adoption, much less for the Internet or, more specifically, Web shopping. The few studies that have investigated the effects of voluntariness have been Iivari (1996) with CASE tools Agarwal and Prasad (1997) with World Wide Web adoption. This research, however, was still conducted in an organizational setting.

For adoption to occur organizationally, Vadapalli and Rammamurthy (1997) contend that consumers, internal groups and external groups must change. In the case of personal adoption, only the consumer must change; organizational factors do not come into play. For this reason, organizational factors will not be variables of this study.

PROPOSED RESEARCH MODEL AND HYPOTHESES

The Proposed Modified TAM for Determining Adoption of Web shopping

Borrowing from many of the research foundations listed above, the TAM introduced here contains the essential and thoroughly supported constructs of perceived ease of use (PEOU) and perceived usefulness (PU). These, combined with two additional variables–perceived information privacy (PIP) and playfulness (PL)–will comprise the major attitudinal component of the model. As will be justified later, the author believes these constructs are strong enough to have direct effects on usage rather than indirect effects mediated by PEOU and PU. In addition to these constructs, two additional latent variables are also proposed, which, when mediated by PEOU and PU, should have indirect effects and/or direct effects on usage. These variables are system quality (SQ), and computer experience (CE). Age, income, and education (Edu) are three additional observed variables that are added to the model to test for and control demographic considerations in the model. Finally, social pressure is introduced as a variable directly affecting usage. Usage will be at three levels (browse, order, pay). Figure 1 shows the conceptual model.

A unique feature of this model is the ability to test usage based upon the original framework (Davis, 1989) of the TAM model to compare and contrast against the original TAM research and this augmented TAM model.

Hypotheses

As with previous TAM studies outlined (Davis, 1989; Davis et. al., 1989; Mathieson, 1991; Adams et al., 1992; Szanja, 1994) the following hypotheses are advanced regarding PEOU, PU and usage:

Figure 1: The Research Model

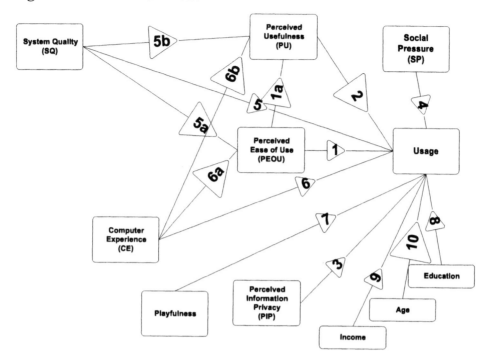

Hypothesis 1 and 1 a–PEOU will directly affect usage and indirectly affect usage through PU. Hypothesis 2–PU will directly affect usage.

These two hypotheses will test and confirm the relationships' validity within the realm of Web shopping. On an exploratory level, the study will examine if the effect of PEOU and PU vary by level of use or dramatically change in relationship to previous TAM studies.

Hypothesis 3–Perceived information privacy will directly affect usage.

A relatively new stream of MIS research, information privacy, defined as "the ability of the individual to personally control information about one's self" (Stone et al., 1983), is becoming critically associated with Internet usage. On the Internet, there are real and perceived dangers that private records can be copied, transactions monitored, and URL activity tracked.

Recently, Smith et al. (1996) have developed an instrument that operationalizes consumer concerns relative to information privacy. By using this scale, this study can examine PIP and its effect on Web shopping usage.

Hypothesis 4–Social pressure, SP, will directly affect usage.

A surrogate for TRA's normative beliefs, SP was proposed by Fishbein and Azjen (1975) and Azjen and Fishbein (1980). Social pressure has been empirically linked to usage by Davis et al. (1989) and Igbaria et al. (1996). On an exploratory level, this study will determine if SP (subjective norm) varies with level of use or varies in comparison to previous studies.

Hypothesis 5, 5a, and 5b–System Quality, SQ, will directly affect usage and indirectly affect usage through PEOU and PU.

Davis (1989) via the TAM and Azjen and Fishbein (1975) via the TRA both contend that external factors affect behavior (or usage) indirectly through influencing beliefs. The TPB, however, asserts external factors can have direct effects on behavior given the level of PBC. The indirect and direct effects of each of the external factors, SQ, G, and CE will be tested.

Hypothesis 6, 6a, and 6b–Computer experience, CE, will directly affect usage and indirectly affect usage through PEOU and PU.

As an external factor and consistent with the reasoning for SQ, CE should show positive correlation with PEOU, PU, and Usage and indirect affect on usage through PEOU and PU. CE and system training have been empirically linked to greater acceptance in several studies (DeLone, 1988; Fuerst & Cheney, 1982; Kraemer et al., 1993; Lee, 1986).

Hypothesis 7–Higher degrees of user playfulness (PL) will directly affect usage.

Many studies have examined intrinsic motivation to use information systems. Most of this research has been limited to microcomputers as a whole. Davis et al. (1989), while pursuing the effect of perceived usefulness and perceived ease of use, found that intrinsic motivators like enjoyment also played a part beyond these two constructs. In addition, other studies (Davis, 1992; Malone, 1981; Webster, 1989) found links of playfulness and usage.

Hypothesis 8–Educational attainment (Edu) will directly affect usage.

Several studies have examined education and age and their effect on IS alienation. Among studies finding such links is Ray (1985). He found that lesser degrees of education resulted in higher levels of computer system alienation. Abdul-Gader and Kozar (1995) examined microcomputer alienation against several other variables, including educational attainment, and found education level inversely related to computer alienation with $r=.6$ and $p<.01$. Intuitively it makes sense that education increases knowledge of computers and both reduces system anxiety and increases usage.

Hypothesis 9–Annual earned income (iIncome) will directly affect usage.

The income gap among Internet users and non-users is well documented. There is recent evidence, however, that this trend is changing. Still, although computers and Internet access are more affordable than ever, there is a substantial financial barrier to entry. In addition, those with lower education levels will, in general, enjoy less income. Accordingly, one would expect a high degree of multicollinearity between income and education.

Hypothesis 10–Age (age) will directly affect usage.

Research examining the effect of age on usage has produced mixed results. For example Steinfield (1986) found a negative link between age and IS usage in computer-mediated environments (older workers used IS less). Yet Ku (1996), examining adoption patterns in e-mail, found no such empirical link.

Methodology

Operationalization of Constructs
* Usage

Consistent with Davis et al. (1989) and Chau (1995), respondents will self-report usage on a 7-point categorical scale, their extent of use of the application. The ranges will also be adopted from Davis et al. The first question was, "How often do you use the Internet to search for products and services?" The second was, "How often do you actually order (but not pay for) products and services directly from the Internet?" Finally, respondents were asked, "How often do you purchase (with credit card authorization) products over the Internet?"
* PEOU and PU

These scales are strictly transformed from the originally proposed (Davis, et al., 1989) scales. The transformations were into the Web shopping context.
* SP or Normative Beliefs

The normative belief or social pressure construct consisted of one question, "Most people who are important to me think I should be using the Internet to buy products and services." This approach is consistent with Fishbein and Azjen's (1979) recommended guidelines. Since this is a one-dimensional scale, tests of reliability will not be possible here. It should be noted, however, that Igbaria et al. (1996), used this construct successfully in a TAM application.

- PIP

PIP was operationalized using Smith et al.'s (1996) previously referenced scales. Its original form consists of 4 dimensions utilizing 15 total
scales. For parsimony, these 15 scales have been reduced to 4 scales with no
subscales. The item with the highest factor loading in each of the subscales has
been taken, with the rest eliminated. In addition, to add a specific dimension
regarding purchasing, a fifth question was added to account for perceived
transaction fear.

- SQ

Davis et al. (1989) suggested that system quality played an important part
on usage as an external factor affecting attitudes. Igbaria et al. (1996), citing
his prior work on system quality as well as that from Lucas (1978), developed
a 5-item scale representing system quality. The 5 dimensions represented
were *functionality, equipment performance, interaction, environment,* and
user interface. It exhibited relatively high reliability and construct validity.

- CE

User experience will be assessed via a 5-item scale, which will record
users' responses to extent of familiarity of several systems related to using the
computer and the Internet. This approach is similar to that proposed by Nelson
and Cheyney (1987) and Igbaria et al. (1995).

- PL

Playfulness was operationalized using a scale developed by Webster and
Martocchio (1992). Termed the computer playfulness scale (CPS), the construct
should measure the degree to which individuals enjoy "cognitive spontaneity"
with the computer interface. The scale exhibited high degrees of test-retest
reliability ($r=.82$ and $p<.001$). The scale consists of 7 items on a 7-point Likert
scale. Individuals are asked their agreement or disagreement with 7 adjectives
(items), namely: spontaneous, unimaginative, flexible, creative, playful, unorigi-
nal and uninventive. Appropriate items are reverse scored to complete the scale.

- Educational Attainment (Edu)

Educational attainment is measured by asking respondents to select their
level of education completed from a 7-item scale.

- Income
- Age

Sampling

Target Population and Survey Instrument

Anyone who has an e-mail address is, in fact, an Internet user of some
degree. Services are available that offer rented lists of e-mail users. In

addition, these lists can partition users among areas of interest (i.e., sites they have visited). Five of these random lists were selected, totaling 2,400 e-mails, via a 100% opt-in list rental site.

An e-mail introducing the study was sent to the target group as described above. A URL was referenced in the e-mail which, if clicked, brings potential respondents to an automated survey form and collection site. In this way, data can be automatically collected from the intended target audience. In addition, because the site collects "hits" from the pages, an additional relative measure of response rate was also collected.

Testing Procedures and Test Results

Testing procedures for this study will involve structural equation model (SEM), a second-generation multivariate technique (Bollen, 1989; Fornell, 1982) that is gaining in use among published MIS studies (Chau, 1996).

Sample Size Response Rate and Power Analysis

Of 2,400 e-mail surveys sent, 428 completed samples were returned. Because the collection procedure did not allow submission of incomplete surveys, no missing data exists. In addition, 10 surveys did not reach their intended recipient. Postmaster Direct tracked click-through rates. The results showed that 597 clicks to the URL containing the survey were obtained. Based upon these parameters, three measures of response were obtained. The click-through response rate was (597/2,390), or 25%. Of those that went to the survey, 428 completed the survey, a yield of (428/587), or 73%. The overall response rate was (428/2,390), or 18%. This approaches the 20% response rate for surveys recommended by Yu and Cooper (1983). The overall e-mail response rate of 18% compares favorably to the range of 6% to 73% suggested by Weible and Wallace (1998). Further, the 18% response rate compares very favorably to the 6% reported by Tse (1998) in his exploratory study of e-mail response rates. In addition, the yield on click-through of 73% suggests the form was designed so as not to discourage most from completing it. The 73% rate compares very favorably with an average rate of 2% for banner ads as reported by Fahey (1998). There was insignificant response bias.

With 428 responses, the sample size far exceeds that recommended by many for achievement of adequate power of testing. This includes the recommended minimum of 100 (proposed by Bollen, 1989), 150 (proposed by Boomsma, 1982) and over 200 (recommended by Anderson & Gerbing, 1988). Finally, (Hair et al., 1992) recommend for multivariate analysis that the sample size should be at least 5 times the number of parameters in the model.

Since the proposed model includes 43 parameters, the minimum response necessary would be (43*5), or 215. The sample size of 428 is far in excess of this recommendation as well.

In addition, power analysis was conducted in accordance with recommendations from Cohen and Cohen (1983). A medium effect size (r=.30) was chosen based upon results from empirical studies shown in the literature search. An alpha of .05 was also chosen. Based on this, the recommended sample size for a power of .80 is n=98. Based on the same formula, the actual power of the test (with a sample size of 428 and an r=.23) is 100%. Power analysis, therefore, also reveals the sample size allows for sufficient power of test.

Validity Tests for the Measurement Model

Confirmatory factor analysis (CFA) and reliability analysis (via Amos 4.0) were performed on the 33 manifest variables representing the 6 latent constructs.

The CFA using Amos 4.0 focused on the 33 manifest variables comprising the latent variables PU, PEOU, PL, CE, SQ, and PIP. The factor structure revealed high and consistent loadings on the six proposed factors. Most SFL were above or approaching the .50 recommended value. In addition 5 of the 6 factors exhibited composite reliabilities close to or above the recommended level of .80. In addition, 4 of the latent constructs exhibited AVEs above the recommended threshold of .50. Still, as suggested by Segars and Grover (1993), manifest variables exhibiting SFLs below the .5 threshold were removed in an attempt to explain more variance and aid in construct parsimony. A second set of similar tests was performed to yielded results shown in Table 1.

The tests show a considerably better measurement model with even more parsimony. The revised measurement model contains 20 manifest variables that appear to measure 6 distinct constructs, as proposed. All variables loaded highly on hypothesized constructs. Factor loadings ranged from a low of .715 to a high of .965. Most loadings occurred well above .85. In addition, SFLs ranged from .511 to .931, all within recommended minimums. AVEs range from .610 to .827, all far exceeding the suggested minimum of .50. Finally, composite reliabilities ranged from .815 to .930, all exceeding the recommended minimum of .80. Based upon these results, the measurement model was fixed and tests for discriminant validity were conducted.

Based upon the outlined procedures, 15 pair-wise comparisons were made to determine the discriminant validity of each latent construct. The tests show strong indicators of discriminant validity. All 15 pair-wise tests show

Table 1: Results of Modified Measurement Model

Standardized Regression Weights Recommended Value >.7				Squared Multiple Correlations Recommended Value >.5		AVE >.50	Composite >.8	Disposition Retain/Remove
CE1	<--	CE	0.804	CE1	0.646	0.698	0.821	Retain
CE3	<--	CE	0.866	CE3	0.750			Retain
PEOU1	<--	PEOU	0.715	PEOU1	0.511			Retain
PEOU2	<--	PEOU	0.812	PEOU2	0.659			Retain
PEOU3	<--	PEOU	0.898	PEOU3	0.806	0.694	0.930	Retain
PEOU4	<--	PEOU	0.838	PEOU4	0.702			Retain
PEOU5	<--	PEOU	0.822	PEOU5	0.676			Retain
PEOU6	<--	PEOU	0.898	PEOU6	0.806			Retain
PIP2	<--	PIP	0.774	PIP2	0.599			Retain
PIP4	<--	PIP	0.715	PIP4	0.511	0.610	0.815	Retain
PIP5	<--	PIP	0.849	PIP5	0.721			Retain
PL2	<--	PL	0.791	PL2	0.626			Retain
PL6	<--	PL	0.965	PL6	0.931	0.827	0.930	Retain
PL7	<--	PL	0.961	PL7	0.924			Retain
PU2	<--	PU	0.896	PU2	0.803			Retain
PU3	<--	PU	0.899	PU3	0.808	0.793	0.842	Retain
PU4	<--	PU	0.876	PU4	0.767			Retain
SQ1	<--	SQ	0.942	SQ1	0.887			Retain
SQ2	<--	SQ	0.884	SQ2	0.781	0.784	0.912	Retain
SQ4	<--	SQ	0.826	SQ4	0.682			Retain

changes in chi-square values between constrained and unconstrained conditions were significant at levels below p<.0001. Based upon these results, the best fitting measurement model was fixed and employed for SEM.

Using Amos version 4.0 (Arbuckle & Wothke, 1999), a structural equation model was developed and testing procedures were employed using maximum likelihood estimation procedures. From the tests, measurements of model fit were generated.

Goodness of Fit Tests

An initial test was performed on the best fitting model and produced AGFIs, Chi-Square/DF, and RMSs all better than the recommended levels for reasonable fit. The modification Indices, a part of the output of Amos 4., suggested that the model also control covariance for (AGE<->INCOME), (INCOME<->EDU), and (CE<->EDU) and (CE<->SQ). These controls make methodological sense as well, as one can see each of these could covary. In addition, the modification indices revealed that the model should also control for indirect effects of SP on both PEOU and PU. This suggests that SP could have significant indirect effects (through PEOU and PU) on usage. This resulted in the final model.

With these changes made, the model was run again. There was an adequate fit of the final structural model, plus the improvement to fit with the adjustment of the measurement model. The final model shows goodness of fit measures exceeding all suggested indices when adjusted for degrees of freedom.

Findings

Within the results from the fixed structural model were standardized regression coefficients, along with their measures of statistical significance. The table appears below. With Table 2, and a confirmed goodness of fit for the associated structural model, which generated it, specific hypotheses were tested.

H1–PEOU and Usage and H1a–PEOU and PU

PEOU showed no significant direct effect on any measure of usage (browse, order, pay). This would seem to contradict earlier studies (Davis, 1989; Davis et. al, 1989; Igbaria, et al., 1997) yet seem to confirm other findings (Adams, et al., 1992; Agarwal & Prasad, 1996; Chau, 1996). Consistent with most prior related studies, there is a strong, positive, statistically significant, and consistent link from PEOU to PU on all three levels of

Table 2: Standardized Regression Estimates and Significance Level

Significance Levels and Standardized Parameter Estimates								
			Browse (Usage1)		Order (Usage2)		Pay (Usage3)	
	Path		Sig. Level	Estimate	Sig. Level	Estimate	Sig. Level	Estimate
PEOU	<--	CE	0.396	(0.044)	0.410	(0.043)	0.398	(0.043)
PEOU	<--	SQ	0.000	0.289	0.000	0.289	0.000	0.289
PEOU	<--	SP	0.000	0.278	0.000	0.278	0.000	0.278
PU	<--	PEOU	0.000	0.194	0.000	0.194	0.000	0.194
PU	<--	SP	0.000	0.396	0.000	0.396	0.000	0.396
PU	<--	SQ	0.001	0.164	0.001	0.164	0.001	0.164
PU	<--	CE	0.641	(0.023)	0.652	(0.022)	0.639	(0.023)
Usage	<--	PIP	0.023	(0.115)	0.020	(0.119)	0.000	0.302
Usage	<--	PU	0.047	0.116	0.035	0.123	0.000	0.199
Usage	<--	SQ	0.327	0.052	0.321	0.053	0.209	0.062
Usage	<--	CE	0.725	(0.019)	0.574	(0.030)	0.423	0.039
Usage	<--	SP	0.814	(0.013)	0.023	0.123	0.073	0.089
Usage	<--	PL	0.001	0.160	0.840	0.010	0.717	(0.016)
Usage	<--	EDU	0.707	0.019	0.158	0.073	0.513	0.031
Usage	<--	PEOU	0.108	0.087	0.661	(0.024)	0.168	0.069
Usage	<--	INCOME	0.008	(0.136)	0.040	(0.106)	0.001	0.165
Usage	<--	AGE	0.732	(0.016)	0.554	(0.028)	0.078	0.078

use. (b=.194, p<.001) which translates into an indirect effect on usage of .022 (browse), .024 (order), and .039 (pay). As postulated in an earlier study by Chau (1996), as technology becomes more user-friendly, learning becomes more immediate and intuitive, making PEOU less of a direct factor. Indeed, Davis (1989) suggested that, when controlled for usefulness, PEOU, as a direct effect, becomes nonsignificant. In voluntary use applications, like Internet shopping, inherent PEOU (to the point of non-differentiation) may become even more critical.

H2–PU and Usage

Confirming the hypothesis, as well as all earlier cited studies, PU had strong, statistically significant, and positive direct effects on all three levels of usage. All parameter estimates were significant at p<.001 and effect increased with levels of usage: (.116 (browse), .123 (order), .199 (pay). This suggests that, as users exploit more capabilities of Web shopping, there is an even stronger link between PU and usage. Contradicting many earlier studies, however, PU did not have the strongest direct effect among all dependent variables.

H3–PIP and Usage

PIP showed strong, statistically significant (p<.001), yet variant direct effects across all usage types. Parameter estimates recorded were -.115 (browse), -.119 (order), and .302 (pay). The significant negative relationship between PIP and two levels of usage (browsing and ordering) is curious and should be a subject of further research. Jarvenpaa and Todd (1996) also noted a negative effect between perceived risk (privacy and credit card risk) and attitude toward Internet shopping. One possible explanation is that users that are more adept at exploiting Internet shopping are also more aware of the privacy issues. Those reporting low usage rates on pay may simply not be aware of privacy concerns. Yet another explanation might be, as supported by an earlier study (Gillett, 1976), that early adopters of retail innovations tend to be more risk-averse to begin with.

Regardless, on the highest involvement measure of usage (pay), PIP was the variable with the strongest direct effect. The direct effect of PIP (.302) was stronger than even that of perceived usefulness (.199). In their study, Jarvenpaa and Todd (1996) also mentioned that the key risk perceived by consumers was "the personal risk associated with credit-card loss." These findings lend further evidence that additional technology-specific constructs like PIP can lead to greater explanatory power than the TAM model alone.

H4–SP and Usage

The only significant direct effect of SP on usage was on the (order) level (b=.123, p=.029). These results would appear to suggest two things. First, in general, usage in voluntary technology, such as Internet shopping, will not be as directly influenced by SP compared to more mandated technology in organizational settings. Second, the presence of direct effect of SP on order, but not pay, might lend some support to Agarwal and Prasad (1997). They contend that perceived voluntariness (perhaps a surrogate for SP) helps in describing initial use, but not sustained use (i.e., going from order to purchase) of information technology in the Internet.

Regardless, significant indirect effects were noted between SP and usage, passed through PEOU and PU. Direct effects of SP on PU and PEOU were all positive, significant at (p<.001), and exactly the same across all levels of usage. Parameter estimates were .396 (SPóPU) and .278 (SPóPU), respectively, consistently across all levels of use. These yielded an indirect effect of .054 across all levels of PU. Indirect effects of SP on usage were (.076, .049, and .109) for browse, order, purchase. These results suggest that, although SP seems to have a reduced direct affect on usage in voluntary technology, SP plays a significant indirect role, mediated through PU and PEOU, as originally proposed by (Davis, 1989).

H5, 5a, 5b–SQ and PEOU and PU and Usage

SQ exhibited no statistically significant direct link with usage. The p values for SQ to usage for browse, order, and pay were .379, .340 and .276, respectively. This seems to contradict earlier findings of Fuerst and Cheney (1982), Igbaria, et al. (1989), Igbaria et al. (1995), O'Reilly (1982). Indirect effects of SQ on Usage were .050 for browse, .020 for order, and .064 for pay. The results suggest that SQ plays a significant role on usage, indirectly through it's effects on PU and PEOU.

H6, 6a, 6b–CE and PEOU and PU and Usage

Surprisingly, CE showed no statistically significant direct or indirect effects on any level of usage. Significance levels for any of these links ranged from .423 to .725. These results contradict the findings of DeLone (1988), Fuerst and Cheney (1982), Kraemer et al. (1993), Lee (1986), and Igbaria, et al. (1995). One possible explanation is, again, the difference of settings (voluntary vs. organizational). Use of technology in voluntary settings must be more inherently easy to use, thereby mitigating the effect of computer experience.

H7–PL and Usage

PL exhibited a significant (p=.001) direct effect on usage in only the browse level of usage. The parameter estimate was .160. This makes intuitive sense. In the three uses of Internet shopping, browsing offers the best opportunity for intrinsic motivation, curiosity, and playfulness. These results suggest that playfulness or intrinsic motivation is important for initial stages of use in Internet shopping, but not at the point of more goal-directed transaction activity.

H8–Education and Usage

The study found no link between Edu and any level of usage. P values range from .158 to .707. In addition, as might be expected, Edu had to be controlled for its covariance with income and CE. These results suggest that the Internet or, specifically, Internet shopping is an education invariant technology. These results also contradict the findings of prior studies (Kirsch & Lengermann, 1972; Seeman, 1975; Allison, 1978; Ray, 1985; and Abdul-Gader & Kozar, 1995). A possible explanation is that, as systems become more accessible and easier to use, education becomes less determinant of both access to and usage of a technology. Indeed a recent study shows the gap for access to the Internet is closing among varying educational, gender and income levels.

H9–Income and Usage

Significant direct effects (p values ranged from .001 to .040) were found between income and all three levels of usage. Income, however, had negative direct effects on the browse (.-.136) and order (-.106) use levels and a positive direct effect on the pay (.165) level. Further, and as predicted, there was significant covariance among income and education and income and age. The findings suggest that lower income users actually demonstrate higher Internet shopping use rates for browsing and ordering than higher income users. Again, and as predicted, income had a significant, direct effect (.165) on pay use. A possible explanation for the varied results across use levels could be the extent to which the Internet population is changing.

H10–Age and Usage

Contrary to previous findings of Steinfield (1986), no significant direct effects were found between age and usage.

CONCLUSIONS

As expected, PU was a significant and strong direct effect across all levels of use. PEOU, however, could only show significant indirect effects through PU. With advances in Web technology and more sophisticated users on the Internet, PEOU may be relegated to an indirect role for this voluntary technology. This research suggests that PEOU is a given among Web users and, thus, its effects are only indirect.

Information privacy seems important only when consumers are paying with their credit card. When consumers browse or order, they do not seem concerned about the effects of relative privacy. More curious still, the research suggests that the more concerned they are about privacy during browsing and ordering, the more they still use Web shopping. Additional research is necessary to review this result. Jarvenpaa and Todd (1996), however, did note similar results.

The study also revealed that intrinsic motivation is only important during the browse mode of usage. This seems intuitive as well. Browsing is an exploratory process and intrinsic motivation is needed to conduct it. When more goal-directed behavior is needed (ordering and paying) the effects of intrinsic motivation vanish.

The only statistically significant demographic variable was income. Age and education showed no direct effects on any level of usage. This would imply that Web shopping is becoming a truly democratic technology. Even income's effects may be questionable, when controlled for credit card ownership. Regardless, these results are consistent not only with Jarvenpaa and Todd (1996), but also a recent study released in December 1999 through the University of Pennsylvania's Wharton Virtual Test Market (Bellman et al., 1999). Both studies found little contribution of demographics on levels of use.

Along a non-demographic level, computer experience and system quality showed no significant direct effects toward any level of usage. They both did, however, show significant indirect effects via links to PEOU and PU. This would seem to suggest that Web shoppers do not consciously link these two items with usage. As Web applications get easier to use and users get more sophisticated, these effects seem to be less direct, passed only through perceptions of usefulness and ease.

By segregating and separately studying three levels of usage (browse, order, pay), the research suggests that a stage approach to Web shopping adoption may be appropriate. This was suggested earlier by Cooper and Zmud (1990) and Chau (1996).

It seems clear that demographics will play a lesser role or effect on Internet and Web adoption scenarios. Regardless, work should continue to explore other demographic variables such as race.

Other suggestions, as a result of the findings in this research, should be applicable for online retail business and managers.

First, Web shopping applications must be useful, above all else. The overwhelming direct effect of usefulness across all levels of use suggests that sites that are playful alone will not ultimately turn Internet users into Web Shoppers, much less into paying customers. Developers of applications don't have a choice between making a site useful or easy. It must be both.

PEOU and SQ should be "givens." The lack of direct effect of ease of use, system quality and even computer experience suggests that these factors are given in the minds of Web shoppers. These attitudes do not appear to be consciously associated with use, only indirectly related through impressions of usefulness and ease of use. This suggests that a site that is not inherently easy to use and/or is too slow or unresponsive will go no further in an environment where choices of other sites abound.

Web Shoppers are ultimately concerned about information privacy, especially when transactions are involved. While the current research suggests that customers at the browse and order level are either unaware or unconcerned about information security and privacy, at the pay level, their awareness and concern is the strongest factor influencing use, even stronger than usefulness.

Use buyer behavior models to sell your products, not purely demographics. Based on the lack of support for most demographics in this study and prior personal Internet use studies, companies should focus on behaviors, not demographics, to prioritize buyers to their site.

REFERENCES

Alba, J., Lynch, J., Barton W., Janiszewski, C., Lutz, R., Sawyer, A. and Wood, S. (1997). Interactive home shopping: Consumer, retailer, and manufacturer incentives to participate in electronic marketplaces. *Journal of Marketing*, July, 6, 38-53.

Anderson, J. C. and Gerbing, D. W. (1988). Structural equation modeling in practice: a review and recommended two step approach. *Psychological Bulletin*, 103(3), 411-423.

Arbuckle, J. L. and Wothke. (1999). *Werner Amos 4.0 User's Guide*. Chicago, IL: SmallWaters Corporation.

Bellman, S., Lohse, G. L. and Johnson, E. J. (1999). Predictors of online buying behavior. *Communications of the ACM*, December, 42(12).

Bollen, K. A. (1989). *Structural Equations with Latent Variables*. New York: Wiley-Innerscience.

Boomsma, A (1982). The robustness of LISREL against small sample sizes in factor analysis models. In Joreskog, K. G. and Wold, H. (Eds.), *Systems Under Indirect Observation: Causality, Structure, Prediction*, 149-173. Amsterdam: North Holland.

Burke, R. R. (1996.). Vrtual shopping: Breakthrough in marketing research. *Harvard Business Review*, March-April, 74, 120-131.

Cohen, J. and Cohen, P. (1983). *Applied Multiple Regression/Correlation Analysis for the Behavioral Sciences* (2nd ed.). Hillsdale, NJ: Erlbaum.

Cope, Nigel. (1996). *Retail in the Digital Age*. London: Bowerdean.

Davis, F. D. (1986). *A Technology Acceptance Model for Empirically Testing New End-User Information Systems: Theory and Results*. Doctoral dissertation. Sloan School of Management, MIT.

Davis, F. (1989). Perceived usefulness, perceived ease of use, and user acceptance of information technology. *MIS Quarterly*, September, 13(3), 319-340.

Davis, F. D. (1993). Extrinsic and intrinsic motivation to use computers in the workplace. *Journal of Applied Social Psychology*, 22, 1111-1132.

DeLone, W. H. (1998). Determinants of success for computer usage in small business. *MIS Quarterly*, 12(1), 51-61.

Fahey, M. J. (1998). The doorway and the billboard. *Marketing Tools*, July. Stamford.

Fornell, C. D. (Ed.). (1982). *A Second Generation of Multivariate Analysis, Volume I and ll: Methods*. New York: Praeger Special Studies.

Gefen, D. and Straub, D. W. (1977). Gender differences in the perception and use of E-mail: An extension to the technology acceptance model. *MIS Quarterly*, December, 4(21), 389.

Gillett, P. L. (1976). In-home shoppers-an overview. *Journal of Marketing*, 10.

Hair, J. F., Anderson, R. E., Tatham, R. L. and Black, W. C. (1992). *Multivariate Data Analysis With Readings*. New York: Macmillan Publishing Company.

Hauser, J. R. and Wernerfelt, B. (1990). An evaluation cost model of consideration sets. *Journal of Consumer Research*, March, 16, 393-408.

Hoffman, D. L. and Novak, T. P. (1996). Marketing in hypermedia computer mediated environments: Conceptual foundations. *Journal of Marketing*, Winter, 60, 50-68.

Igbaria, M., Parasuraman, S. and Baroudi, J. J. (1996). A motivational model of microcomputer usage. *Journal of Management Information Systems*, Summer, 13(1),127-43.

Iivari, J. (1996). Why are CASE tools not used?. *Communications of the ACM*, October, 39(10).

Jarvenpaa, S. L. and Todd, P. A. (1996). Consumer reactions to electronic shopping on the World Wide Web. *International Journal of Electronic Commerce*, Winter 96-97, 1(2), 59-88.

Kraemer, L., Danziger, N., Dunkle, D. E. and King, J. L. (1993). The usefulness of computer-based information to public managers. *MIS Quarterly*, 17(2), 129-148.

Ku, L. (1996). Social and nonsocial uses of electronic messaging systems in organizations. *Journal of Business Communication*, July, 33(3), 297-325.

Lee, D. S. (1986). Usage patterns and sources of assistance to personal computer users. MIS *Quarterly*, 10(4), 313-325.

Lucas, H.C. (1978). Empirical evidence for a descriptive model of implementation. *MIS Quarterly*, 2(2), 27-41.

Malone, T. W. (1981). Toward a theory of intrinsically motivating instruction. *Cognitive Science*, 4 , 333-369.

Nelson, R. and Cheney, P. (1987). Training end-users: An exploratory study. *MIS Quarterly*, 11(4), 547-559.

Peterson, R. A. (Ed.). (1997). Electronic marketing: Visions, definitions and implications. In *Electronic Marketing and the Consumer*, 1-16. Thousand Oaks, CA: Sage.

Phillips, F., Donoho, A., Keep, W. W., Mayberry, W., McCann, J. M., Shapiro, K. and Smith, D. (1997). Electronically connecting retailers and customers: Interim summary of an expert roundtable. In Peterson, R. A. (Ed.), *Electronic Marketing and the Consumer*, 101-122. Thousand Oaks, CA: Sage.

Pine, B. J. II, Peppers, D. and Rogers, M. (1995). Do you want to keep your customers forever? *Harvard Business Review*, March/April, 73, 103-114.

Ray, N. (1985). *Channel Alienation: Sources and Consequences*. Unpublished PhD Dissertation, Texas Tech University, Lubbock, TX.

Schor, J. (1989). *The Overworked American: The Unexpected Decline of Leisure*. New York: Basic Books.

Smith, J. H. and Milberg, S. J. and Burke, S. J. (1996). Information privacy: Measuring individuals' concerns about organizational practices. *MIS Quarterly*, June, 167-96.

Steinfield, C. W. (1986). Computer-mediated communication in an organizational setting: Explaining task related and socioeconomic uses. In McLaughlin, M. L. (Ed.), *Communication Yearbook*, 9, 777-804. Beverly Hills, CA: Sage.

Stone, E. F., Gardner, D. G., Gueutal, H. G. and McClure, S. (1983). A field experiment comparing information-privacy values, beliefs and attitudes across several types of organizations. *Journal of Applied Psychology*, August, 68(3), 459-468.

Webster, J. (1989). *Playfulness and Computers at Work*. PhD Dissertation, New York University.

Webster, J. and Martocchio, J. J. (1992). Microcomputer playfulness: Development of a measure with workplace implications. *MIS Quarterly*, 16(1), 201-224.

Weible, R. and Wallace, J. (1998). Cyber research: The impact of the Internet on data collection. *Marketing Research*, Fall. Chicago.

Yu, J. and Cooper, H. (1983). A qualitative review of research design effects on response rates to questionnaires. *Journal of Marketing Research*, 36, 36-44.

SECTION II

Chapter VII

Organizational Impacts and Social Shaping of Web Management Practice

Kristin R. Eschenfelder
University of Wisconsin-Madison, USA

INTRODUCTION

The extraordinary growth of individual and organizational use of the Internet, particularly the Web, during the past decade has led scholars to question the social impacts of this incredible technology diffusion. In this chapter, I discuss a currently under-explored aspect of the social impacts of Web usage–the impacts of ongoing Web information system management (Web management) on the organizations and employees that maintain commercial Web sites (Web managers).

This chapter is organized in the following manner. In the first section, I describe how this chapter supports the book's theme. I then introduce key principles of social informatics and my general research approach and discuss the objectives of the study. In the second section, I define key constructs, review relevant literature, introduce the study's theoretical framework, and summarize the methodology. In the third section, I describe the research results. In the fourth section, I draw on the data to present a summary model of Web management, suggest specific improvements to Web management practice, and discuss future impacts of Web information systems (Web IS) and trends in Web management. I conclude the chapter with sections on future research and final comments.

Relation to the Book's Theme

In this chapter, I investigate the collection's theme–the impact of Web usage–in terms of the consequences to organizations of providing ongoing management and maintenance of Web IS in the years following the systems' initial implementation. Generally, the information systems research community acknowledges that the Web "will likely bring turmoil to the information management function in organizations" (Jarvenpaa & Ives, 1996, p. 96). Nevertheless, currently there is only a small (but growing) empirical understanding of long-term organizational impacts of post-implementation Web IS (Lamb, 1999; Lamb & Davidson, 2000, Scheepers, 1999; Bieber et al., 1998).

The Social Informatics Approach

I use a social informatics approach to investigate the consequences of ongoing Web management. Social informatics refers to cross-disciplinary work that recognizes and focuses on the reciprocal shaping relationship between technology and its social context (Sawyer & Eschenfelder, 2001; Kling 1999, 2000).

This study draws heavily on two principles of social informatics. The first principle is that technology is conceived, developed, configured, used, maintained, and reconfigured within a social context. Theorists have conceptualized this context as patterns of interaction mediated by, embedded in, or embedding technologies, and occurring within and between organizations and within and between societies (Davidson and Lamb, 2000). They have conceptualized these interactions as interdependent and multilevel systems of nodes and "socio-technical" links (Castells, 1991; Lamb & Kling, forthcoming). Socio-technical links are both social and technological because humans use technology to construct and enforce views of reality through symbolic and material bonds (Strum & Latour, 1999; MacKenzie & Wajcman, 1999).

The second principle is that technology and its contexts are in a constant process of reciprocal shaping (Kling, 1999; Kling, McKim, Fortuna & King 2001; Orlikowski & Baroudi, 1991; Bijker, 1995). That is, technology has certain impacts on its context, and a technology's context shapes the technology's development, use, management, and reconfiguration (Sawyer and Eschenfelder, 2001).

In this chapter I describe Web IS and Web management practice as situated in a context composed of socio-technical links. I describe both the organizational impacts of ongoing Web management (i.e., the impact of the technology management practice on the organizational context) and how organizational context shapes ongoing management practice.

Objectives

In this chapter, I pursue three major objectives. First, I seek to expose Web management as a deeply social activity. Both the trade press and researchers have published many articles about Web IS. Much of this writing, however, presents Web IS as cohesive, socially insulated, and purely technological entities (for examples, see Destounis, Garofalakis, Kappos and Tzimas, 2001; Randall, 2001). While this literature provides many useful lessons, it does not inform readers of the social nature of Web IS and Web management practice. In contrast, this chapter adds to the small stream of research that treat Web IS as fractious and socially embedded systems (Lamb, 1999; Lamb & Davidson, 2000; Scheeper, 1999; Vadapalli & Ramamurthy, 1998).

Second, I seek to describe the organizational impacts of Web IS and the characteristics of the social context which shape Web management practice. Drawing on my social analysis of Web management, my third objective is to make recommendations for the improvement of Web management practice.

BACKGROUND

Definitions and Discussions

In order to understand the boundaries of the study and the limitations of its results, it is important to define both Web IS and Web management. I define Web IS as externally oriented (Internet- or extranet-based) information systems developed using Internet protocols and architectures. The case-site Web IS in this study are best characterized as highly distributed systems, with multiple quasi-independent linked parts (Lamb, 1999). That is, a Web IS is composed of multiple interlinked, but independently controlled, component Web sites or modules of content.

I broadly defined Web management as all post-implementation maintenance and enhancement activities required to keep a Web IS operational and meeting customer needs. Maintenance tasks included those required to keep a Web site functioning correctly and to keep content accurate. Enhancement activities included tasks to improve the functionality of a Web site or to develop new content. This includes systems redesign or development (Eschenfelder & Sawyer, 2001).

Dependency Theory Framework

Dependency analysis constitutes one method of illustrating the socio-technical links that constitute Web management context. A dependency approach had several advantages. First, dependencies provide a manageable focus for data collection, analysis, and presentation. Second, they can illuminate interactions between actors (either human or non human) or groups. Third, they can uncover both explicit and implicit organizational connections, process flows, and social interactions. Finally, they can highlight management problem areas which process or structural redesign can then alleviate.

The study's theoretical framework focuses on two types of dependencies, listed here as resource dependencies and social benchmarking dependencies (see Figure 1).

The theoretical basis for these two dependency types draws on the conceptualizations of dependencies across several research fields. For instance, researchers in management science and administration science use resource dependency theory to understand how organizations react to pressures in their external environment to secure resources needed for survival (for examples, see Pfeffer & Salancik, 1978; Tolbert, 1985; Vandeven & Walker, 1984). Psychology and public health researchers use a Social Dependency approach to analyze how affiliations with others shape an individual's actions (Van Duuren & Di Giacomo, 1996; Jacoben & Robins, 1989). Coordination theory, in the information systems literature, analyzes complex system processes in terms of their underlying dependencies (Malone & Crowston, 1994; Crowston, 1996; Crowston & Kammerer, 1998). Finally, the socio-technical interaction network (STIN) approach sees dependencies as one of many constructs useful for understanding a technology's context (Kling et al., 2000, 2001).

This study draws on these conceptualizations of dependencies for its theoretical framework. I based the framework's "resource dependency" on the conceptualization of dependencies used in the dependency theory, coordination theory, and the STIN approach. I developed the "social benchmarking" dependencies from conceptualizations of dependencies used in the social dependency and STIN approaches.

Figure 1: Theoretical Dependency Framework

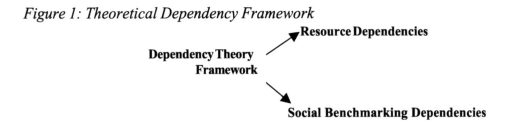

Conducting the Research

I conducted field research at four large, traditional US manufacturing companies. I used criteria sampling to select traditional manufacturing companies that had maintained Internet and/or extranet sites for at least two years. The time criteria guaranteed that Web managers would have post-implementation experiences to discuss. The organizational-type criteria ensured that participants could comment about the impact of Web manage-ment on a common set of preexisting processes and structures and describe how the processes and structures shape Web management practice. I defined Web managers as individuals who make management decisions for Web IS or Web sites, as opposed to individuals who focus on purely technical, design or content creation for Web sites. Finally, I recruited participants through a criteria-based snowball sampling technique.

My research sites included Blue Co., a manufacturer of environmental control equipment, Green Co., a manufacturer of agricultural production and consumer products, Grey Co., a manufacturer of computer peripherals and publication equipment, and Red Co., a producer of distribution systems and machinery. Each company had over 5,000 employees in order to control for size. Each had a decentralized management style, allowing organizational groups considerable freedom in experimentation with Web IS.

Data elicitation consisted of semi-structured interviews lasting between 40 and 90 minutes with 18 Web managers from across the four companies, and observation of company Web management meetings. Data analysis employed the analytic induction technique, a cyclical process involving the creation of themes from the data, and the subsequent testing and reanalysis of those themes on new data until the researcher achieves theoretical saturation (Glaser & Strauss, 1967; Shelley & Silbert, 1992).

STUDY RESULTS

In this section, I present the study results. I first introduce the major actor groups involved with, affected by, or influencing Web management. I then define and discuss the major categories of identified dependencies.

Actor Groups and Dependencies

Table 1 introduces and defines 12 major actor groups involved with, affected by, or influencing Web management. These actors represent the nodes of the socio-technical network conceptualized by the social informatics approach. The nodes include both human and nonhuman actors, and actors internal to the organization and external to the organization.

The table shows that important human organizational actors include both technical and nontechnical personnel. The important roles of nontechnical personnel such as business managers, corporate strategists, content contributors, and internal customers show that the Web IS and Web management practice are not isolated within information systems units. Instead, many different actors within the organization shape Web IS and Web management and are influenced by the Web IS and Web management.

Table 1 also illustrates the number of important external actors. This indicates that the socio-technical context surrounding Web IS extends beyond traditional organizational boundaries. External nodes, such as external customers, peer organizations, investors, suppliers, third-party Web tools, professional peers, and the IT trade press, influence the configuration of Web IS and Web management practice within organizations. This data further undermines the view of Web IS and Web management as isolated technical phenomenon. It instead presents them as socially malleable and suspended in, shaped by, and affecting a large network of organizational and industrial influences.

Table 2 outlines the major groups of dependencies identified in the analysis. Study participants described these dependencies as inherent to Web

Table 1: Key Actor Groups

Actor Group	Description
Internal Actors	
Corporate Web Manager	Work for a corporate unit.
Division/Business Group Web Manager	Work for a business group or a division of a company.
Business Manager	Managers that lead a business group or division of a company.
Corporate Strategist	Sets overall direction and goals for web IS.
Content Contributor	Contribute to the content management process either by creating, editing, or maintaining content.
Internal Customer	Request web IS enhancement or maintenance work.
External Actors	
External Customers	Purchase products or services.
Investors	Buy company stock.
Peer Organizations	Organizations in the same line of business.
Suppliers/Vendors	Sell products or services to the case site.
Third Party Web Tools	Create web applications.
Professional Peers/Trade Press	Web managers in other organizations. Magazines and web sites that write about web projects, trends and new products.

management practice. They compose the socio-technical linkages between the actors, or nodes, described above. Examining Table 2, the reader should notice it includes both the resource dependencies and social benchmarking dependencies outlined by the theoretical framework.

In analyzing the resource dependencies, I found that traditional conceptions of resources (such as time, money, staff and expertise) acted as important socio-technical links. I also found three dependencies based on less traditional conceptions of resources such as attention, understanding and reputation. I call these "social resources."

In analyzing the social benchmarking dependencies, I found three major patterns of social account-taking. These dependencies occur both within an organization and across organizational boundaries.

Examples of resource dependencies and social benchmarking dependencies illustrate the highly socially embedded nature of Web IS. As I show in the next section's examples, typically these dependencies are themselves effects

Table 2: Web Management Dependencies

Dependency Type	Definition
RESOURCE DEPENDENCIES	A relationship between individuals or groups where one party's intentional or unintentional control of a resource influences the range of possible actions other parties' can take or the value of some desired output.
Maintenance Funds	Dependencies related to traditional resources: money, time, staff, and expertise.
Brainshare	Dependencies requiring attention or commitment.
Web Understanding	Dependencies related to business managers' level of knowledge of Web technology, Web design, or Web IS management.
Good Name	Dependencies related to the public image of the organization as a whole or to the public image of individuals or groups within the organization.
SOCIAL BENCHMARKING DEPENDENCIES	When individuals or groups consciously or unconsciously benchmark their actions, performance or outputs to the perceived desires, actions, performance, or outputs of other groups or individuals.
Being Left Behind/ Lost Opportunity	Benchmarking work activities and accomplishments to external others' work activities or accomplishments or to idealized activities and accomplishments presented in the trade press or by software vendors.
Web Evaluation Criteria	Benchmarking Web IS activity to a corporate-defined standard of assessment.
Organizational Web Policies	Social referencing and negotiating inherent in the creation and enforcement of organizational Web IS management policies.

of organizational use of the Web. That is, organizational use of the Web creates the dependencies. Further, the availability or unavailability of the resources associated with the dependencies shapes Web management practice.

Resource Dependencies

This section defines, describes, and provides examples of three types of resource-based Web management dependencies: brainshare dependencies, Web understanding dependencies and good name dependencies. For each, I explain how organizational use of the Web creates the dependency and how the social context surrounding the Web IS shapes Web management practice through the dependency.

Brainshare

Brainshare dependencies are those dependencies requiring attention or commitment of others. The study results show brainshare dependencies act as key shapers of the content management aspects of Web management because Web managers must rely on the attention and commitment of others in order to maintain quality content. To explain further, content management requires accomplishment of multiple interrelated tasks (e.g., considering or evaluating potential content, converting content forms, consolidating new content with the previously existing content, physically posting the content to the Web server, and reviewing, correcting and weeding posted content.) Typically, Web managers share responsibility for these tasks with other employees, whom I refer to as "content contributors" (Scheepers, 1999; Lamb, 2000).

The creation of the content contributor position is an important organizational impact of Web IS and Web management. Before organizational use of the Web, content contributors had other job responsibilities, and data suggest that content contributors still typically have primary job responsibilities in areas other than Web management (e.g., clerical, secretarial, publications). Further, their companies often do not compensate the addition of their new content responsibilities with pay raises or promotions. Accordingly, data suggest these part-time contributors do not always welcome their additional responsibilities and sometimes consider their content contribution tasks as low priority work. One Web manager explained the difficulty of depending on distributed contributors. "They [contributors] just don't have the time. The content is somewhere, but they don't have the time to gather it and it's just not a priority for them." This work's under-rewarded status shapes Web management practice by requiring Web managers to worry about whether the content contributors will perform their tasks and take actions to ensure the work is completed.

Web Understanding

The second type of resource dependency relates to business managers' level of knowledge of Web technology, Web design, or Web management–their "Web understanding." Good Web management requires a thorough understanding of the communications limitations of Web IS technology and basic design principles for Web sites. One social impact of Web management is that business managers who oversee Web IS must educate themselves about the technology. Many business managers, however, currently lack Web understanding. This knowledge gap may lead them to have unreasonable expectations of how Web IS can perform and to propose inappropriate or technologically unfeasible projects. For example, one research participant described how some business managers in his organization did not have sufficient Web understanding to propose suitable projects. "You just missed the last meeting where the boss pulled me aside because one of the VPs in the organization wants to create a television site on the Web and wants all the real-time video of what's going on in Grey Co. to be available on the Web. Our customers, 85% are 28.8 modem users. It's not something that's really viable." This lack of business manager understanding shapes Web manage-ment practice because it requires Web managers to spend time working on inappropriate projects, or it requires them to develop and use sophisticated political skills in order to avoid implementing the inappropriate projects.

Good Name

Good name dependencies are the third example of resource dependen-cies. They are dependencies related to the public image of the organization as a whole or to the public image of individuals or groups within the organiza-tion. One impact of the increased importance of the Web on organizations has been the growth of "look and feel" policies or corporate-sponsored templates within organizations. These new structures attempt to standardize the appear-ance and navigation of the component Web sites in a Web IS.

As a distributed information system, Web IS are often composed of quasi independent but interlinked Web sites (Lamb, 1999). The quality of these component Web sites may vary within a larger Web IS. For instance, within one company, one division may invest many resources in its portion of the Web IS, while another division may not invest and its Web sites may languish with outdated content or broken links. Poor impressions created by one under-maintained portion of the site may affect visitors' impressions of the company as a whole.

Further, poorly maintained Web sites may also negatively affect the reputations of individual Web managers. Although Web managers often did not control all of the content on their sites, they perceived that content quality affected their professional reputations. One Web manager explained, "I just got a call yesterday, you know, 'You have the wrong phone number [on the Web page].' Well, it's not up to me to maintain it, call so-and-so. But it's reflected on me."

Social Benchmarking Dependencies

Table 2 includes a second set of dependencies called social benchmarking dependencies. These dependencies form when individuals or groups consciously or unconsciously benchmark their actions, performance, or outputs to the perceived desires, actions, or performance of other groups or individuals. The dependency influences actions or decision making as the benchmarkers adjust their behavior in response to the observed attributes of the benchmarkees. Here I describe three types of social benchmarking dependencies that illustrate how Web IS impact organizations and how the social context surrounding Web IS shape their design, use, reconfiguration and management.

Lost Opportunity/Being Left Behind

The first example of account-taking dependencies explains how Web managers benchmark their work activities and Web accomplishments to others both inside and outside the organization. Web managers judge their own accomplishments and the accomplishments of their company's Web efforts in comparison to projects done by Web managers at other companies, projects celebrated in the trade press and in professional conferences, and projects suggested by software vendors' products and third-party Web tools such as portals or integrated catalog sites.

This benchmarking shapes Web management practice by encouraging greater Web activity. It may lead Web managers to believe that if their company does not keep up with the types of projects done by others, the company will lose business opportunities. Further, Web managers' skill sets may become quickly antiquated if they are not able to work on state of the art projects.

Web IS Evaluation Criteria

The second example of account-taking dependencies involves business managers benchmarking their groups' Web IS activity to a corporate-defined standard of desired activity. Another impact of ongoing Web management is the inclusion of Web activity reports in evaluations for business or divisional managers with the aim of encouraging faster business-unit adoption of e-business. These reports typically measure the degree to which the business units have incorporated the Web in business strategies and processes.

Data suggests that formal assessments had both positive and negative impacts on Web IS and Web management practice. On one hand, assessment encouraged some disinterested business managers to consider developing Web activities. Further, continual evaluation might encourage these business managers to commit resources to maintaining high-quality sites. On the negative side, Web managers believed that some business managers would initiate Web activity for the sole purpose of receiving a good evaluation and would then abandon it unless forced by continued assessment.

Web Management Policies

The third example of account-taking dependencies describes the complex social referencing and negotiating inherent in the creation and enforcement of organizational Web management policies. In another example of the organizational impacts of Web use, the increased importance of the Web to organizations has led them to create management policies to control certain aspects of Web IS such as choice of Web hosting or design company, publication approval of new content, overall look and feel, and choice of development software package or server operating system.

Web managers use social referencing to determine to what extent they should comply with these policies. Divisional/business group Web managers reported they sometimes ignored, undermined, or actively lobbied to change rules they perceived as impeding their business goals. In the following quote, a Web manager explains how his Web team undermined an obtrusive rule. "We are finally breaking their rules that there will be no NT servers … So we battled all of '99 for the fact that we could have an NT server."

Nevertheless, the organizational social context does not leave Web managers free to ignore all rules. Ignoring rules extracts a social cost and negatively shapes the organizational reputation of the rule breakers. As one Web manager described, "We're viewed as kind of the bad boys on the block … and it becomes a political issue because you get the mongrel of not being part of a team or not fitting in with the corporate policy or whatever."

ANALYSIS AND DISCUSSION

In this section I draw on the study data, the conceptual approach and the initial theoretical framework to present a model of Web management and discuss specific recommendations to improve Web management practice.

Web Management Model

I used the study's social informatics approach, theoretical framework and the analyzed data to develop a model of the socio-technical context of Web IS and Web management. The model, Figure 2 shown below, applies the first social informatics principle that technology is conceived, created, used, managed, and reconfigured within a socio-technical context. Figure 2 illustrates the nodes and links of that context. It places Web mangers in the center of the model because data collection focused on the experiences of Web managers.

The model illustrates how the context of Web IS and Web management practice extends beyond traditional organizational boundaries. It shows how Web managers are employees of a particular organization, but they are also part of a profession (IT professionals, Web managers) and members of a given industry (e.g., light agricultural supply manufacturing).

The model's double-headed arrows signify the second social informatics principle–that technology and its context exist in a relationship of reciprocal shaping. Within the inner oval, the model shows the reciprocal linkages between corporate Web managers and business/divisional Web managers. It also shows the reciprocal linkages between Web managers and business managers, content contributors, and corporate strategists. Outside the oval illustrates the linkages between Web management and industry level influences such as peer Web managers at other organizations, customers, vendors, competitors, third-party Web tools, and investors.

Figure 2: Web IS Management Dependencies

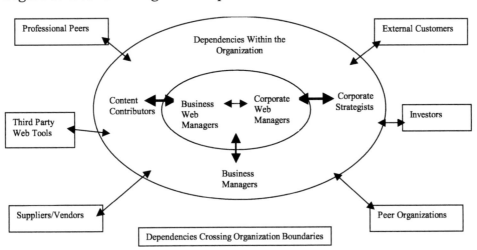

Solutions and Recommendations

The model presented in this paper illustrates the key nodes and linkages that compose the socio-technical context surrounding a Web IS and Web management practice. This section draws on the study findings and the model to present informed recommendations to improve Web management practice.

Business Managers' Understanding

The social informatics perspective and the study model illustrate how organizational use of the Web requires business managers to develop Web understanding. It also illustrates the dependency between Web management practice and the interest and understanding of business managers, who control resources and make decisions about the systems. The model suggests that some management education will occur informally, through the social benchmarking network ties between peer business managers, business managers and industry trade magazines, and business managers and professional conferences. Companies wishing to aggressively initiate Web-based process change, however, may want to take more active steps to educate business managers such as sponsoring training seminars, conference attendance or continuing information technology management education.

The dependencies presented in the model also suggest that if companies evaluate business managers on their use of the Web, they must evaluate them in terms of the long-term quality and usefulness of their Web sites–not just on the number of projects they have initiated. This will discourage managers from beginning Web projects solely in order to fulfill organizational evaluation criteria.

Rewarding Content Contributions

The social informatics perspective and the study model reveal how ongoing management of organizational Web resources has led to the creation of content contributor positions. Further, the analysis reveals how the under-rewarded nature of these positions affects the overall quality of content, an organization's reputation, individual Web managers' reputations, and the types of tasks inherent in Web management.

Content management requires the development of mechanisms and processes to support content. These include, but are not limited to:

- Processes to identify potential content from the material already produced by the organization;
- Processes to develop content if it is not already created by another process (e.g., encouraging employees to think of their work as potential Web content);

- Procedures and guidelines to evaluate potential content for appropriateness;
- Content editing; and
- Periodic review of posted content for accuracy.

Organizations must identify parties responsible for the maintenance of content and provide incentives to ensure timely completion of the work. Content contributors with other primary responsibilities should be recognized and rewarded for their role in maintaining the Web IS.

FUTURE TRENDS

In this section, I discuss three potential future problem areas in Web management: the growing number of actors involved with Web management, the need for coordination among all these actors, and the impending need for greater maintenance task support. The section concludes with a discussion of future research opportunities.

More People Involved in Web Work

As more organizational processes become Web-enabled, more people will become involved with Web-related work. This has several implications. First, it suggests that there will be greater demand for Web managers and content contributors. Organizations will need to hire or train more personnel to fill these roles. It also implies that more business managers will require training about the potential and limitations of Web technology.

Increased Need for Communications and Coordination

This second point relates to the first. The addition of more and more actors to the socio-technical networks surrounding Web management will require development of new relationships and lines of communications. This problem was already occurring within some of the study sites. As one Web manager explained, "It's a problem just identifying all the people involved in a given process." Further, certain cross-organization effects of Web management such as the development of look and feel standards, cross-site navigation strategies, and company-wide product databases require more interpersonal linkages across organizational and geographical boundaries. Web managers in different cities or different countries who contribute to the same Web IS will need to coordinate their work.

System Maintenance Responsibilities

The proliferation of Web IS and Web IS content in organizations and organizations' growing dependence on Web IS as a communications media will strain current Web IS maintenance processes. High-quality systems require intensive maintenance. At the same time, the trade press and professional conferences will continue to celebrate Web development at the expense of Web maintenance. This will decrease the value of maintenance work for Web managers. Consequently, organizations may find it difficult to ensure adequate maintenance. Web managers may try to avoid these responsibilities or shunt them off onto others. Web managers who are "stuck" doing maintenance may feel dissatisfied and try to move to other positions or change their job responsibilities.

Future Research

Future social informatics research into the impacts and influencers of Web management could take several approaches. First, we need further studies to elaborate the model presented in this chapter. Research could add to this study's largely organizational-level analysis by identifying more socio-technical linkages at industry, national and societal levels. Future research could also provide alternative perspectives on Web management, gathering data from other actors with different organizational viewpoints. Finally, a longitudinal study would complement this study's snapshot approach. It could answer questions like, "How does Web management practice change over time?"

CONCLUSION

This chapter presented the results of a study that explored the consequences of ongoing Web management to organizations that maintain these systems. This represents an under-explored, but crucial aspect of the effects of continued Web usage by our society. Organizations are currently investing large sums of money in Web IS, with little knowledge of the burdens and organizational changes the systems will create.

I used a social informatics approach to investigate the social impacts of ongoing Web management and the organizational factors that shape Web management practice. My model draws on dependency theories to show the socio-technical linkages that encompass and shape Web management practice. The model identifies key actors within and outside of organizational boundaries and explains the linkages between actors in terms of resource-based dependencies and social benchmarking dependencies. Resource dependencies include both traditional conceptions of resources (e.g., money, staff, time, inputs) and nontraditional conceptions of resources such as attention, understanding, and reputation. Social benchmarking dependencies include comparisons to both internal standards of behavior or accomplishment (e.g., organizational goals for Web IS usage and organizational Web management policies) and external standards of behavior or accomplishment (e.g., competitors, third-party Web-related tools, Web management ideals presented in the trade press).

The richness and breadth of the socio-technical links of the Web IS social context suggest that Web management has many impacts on organizational life and that many intra- and interorganizational forces shape Web management practice.

REFERENCES

Bieber, M., Conger, S., Ives, B., Janko, W. and O'Keefe, B. (1998). What's so different about the World Wide Web anyway? In Newman, M. and DeGross, J. I. (Eds.), *Proceedings of the 19th Annual International Conference of Information Systems*, 415-419.

Bijker, W. (1995). *Of Bicycles, Bakelites, and Bulbs: Toward A Theory Of Sociotechnical Change*. Cambridge: MIT Press.

Castells, M. (1991). *The Information City: A New Framework for Social Change*. Research Paper #184. University of Toronto: Centre for Urban and Community Studies.

Crowston, K. (1996). A coordination theory approach to organizational process design. *Organizational Science*, 8(2),157-175.

Crowston, K. and Kammerer, E. E. (1998). Coordination and collective mind in software requirements development. *IBM Systems Journal*, 37(2), 227-245.

Destounis, P., Garofalakis, J., Kappos, P. and Tzimas, J. (2001). Measuring the mean Web page size and its compression to limit latency and improve download time. *Internet Research*, 11(1), 10-17.

Eschenfelder, K. R. and Sawyer, S. (2001). Web information systems management: Active or reactive emergence? In the *Proceedings of the IFIP 8.2 Conference Realigning Research and Practice in IS Development: The Social and Organisational Perspective*.

Glaser, B. G. and Strauss, A. L. (1967). *The Discovery of Grounded Theory: Strategies for Qualitative Research*. Hawthorne, NY: Aldine de Gruyter.

Jacoben, R. and Robins, C. J. (1989). Social dependency and social support in bulemic and non bulemic women. *International Journal of Eating Disorders*, 8(6), 665-670.

Jarvenpaa, S. L. and B. Ives (1996). Introducing transformational information technologies: The case of the World Wide Web technology. *International Journal of Electronic Commerce*, 1(1), 95-126.

Kling, R. (2000). Learning about information technologies and social change: The contributions of social informatics. *The Information Society*, 16(3), 217.

Kling, R. (1999). What is social informatics and why does it matter? *D-Lib Magazine*, 5(1). Available on the World Wide Web at: http://www.d-lib.com.

Kling, R., McKim, G., Fortuna, J. and King, A. (2001). *A Bit More to IT: Scientific Communication Forums and Socio-Technical Interaction Networks*. Manuscript submitted for publication. Available on the World Wide Web at: http://www.slis.india.edu/SCIT.

Kling, R., McKim, G., Fortuna, J. and King, A. (2000). Scientific collaboratories as socio-technical interaction networks: A theoretical approach. In Chung, H. M. (Ed.), *Proceedings of the Americas Conference on Information Systems*, August 10-13, Long Beach California.

Lamb, R. (1999). Using intranets: Preliminary results from a socio-technical field study. *Proceedings of the 32nd Hawaii International Conference on Systems Sciences*. 32nd Hawaii International Conference on Systems Sciences.

Lamb, R. and E. Davidson (2000). The new computing archipelago: Internet islands of practice. In Baskerville, R., Stage, J. and De Gross, J. I. (Eds.), *Organizational and Social Perspectives on Information Technology*.

Lamb, R. and Kling, R. (2001) *Socially Rich Interaction Through Information and Communication Technology: Moving Beyond the Concept of Users*. Manuscript submitted for publication.

MacKenzie, D. and Wajcman, J. (1999). *The Social Shaping of Technology*. 2nd Edition. Buckingman: Open University Press.

Malone, T. W. and Crowston, K. (1994). The interdisciplinary study of coordination. *ACM Computing Surveys*, 1, 87-119.

Orlikowski, W., and Baroudi, J. J. (1991). Studying information technology in organizations. Research approaches and assumptions. *Information Systems Research*, 2(1), 28.

Pfeffer, J. and Salancik, G. R. (1978) *External Control of Organizations: A Resource Dependence Perspective*. New York: Harper and Row.

Randall, N. (2001). Content management–Don't let large sites get out of hand. *PC Magazine*, January 2, 1a.

Sawyer, S. and Eschenfelder, K. R. (forthcoming) Social informatics in the information sciences. In Cronin, B. and Shaw, D. (Eds.), *Annual Review of Information Science and Technology (ARIST)*.

Scheepers, R. (1999). Key roles in the initiation and implementation of Intranet technology. In Ojelanki Ngwenyama et al. (Ed.) *New Information Technologies in Organizational Processes: Field Studies and Theoretical Reflections on the Future of Work*. Boston: Kluwer Academic Publishers.

Shelly, A. and Silbert, E. (1992). Qualitative analysis: A cyclical process assisted by computer. In Hueber, G. L. (Ed.), *Qualitative Analyse: Computereinstaz Inder Socioalforshung*, 71-114. Munich, Vienna: R. Oldenbourg Verlag.

Strum, S. and Latour, B. (1999). The meanings of the social: From baboons to humans. In MacKenzie, D. and Wajcman, J. (Eds.), *The Social Shaping of Technology 2nd Edition*. Buckingman: Open University Press.

Tolbert, P. S. (1985). Institutional environments and resource dependencies. *Administrative Science Quarterly*, 30(1), 1-13.

Vadapalli, A. and Ramamurthy, K. (1998) Business use of the Internet: An analytical framework and exploratory case study. *International Journal of Electronic Commerce*, 2(2), 77-94.

Vandeven, A. H. and Walker, G. (1984). Dynamics of interorganizational coordination. *Administrative Science Quarterly*, 29(4), 598-621.

VanDuuren and DiGiacomo (1996). Degrading situations and antisocial behavior. *European Journal of Social Psychology*, 26(5), 763-776.

Chapter VIII

Internet Gambling in the Workplace

Mark Griffiths
Nottingham Trent University, UK

According to a recent report carried out by the company *SurfControl* (Snoddy, 2000), office workers who while away one hour a day at work on various nonwork activities (e.g., trading shares, booking holidays, shopping online, etc.) could be costing businesses as much as $35 million a year. Their survey found that 59% of office Internet use was not work-related and that those who traded in shares, played sport, shopped, and bought holidays cost companies the most. One activity that may play an ever-increasing part of Internet use at work is Internet gambling.

Most gamblers are what might be termed "normal" or "social" gamblers who occasionally bet on a horse race, play bingo or buy a lottery ticket. However, for a small proportion of the population, gambling is an activity that takes over their whole life and can cause major problems. A new area of potential concern is Internet gambling--particularly in the workplace. Many people believe the future lies in the Internet, and the gaming industry—like most other companies with a service to sell—is itself starting to go online. Technology *is* the future and electronic gambling is where the action is and will continue to be. No one is really sure how the Internet will develop over the next 5 to 10 years but Internet gambling as a commercial activity has the potential for large financial rewards for the operators.

Gambling is undergoing mass expansion all over the world. The global growth of gambling is particularly noteworthy in the area of Internet gambling. In many countries there appears to be a slow shift from gambling being taken out of gambling environments and into the home and the workplace (and in the case of Internet gambling it has gone from being site specific to being in cyberspace). What is being witnessed is a shift from destination resorts (e.g., Las Vegas, Atlantic City), to individual gaming establishments (e.g., casinos, amusement arcades, betting shops, etc.), to single-site gambling opportunities (e.g., slot machines in cafes, cinemas, restaurants, etc.), to gambling from home or work (e.g., Internet gambling, telephone betting, etc.). There also appears to be some standardization of the market in that many of the same types of gambling games are appearing all over the world and gambling in itself is becoming more socially acceptable and legitimate. The success of gambling depends on many factors including diversity, accessibility and advertising. Internet gambling is global, accessible, has no geographical borders, and has 24-hour availability. It therefore has the potential to utilize these factors to maximum effect.

Nowadays, employees do not even have to leave their desks as they can set up endless Internet accounts with two or three different bookmakers. Part of the problem stems from the fact that employers are reluctant to acknowledge gambling as a workplace issue and the possible implications that may arise from it. Internet gambling is perhaps one of the fastest growing areas in the gambling world and highlights the ease with which gambling can intrude in the workplace. This chapter therefore outlines a number of important and interrelated areas including overviews of (i) gambling, (ii) problem gambling, (iii) technological addictions, (iv) Internet gambling, (v) types of gambling at work and implications for employers, (vi) workplace gambling issues and implications for Internet gambling, and (vii) identification of gambling problems in the workplace and implications for the identification of Internet gamblers.

GAMBLING: A BRIEF OVERVIEW

The National Centre for Social Research recently carried out the biggest ever survey of adult gambling behaviour in Britain, which was the first nationally representative survey of its kind (Sproston, Erens & Orford, 2000). Of the almost 8,000 people who participated, it was found that three in four adults in Britain gamble every year. Unsurprisingly, the national lottery was the most popular gambling activity in the country, with 65% of the population buying lottery tickets in the past year. The percentage of the population participating in other types of gambling over the past year included: scratchcards (22%); fruit machines (14%); horse race betting (13%); making private bets with friends or workmates (11%); the football pools (9%); bingo (7%); and casino gambling (3%). New types of gambling, including spread betting and

Internet gambling, were still very much a minority interest, played by about 1% of the population. The survey found that over a quarter of a million people (0.6% to 0.8% of the population) were problem gamblers. While some of these people were aware that they have difficulties controlling their gambling, the survey showed that at least half the people who were identified as problem gamblers did not recognize they had a problem.

Gambling (and more specifically Internet gambling) is a hidden activity. The growing availability of Internet gambling, telephone betting and spread betting is making it easier to gamble from the workplace. For most people gambling is not a serious problem and in some cases may even be of benefit in team building and/or creating a collegiate atmosphere (e.g., national lottery syndicates, office sweepstakes). However, for those whose gambling starts to become more of a problem, it can affect both the organization and other work colleagues. Typically, problem gambling at work can lead to many negative "warning signs" such as misuse of time, mysterious disappearances, long lunches, late to work, leaving early from work, unusual vacation patterns, unexplained sick leave, telephone misuse, etc. However, Internet gambling at work means that many of these warning signs will not be picked up.

Problem Gambling: A Brief Overview

In 1980, pathological gambling was recognized as a mental disorder in the third edition of the Diagnostic and Statistical Manual (DSM-III; American Psychiatric Association, 1980) under the section "Disorders of Impulse Control" along with other illnesses such as kleptomania and pyromania. Adopting a medical model of pathological gambling in this way displaced the old image that the gambler was a sinner or a criminal.

In diagnosing the pathological gambler, the DSM-III stated that the individual is chronically and progressively unable to resist impulses to gamble and that gambling compromises, disrupts or damages family, personal, and vocational pursuits. The behaviour increases under times of stress and associated features include lying to obtain money, committing crimes (e.g., forgery, embezzlement, fraud, etc.), and concealment from others of the extent of the individual's gambling activities. In addition, the DSM-III stated that to be a pathological gambler, the gambling must not be due to antisocial personality disorder. These criteria were criticized for (i) a middle-class bias, i.e., criminal offences like embezzlement and income tax evasion were "middle class" offences, (ii) lack of recognition that many compulsive gamblers are self-employed, and (iii) exclusion of individuals with antisocial personality disorder (Lesieur, 1988).

Lesieur (1988) recommended the same custom be followed for pathological gamblers as for substance abusers and alcoholics in the past, i.e., allow for simultaneous diagnosis with no exclusions. In addition, the criteria leave out the "problem gambler" who by self-admission, or by others' testimony spends a disproportionate amount of time gambling but has yet to produce the serious consequences laid down in the DSM-III. The newer DSM-III-R criteria (American Psychiatric Association, 1987) were subsequently changed, taking on board the criticisms, and modelled extensively on substance abuse disorders due to the growing acceptance of gambling as a bona fide addictive behaviour.

However, in 1989, Rosenthal conducted an analysis of the use of the DSM-III-R criteria by treatment professionals. It was reported that there was some dissatisfaction with the new criteria, and that there was some preference for a compromise between the DSM-III and the DSM-III-R. As a consequence, the criteria were changed again for DSM-IV (American Psychiatric Association, 1994). The new criteria, presented in Table 1 represent a combination of DSM-III (criteria 6-9) and DSM-III-R (criteria 1-3 and 5) and the addition of "escape" (criteria 4), which was added on the basis of recent research.

It is obvious that addictions like problem gambling always result from an interaction and interplay between many factors including the person's biological and/or genetic predisposition, their psychological constitution, their social environment and the nature of the activity itself. However, in the case of gambling, it could be argued that technology and technological advance can be important contributory factors. Since technology has played (and will continue to play) a critical role in the development of increased gambling opportunities (e.g., Internet gambling), this will lead to increased accessibility. What has been clearly demonstrated from research evidence in other countries is that where accessibility of gambling is increased there is an increase not only in the number of regular gamblers but also an increase in the number of problem gamblers (Marcum & Rowen, 1974; Weinstein & Deitch, 1974; Skolnick, 1978; Dielman, 1979; Kallick-Kaufmann, 1979; Custer, 1982; Rosecrance, 1985). This obviously means that not everyone is susceptible to developing gambling addictions but it does mean that, at a societal (rather than individual) level, the more gambling opportunities, the more problems.

Problem Gambling: Factors and Phases

The acquisition, development and maintenance of problem gambling is an area that is continually disputed. The exact causes and reasons for

Table 1: DSM-IV Criteria for Pathological Gambling (American Psychiatric Association, 1994)

> The revised criteria now state that persistent and maladaptive gambling behaviour is indicated by five (or more) of the following:
>
> (1)　is preoccupied with gambling (e.g., preoccupied with re-living past gambling experiences, handicapping or planning the next venture, or thinking of ways to get money with which to gamble)
>
> (2)　needs to gamble with increasing amounts of money in order to achieve the desired excitement
>
> (3)　has repeated unsuccessful efforts to control, cut back, or stop gambling
>
> (4)　is restless or irritable when attempting to cut down or stop gambling
>
> (5)　gambles as a way of escaping from problems or of relieving a dysphoric mood (e.g., feelings of helplessness, guilt, anxiety, depression)
>
> (6)　after losing money gambling, often returns another day in order to get even ("chasing" one's losses)
>
> (7)　lies to family members, therapist, or others to conceal the extent of involvement with gambling
>
> (8)　has committed illegal acts such as forgery, fraud, theft, or embezzlement to finance gambling
>
> (9)　has jeopardized or lost a significant relationship, job, or educational or career opportunity because of gambling
>
> (10)　relies on others to provide money to relieve a desperate financial situation

continuing gambling behaviour seem to be dependent upon the individual, but there do seem to be some general underlying factors and reoccurring themes. Problem gambling generally begins in adolescence and may start following a major life stress (Wolkowitz, Roy & Doran, 1985). Such events may induce a need to escape from the problems of reality. Prior to the age of 15, other predisposing factors may include serious family problems (e.g., divorce of parents), inappropriate school or parental discipline, exposure to gambling in childhood and/or adolescence (by family and/or peers), and even familiar emphasis on material symbols rather than savings (American Psychiatric Association, 1980).

Lesieur and Rosenthal (1991) also summarized a number of factors which they believe to be intrinsic and extrinsic to gambling situations and the progression of gambling. The intrinsic factors include (i) a big win, (ii) chasing behaviour, (iii) a bailout (Custer, 1982), and (iv) going on tilt. (Going on tilt is a gambling expression for an acute deterioration in play or loss of control.) The extrinsic factors include (i) use of alcohol or other drugs, (ii) death of a close relation or divorce, (iii) birth of a child, (iv) physical illness or a threat to one's life, (v) difficulties in relationships, and/or (vi) job or career disappointment and/or (paradoxically) success. There also appear to be several "soft signs" of pathological gambling including a higher than average IQ, being lively and energetic, a risk taker, a lack of hobbies and interests, low boredom threshold, episodic insomnia and "workaholic" tendencies.

Lesieur and Custer (1984) concluded that pathological gambling behaviour consists of three stages—the winning phase, the losing phase and the desperation phase. However there is controversy as to whether it is the "big win" (Lesieur, 1984; Custer, 1982) or a "big loss"—termed a "bad beat" (Rosecrance, 1986) that facilitates continued gambling in the losing phase. The winning phase normally begins with small but successful bets in adolescence. Early wins prompt more "skillful" gambling, which usually leads to larger winnings. Custer (1982) reports that most social gamblers stop at this stage. However, after a considerable big win maybe equalling or exceeding the individual's annual salary, the gambler accepts the thought that the occurrence can happen again.

The next stage—the losing phase—is characterized by unrealistic optimism on the gambler's part, and all bets are in an effort to recoup their losses (which has been termed "the chase" by Lesieur, 1984). The result is that instead of "cutting their losses," gamblers get deeper into debt, preoccupying themselves with gambling, determined that a big win will repay their loans and solve all their problems. Family troubles begin (both marital and with relatives) and illegal borrowing and other criminal activities in an effort to get money usually start to occur. At this point in the pathological gambler's career, family and/or friends may "bail out" the gambler. Alienation from those closest to the pathological gambler characterizes the appearance of the final stage—the desperation phase. In a last ditch frenzied effort to repay their debts, illegal criminal behaviour reaches its height and when there are finally no more options left the gambler may suffer severe depression and have suicidal thoughts.

It is then, usually at the insistence of the family (if not the courts), that the gambler must seek help. Because the pathological gambler is impatient, requiring immediate results, Custer (1982) suggested that help should be aimed at priority areas, i.e., legal and financial difficulties, counselling to resolve family and marital problems, and most importantly hospitalization for desperate patients who are depressed and suicidal. More recently, Rosenthal (1989) has described a fourth phase called the "hopeless" or "giving up" phase. This is where gamblers know they cannot possibly retrieve their losses and they do not care, leading to play for play's sake: "Like laboratory animals with electrodes planted in their pleasure center, they gamble to the point of exhaustion" (Lesieur & Rosenthal, 1991, pp. 14-15).

Adverse health consequences (for both the gambler and their partner) include depression, insomnia, intestinal disorders, migraines, and other stress-related disorders (Lorenz & Yaffee, 1986, 1988). Gambling disrupts families through lies, deception, arguments, and money spent. Gambling eventually leads to indebtedness and crime to support their addiction (forgery, fraud, employee theft, bookmaking, larceny).

Technological Addictions

Before looking at Internet gambling in more detail, it would seem appropriate to briefly examine the growing area of technological addictions as these have overlapping links with both gambling and the Internet. Ajayi (1995) has reported that where the Internet is concerned what we are seeing is merely the continuation of a decades-long trend of people spending increasingly more time with technology than with humans. She argues that the shift away from family and peers to mass media technology as the primary socialization agents can be traced to the advent of radio in the 1930s, followed by television in the 1950s and computer networks today. Ajayi further argues that for many people, going online is a way of dealing with a society where people are becoming increasingly more isolated from one another.

Over the past decade, it has been alleged that social pathologies are beginning to surface in cyberspace, i.e., "technological addictions" (e.g., Griffiths, 1995a, 1995b, 1996a, b; 1998). Technological addictions are operationally defined as non-chemical (behavioural) addictions which involve human-machine interaction. They can either be passive (e.g., television) or active (e.g., computer games) and usually contain inducing and reinforcing features which may contribute to the promotion of addictive tendencies. Technological addictions can be viewed as a subset of behavioural addictions (see Marks, 1990) and feature all the core components of addiction (e.g., salience, euphoria, tolerance, withdrawal, conflict and relapse—see Griffiths, 1995b, 1995c, 1996b) and as such are bona fide addictions. It is assumed that the effects of behavioural excess are very similar to the effects found with more established addictions like drinking alcohol, drug taking and gambling.

There are, of course, important theoretical questions. In the case of "Internet addiction," what are people actually addicted to? Is it the process of typing? The medium of communication? Aspects of its specific style (e.g., an anonymous, disinhibiting, nonthreatening, non-face-to-face interaction)?

The information that can be obtained (e.g., pornography)? Specific types of activity (playing role-playing games, playing computer games, gambling etc.)? Talking to others (in chat rooms)? This has led to much debate amongst those working in the field. For instance, Young (1999) claims Internet addiction is a broad term which covers a wide variety of behaviors and impulse control problems. This is categorized by five specific subtypes:

- *Cybersexual addiction:* compulsive use of adult Web sites for cybersex and cyberporn.
- *Cyber-relationship addiction:* over-involvement in online relationships.
- *Net compulsions:* obsessive online gambling, shopping or day trading.
- *Information overload:* compulsive Web surfing or database searches.
- *Computer addiction:* obsessive computer game playing (e.g., *Doom, Myst, Solitaire,* etc.)

In reply to Young, Griffiths (1999a, 2000a) states that many of these excessive users are not "Internet addicts" but just use the Internet excessively as a medium to fuel other addictions. Put very simply, a gambling addict or a computer game addict who engages in their chosen behaviour online is not addicted to the Internet. The Internet is just the place where they engage in the behaviour. However, in contrast to this, there are case study reports of individuals who appear to be addicted to the Internet itself (e.g., Young, 1997; Griffiths, 2000b). These are usually people who use Internet chat rooms or play fantasy role-playing games--activities that they would not engage in except on the Internet itself. These individuals to some extent are engaged in text-based virtual realities and take on other social personas and social identities as a way of making themselves feel good about themselves. In these cases, the Internet may provide an alternative reality to the user and allow them feelings of immersion and anonymity which may lead to an altered state of consciousness. This in itself may be highly psychologically and/or physiologically rewarding. It has also been speculated (Griffiths, 1995a) that structural characteristics of the software itself might promote addictive tendencies. Structural characteristics (i.e., features which manufacturers design into their products) promote interactivity and to some extent define alternative realities to the user and allow them feelings of anonymity--features which, as argued above, may be very psychologically rewarding to such individuals. There is no doubt that Internet usage among the general population will start to increase over the next few years and that if social pathologies exist then there is a need for further research. This area has particular relevance to the area of workplace gambling in the shape of Internet gambling. This will be examined more closely in the next section.

Internet Gambling

The Internet is the fastest growing telecommunications medium in history and could be argued as the future of communications, information and entertainment. Almost any commodity—including gambling—is now being offered on the Internet. Gambling has entered the digital age and is undergoing global mass expansion. The number of Internet users and their willingness to engage in Internet commerce is growing. According to a recent report, 18% of Internet users are comfortable about transmitting financial information over the Internet, as witnessed by the explosive growth in online consumer spending on books, music and travel (Sinclair, 2000). However, it is not known how many of them would also be willing to gamble.

Cyber Dialogue.com, a New York firm that publishes a monthly report of topical data relating to the Web, estimates that 43.1 million US adults use entertainment content Web sites or services. The most popular are sports (22.4 million adult users), movies (22.1 million), music (19.7 million) and (non-gambling) games (18 million). *Cyber Dialogue.com's* estimate of the number of US adult users of Internet gambling services is 1.4 million. The market for at-home gambling over the Internet will continue to grow with the medium itself and is unlikely to stop until the Internet is as ubiquitous as telephones and televisions. Some observers predict that Internet casinos could become a $10 billion industry (Dwek, 1997). Internet gambling is still in its infancy but things are changing fast. At present there are about 800 sites where people can gamble for money. These are all listed by type (online casinos, lotteries, sports books, etc.) at the *Rolling Good Times* homepage (rgtonline.com), which indicates that just over half of all sites are online casinos.

Internet Gambling: Social Issues

The rise of Internet gambling provides both marketing opportunities and marketing threats. This will have implications for other forms of gambling and existing licence-holders. Some parts of the gaming industry will almost certainly lose market share. Many may start to set up their own Internet gambling sites because the initial setup costs will be minimal in comparison to (say) a casino. This will have implications for the social impact of Internet gambling in both the home and the workplace.

Some observers (e.g., O'Neill, 1998) have argued that Internet gambling provides "a natural fit for compulsive gamblers." However, there are some problems. According to Tottenham (1996), these problems include those of a technical, management and regulatory nature. However, over time, the

Internet will become technologically more sophisticated, allowing faster speeds and better graphics, etc. and issues surrounding security and marketing will be tightened up. Griffiths (1999b) points out that there are also a number of relevant social issues such as (i) How do we protect vulnerable and "at risk" populations from Internet gambling (e.g., adolescents, the intoxicated, problem gamblers)? (ii) What do we do about Internet gambling in the workplace? (iii) What are the implications of an activity that has 24-hour accessibility all year round? (iv) Will people gamble more with e-cash on credit cards than they would with real money? (v) How can gamblers be sure that they receive winnings from operators in unregulated countries? and (vi) How can exploitative Internet practices be stopped (e.g., the use of sexual services to sell gambling sites, the abuse of "meta-tags" on Internet gambling sites).

The issue of Internet gambling has received very little in the way of public debate. It is quite obvious that the driving force behind Internet gambling is not consumer demand but market supply. The gaming industry is itself setting the pace. Today's gambler can gamble in a variety of places including casinos, betting shops, amusement arcades and bingo halls. Most of these types of gambling are currently available in some form on the Internet. One of the major influences of technology appears to be the shift from social to asocial forms of gambling. Is this something we should be worried about? Research has consistently shown that those who experience problems are more likely to be those playing on their own (e.g., those playing to escape) (e.g., Griffiths, 1990; Griffiths, 1991; Fisher, 1993). A study by the UK Home Office (1988) also made the point that those people who played in groups often exerted social influence on problem gamblers in an effort to reduce the problems faced. Retrospectively, most problem gamblers report that, at the height of their problem gambling, it is a solitary activity (e.g., Griffiths, 1995c).

Gambling in a social setting could potentially provide some kind of "safety net" for overspenders, i.e., a form of gambling where the primary orientation of gambling is for social reasons with the possibility of some fun and chance to win some money. However, it could be speculated that those individuals whose prime motivation was to constantly play just to win money would possibly experience more problems. From this it could be speculated that as gambling becomes more technological, gambling problems would increase due to its asocial nature.

GAMBLING IN THE WORKPLACE

Gambling in the workplace is a little-researched area despite the potential far-reaching consequences. Part of the problem stems from the fact that employers are reluctant to acknowledge gambling as a workplace issue and the possible implications that may arise from it. This section examines the major issues surrounding gambling in the workplace, including the most common types of gambling in the workplace, general issues, and the specific implications for Internet gambling in the workplace.

Types of Workplace Gambling

Office sweepstake—This is perhaps the most minor form of gambling in the workplace and takes place only occasionally. Traditional office sweepstakes include horse races. In general, this type of gambling is containable and short-term and could have the possible positive outcome of team-building value.

National lottery syndicates—This appears to be very popular since the introduction of lotteries. Time spent away from work-related activities is minimal in most cases, although one or two employees may take a small proportion of their work time to collect stakes, sort numbers, purchase tickets, etc. Like office sweepstakes, lottery syndicates may also have some team-building value. On the negative side—and only in very extreme cases—work morale may be shattered when the syndicate wins major or minor prizes only to discover the tickets were not bought in the first place by the organizer(s). Tension can also occur if there are rival lottery syndicates in which one syndicate consistently does better than the other one. This too can have an effect on work morale. Another extreme consequence may be a winning syndicate who resigns *en masse*.

Telephone betting—This is a growth area for the betting industry. It is easy for an employee to have an account with the bookmaker and place bets from the office. In some cases staff may also follow races on the television, radio and/or the Internet at work. There are financial costs to the organization (e.g., frequent telephone calls) and reduced work productivity if this happens frequently. Being a somewhat solitary activity this can happen without the knowledge of both management and the employee's coworkers and therefore remain a hidden problem for a long time.

Internet gambling—Internet gambling is one of the newer opportunities for gambling in the workplace. There are now a huge number of Web sites offering opportunities for gambling on the Internet by using a credit card. At present there are few legal restrictions to stop this form of gambling taking place. An increasing number of organizations have unlimited Internet access for all employees, and many employees have their own computer terminal in their own office (e.g., higher education), which allows such activity to take place without arousing suspicion. Like telephone betting, Internet gambling is a somewhat solitary activity that can happen without the knowledge of both management and the employee's coworkers.

Spread betting—This type of gambling is becoming increasingly popular and can be done over the Internet or telephone from work. If the spread bet is related to an ongoing event (such as a 5-day international cricket match), there may be an increased temptation to follow the event instead of working and an increased temptation to make further bets. This may have time and cost implications (cost of telephone calls and significantly reduced productivity). Like telephone betting and Internet gambling, spread betting can be a hidden solitary activity.

Card schools—These usually take place in work breaks or during downtime (i.e., less busy periods). This is probably not a big problem for most employers and will usually only involve small numbers of workers. There may be implications regarding those who owe debts and/or are problem gamblers.

Other Gambling Issues in the Workplace and Implications for Internet Gambling

Lunch-break gambling—Employees who are heavy gamblers may frequently visit arcades and bookmakers during their lunch breaks. Those who are problem gamblers are likely to linger in the venue and overrun their break time. This can become easy to do in those organizations that offer great flexibility in work schedules (e.g., higher education). Obviously, for Internet gamblers, this is not an issue, as they can do it without having to even leave the office. This also means that Internet problem gamblers are even harder to identify.

Night-time gambling—Casino gamblers (and those who take part in private card-schools) can spend large amounts of time gambling into the small hours of the morning and/or through the night. Heavy gamblers are prone to doing this frequently, and if they have a day job, punctuality and efficiency may suffer considerably due to absenteeism. This is an area that can potentially affect Internet gamblers. For instance, in many places (like the UK), Internet access at home is paid for by the minute, and it is in evenings and through the night (during off-peak hours) that call charges are the cheapest. This means that Internet gamblers are more likely to use the medium when the cost is lower.

Illegal bookmaking—This can be a significant problem. Running a book in the workplace is fairly easy to do and bets can be taken on almost anything, including work-related matters (e.g., which candidate will get a job, who is next for promotion, etc.) as well as more traditional bets (e.g., the outcome of a football match). There may be implications around crime, problem gambling, debt and encroachment on work time. This is one of the few areas where there appear to be few implications, if any, for Internet gamblers.

Jobs with unaccountable time—The element of trust in an employer-employee relationship is particularly tested in jobs where there is an element of unaccountable time (e.g., sales reps, people who work from home). A gambler may be tempted to use some of that time to pursue their interest, and a problem gambler would find it almost irresistible. This obviously has implications for productivity. With regards to Internet gambling, again, there appear to be few implications. However, the widespread use of portable laptops and mobile phones means that Internet gamblers can engage in their behaviour from almost anywhere.

Criminal acts in the workplace—One of the most common offences committed by problem gamblers is theft from an employer (embezzlement, fraud, etc.). Very often a gambler may be in a position of financial trust and, as their gambling problem develops, the employee "borrows" from the organization in order to cover debts and/or to "chase" losses. Such a situation can have serious financial implications for the organization. It is not uncommon for a whole company to go out of business because of the criminal actions of one problem gambler. A key indicator here can be employees who do not take holidays other than a couple of days here or there (so that no one needs to cover during absence). Internet gamblers are no more immune to committing criminal acts than any other type of gambler.

Gambling dependency—For anyone who has a gambling problem or a severe gambling dependency, this activity will be the most important thing in their lives which they will do to the detriment of everything else including their job. A problem gambler in the workplace will spend most of their time thinking about the next gamble rather than the work issues in hand. This obviously impacts on productivity. At present, there is no evidence to suggest that Internet gamblers are any less likely to become problem gamblers than other forms of gamblers. However, it is worth pointing out that Internet gambling currently has a low prevalence rate and therefore the number of Internet gamblers with problems is likely to be small.

Effects on other people—Gambling dependency may also have the knock-on effects for other people that the gambler comes into contact with. For instance, a problem gambler may abuse a position of authority at work after a serious loss and start to borrow or steal money from fellow workers. A problem gambler may also reduce their partner's effectiveness in the workplace since their thoughts will be preoccupied with worry over the gambler. Again, there is no evidence to suggest that Internet gamblers are any less likely to cause problems to other people than other forms of problem gamblers.

Gaming industry and associated gaming industry personnel—Any gaming organization (e.g., casino, amusement arcade, etc.) or any organization which houses a gambling facility (e.g., slot machines in pubs, restaurants, cafes, etc.) has the potential for employees to use/abuse those facilities, particularly during break times. What may start off as something to pass the time could lead to a potential problem. Gambling will be attractive to many staff—including those in supervisory or managerial positions. This raises a number of issues in those organizations, especially because problem gamblers often seek out employment where they can additionally gamble. Internet gambling has the potential to exacerbate such problems because it effectively makes any environment a gambling environment if employees have Internet access.

Financial dealing—Finally, it is worth mentioning that for those organizations who deal in financial markets, "gambling" (i.e., speculating) with other people's money is commonplace. The whole birth of sports spread betting originated from the methods of stock market speculating because traders wanted to apply their "gambling" skills to other domains. Speculating can become problematic if an employee starts using other people's money for their own financial benefit and can in some cases severely affect or bring down a company (e.g., Nick Leeson who single-handedly brought down *Barings Bank*).

Gambling in the Workplace—What Are the Effects?

Problem gambling has few observable signs and symptoms that are commonly associated with other addictions (e.g., alcoholism, drug addiction, etc.) and has commonly been described as a "hidden" addiction. This makes identification of problem gamblers hard for employers. However, there are a number of behaviours and "warning signs" that might be indicative of a gambling problem. Many of these involve the exploitation of time and finances and are listed in more detail below. It is also worth highlighting that the identification of problem Internet gamblers may be even harder than other problem gamblers. This is because many of the behaviours concerning the exploitation of time may simply not apply, as Internet gamblers will be gambling from within the work environment rather than gambling at an outside gambling establishment. The lists below outline in more detail the indicative behaviours of a gambling problem at work that can be used by both managers and work colleagues.

Time Exploitation (Abuses of Time)
- arriving late to work (gambling into the late evening)
- leaving early from work (to go gambling)
- long lunch hours (to accommodate gambling)
- gambling on company time (e.g., cards, bookmaking)
- increased absenteeism
- mysterious disappearances
- unusual or predictable sick-leave pattern

Productivity and Efficiency
- irritability, moodiness, poor concentration
- potential morale problem
- gambler's mind is on other things (heavy losses, indebtedness, chasing)
- unfinished projects, productivity changes
- interference with agency operations
- greater need for internal support services
- telephone misuse/excessive use of the telephone
- Internet misuse/excessive use of the Internet

Financial
- constantly borrows money from fellow work colleagues
- fellow work colleagues constantly approached for financial loans
- employers constantly approached for cash advances on salary
- repeated credit loans
- owes money to loan sharks

Criminal Activity
- higher incidence of general illegal activity
- running books (to make extra money)
- stealing money from work colleagues
- fraudulent expense claims
- embezzlement
- selling stolen goods at work
- selling drugs at work (to make extra money)

Miscellaneous
- unusual vacation pattern (takes no holiday so financial irregularities are not discovered by others)
- has sporting newspapers or racing form guides on work desk

GUIDELINES FOR MANAGERS

As has been demonstrated, being able to spot a gambler can be very difficult, and trying to spot an Internet gambler may be even harder. However, there are some practical steps that can be taken to help minimize the potential problem.

(1) *Take the issue of gambling seriously.* Gambling in all its forms has not been viewed as an occupational issue at any serious level. Managers, in conjunction with personnel departments, need to ensure they are aware of the issue and the potential risks it can bring to both their employees and the whole organization. They also need to be aware that for employees who deal with finances, the consequences for the company, should that person be a problem gambler, can be very great.

(2) *Raise awareness of gambling issues at work.* This can be done through e-mail circulation, leaflets, and posters on general notice boards. Most countries will have national and/or local gambling agencies that can supply useful educational literature (including posters). Telephone numbers for these organizations can be found in most telephone directories.

(3) *Ask employees to be vigilant.* Problem gambling at work can have serious repercussions not only for the individual but also for those employees who befriend a problem gambler, and the organization itself. Fellow staff need to know the signs and symptoms of gambling (outlined in the previous section). Employee behaviors such as asking to borrow money all the time might be indicative of a gambling problem.

(4) *Give employees access to diagnostic gambling checklists.* Make sure that any literature or poster within the workplace includes a self-diagnostic checklist so that employees can check themselves to see if they might have (or be developing) a gambling problem (e.g., such as the DSM-IV checklist in Table 1 or the GA Twenty Questions in Table 2).

(5) *Check monthly telephone bills of your staff.* Although it will be hard to spot the occasional gambler, those staff with a gambling problem are likely to have set up a telephone account with one or more bookmakers and are probably more likely to have Internet gambling accounts if they have Internet access at work too.

(6) *Check Internet "bookmarks" of your staff.* In some jurisdictions across the world, employers can legally access the e-mails and Internet content of their employees. One of the most simple checks is to simply look at an employee's list of "bookmarked" Web sites. If they are gambling on the Internet regularly, Internet gambling sites are almost certainly likely to be bookmarked.

Table 2: The twenty questions of Gamblers Anonymous

(1) Do you lose time from your work because of gambling?
(2) Is gambling making your home life unhappy?
(3) Is gambling affecting your reputation?
(4) Have you ever felt remorse after gambling?
(5) Do you ever gamble to get money with which to pay debts or to otherwise solve financial difficulties?
(6) Does gambling ever cause a decrease in your ambition or efficiency?
(7) After losing, do you feel you must return as soon as possible to win back your losses?
(8) After you win, do you have a strong urge to return to win your money?
(9) Do you often gamble until your last dollar is gone?
(10) Do you ever borrow to finance your gambling?
(11) Have you ever sold any real or personal property to finance your gambling?
(12) Are you reluctant to use "gambling money" for normal expenditures?
(13) Does gambling ever make you careless of the welfare of your family?
(14) Do you ever gamble longer than you planned?
(15) Do you ever gamble to escape worry and trouble?
(16) Have you ever committed or considered committing an illegal act to finance gambling?
(17) Does gambling cause you to have sleeping difficulty?
(18) Do arguments, disappointments, or frustrations cause you to gamble?
(19) Do you have an urge to celebrate any good fortune by a few hours of gambling?
(20) Have you ever considered self-destruction as a result of your gambling?

Answering "yes" to seven or more questions may be indicative of a gambling problem. Internet gambling can be assessed separately by replacing the word "gambling" with "internet gambling."

(7) *Develop a "Gambling at Work" policy.* Many organizations have policies for behaviours such as smoking or drinking alcohol. Employers should develop their own gambling policies by liaison between personnel services and local gambling agencies.

(8) *Give support to identified problem gamblers.* Most large organizations have counselling services and other forms of support for employees who find themselves in difficulties. Problem gambling needs to be treated sympathetically (and like other more bona fide addictions such as alcoholism). Employee support services must also be educated about the potential problems of workplace gambling.

CLOSING REMARKS

Problem Internet gambling can clearly be a hidden activity and the growing availability of Internet gambling is making it easier to gamble from the workplace. Thankfully, it would appear that for most people Internet gambling is not a serious problem; although, even for social Internet gamblers who gamble during work hours, there are issues about time wasting and impact on work productivity. For those whose gambling starts to become more of a problem, it can affect both the organization and other work colleagues. Managers clearly need to have their awareness of this issue raised, and once this has happened, they need to raise awareness of the issue among the work force. Employers should seek to introduce a gambling policy at work which includes Internet gambling (see guidelines outlined above). This should include a checklist (see tables 1 and 2) so that employees can assess themselves but also include the list of behaviors and warning signs outlined earlier in this chapter.

In this chapter, major issues that surround gambling and Internet gambling in the workplace have been highlighted. Knowledge of such issues can then be applied individually to organizations in the hope that they can develop a gambling policy in the same way that many organizations have introduced smoking and alcohol policies. Gambling (including Internet gambling) is a social issue, a health issue *and* an occupational issue.

REFERENCES

Ajayi, A. (1995). Cited in Griffiths, M. D. (1995a). Technological addictions. *Clinical Psychology Forum*, 76, 14-19.

American Psychiatric Association (1980). *Diagnostic and Statistical Manual of Mental Disorders* (3rd Edition). Washington DC: Author.

American Psychiatric Association (1987). *Diagnostic and Statistical Manual of Mental Disorders* (3rd Edition-Revised). Washington DC: Author.

American Psychiatric Association (1994). *Diagnostic and Statistical Manual of Mental Disorders* (4th Edition). Washington D.C: Author.

Cornish, D. B. (1978). *Gambling: A review of the literature and its implications for policy and research*. London: Her Majesty's Stationery Office.

Custer, R. L. (1982). An overview of compulsive gambling. In Carone, P., Yoles, S., Keiffer, S. and Krinsky, L. (Eds.), *Addictive Disorders Update*, 107-124. New York: Human Sciences Press.

Dielman, T. E. (1979). Gambling: A social problem? *Journal of Social Issues*, 35, 36-42.

Dwek, R. (1997). Is on line gambling on or off? *Escape*, May/June, 48.

Eadington, W. (1998). The spread of gaming devices outside of casinos: benefit-cost considerations and political backlash. Paper presented at the *Third European Association for the Study of Gambling Conference*, Munich, Germany.

Fisher, S. (1993). The pull of the fruit machine: A sociological typology of young players. *Sociological Review*, 41, 446-474.

Griffiths, M. D. (1990). The acquisition, development and maintenance of fruit machine gambling in adolescence. *Journal of Gambling Studies*, 6, 193-204.

Griffiths, M. D. (1991). The observational analysis of adolescent gambling in UK amusement arcades. *Journal of Community and Applied Social Psychology*, 1, 309-320.

Griffiths, M. D. (1995a). Technological addictions. *Clinical Psychology Forum*, 76, 14-19.

Griffiths, M. D. (1995b). Netties anonymous. *Times Higher Educational Supplement*, April 7, 18.

Griffiths, M. D. (1995c). *Adolescent Gambling*. London: Routledge.

Griffiths, M. D. (1996a). Internet addiction: An issue for clinical psychology? *Clinical Psychology Forum*, 97, 32-36.

Griffiths, M. D. (1996b). Behaviourial addictions: An issue for everybody. *Employee Counselling Today*, 8(3), 19-25.

Griffiths, M. D. (1998). Gambling in the 1990s: Issues of concern. Paper presented to *GamCare National Conference*, May. London, UK.

Griffiths, M. D. (1998). Internet addiction: Does it really exist? In Gackenbach, J. (Ed.), *Psychology and the Internet: Intrapersonal, Interpersonal and Transpersonal Applications*, 61-75. New York: Academic Press.

Griffiths, M. D. (1999a). Internet addiction: Internet fuels other addictions. *Student British Medical Journal*, 7, 428-429.

Griffiths, M. D. (1999b). Gambling technologies: Prospects for problem gambling. *Journal of Gambling Studies*, 15, 265-283.

Griffiths, M. D. (2000a). Internet addiction—Time to be taken seriously? *Addiction Research*, 8, 413-418.

Griffiths, M. D. (2000b). Does Internet and computer "addiction" exist? Some case study evidence. *CyberPsychology and Behavior*, 3, 211-218.

Kallick-Kaufmann, M. (1979). The micro and macro dimensions of gambling in the United States. *Journal of Social Issues*, 35, 7-26.

Lesieur, H. R. (1984). *The Chase: Career of the Compulsive Gambler*. Cambridge, MA: Schenkman Books.

Lesieur, H. (1988). Altering the DSM-III Criteria for pathological gambling. *Journal of Gambling Behavior*, 4, 38-47.

Lesieur, H. R. and Custer, R.L. (1984). Pathological gambling: Roots, phases and treatment. *Annals of the American Academy of Political and Social Sciences*, 474, 146-156.

Lesieur, H. R. and Rosenthal, R. J. (1991). Pathological gambling: A review of the literature. *Journal of Gambling Studies*, 7, 5-39.

Lorenz, V. C. and Yaffee, R. A. (1986). Pathological gambling: Psychosomatic, emotional and marital difficulties as reported by the gambler. *Journal of Gambling Behavior*, 2, 40-45.

Lorenz, V. C. and Yaffee, R. A. (1988). Pathological gambling: Psychosomatic, emotional and marital difficulties as reported by the spouse. *Journal of Gambling Behavior*, 4, 13-26.

Marcum, J. and Rowen, H. (1974). How many games in town? The pros and cons of legalized gambling. *Public Interest,* 36, 26-52.

Marks, I. (1990). Non-chemical (behaviourial) addictions. *British Journal of Addiction*, 85, 1389-1394.

McMillen, J. (1998). Interactive gambling and society: trends and issues. Paper presented at the *Third European Association for the Study of Gambling Conference*, July. Munich, Germany.

O'Neill, K. (1998, June). Internet gambling. Paper presented at the 13th *National Council on Problem Gambling Conference*, Las Vegas, USA.

Rosecrance, J. (1985). Compulsive gambling and the medicalization of deviance. *Social Problems,* 32, 275-284.

Rosecrance, J. (1986). "The next best thing": A study of problem gambling. *International Journal of the Addictions*, 20(11-12), 1727-1739.

Rosenthal, R. J. (1989, November). Compulsive gambling. Paper presented at the *California Society for the Treatment of Alcoholism and Other Drug Dependencies*. San Diego.

Sinclair, S. (2000). *Wagering on the Internet*. Available on the World Wide Web at http://www.rivercitygroup.com.

Skolnick, J. (1978). *House of Cards*. Boston: Little Brown.

Snoddy, J. (2000). Bill's up for office surfers. *The Guardian*, October 18, 28.

Sproston, K., Erens, R. and Orford, J. (2000).*Gambling Behaviour in Britain Results from the British Gambling Prevalence Survey*. London: National Centre for Social Research.

Tottenham, A. (1996). Gaming on the Internet. Paper presented at the *Second European Association for the Study of Gambling Conference*, September. Amsterdam, Holland.

Wolkowitz, O. M., Roy, A. and Doran, A. R. (1985). Pathological gambling and other risk-taking pursuits. *Psychiatric Clinics of N. America*, 8, 311-22.

Chapter IX

Internet User Satisfaction, Job Satisfaction and Internet Background: An Exploratory Study

Claire A. Simmers
St. Joseph's University, USA

Murugan Anandarajan
Drexel University, USA

The relationships among Internet user satisfaction (IUS), job satisfaction, and user's Internet background are examined. Internet user satisfaction and job satisfaction are positively correlated. There are significant differences in IUS (but not job satisfaction) based on demographic factors (age, gender, and organizational position). Usage and general Internet experience differentiate levels of IUS and job satisfaction. Self-training is a key variable in both IUS and job satisfaction.

INTRODUCTION

The rapid growth and increasing importance of the Internet represents a significant development and is prompting a growing interest in understanding and managing Internet usage at work. Realizing the enormous potential of the Internet, many businesses have embraced it as a tool to help them achieve a competitive edge. Enterprises are using the Internet to link directly to suppliers, factories, distributors, as well as customers. In the US, Internet commerce will account for approximately $17 billion in goods and services in 1998, more than twice the amount in 1997. By 2002, that's expected to be over $325 billion (Hof, McWilliams, & Saveri, 1998). This business explosion has made Internet usage a significant activity in firms.

User information satisfaction in prior research referred to the extent that users believe the information systems they used met their information needs (Delone & McLean, 1992; Igbaria & Chakrabrati, 1990). Studies on user information satisfaction examined: a) the conceptual support and validity of the construct (Hendrickson, Glorfield, & Cronan, 1994; Kettinger & Lee, 1994), b) UIS as one of the factors influencing information system success (Cheney, Mann, & Amoroso, 1986; DeLone & McLean, 1992; Straub, Limayem, & KarahannaEvaristo, 1995), and c) the relationship of UIS with user involvement (Lawrence & Low, 1993) and job satisfaction (Ang & Soh, 1997). It has been suggested that information success, through user satisfaction, can improve organizational productivity (Schroeder, Anderson, & Scubber, 1986) and enhance managerial decision-making (McLeod & Jones, 1987).

A growing body of empirical evidence suggests that information systems affect the nature of office work, job satisfaction and the quality of work life. Office workers' interactions with clients, perceived task environment, and well-being were influenced by the type of system interface used (Turner, 1984). Coates (1988) and Kaye and Sutton (1985) found that computerization had affected office work productivity as well as the quality of work life. Millman and Hartwick (1987) discovered that middle managers believe that office automation had given them increased autonomy, more freedom to do their work, and greater ownership of the results. While the majority of studies find positive relationships with information systems and job satisfaction, there have been some contradictory findings of less positive effects on individuals' work experiences (Attewell & Rule, 1984). These contradictory findings, coupled with the dearth of research on the relationships of Internet usage with cognitive and affective components of work—in particular—job satisfaction suggests a gap in our knowledge, which the present study seeks to address.

Empirical work on the impact of the Internet in the work environment is in the early stages. Most organizations are just beginning to grapple with the complex issues of work-related Internet usage (McWilliams & Stepanek, 1998). A study conducted in a manufacturing firm found that in a typical 8-hour working day, over 250,000 Internet sites were accessed by a workforce of 386 employees. Of particular concern was the discovery that approximately

90% of the accessed sites were non-work-related (LaPlante, 1997). This rapid growth and increasing importance of the Internet represents a significant development and is prompting a growing interest in understanding and managing Internet usage at work. With Internet usage becoming as widespread in the work environment as the telephone and personal computer, businesses need to understand user/Internet interface so that usage on the job effectively matches business priorities. If businesses are to span the gap between simply connecting to the Internet and harnessing its power for competitive advantage, a more complete understanding of the mechanisms affecting Internet usage needs to be made (Cronin, 1996). This study begins to address this gap by examining the relationships among Internet user satisfaction, job satisfaction, and contextual variables (Internet background and demographic variables). Thus, the research extends previous work by investigating the network of relationships among demographic, experiential, background, user satisfaction and individual impact. We developed and tested an integrated model of Internet impact, which incorporates those variables found to predict or explain the impact of the information technology, specifically the Internet.

RESEARCH MODEL AND HYPOTHESES

In developing our model, we built on the theoretical frameworks used in previous research. DeLone and McLean's (1992) model of information success emphasized that use and user satisfaction impacted the individual user. The technology acceptance model by Davis, Bagozzi, and Warshaw (1989) highlighted the importance of external factors such as training and experience, as well as individuals' perceptions and attitudes. The research model in this study represents an integration of these theoretical perspectives and prior research (Ang & Soh, 1997). It focuses on the links among Internet user satisfaction, job satisfaction, and users' demographic variables and Internet background. Figure 1 presents the research model examined here. It hypothesizes that contextual factors (demographic variables and Internet background) account for significant differences in Internet user satisfaction and job satisfaction. Additionally, the model proposes that there is a positive relationship between user satisfaction and job satisfaction. The total network of relationships among the variables in the model and the rationale for the proposed linkages are explained in the following sections.

Figure 1: Research Model

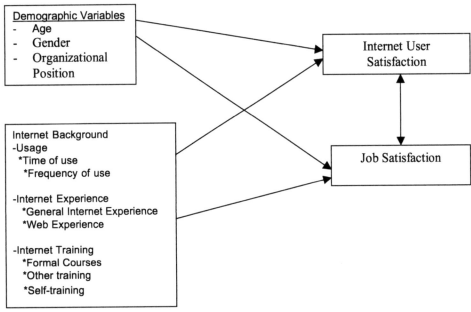

Job Satisfaction

Job satisfaction may best be understood as a function of the degree to which psychological, social, and task knowledge needs are met in the workplace (Kaye & Sutton, 1985). Meeting these needs revolves around situational or job characteristics (Hackman & Oldham, 1980; Herzberg 1966), or relatively stable dispositional characteristics of the person independent of work characteristics (Locke, 1976; Staw & Ross,1985; Staw, Bell, & Clausen,1986), or the interaction of the situation and the person (Dawis & Lofquist, 1984; Holland, 1985). In this study, we focus on the situational characteristics (Ostroff 1992). Earlier research (Cheney & Dickson, 1982) bolsters this viewpoint. Additionally, understanding the causes of job satisfaction has intrigued researchers even though the bulk of evidence shows the correlation between satisfaction and individual performance to be relatively low (Iaffaldano & Muchinsky, 1985). However, Ostroff (1992) found that the satisfaction-performance relationship was positive for organizational performance and organizational prosocial or citizenship-type behaviors (Organ, 1988). The intuitive belief, especially among practitioners, is that job satisfaction is an important determinant of productivity (Organ, 1988) hence, the interest in understanding the antecedents of job satisfaction continues.

Internet User Satisfaction

Internet user satisfaction is a widely used measure of information systems success (DeLone & McLean, 1992) and relates to how well information needs are being met. The importance of Internet user satisfaction derives from DeLone and McLean's (1992) I/S success model of information system success and the technology acceptance model (TAM) by Davis, Bagozzi, and Warshaw (1989). The I/S model posits that user satisfaction, coupled with use, will impact the individual user. The attitudinal determinants in the TAM model, coupled with demographic and experiential factors, will also define Internet success in terms of increased user satisfaction and positive individual outcomes, such as increased job satisfaction. Therefore, the following hypothesis is proposed:

H1: There is a positive relationship between Internet user satisfaction and job satisfaction.

Internet Background Factors

System usage, as measured by time spent on the Internet and frequency of use, is often used as an indicator of personal computer acceptance (Adams, Nelson, & Todd, 1992; Davis, Bagozzi, & Warshaw, 1989). System usage has practical value for managers who want to evaluate the impact of information technology (Straub et al., 1995). In the Delone and McLean model of information success, there is a linkage between system usage and user satisfaction. This model posits that if using the system is satisfactory, more system usage will occur. This is particularly true when system usage is voluntary (Hiltz & Johnson, 1989).

Internet experience was defined as a user's knowledge or expertise in performing tasks on the Internet. Internet experience was likely to promote more favorable beliefs about the usefulness of the Internet in the work environment. Studies of microcomputer usage provided empirical support for this linkage (Harrison & Rainer, 1992; Igbaria, Parasuraman, & Baroudi, 1996; Taylor & Todd, 1995b; Thompson, Higgins, & Howell, 1994).

Internet training refers to instruction on the use of the Internet and focuses on efforts to transfer knowledge (Nelson & Cheney, 1987). Training is posited to increase confidence in user perceptions about the ease of use and benefits of the Internet. Prior research on end-user training reported that training promoted greater understanding and more favorable attitudes. Training was found to have a positive impact on perceived ease of use (Davis & Bostrom, 1993) and perceived usefulness (Igbaria, Guimaraes, & Davis,

1995). There has been some support for a direct link between training and technology acceptance (Amoroso & Cheney, 1991; Nelson & Cheney, 1987), but development of appropriate motivational levels may be as important as knowledge acquisition (Sein, Bostrom & Olfman, 1987). This is particularly true with novice end-users and with new technology.

Thus the following hypotheses concerning Internet background are proposed:

H2a: Usage and frequency of use account for significant differences in IUS.

H2b: Usage and frequency of use account for significant differences in job satisfaction.

H3a: Internet experience accounts for significant differences in IUS.

H3b: Internet experience accounts for significant differences in job satisfaction.

H4a: Internet training accounts for significant differences in IUS.

H4b: Internet training accounts for significant differences in job satisfaction.

Demographic Factors

Prior research strongly supported the importance of demographic factors in examining information systems (Harrison & Rainer, 1992; Zmud, 1979). Age, gender, and organizational position were examined as relevant demographic factors likely to influence Internet user satisfaction and job satisfaction.

Age is an important factor of work behavior in general (Terborg, 1981) and end-user computing specifically (Igbaria & Parasuraman, 1989). Although there is some support for older employees reporting more favorable beliefs and outcomes in system usage (Ang & Soh, 1997), stronger support has been reported for older employees having less favorable beliefs and outcomes than younger workers (Czara, Hammond, Blascovich, & Swede, 1989; Harrison & Rainer, 1992; Nickell & Pinto, 1986).

Gender has been a key variable in the acceptance of technology (Gefen & Straub, 1997; Truman & Baroudi, 1994). The gender model of work predicts asymmetries in intentions of men and women, and computer usage has been generally been viewed as a masculine activity (Gefen & Straub, 1997; Harrison, Rainer, & Hochwarter, 1997; Williams, Ogletree, Woodburne, & Raffeld, 1994). On the other hand, the job model of work predicts that gender is not as salient a factor in the work environment as job type and individual qualifications. Recent research has been conflicting on the gender differences. Although the job model of work has received some support (Gefen & Straub, 1997), stronger support has been reported for the gender model of work (Harrison et al., 1997; Loch &

Conger, 1996). Based on gender role expectations and previous research, the following are proposed:

H5a: Age accounts for significant differences in IUS.

H5b: Age accounts for significant differences in job satisfaction.

H6a: Gender accounts for significant differences in IUS.

H6b: Gender accounts for significant differences in job satisfaction.

Organizational position is an important variable in both organizational theory (Cyert & March, 1963) and information systems research (Ang & Pavri, 1994; Orlikowski & Robey, 1991). Information systems may impact employees differently as information needs may vary by position. Thus satisfaction with the Internet may vary depending upon one's position in the organization.

The following are proposed:

H7a: Significant differences in IUS exist among users at different organizational positions.

H7b: Significant differences in job satisfaction exist among users at different organizational positions.

RESEARCH METHODOLOGY

Sample

Data for this study were collected in 1998 using a questionnaire sent to a random sample of 3,000 undergraduate alumni of a university in the northeastern United States. The survey was pilot tested with MBA students (Anandarajan, Simmers, & Igbaria, 2000). Three-hundred and twenty five surveys were returned within two weeks and another 170 received within a month after a follow-up postcard. There were 445 useable surveys, after discarding 50 incomplete surveys. The participation rate was consistent with other studies where potential respondents were not screened prior to participation (Miller, Burke, & Glick, 1998; Scandura & Lankau, 1997). Of the 445 individual responses, 334 had Internet access at work and formed the sample for this study. Users came from a range of businesses, including: services (20.1%), manufacturing (16.2%), finance/insurance/real estate (14.1%), education (11.7%), government (10.8%), self-employed (3.3%), and wholesale or retail trade (2.1%). Forty-one percent of the respondents worked in companies with fewer than 500 employees and 59% worked in companies with more than 500 employees. The length of time employed in the company ranged from 1 to 38 years, with an average of 8.7 years (S.D. = 8.19). Table 1 shows their profiles.

Table 1: Respondent Profiles

Age		Gender	
Below 26	27	Male	212
26-30	42	Female	122
31-35	61		
36-40	43		
41-45	42		
46-50	45		
51-55	29		
56-60	23		
61 and above	15		
missing	07		

Organizational Position

Top level manager	57
Middle level manager	66
Lower level manager	30
Professional	130
Administrative support	21
Other	29
Missing	01

Company has a website

Yes	282 (84.4%)
No	051
Missing	001

Internet usage outside of work

Yes	253 (75.7%)
No	081

To evaluate nonresponse bias, comparisons between respondent and nonrespondent individuals and between early responses and late responses were made on the basis of two objective measures (age and gender). No statistically significant differences were found, strengthening confidence in the representativeness of the sample.

Measures

The measures used to operationalize the variables were selected from the literature. Table 2 shows the variable means, standard deviations, and scale

Table 2: Variable Means, Standard Deviations and Scale Reliabilities

Variable	Number Of Items	Mean	Standard Deviation	Cronbach's Alpha	Factor Loadings	Eigenvalues
Age	1	40.501	11.316			
Time usage	1	2.955	1.236			
Frequency	1	4.720	1.342			
General Internet experience	3	3.422	1.051	.854	.916, .891, .790	1.478
Web experience	3	1.473	0.923	.924	.914, .906, .915	3.507
Formal courses	1	1.189	0.562			
Other training	3	1.697	0.719	.575	.723, .775, .684	1.729
Self-training	1	3.855	1.161			
Internet User Satisfaction	8	3.385	0.739	.906	.834, .862, .847, .856, .790, .763, .737, .544	4.935
Job Satisfaction	7	3.404	0.464	.860	.688, .527, .833, .845, .753, .679, .778	3.794

Gender coded: 1 = Male
                      2 = Female

reliabilities. Multi-item scales were constructed using principal components factor analysis with varimax rotation. We used Hair, Anderson, Tatham, and Black's (1995) guidelines in determining the relative importance of the factor loadings.

Job satisfaction was measured by a seven-item scale derived from Hackman and Oldham (1980) and represented an index of overall job satisfaction. The items were modified to evaluate how the Internet had changed respondents' job satisfaction. Examples are: "Evaluate how the Internet has changed: general satisfaction with your job, general satisfaction with the kind of work you do in your job, and your overall productivity." The response anchors for the questions ranged from (1) greatly decreased to (5) greatly increased.

Internet user satisfaction was adapted from microcomputer user satisfaction (Doll & Torkzadeh, 1988; Igbaria, 1990, 1992). It was modified to provide a measure of the degree of satisfaction in the way the Internet met the user's requirements for information content, accuracy, output, format, ease of use, and timeliness. Each of the eight items was measured on a 5-point Likert scale ranging from 1 (not at all) to 5 (most often).

Two indicators of Internet usage were used: (1) actual daily use of the Internet at work; and (2) frequency of use. Daily usage and frequency of usage were adapted from studies of microcomputer usage (Cheney & Dickson, 1982; Igbaria et al., 1996).

Daily usage of the Internet was ascertained by asking individuals to indicate the amount of time spent on the Internet per day, using a 6-point scale ranging from 1 (almost none) to 6 (more than 3 hours per day).

Frequency of use was measured on a 6-point scale ranging from 1 (less than once a month) to 6 (several times a day).

Self-report indicators are often used to operationalize system use, particularly where objective use metrics are not readily available. Since respondents accessed the Internet from a variety of organizations, objective logs were not obtainable. Self-reported usage and impact are not precise measures, but prior research suggests they are suitable as relative measures (Blair & Burton, 1987).

Internet experience was assessed by asking the participants to indicate the extent of their experience with using the Internet on a 5-point scale from 1 (none) to 5 (very extensive). Factor one, labeled "Web page experience," contained three items, including: (1) creating Web pages, (2) programming in hypertext-based software, and (3) maintaining Web pages. The mean of the three items was used to create an index of Web page experience. The second factor, labeled "general Internet experience," consisted of three items: (1)

accessing the Internet, (2) using Internet search engines, and (3) downloading files from the Internet. The mean was used as a measure of general Internet experience.

Internet training, based on a factor analysis, consisted of three indicators: (1) courses at a community college or university; (2) other training from vendors, outside consultants, in-house company courses, or by a fellow worker; and (3) self-training. The first indicator was labeled "formal courses." The second indicator, "other training," was calculated from the mean of three items. The third indicator was a single item, "self-training." The items had a 5-point rating scale ranging from (1) very little to (5) very extensive. Both Internet experience and Internet training measures were derived from Igbaria et al. (1996).

Single-item questions were used to ascertain age, gender and organizational position. *Age* consisted of one question where respondents were asked to record their age to the nearest year. *Gender* was assessed with a fixed response item (1 = male; 2 = female). Respondents were asked which category best described their current position from top-level manager (1) to other (6).

RESULTS

Bivariate correlation analysis and analyses of variance were performed to test the seven hypotheses. Table 3 shows the Pearson correlation coefficients among all the study variables. Internet user satisfaction and job satisfaction are strongly correlated ($r = .40, p > .001$), supporting H1. Time of use, frequency of use, general Internet experience, Web experience, other training, and self-training are positively correlated with both Internet user satisfaction and job satisfaction.

Table 3: Pearson Correlations

	1	2	3	4	5	6	7	8	9	10	11	12
1. Age	1.000											
2. Gender	-.269	1.000										
3. Organizational Position	-.279	.280	1.000									
4. Time of use	.021	.005	.035	1.000								
5. Frequency	-.029	-.036	.010	.685	1.000							
6. General experience	-.218	-.048	.075	.449	.556	1.000						
7. Web experience	-.183	-.009	.093	.311	.225	.419	1.000					
8. Formal courses	-.168	.001	-.025	.035	.063	.126	.053	1.000				
9. Other training	.049	.120	.042	.249	.155	.134	.112	.157	1.000			
10. Self-training	-.216	.034	.041	.410	.412	.597	.265	-.029	.036	1.000		
11. Internet satisfaction	-.232	.132	.145	.308	.278	.437	.204	.068	.112	.375	1.000	
12. Job satisfaction	-.053	.068	.046	.334	.278	.260	.217	.015	.121	.232	.400	1.000

r > .11, p < .05
r > .14, p < .01
r > .20, p < .001

n = 305

Table 4: Analyses of Variance Results

Satisfaction Variables	Demographic & Background Variable	Degree of Freedom	*F*-value	Prob > *F*
Internet User Satisfaction	Age	46	1.49	0.03
	Gender	01	5.41	0.02
	Organizational Position	05	2.31	0.04
	Time of use	05	8.07	0.00
	Frequency of use	05	5.84	0.00
	General Internet Experience	13	7.90	0.00
	Web Experience			ns
	Courses			ns
	Other training			ns
	Self-training	4	13.12	0.00
Job Satisfaction	Age			ns
	Gender			ns
	Organizational Position			ns
	Time of use	5	8.24	0.00
	Frequency of use	5	6.37	0.00
	General Internet Experience	13	2.81	0.001
	Web Experience	12	1.93	0.03
	Courses			ns
	Other training			ns
	Self-training	4	5.04	0.001

ns = not significant

Analyses of variance (ANOVA) were performed to test the differences in the IUS and job satisfaction by demographic factors (age, gender, and organizational position) and by Internet background (usage, experience, and training). Table 4 shows the ANOVA results. There are significant differences in Internet user satisfaction based on age (H5a), gender (H6a), organizational position (H7a), and time and frequency of use (H2a). Hypotheses 3a and 4a are partially supported with significant differences in IUS based on general Internet experience and self-training.

There are significant differences in job satisfaction based on time and frequency of use (H2b), general Internet and Web experience (H3b), and self-training (partially supporting H4b). No significant differences were found in job satisfaction for the demographic variables.

DISCUSSION

This study breaks new ground in research in managing in the information age by examining Internet user satisfaction and job satisfaction. This research integrated DeLone and McLean's (1992) model of information system success and the technology acceptance model with empirical findings of research on personal computing. The results show strong support for the proposed linkages among the model variables.

The results provide interesting insights into the relation of demographic and Internet background factors associated with attitudes about the Internet and the work environment. In line with our expectations, but contrary to the findings of Ang and Soh (1997), demographic variables accounted for significant variation in Internet user satisfaction. Older workers may have less IUS than younger workers, as evidenced by the negative correlation between age and Internet user satisfaction. This supports previous research and suggests that management of the Internet may need to account for age differences among users. Surprisingly, gender is positively correlated with IUS, suggesting that women have a more positive attitude towards the Internet. Demographic factors are not significant in explaining differences in job satisfaction; their impact may be through Internet user satisfaction, suggesting a mediational model like the technology acceptance model.

There is a strong positive association between IUS and job satisfaction, which supports our hypothesis (H1) and is similar to previous findings on computer-mediated use (Ang & Soh, 1997). This has important implications for managers since improving satisfaction with Internet use could spill over to general job satisfaction. This may become particularly salient as Internet usage permeates the work environment, and the Internet increases in importance as a competitive weapon used by all employees (Bremer, 1996).

The results also show that the training reported by the respondents is currently largely self-directed and is an important factor in Internet user satisfaction and job satisfaction. This strong relationship of training, as well as experience, leads to the suggestion that replacement of self-training by organizationally endorsed training might foster a better balance between control and encouragement of the Internet. However, since other training did not significantly impact IUS and job satisfaction, organizationally endorsed training should be planned and implemented so that the positive attributes of self-training (flexibility, moving at one's own pace, freedom, and autonomy) can be blended with organizational requirements.

There are limitations in this study. The relatively low response rate (15%) calls into question generalizability of the findings; additional research is required to see if similar results are obtained. A few possible extensions of this work include examining additional work environments both in the United States and globally and conducting experiments. Expanding the analysis to include additional variables, as well as models of analysis such as structural equation modeling and regression, will build on the exploratory work done in this paper. Additionally, while cross-sectional studies, such as the present one, are useful for identifying patterns of relationships among relevant variables, longitudinal research design is essential to confirm causal linkages. The strengths of the findings would also be enhanced by the use of both subjective and objective measures, as common method variance contributing to the results cannot be ruled out.

In conclusion, the study extends prior research on information technology acceptance in a number of ways. It is among the first studies of Internet usage in the work environment. The study illustrates the importance of experience and training in influencing Internet user satisfaction and job satisfaction. The findings indicate that the type of training is important, as self-training plays an important role. The Internet-mediated work environment has many challenges for both researchers and managers as we grapple with how to harness the Internet's tremendous potential.

REFERENCES

Adams, D. A., Nelson, R. R. and Todd, P. A. (1992). Perceived usefulness, ease of use, and usage of information technology: A replication. *MIS Quarterly*, 16(2), 227-247.

Ajzen, I. (1991). The theory of planned behavior. *Organizational Behavior and Human Decision Processes*, 50, 179-211.

Ajzen, I. and Fishbein, M. (1980). *Understanding Attitudes and Predicting Behavior*. Englewood Cliffs, NJ: Prentice-Hall.

Amoroso, D. L. and Cheney, P. H. 1991. Testing a causal model of end-user application effectiveness. *Journal of Management Information Systems*, 8(1), 63-89.

Anandarajan, M., Simmers, C. A. and Igbaria, M. (2000). An exploratory investigation of the antecedents and impact of Internet usage: An individual perspective. *Behavior and Information Technology*.

Ang, J. and Pavri, (1994). A survey and critique of the impacts of information technology. *International Journal of Information Management*, 14(2), 122-133.

Ang, J. and Soh, P. H. (1997). User information satisfaction, job satisfaction and computer background: An exploratory study. *Information & Management*, 32, 255-266.

Attewell, P. and Rule, J. (1984). Computing and organizations: What we know and what we don't know. *Communications of the ACM*, 27(12), 1184-1192.

Blair, E. and Burton, S. (1987). Cognitive processes used by survey respondents to answer behavioral frequency questions. *Journal of Consumer Research*, 14, 280-288.

Bremer, M. (1996). Productivity, policy, and Internet training issues. In Cronin, M. (Ed.), *The Internet Strategy Handbook*, 191-210. Boston: Harvard Business School Press.

Cheney, P. and Dickson, G. B. (1982). Organizational characteristics and information systems success: An extrapolation investigation. *Academy of Management Journal*, 25(1), 170-184.

Cheney, P., Mann, R. and Amoroso, D. (1986). Organizational factors affecting the success of end-user computing. *Journal of Management Information Systems*, 3(1), 65-80.

Coates, V. T. (1988). Office automation: Productivity, employment and social impacts. *Office: Technology and People*, 3, 315-326.

Cronin, M. J. (1996). The Internet as a competitive business resource. In Cronin, M. (Ed.), *The Internet Strategy Handbook*, 1-23. Boston: Harvard Business School Press.

Cyert, R. N. and March, J. G. (1963). *A Behavioral Theory of the Firm*. Englewood Cliffs, NJ: Prentice-Hall.

Czara, S. J., Hammond, K., Blascovich, J. J. and Swede, H. (1989). Age related differences in learning to use a text-editing system. *Behavior and Information Technology*, 8(4), 309-319.

Davis, F. D., Bagozzi, R. P. and Warshaw, P. R. (1989). User acceptance of computer technology: A comparison of two theoretical models. *Management Science*, 35(8), 982-1003.

Davis, S. A. and Bostrom, R. P. (1993). Training end-users: An experimental investigation of the roles of the computer interface and training methods. *MIS Quarterly*, 17(1), 61-85.

Dawis, R. W. and Lofquist, L. H. (1984). *A Psychological Theory of Work adjustment*. Minneapolis, MN: University of Minnesota Press.

DeLone, W. H. and McLean, E. R. (1992). Information systems success: The quest for the dependent variable. *Information Systems Research*, 3(1), 60-95.

Doll, W. J. and Torkzadeh, G. (1988). The measurement of end-user computing: An exploratory study. *Information Resources Management Journal*, Fall, 1, 39-46.

Fishbein, M. and Ajzen, I. (1975). *Belief, Attitude, Intentions, And Behavior: An Introduction To Theory And Research*. Reading, MA: Addison–Wesley.

Gefen, D. and Straub, D. W. (1997). Gender differences in the perception and use of e-mail: An extension to the technology acceptance model. *MIS Quarterly*, 21(4), 389-400.

Hackman, J. R. and Oldham, G. R. (1980). *Work Redesign*. Reading, MA: Addison-Wesley.

Hair, J. F., Anderson, R. E., Tatham, R. L. and Black, W. C. (1995). *Multivariate Data Analysis With Readings* (4th ed.). Englewood Cliffs, NJ: Prentice-Hall.

Harrison, A. W. and Rainer, R. K. (1992). The influence of individual differences on skill in end-user computing. *Journal of Management Information Systems.* 9(1), 93-111.

Harrison, A. W., Rainer, R. K. and Hochwarter, W. A. (1997). Gender differences in computing activities. *Journal of Social Behavior and Personality*, 12(4), 849-868.

Hendrickson, A. R., Glorfield, K. and Cronan, T. P. (1994). On the repeated test-retest reliability of end-user computing satisfaction instrument: A comment. *Decision Sciences*, 25(4), 655-667.

Herzberg, F. (1966). *Work and the Nature of Man.* Cleveland: World Publishing.

Hiltz, S. R. and Johnson, K. (1989). Measuring acceptance of computer-mediated communication systems. *Journal of American Society for Information Science*, 40(6), 386-397.

Hof, R. D., McWilliams, G. and Saveri, G. (1998). The "click here" economy. *Business Week*, June 22, 122-128.

Holland, J. L. (1985). *Making Vocational Choices: A Theory of Careers* (2nd ed.). Englewood Cliffs, NJ: Prentice Hall.

Iaffaldano, M. T. and Muchinsky, P. M. (1985). Job satisfaction and job performance: A meta-analysis. *Psychological Bulletin*, 97, 251-273.

Igbaria, M. (1992). An examination of microcomputer usage in Taiwan. *Information & Management*, 22, 19-28.

Igbaria, M. and Chakrabrati, A. 1990. Computer anxiety and attitudes towards microcomputer use. *Behavior and Information Technology*, 9(3), 229-241.

Igbaria, M., Guimaraes, T. and Davis, G. B. (1995). Testing the determinants of microcomputer usage via a structural equation model. *Journal of Management Information Systems*, 11(4), 87-114.

Igbaria, M. and Nachman, S. A. (1990). Correlates of user satisfaction with end user computing. *Information and Management*, 19, 73-82.

Igbaria, M. and Parasuraman, S. (1989). A path analytic study of individual characteristics, computer anxiety, and attitudes toward microcomputers. *Journal of Management*, 15(3), 373-388.

Igbaria, M., Parasuraman, S. and Baroudi, J. (1996). A motivational model of microcomputer usage. *Journal of Management Information Systems*, 13(1), 127-143.

Kaye, A. R. and Sutton, M. J. (1985). Productivity and quality of working life for office principals and the implications for office automation. *Office: Technology and People*, 2, 257-286.

Kettinger, W. J. and Lee, C. C. (1994). Perceived service quality and user satisfaction with the information services function. *Decision Sciences*, 25(5-6), 737-766.

LaPlante, A. (1997). Start small think infinite. *Computerworld*, 31(8), 24-30.

Lawrence, M. and Low, G. (1993). Exploring individual user satisfaction with user-led development. *MIS Quarterly*, 17(2), 19208.

Loch, K. D. and Conger, S. (1996). Evaluating ethical decision making and computer use. *Communications of the ACM*, 39(7), 74-83.

Locke, E. A. (1976). The nature and causes of job satisfaction. In Dunnette, M. D. (Ed.), *Handbook of Industrial and Organizational Psychology*, 1297-1343. Chicago: Rand McNally.

McLeod, R. and Jones, J. W. (1987). A framework for office automation. *MIS Quarterly*, 11(1), 86-104.

McWilliams, G. and Stepanek, M. (1998). Taming the info monster. *Business Week*, June 22, 170-172.

Miller, C. C., Burke, L. M. and Glick, W. H. (1998). Cognitive diversity among upper-echelon executives: Implications for strategic decision processes. *Strategic Management Journal*, 19(1), 39-58.

Millman, Z. and Hartwick, J. (1987). The impact of automated office systems on middle managers and their work. *MIS Quarterly*, 11(4), 479-491.

Moore, G. C. and Benbasat, I. (1991). Development of an instrument to measure the perceptions of adopting an information technology innovation. *Information Systems Research*, 2(3), 192-222.

Nelson, R. and Cheney, P. (1987). Training endusers: An exploratory study. *MIS Quarterly*, 11(4), 547-559.

Nickell, G. S. and Pinto, J. N. (1986). The computer attitude scale. *Computers in Human Behavior*, 2, 301-306.

Organ, D. W. (1988). A restatement of the satisfaction-performance hypothesis. *Journal of Management*, 14(4), 547-557.

Orlikowski, W. J. and Robey, D. (1991). Information technology and the structuring of organizations. *Information Systems Research*, 2(2), 143-169.

Ostroff, C. (1992). The relationship between satisfaction, attitudes and performance: An organizational level analysis. *Journal of Applied Psychology*, 77(6), 963-974.

Scandura, T. A. and Lankau, M. J. (1997). Relationships of gender, family responsibility and flexible work hours to organizational commitment and job satisfaction. *Journal of Organizational Behavior*, 18(4), 377-391.

Schroeder, R., Anderson, J. C., and Scubber, G. D. (1986). White-collar productivity measurement. *Management Decision*, 24(5), 3-7.

Sein, M. K., Bostrom, R. P. and Olfman, L. (1987). Training end users to computers: Cognitive, motivational, and social issues. *INFOR (Information Systems and Operational Research)*, 25(3), 236-254.

Staw, B. M. and Ross, J. (1985). Stability in the midst of change: A dispositional approach to job attitudes. *Journal of Applied Psychology*, 70, 469-480.

Staw, B. M., Bell, N. E. and Clausen, J. A. (1986). The dispositional approach to job attitudes: A lifetime longitudinal test. *Administrative Science Quarterly*, 31, 56-77.

Straub, D., Limayem, M. and KarahannaEvaristo, E. (1995). Measuring system usage: Implications for IS theory testing. *Management Science*, 41(8), 1328-1342.

Taylor, S. and Todd, P. A. (1995a). Understanding information technology usage: A test of competing models. *Information Systems Research*, 6(2), 144-146.

Taylor, S. and Todd, P. A. (1995b). Assessing IT usage: The role of prior experience. *MIS Quarterly*, 19(4), 561-570.

Terborg, J. R. (1981). Interactional psychology and research on human behavior in organizations. *Academy of Management Review*, 6(4), 569-576.

Thompson, R. L., Higgins, C. A. and Howell, J. M. (1994). Influence of experience on personal computer utilization: Testing a conceptual model. *Journal of MIS*, Summer, 167-187.

Truman, G. E. and Baroudi, J. J. (1994). Gender differences in the information systems managerial ranks: An assessment of potential discriminatory practices. *MIS Quarterly*, 18(2), 129-141.

Turner, J. A. (1984). Computer mediated work: The interplay between technology and structured jobs. *Communications of the ACM*, 27(12), 1210-1217.

Williams, S. W., Ogletree, S. M., Woodburne, W. and Raffeld, P. (1994). Gender roles, computer attitudes, and dyadic computer interaction: Performance in college students. *Sex Roles: A Journal of Research*, 29(7-8), 515-526.

Zeffane, R. M. (1994). Correlates of job satisfaction and their implications for work redesign: A focus on the Australian telecommunication industry. *Public Personnel Management*, 23(1), 61-75.

Zmud, R. W. (1979). Individual differences and MIS success: A view of the empirical literature. *Management Science*, 25(10), 966-979.

Chapter X

The Measurement of Telecommuting Performance

Magid Igbaria
Claremont Graduate University, USA
Tel Aviv University, Israel

Patrick W. Devine
Drexel University, USA

Eunyoung Cheon
TA Wood Corporation, South Korea

Telecommuting provides various benefits to a number of constituents. However, the rate of telecommuting implementation is low due to the difficulty of measuring telecommuting performance. A new approach is needed to measure telecommuting activities. This paper analyzes the characteristics of telecommuting in order to establish a clearer understanding of the many facets of telecommuting. Based on this analysis, a conceptual framework for measuring its performance is presented.

INTRODUCTION

The recent proliferation of personal computers and communication networks has enabled organizations to acquire and retain their distributed organizational structures. As a result of these telecommunications networks, geographically distributed people can communicate, coordinate, and collaborate their work efforts across time and space barriers. These advancements have contributed to the creation of "the virtual workplace" (Cascio, 2000), a recent phenomenon that has changed the way people work. One of the related business practices of the virtual workplace is "telecommuting."

Despite years of effort, the definition of telecommuting is still not clear. Though often used interchangeably, the terms telecommuting and teleworking are generally considered to be two distinct constructs. The broad term for working away from the main office using telecommunications is generally regarded as "telework" (Hill, Miller, Weiner, & Colihan, 1998). Teleworking includes any form of substitution of information technologies for work-related travel (Nilles, 1998). Under this definition, even the use of telephones or facsimile transmission is regarded as telework.

Telecommuting is generally considered to be a subset of teleworking. Coined by Jack Nilles in 1973, telecommuting was defined as "periodic work out of the principal office, one or more days per week either at home, a client's site, or in a telework center" (Nilles, 1998). Telecommuting emphasizes as one if its major benefits the ability to reduce or eliminate daily travel to a work location. In the United States, practitioners and researchers have shown increasing interest in commuting problems like traffic congestion so that the term "telecommuting" has been dominant over the term "telework."

Various paradigms of telework related to work arrangement exist. Büssing (1998) structured organizational forms of teleworking into four types: "mobile telework, alternating telework, collective telework, and home-based telework." Among these forms, the dominant type of teleworking in most countries is the alternating of telework between home and organization (Büssing, 1998), which has come to be known as "telecommuting." The focus of this analysis is grounded in this definition, and thus, self-employed telecommuters and the employees who work overtime at home are not examined.

Although remote work was foreseen as early as 1950, the practices of telework did not start until the availability of telecommunications technology in the early 1970s (US Department of Transportation, 1993). After the introduction of telecommuting by Nilles in 1973, companies started to consider telecommuting as a new business form, and several companies set up telecommuting trials during the early 1970s (Katz, 1987). Organizations continued to experiment with telecommuting, and the number of telecommuters reached about 10,000 by the middle of the 1980s (Gordon, 1986).

The practice of telecommuting has been dramatically increasing during the last decade. The number of telecommuters has grown to more than 10 million in the US (Shellenbarger, 1997; Nilles, 1997) and equivalent numbers in the rest of the world (Nilles, 1997). Most researchers expect that this growth rate will only continue to increase in the foreseeable future. Using a mathematical forecasting model he developed to project U.S. growth of telecommuting and worldwide growth of telework, Nilles (1998) estimated that the number of telecommuters in the US will grow to more than 35 million by year 2010 and the number of teleworkers worldwide will grow to more than 125 million by the year 2010.

As the number of telecommuters continues to grow, there has been increased emphasis by researchers to more fully understand the many facets of telecommuting (Mokhtarian et al., 1998; Fairweather, 1999). Despite the growing number of articles and books on telecommuting, academics as well as business practitioners are still struggling to comprehend the many unknown and vague dimensions of telecommuting. Topics such as "how to appraise the work performance of telecommuters," "how to control productivity of telecommuters," and "how to measure the success and effectiveness of telecommuting" are still little understood and have only recently begun to be explored.

This analysis aims to provide a conceptual framework for measuring the performance of telecommuting. The article is structured as follows: (1) demands of telecommuting measurements; (2) characteristics of telecommuting; (3) conceptual telecommuting performance measurement (TPM) model; and (4) conclusions.

IMPORTANCE OF TELECOMMUTING PERFORMANCE MEASUREMENTS

Telecommuting meets the demands of three constituents: employees, organizations, and society (McCloskey & Igbaria, 1998). Many researchers have focused their efforts and time on exploring the benefits of telecommuting (e.g., Nilles et al., 1976; Kugelmass, 1995; Piskurich, 1996; Shaw, 1996; Dombrow, 1998; Igbaria & Guimaraes, 1999). As we can see from Table 1, telecommuting provides various benefits to individuals, organizations, and society. Contrary to some beliefs that work experiences of men and women who telecommute differ, prior research has shown that the men and women who telecommute experience an equitable work experience (McCloskey et al., 1998). Although telecommuting offers many economic, societal and environmental benefits and despite the growing acceptance of telecommuting by the business world, the overall usage of telecommuting is still quite low. According to Jack Nilles, president of JALA International, Inc., about 48% of today's workers could be telecommuting at least part of the time, but only 10 percent are doing so (ITAC, 1999).

Table 1: The Benefits of Telecommuting

The Benefits		
Employees	**Organization**	**Society**
• Increased family interaction • Reduced commuting time and costs • Employment opportunities • Flexible work arrangements • Improved employee safety • Personal control over working conditions • Eliminated unplanned or unproductive meeting • Flexibility of child and elder care options • Increased privacy • Reduced stress of commuting • Enhanced communication with supervisor • Improved ability to work without interruption • Less stress, better health • Less money spent on gas, clothes, and meals out	• Increased productivity • Improved customer service • Improved morale and job satisfaction • Improved employee commitment • Increased retention rate • Improved recruiting opportunities • Reduced contention for space or computer time • Disaster mitigation • Helps in ADA compliance and various EPA regulations • Reduced absenteeism and sick time • Maximized office spaces • Decreased relocation costs • Reduced overtime • Reduced cost on office rent, utilities, and other in-office expense • Decreased recruiting costs • More competitive in the market • Enhanced computer literacy • Improved communication	• Energy conservation • Improved air quality • Reduced traffic congestion • Better use of existing transportation infrastructure • Decreased environmental impact of commuting • Reduced need for road repair • Reduced pressure from public transportation

Thus, a key question to be answered is, despite the various benefits of telecommuting, why aren't more companies and individuals taking advantage of it? The low usage of telecommuting is greatly influenced by other personal and organizational factors (Westfall, 1997). Managers in many organizations have traditionally been reluctant to support telecommuting (Fairweather, 1999). Supervisory control and direct control are key issues for organizations, and management's perception that telecommuting will cause organizations to lose this control is a major obstacle to its acceptance (Fitzer, 1997; Kugelmass, 1995). In essence, managers are uncomfortable with supervising employees they cannot see. Many managers believe that productivity lies in management's emphasis on observing and monitoring tasks, as opposed to placing an emphasis on results and measurement (Harler, 1998). While the effectiveness of this controlling approach to management has often been debated regarding the traditional work setting, it clearly is not appropriate as a means of supervising telecommuters. Management cannot watch over each telecommuter at his or her home in an effort to assess productivity. They can, however, assess the final product or end result of the telecommuter's efforts.

Thus, managers must retool their role as supervisors in an effort to switch to a more project-oriented management style (Cascio, 2000).

Becoming more project- or performance-oriented is only the first step, as without effective measurement tools in place, the effectiveness of the individual telecommuter, as well as the effectiveness of the organization's telecommuting program as a whole, cannot be evaluated. The development of effective measurement tools is of key importance (Segal, 1998), as if management knows specifically what to measure and how to measure it, the effectiveness of telecommuting can be evaluated, assessed, and improved upon. Developing these tools is no easy task, as it involves not only assessing the tangible benefits and costs of telecommuting, but also the intangible benefits and costs as well. Merely looking at "the bottom line" does not actually give an accurate assessment of telecommuting, as typical accounting systems are not fit to measure the intangible costs and benefits of telecommuting. Though attempting to quantify intangible costs and benefits relating to social, psychological, ethical, legal, and environmental issues is an arduous task, it is no less important than the tangible costs and benefits in assessing the success or failure of telecommuting in an organization.

Though the key stakeholders who participate in telecommuting recognize the importance of telecommuting measurement, agreement over the development, implementation, and dimensions of these measures has been rare (Ashton & Ashton, 1999). Past research has tangentially addressed this issue, as there have been many articles about cost-benefits analysis and economic issues for telecommuting (e.g., Gordon, 1997; Nilles, 1998; Westfall, 1998). However, telecommuting suffers from the lack of a coherent and agreed upon model for measuring its performance. Nilles (1998) attempted to measure telecommuting using costs and benefits but failed to provide a comprehensive model of telecommuting measurements. Westfall (1998) also developed a framework of telecommuting measurements but did not consider nonmonetary issues. This article seeks to address this problem by covering a broad conceptual perspective on telecommuting measurements within the context of individual, organizational, and environmental studies.

THE CHARACTERISTICS OF TELECOMMUTING

As noted earlier, advances in information systems and communication technologies have enabled a new work setting known as telecommuting. The different characteristics that stem from this new work setting necessitate different ways to measure its success (Capowski, 1998). Just as a carpenter knows that one type of ruler will not work for every object that needs to be measured, businesses must also recognize that they must employ different measurement techniques based upon the type of work that is to be evaluated. Understanding the characteristics of the objects you will measure is critical for selecting the correct measurement tools. Though a ruler is effective for measuring various lengths, a carpenter would choose a tape measure over a ruler when attempting to measure the circumference of a ball. In a similar fashion, though traditional measurements of performance and productivity are useful, it would be inappropriate to use these methods for the evaluation of telecommuting. Thus, this section attempts to review the aspects that characterize telecommuting and tries to identify the key dimensions that must be considered for its evaluation. Time, place, structure, technology, people, and tasks are suggested as factors to be included in the formulation of telecommuting characteristics.

Time and Place

Johansen (1988) provides two dimensions for understanding the concepts of time and place. In considering time, people can meet either at the same time (synchronous) or at different times (asynchronous). In considering place, people can meet either in the same location or in different locations. With telecommuting, time regulates a period in which work is done, and place determines the location that work is done.

As computer and telecommunications technologies are advanced, telecommuting increasingly adds allowances for different working times and places. Brandt (1983) identifies worker's location and affiliation as key dimensions of telework. Kugelmass (1995) characterized telecommuting as the combination of flextime and flexiplace. Telecommuters can work at home or other approved sites away from their main office and do not need to work within the confines of the regular office schedule and time. They can shift their working hours and locations to more productive working hours and location. As a consequence, the utilization rates of time and place are increased. Figure 1 shows the time and place in telecommuting compared to on-site working.

Structure

Structure refers to the manner in which the work and workers are organized. As telecommuting is independent from time and place, telecommuting also allows for connecting employees at central business districts and residential areas. Telework allows greater organizational flexibility (Nilles, 1998), as the jobs can be distributed at different work sites.

Figure 1: The Time and Place in Telecommuting

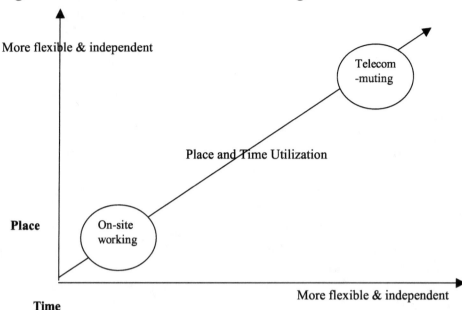

Telecommuting is the ultimate extension of decentralization as the employees are placed in different sites from the organization (Wright & Oldford, 1993). Employees can work at various locations and still participate in the work of the organization (Igbaria et al., 1998). Telecommuters can work away from their main office but their professional life is still aligned with the organization. The structure of telecommuting more and more is viewed as decentralized or dispersed and as a part of a virtual organization. This is especially beneficial for multinational companies that have subsidiaries existing across the globe in many different time zones (Reese, 2000). Communications with employees, managers, customers and clients across time zones is much more easily facilitated with telecommuting (Shellenbarger, 1998) than it is with non-telecommuting, where on-site employees are confined to the limitations of traditional business hours.

Technology

Some telecommuters need no more than a telephone line, whereas others may need complicated telecommunications capabilities like T1, ISDN links, LAN access, etc. Appropriate technology is a necessary condition for telecommuting. The face-to-face requirements of telecommuting may even be dependent on the sophistication of the technology available to you (Nilles,

1998). In other words, people who don't even have a telephone may need a lot of face-to-face interactions while people who have a full-motion video teleconferencing system can decrease the face-to-face interactions significantly.

Telecommuting is changing communication paths from physically oriented to nonphysically-oriented communication structures. Within the traditional working setting, people are more likely to communicate face-to-face, but with telecommuting, some (and in some cases almost all) of meetings are carried out by using some form of telecommunications technology like telephone or videoconferencing (Nilles, 1997). Telecommuters make the most of the limited face-to-face contact with their supervisors and coworkers (Humble et al., 1995). Telecommuters need to document their work and generally transfer the work and receive required information electronically. Such characteristics greatly differentiate telecommuting from traditional working. Thus, computers and advanced telecommunications technology play a powerful role in telecommuting.

People

People refer to the employees who work for their organizations. Telecommuting changes employees' behavior in terms of reporting procedures, direct supervision, personal interaction, etc. Telecommuting permits a higher level of autonomy (Wright & Oldford, 1993) and control over their time than on-site working. Scheduling and directing their own jobs are part of telecommuters' responsibilities. Telecommuters often perform jobs that would be done for them by others in the office such as testing the quality of their work, estimating the time to complete a job, bookkeeping and secretarial jobs (Humble et al., 1995). As telecommuters becomes more independent and remote from the organization, they are perceived to be self-motivated, self-disciplined, and self-starters.

Tasks

Tasks refer to the work assigned to the employees. Since telecommuters perform their jobs one or more days per week at other sites like home or telework centers away from the central business office, the tasks are often transferred electronically. Telecommuting fits well with occupations based on information where the products can be shipped easily through telecommunications technology (Ramsower, 1985). Industries such as manufacturing, which require physical access to special or fixed resources, are generally not suitable for telecommuting. Similarly, industries or jobs where face-to-face meetings are a major component of the job are also less likely to utilize telecommuting. Additionally, the nature of the tasks for telecommuting requires less direct supervision and control because the jobs will be done at remote sites without physical presence in the traditional office. The characteristics of telecommuting with four factors—structure, technology, people, and tasks—are summarized in Table 2.

CONCEPTUAL TELECOMMUTING MEASUREMENT MODEL

Figure 2 describes a model conceptualizing measurement for telecommuting and summarizes both positive and negative indicators that are critical elements of this model. Reading the framework top to bottom, one can see that telecommuting is directed toward success through improvements.

Telecommuting should be successful in terms of surviving economically and fulfilling the requirements of its key stakeholders: employees, organizations, and society. Though no single measurement of employees, organizations, and society will lead to an accurate measurement of telecommuting, a comprehensive approach, where the measurements consider all key stakeholders, will provide a more accurate performance evaluation of telecommuting. Typical analyses of measuring examine what you gain (benefits) vs. what you lose (costs). This model provides both positive and negative indicators for the measurements, examining both the tangible, as

Table 2: The Characteristics of Telecommuting

Factors	Traditional On-site Working	Telecommuting
Structure	• Centralized fashion	• Decentralized/dispersed
Technology	• Technology dependence and requirements varies based on the characteristics of business	• Dependence on technology (e.g. IT, IS, computers & telecommunications) • Requires data and communications capability
People	• Need of feedback and constant supervision	• Autonomy over their time • Control over their time • Self-motivated, self-disciplined & self-starter
Tasks	• Physical contact • Close scrutiny • Need of various physical facility • Production/information	• Easy to be transferred electronically • Little face-to-face interactions & close scrutiny • Minimal physical facility • Information/knowledge

Figure 2: Telecommuting Performance Measurement (TPM) Model

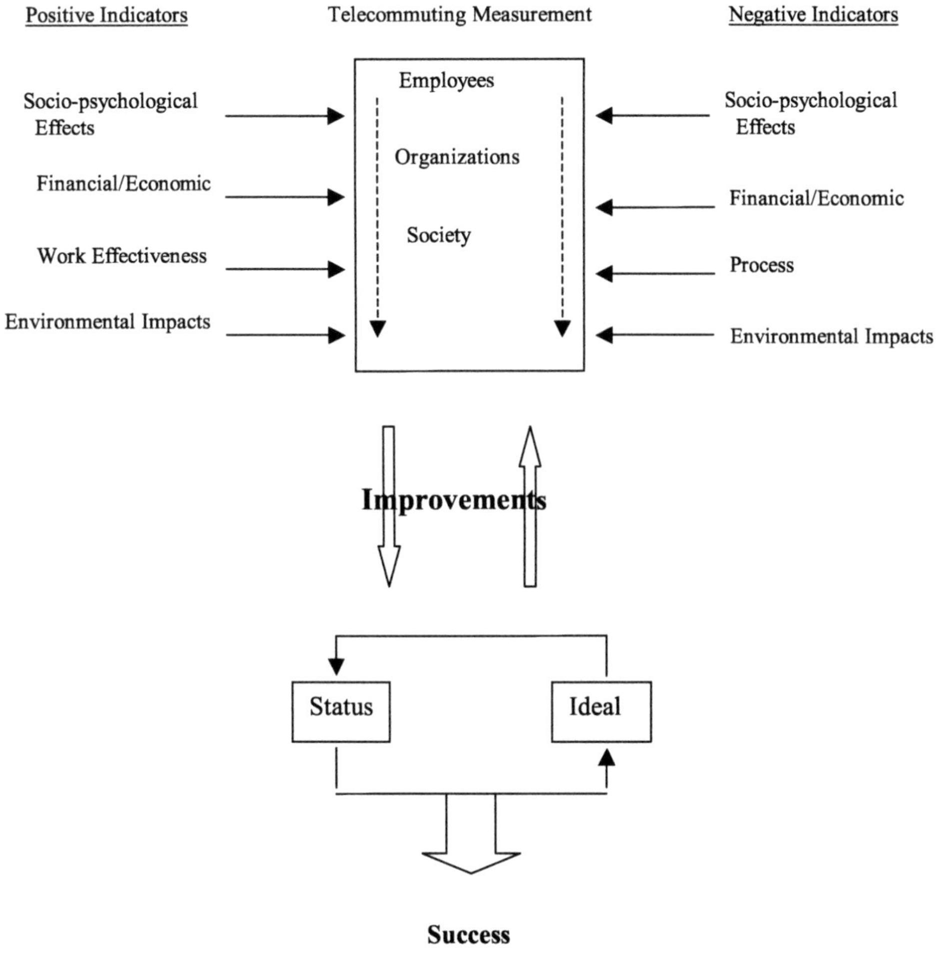

Positive Indicators	Telecommuting Measurement	Negative Indicators

Employees

Socio-psychological Effects → | Organizations | ← Socio-psychological Effects

Financial/Economic → | Society | ← Financial/Economic

Work Effectiveness → | | ← Process

Environmental Impacts → | | ← Environmental Impacts

Improvements

Status   Ideal

Success

well as the intangible, benefits and costs. Both indicators can be used as a performance index for evaluators.

Telecommuting Measurement

In order to better manage telecommuting to maximize its advantages and minimize its disadvantages, organizations need to undertake certain measures. This analysis looks at all possible variables regardless of whether they are monetary or nonmonetary, tangible or intangible, and quantitative or qualitative.

Intangible factors are more likely ignored than monetary or tangible values because intangible factors are not easily measured. Yet, even if the factors to be measured are not economic values, the comparisons of these factors before and after telecommuting allows for the assessment of the intangible benefits and or costs. An evaluator can assess changes on effects rather than absolute values of the factors. Interviews with the employees and/ or questionnaires will be the best method to measure the effects because the factors to be assessed are intangible and the perception of the factors is subjective based on people. To observe the changes on the effects, an evaluator needs to measure both the telecommuter's and non-telecommuter's perceptions before and after the telecommuting is introduced.

Similar to other economic terms, the monetary variables related to telecommuting, such the costs for computer hardware and software, telecommunications, etc., can be measured by typical accounting systems. The quantitative, but nonmonetary, variables can be measured based on the quantitative changes of the amount both for telecommuters and non-telecommuters before and after the telecommuting is introduced.

A key issue in telecommuting measurements is whether the changes attributable to the introduction of telecommuting are beneficial and whether the net economic result is positive. Using the model proposed in this analysis, an evaluator is able to assess this issue and identify whether the overall result is positive or negative. Comparing the ideal and current situation, the evaluator can improve the performance of telecommuting toward the goal of an overall successful telecommuting program. As the organization starts small and evaluates results, it can improve the performance of telecommuting by building on what works and modifying what does not.

Positive Indicators

This section reviews positive indicators in an attempt to identify the factors that will lead to successful telecommuting. It focuses on the indicators attributable to socio-psychological effects, financial, work effectiveness and environmental impacts.

Socio-Psychological Effects

Aside from the quantitative effects of telecommuting, there is the issue of the socio-psychological effects of telecommuting. The socio-psychological effects involve various intangible factors which are difficult to quantify and measure. As noted earlier, the best way to measure the variables is through observing the changes caused by telecommuting. There is a large body of literature available which addresses various socio-psychological effects of telecommuting and upon which this analysis draws (e.g., Katz, 1987; Duxbury et al., 1992; Galinsky et al., 1993; Humble et al., 1995; Piskurich, 1996; Shaw, 1996; Duxbury et al., 1998; Hill et al., 1998; Nilles, 1998; Igbaria & Guimaraes, 1999).

The survey by Nilles (1998) showed the quality of telecommuter's life changes were more positive than those of non-telecommuters. With the flexibility of work time and place, telecommuters can have more time for other things like family interaction, child or elder care, community events, etc.(Shellenbarger, 1998; Greenbaum, 1998). Telecommuting has been shown to facilitate a balance between work and family commitments and demands (Galinsky et al., 1993; Hill et al., 1996; Humble et al., 1995; Duxbury et al., 1998). Reduced commuting time to the office helps telecommuters to reduce the stress from traffic congestion (Nilles, 1998; Shaw, 1996) and improve health condition (Shaw, 1996). Telecommuting provides positive changes on feelings of control of one's life (Nilles, 1998; Piskurich, 1996; Hill et al., 1998), ability to work without interruption (Piskurich, 1996), job satisfaction (Igbaria & Guimaraes, 1999), and morale (Kugelmass, 1995).

Financial/Economic
The values of financial/economic factors are obviously more easily measured than noneconomic factors. Possible variables of financial/ economic factors are the focus of this section. The monetary benefits of telecommuting are generally in the form of reduced operating costs. Organizations can reduce real estate cost and office expense cost due to the reduced number of on-site workers (Fitzer, 1997; Shaw, 1996). Potential occupancy costs savings that occur from reducing office space is critical to the economic viability of telecommuting (Westfall, 1998; Cascio, 2000). The retention rate of employees can be improved because the employees are satisfied with their flexible work arrangements (Kugelmass, 1995). Working from home made telecommuters reduce their likelihood of leaving the company (Igbaria & Guimaraes, 1999). In other words, turnover in a company is decreased, thus saving the costs for additional recruiting (Dombrow, 1998; Shaw, 1996; Gemignani, 2000), and retraining. Additionally, when companies do need to recruit new employees, telecommuting frees them from the limitations of geography, as they can hire employees without regard to issues such as availability of "local" talent, employees' proximity to the office, relocation expenses, etc. (Peltin & Crowder, 2000). Fuel, clothes, and meals expenses can be reduced due to the fact that telecommuters go to their company less than before (Shaw, 1996). Since the reduced traffic flow through telecommuting would reduce roadway wear and tear, it would decrease costs for repairing roads (Piskurich, 1996; Nilles, 1998).

One of the powerful driving forces of telecommuting is potential cost saving. Although other factors like socio-psychological factors are more likely subjective, the financial/economic variables can be easily quantified and converted to monetary values. An evaluator can apply the typical accounting systems that usually measure economic terms to measure monetary values.

Work Effectiveness

The impact on employee effectiveness is an important criteria in assessing the desirability of telecommuting (Nilles, 1998). In measuring work effectiveness, organizations need to look at the full scope of work performed. Possible variables of work effectiveness indicators are explored below.

One of the most cited benefits of telecommuting is increased productivity of the telecommuters (e.g., Kugelmass, 1995; Nilles, 1998; Piskurich, 1996; Weiss, 1994; Westfall, 1998; US Department of Transportation, 1997, etc.). Even though the evidence of productivity gains noted in many sources like literature, trade, and popular press is not highly compelling in detailed terms such as increased amount or methods of evaluation (Westfall, 1998), the overall productivity gains attributable to telecommuting are compelling. Many case studies and many researchers have focused on this issue and asserted that telecommuting increases productivity (e.g. Kugelmass, 1995; Nilles, 1998; Piskurich, 1996; Weiss, 1994; Westfall, 1998; US Department of Transportation, 1997, etc.).

Though increased productivity in and of itself is a key factor, other work effectiveness factors surrounding increased productivity should also be examined. Flexible work time and place management has been shown to contribute to increased work effectiveness. The ability of telecommuters to work from home on days when they are not feeling good enough to commute to their company has allowed companies to reap productivity gains which would have otherwise been lost in a "non-telecommuting" work environment (US Department of Transportation, 1997). Telecommuters also have more control over their working conditions than they would in a traditional work setting. Though the telecommuter's environment may not be completely ideal due to potential distractions such as family members, televisions, and other in-home diversions (Bernardi, 1998), with proper diligence many telecommuters find that these are more easily managed than the inherent problems faced in an office-related environment. As a result, the telecommuters can work with fewer distractions from telephones, meetings, and colleagues, which also increases work effectiveness.

Most variables of work effectiveness are associated with work performance of employees. The occupations of most telecommuters involve information work. Their contributions are intangible and thus are not easily measured. Telecommuting requires a change in the process of employee performance appraisal. Many authors suggest that managers of telecommuters may benefit from changing management style from observational to an output oriented evaluation mode (e.g., Fitzer, 1997; Fillipczak, 1992; Hamilton, 1987; Katz, 1987; Nilles, 1994; Rotter and Center for Transportation Studies and Research, 1996). Management by objectives (MBO) or output controls has been suggested as appropriate for telecommuting. Output controls direct employees by specifying output goals and standards while leaving the choice of methods and procedures to the employees themselves (Johnson, 1998). For a telecommuting program to be effective, telecommuters should be evaluated based on the results they provide, not on time they spend in their office, procedures they follow, or behaviors they show.

Work effectiveness is a broad view; it is not just about measuring the quantity of work. This kind of approach includes how much and how well it gets done, when it gets done, and how many things can be done at once (Gordon, 1997). According to Gordon, an effective telecommuter is one who scores well on these four criteria.

Environmental Impacts

Telecommuting provides benefits to communities as well as society in general. Benefits such as air quality enhancement, energy reduction, reduced traffic congestion, development of areas, etc., are the interests here. Potential variables of environmental impacts are indirect benefits that are associated with reduced use of automobile transportation. Some of them can be easily quantified. For example, the pollution reduction can be measured using ratio of pollutant per automobile mile; reduced traffic congestion can be calculated using ratio of reduced miles per telecommuter. The environmental impacts involve various factors to be measured.

Two of the most important environmental impacts of telecommuting are the reduction of air pollution and energy consumption. Since telecommuters drive less or do not drive during telecommuting days, they reduce daily air pollution and energy use (Nilles, 1998). Besides these factors, there is reduced traffic congestion (Nilles et al., 1976; Kugelmass, 1995; Piskurich, 1996) as a consequence of reduced commuting time. The benefits–decreased air pollution, reduced energy consumption, and reduced traffic congestion–help organizations, agencies, and geographic areas meet air-quality legislative requirements and other policy directives (US Department of Transportation, 1997). These benefits are supported by many case studies (e.g., Korte & Wynne, 1996; Nilles, 1988; Sampath et al., 1992).

Telecommuting also promotes more efficient use of existing transportation infrastructure (Kugelmass, 1995). Roads, highways, and public transportation systems of many growing metropolitan and suburban areas have been utilized far beyond their capacity for getting workers to and from the office. Due to the ability of telecommuters to work from home, many of these overburdened systems are relieved of this strain and can operate much more efficiently. Telecommuting programs may have secondary benefits related to enhancing vibrancy of communities (Korte & Wynne, 1996). Since more people stay at home or in their local area, they are more likely to have interactions with their communities.

Negative Indicators

This section reviews negative indicators in an attempt to identify significant detrimental factors of telecommuting. It focuses on the indicators attributable to socio-psychological effects, financial, process, and environmental impacts.

Socio-Psychological Effects

Similar to the socio-psychological effects of positive indicators, the variables here are related to the human factors. Psychological problems like social isolation, loss of organizational structure, or workaholism are widely cited as the drawbacks to telecommuting (e.g., Crossan & Burton, 1993; Dombrow, 1998; Fitzer, 1997; Flilipczak, 1992; Kugelmass, 1995; Moss & Carey, 1994; Piskurich, 1996; Shaw, 1996). These concerns turn out to be important factors at least equal to monetary costs in measuring telecommuting.

Social isolation is one of the most often cited drawbacks of telecommuting. Since the visibility of telecommuters is reduced for their colleagues and managers, the interactions among them are decreased. Feelings of isolation may occur to the home-based telecommuters because they do not have the daily interaction with other employees (Bernardi, 1998). The lack of physical and personalized status in an office of the telecommuter's organization can give the telecommuters a sense of loss of organizational structure and give rise to the perception that they are at a disadvantage when compared to their in-office peers (Dunham, 2000). Lower levels of presence in the office have been shown to reduce the levels of satisfaction with peers, as well as satisfaction with advancement within the organization (Igbaria & Guimaraes, 1999). Resentment or jealousy by telecommuters' colleagues who do not telecommute has occurred in some cases where telecommuting has been implemented (Moss & Carey, 1994; Piskurich, 1996). Telecommuters may also have a more productive home-work environment than their in-office peers and, thus, it becomes easier for the telecommuters to work overtime and more intensively. As a result of this, in addition to furthering resentment and jealousy, it is possible that telecommuters become workaholics (Kugelmass, 1995; Dombrow, 1998; Piskurich, 1996). As the line between work-life and home-life becomes blurred, marital and family tensions can also increase (Agres et al., 1998; Snizek, 1995) From a business viewpoint, many critics fear that miscommunication and diminished feelings of trust may also occur between telecommuters and their customers and clients, as well as fellow employees, as personal interaction is diminished through telecommuting (Nie, 1999; Minerd, 1999).

Financial/Economic
The financial and economic costs of telecommuting are highlighted in this section. Although it is widely believed that a telecommuting program is expensive to implement and maintain, very few studies outlining these costs have been published. Some literature and case studies have indicated that the various cost factors associated with telecommuting are computer hardware and software, furniture and other nontechnical office equipment, telecommunications, and training (e.g., Nilles, 1998; Westfall, 1998; Korte & Wynne, 1996; Gjertsen, 2000). But given the differences in telecommuting programs that exist from organization to organization, the costs of participating in telecommuting will vary on a case-by-case basis; some telecommuting programs may cost more than others depending on the level of technology to be applied, number of employees involved, and the nature of the organization implementing the program. Similar to the financial/economic factors of positive indicators, the expenses or cost factors are related to monetary costs that can generally be measured by typical accounting systems.

In its broadest perspective, telecommuting is the idea of moving the work to the workers instead of moving the workers to the work (Harler, 1998). The idea is largely accomplished by technologies related to telecommunications and computer hardware and software. Obviously these factors turn out to be significant costs of telecommuting. The reliance of telecommuters on telecommunications rather than on physical personal contact is a significant change from the typical office culture (Katz, 1987). This creates a demand for additional training in effective communication through telecommunications. Managers and employees alike must be trained in effective management techniques, procedures, and communications through telecommunications (Korte & Wynne, 1996; McCune, 1998). The cost of this training must also be factored into the overall expense of the telecommuting program.

Additional costs that must also be considered are the expenses of moving existing equipment from offices to the telecommuters' homes or satellite centers, facilities leasing and furniture (Nilles, 1998), and increased telephone, air conditioning, and heating costs for the telecommuters (Moss & Carey, 1994).

Intangible setup costs must also be factored into the cost of telecommuting. Due to the fact that telecommuting is in its relative infancy, many legal issues which have been settled regarding traditional office work have yet to be resolved. Companies must consider and prepare for discrimination, safety, compensation, confidentiality, and termination issues to arise and attempt to factor in the costs for these issues as well (Peltin & Crowder, 2000; Segal, 1998; Greenbaum, 1998). Planning for these factors and documenting all policies and procedures before the implementation of a telecommuting program are essential steps toward the dual goals of protecting the company and implementing a successful telecommuting program (Berry, 1998; Gjertsen, 2000). This is no easy task as many legislative issues regarding telecommuting are still being revised and debated in various state and federal governmental branches and agencies. The US Occupational Health and Safety Administration (OSHA) exemplified this uncertainty when it set strict guidelines regarding companies' responsibilities for the safety of their telecommuters on November 15, 1999, and then, in the midst of huge criticism from the business world, backed away from its position less than eight weeks later (Howard, 2000). Thus, companies face an uncertain legal landscape for their telecommuting programs and must develop contingency plans and policies in order to minimize their exposure to risk (Hawkins, 2000). The cost of these policies and procedures, as well as the increased cost of legal, risk management, and human resources expertise to develop these policies, must also be considered (Prince, 2000).

Process

While the variables of financial/economic under negative indicators are more likely explicit costs, the variables of this section are centered around implicit costs. The variables are related to the maintenance and facilitation of the telecommuting process. These include additional administrative works, increased need for security, and lack of informal communication.

Telecommuters create increased demands on the time of their managers and coworkers (Westfall, 1998). Telecommuting leads to extra work for the managers (Fritz et al., 1995), as questions that may have previously been resolved with a quick conversation in the hall may now require e-mails, follow-up e-mails, videoconferencing, telephone calls, etc. The majority of participants in case studies collected by Korte and Wynne (1996) see the lack of informal communications as a disadvantage of telecommuting. The amount of informal communications varies with level of telecommuting–i.e., telecommuters who telecommute five or more days per week have less informal communication than those who telecommute one day per week. For entirely home-based telecommuters, since all meetings are scheduled in advance, it is not easy to have informal communications.

While most communications within the traditional work setting are performed by face-to-face communication, communications with telecommuting generally happen through telecommunications technology. Some (and in many cases almost all) meetings are carried out through the use of the telephone or videoconferencing (Nilles, 1997). With this new paradigm of communication, the use of electronic computer-mediated communications systems (CMCS) has been increasing. The use of CMCS mandates that an adequate technical support policy be implemented to facilitate and protect communications with the home office, managers, supervisors, etc. (Lamont, 2000). In light of the fact that many telecommuters do not work traditional hours, for many companies, around the clock support may not only be necessary, but critical (York, 1999). Since telecommuters work outside of their central office, significant amounts of organizational data and information also "walk away" from the main office to the telecommuters' homes or telework centers. As more and more individuals telecommute, there are increased security threats brought on by employee theft, hackers, and computer viruses (Sliwa, 2000; Fairweather, 1999). This phenomenon necessitates increased time and resources regarding data security (Prince, 2000). The need for technological support for the telecommuter, as well as to ensure data security, translates into additional costs which must be considered when assessing any telecommuting program.

Though telecommuters make the most of the limited face-to-face contact with their supervisors and coworkers (Humble et al., 1995), generally they need to document their work and transfer it, as well as receive required information, electronically. Such characteristics differentiate greatly telecommuting from traditional working, and telecommuting requires significantly more organizational and administrative resources if it is to be used effectively.

Environmental Impacts

Telecommuting does not provide much negative impact to our society and community. According to Dombrow (1998), who pointed out a possible negative impact of telecommuting on society, telecommuting causes the potential loss of jobs that are related to traditional commuters, like bus drivers, toll collectors, dry cleaners or restaurant employees. The possible variables of positive and negative indicators for telecommuting measurements are summarized in Table 3.

CONCLUSIONS

Telecommuting provides economic, societal, and environmental benefits to individuals, organizations, and society. However, despite these benefits, telecommuting is still underutilized by the majority of organizations in the business world. The major reason is the difficulty of measuring telecommuting performance. The traditional methods of measuring performance are inadequate and, thus, to measure the performance of telecommuting, a new approach is demanded.

The TPM model proposed in the paper provides an important insight into the consideration of both benefits and costs, tangible and intangible factors, and monetary and nonmonetary values in measuring telecommuting performance. The model conceptualizes the measurement of telecommuting performance, consisting of positive and negative indicators. Evaluators can use the identified positive and negative indicators as a performance index upon which to assess their organization's telecommuting program. In order to justify and

Table 3: Possible Variables for Telecommuting Measurements

Indicators	Possible Variables
Positive Indicators	
Socio-psychological Effects	Quality of life, flexible work arrangements, flexibility of child and elder care options, increased privacy, reduced stress of commuting, better health, improved ability to work without interruption, increased job satisfaction, increased morale, feelings of control of one's life, etc.
Financial/Economic	Reduced occupancy costs, less money spent on gas, clothes, and meals out, decreased employee turnover, reduced recruiting cost, reduced need for road repair, etc.
Work Effectiveness	Increased productivity, increased commitment, timeliness, quality of work, quantity of work, reduced absenteeism, reduced sick time, fewer interruptions, etc.
Environmental Impacts	Air quality enhancement, reduced energy consumption, reduced traffic congestion, better use of existing transportation infrastructure, increased vibrancy within local communities, etc.
Negative Indicators	
Socio-psychological Effects	Social isolation, loss of organizational structure, reduced satisfaction with peers, decreased satisfaction with promotion, jealousy or resentment of co-workers, workaholism, miscommunication, mistrust, etc.
Financial/Economic	Computer hardware and software cost, IT communication cost, training cost, recurring operating cost, legal costs, miscellaneous costs (e.g., moving expense, furniture, other facilitates cost, telephone bills, air conditioning bills, etc.), etc.
Process	Additional support or work, increased need for security, lack of informal communications, etc.
Environmental Impacts	Loss of some jobs, etc.

continue a telecommuting program, it must be successful not just according to financial indicators; rather, the evaluation must incorporate the intangible and nonmonetary costs and benefits as well. Telecommuting, as well as its evaluation and assessment, should not be a static process. Rather, as the proposed model illustrates, telecommuting is directed toward success through continual improvements. Additional research is needed to prove and refine the TPM model empirically. We hope that the paper contributes to the understanding and measuring of telecommuting and will stimulate research on measuring telecommuting.

REFERENCES

Agres, C., Edburg, D. and Igbaria, M. (1998). Transformation to virtual societies: Forces and issues. *Information Society*, 14(2), 71-82.

Ashton, A. and Ashton, R. (1999). What would you do? *Home Office Computing*, 17(9), 99-100.

Bernardi, L. (1998). Telecommuting: Legal and management issues. *The Canadian Manager*, 23(3), 18-28.

Berry, J. (1998). Remote rights raise a legal flag. *Internetweek*, 731, 27-28.

Brandt, S. (1983). Working at home: How to cope with spatial design possibilities caused by the new communication media. *Office Technology and People*, 2, 1-13.

Büssing, A. (1998). Teleworking and quality of life. In Jackson, P. and van der Wielen, J. (Eds.), *Teleworking; International Perspectives*, 144-165.

Capowski, G. (1998). Telecommuting: The new frontier. *HRFocus*, 75(4), 2.

Cascio, W. (2000). Managing a virtual workplace. *Academy of Management Executive*, 14(3), 81-90. 2000.

Crossan, G. and Burton, P. (1993). Teleworking stereotypes: A case study. *Journal of Information Science*, 19, 349-362.

Dombrow, J. (1998). Electronic communications and the law: Help or hindrance to telecommuting? *Federal Communications Law Journal*, 50(3), 685-709.

Drucker, P. (1973). *Management: Tasks, Responsibilities, Practices*. New York: Harper & Row Publishers.

Dunham, K. (2000). Telecommuter's lament: Once touted as the future, work-at-home situations lose favor with employers. *Wall Street Journal*.

Duxbury, L., Higgins, C. and Mills, S. (1992). After-hours telecommuting and work-family conflict: A comparative analysis. *Information Systems Research*, 3(2), 173-190.

Duxbury, L., Higgins, C. and Neufeld, D. (1998). Telework and the balance between work and family: Is telework part of the problem or part of the solution? In Igbaria, M. and Tan (Eds.), *The Virtual Workplace*, 218-255.

Fairweather, N. (1999). Surveillance in employment: The case of teleworking. *Journal of Business Ethics*. 22(1), 39-49.

Filipczak, B. (1992). Telecommuting: A better way to work? *Training*, 29(5), 53-61.

Fitzer, M. (1997). Managing from afar: Performance and rewards in a telecommuting environment. *Compensation and Benefits Review*, 29(1), 65-73.

Fritz, M., Higa, K. and Narasimhan, S. (1995). Toward a telework taxonomy and test for suitability: A synthesis of the literature. *Group Decision and Negotiation Support*, 4(4), 311-334.

Galinsky, H., Bond, J. and Friedman, D. (1993). *The Changing Workforce: Highlight of the National Study*. Family and Work Institute, New York.

Gemignani, J. (2000). There is no place like home for today's teleworkers. *Business and Health*, 18(5), 30-36.

Gjertsen, L. (2000). Employers, insurers grapple with risks of telecommuting. *National Underwriter*, 104(17), 28-30.

Gordon, G. (1986). *Personal Communication*.

Gordon, G. (1997). *The Last Word on Productivity and Telecommuting*. Gill Gordon Associates.

Greenbaum, T. (1998). Avoiding a virtual disaster. *HRFocus*, 75(2), 11-12.

Hamilton, C. Telecommuting. (1987). *Personnel Journal*, 66, 91-101.

Harler, C. (1998). The good, the bad and the fattening. *America's Network*, 102(6), 26-28.

Hawkins, C. (2000). Settle out of court. *Home Office Computing*, 18(3), 96-97.

Hill, J., Hawkins, A., and Miller, B. (1996). Work and family in the virtual office: Perceived influences of mobile telework. *Family Relations*, 45, 293-301.

Hill, J., Miller, B., Weiner, S. and Colihan, J. (1998). Influences of the virtual office on aspects of work and work/life balance. *Personnel Psychology*, 51(3), 667-683.

Howard, J. (2000). At-home work spurs risk management concerns. *National Underwriter*, 104(18), 57.

Humble, J., Jacobs, S., and Van Sell, M. (1995). Benefits of telecommuting for engineers and other high-tech professionals. *Industrial Management*, 37(2), 15-19.

Igbaria, M. and Guimaraes, T. (1999). Exploring differences in employees turnover intention and its determinants among telecommuters and non-telecommuters. *Journal of Management Information Systems,* 16(1), 147-164.

Igbaria, M., Olfman, L., and Shayo, C. (1998). Virtual Societies: Their Prospects and Dilemmas in Psychology and the Internet: Intrapersonal, Interpersonal and Transpersonal Implications. Gackenbach, J. (Ed.), Academic Press, San Diego and London.

International Telework Association and Council. (1999). Available on the World Wide Web at: http://www.telecommute.org/TeleworkAmerica/millions_twa.htm.

Johansen, R. (1988). *Groupware: Computer Support for Business Teams.* Free Press, New York.

Jonson, S. (1998). Teleworking service management: Issues for an integrated framework, In Jackson, P., Wielen, J. and van der, J. M. (Eds.), *Teleworking: International Perspectives from Telecommuting to the Virtual Organization.* Routledge, London, New York.

Katz, A. (1987). The management, control, and evaluation of a telecommuting project: A case study. *Information and Management,* 13(4), 179-190.

Korte, W. and Wynne, R. (1996). *Telework: Penetration, Potential and Practice in Europe.* Amsterdam, Oxford, IOS.

Kugelmass, J. (1995). *Telecommuting: A Manager's Guide to Flexible Work Arrangements.* New York: Lexington Books.

Lamont, I. (2000). Taming telecommunications. *Network World,* July 3, 55.

McCloskey, D. and Igbaria, M. (1998). A review of the empirical research on telecommuting and directions for future research. In Igbaria, M. and Tan (Eds.), *The Virtual Workplace,* 338-358.

McCloskey, D., Igbaria, M. and Parasuranman, S. (1998). The work experience of professional men and women who telecommute: Convergence or divergence? *Journal of End User Telecommuting,* 10(4), 15-22.

McCune, J. (1998). Telecommuting revisited. *Management Review,* 87(2), 10-16.

Minerd, J. (1999). The decline of conversation. *The Futurist.* 33(2), 18-19.

Mokhtarian, P., Bagley, M. and Salomon, I. (1998). The impact of gender, occupation, and presence of children on telecommuting motivations and constraints. *Journal of the American Society for Information Science,* 49(12), 1115-1134.

Moss, M. and Carey, J. (1994). Telecommuting for individuals and organizations. *The Journal of Urban Technology,* 17-29.

Nie, N. (1999). Tracking our techno-future. *American Demographics*, 21(7), 50-52.

Nilles, J. (1988). Traffic reduction by telecommuting: A status review and selected bibliography. *Transportation Resources*, 22A(4), 301-317.

Nilles, J. (1994). *Making Telecommuting Happen: A Guide for Telemangers and Telecommuters*. New York, NY: Van Nostrand Reinhold.

Nilles, J. (1997). Telework: Enabling distributed organizations. *Information Systems Management*, 14(4), 7-14.

Nilles, J. (1998). *Managing Telework: Strategies for Managing the Virtual Workforce*. New York: Wiley.

Nilles, J., Carlson, F., Jr., Gray, P. and Hanneman, G. (1976). *The Telecommuting-Transportation Tradeoff*. New York, NY: John Wiley & Sons, Inc.

Peltin, S. and Crowder, J. (2000). Reducing telecommuting management risks. *National Underwriter*, 104(18), 14-20.

Piskurich, G. (1996). Making telecommuting work. *Training & Development*, 50(2), 20-27.

Prince, M. (2000). Telecommuters present unique risks to employers. *Business Insurance,* 34(20), 22-24.

Ramsower, R. (1985). *Telecommuting: The Organizational and Behavioral Effects of Working at Home*. Michigan: University of Michigan Research Press.

Reese, S. (2000). Productivity plus. *Business and Health*, 18(4), 71-72.

Rotter, N. (1996). Center for transportation studies and research. Performance appraisal and telecommuting: insights form an information processing approach. Paper presented at the *Telecommuting '96*, Jacksonville, FL.

Sampath, S., Saxena, S. and Mokhtarian, P. (1992). The effectiveness of telecommuting as a transportation control measure. *Transportation Planning and Air Quality*. American Society of Civil Engineers, New York.

Segal, J. (1998). Home sweet office? *HRMagazine*, 43(5), 119-129.

Shaw, L. (1996). *Telecommute!: Go to Work Without Leaving Home*. New York: John Wiley.

Shellenbarger, S. (1997). Madison Avenue may need to alter image of '90s telecommuter. *The Wall Street Journal*, B1.

Shellenbarger, S. (1998). Families, communities can benefit from rise in home based work. *The Wall Street Journal*, Pp. B1.

Sliwa, C. (2000). Users react sympathetically to Microsoft security breach. *ComputerWorld*, 89.

Snizek, W. (1995). Virtual offices: Some neglected considerations. *Communications of the ACM*, 38(9),15-7.

US Department of Transportation. (1993). *Transportation Implications of Telecommuting*, April. Washington DC.

US Department of Transportation. (1997). *Successful Telecommuting Programs in the Public and Private Sectors: A Report to Congress.*

Weiss, J. M. (1994). Telecommuting boots employee output. *HRMaganize.* 51-53.

Westfall, R. (1998). The microeconomics of remote work. In Igbaria, M. and Tan (Eds.), *The Virtual Workplace*, 257-287.

Westfall, R. (1997). *Remote Work: A Conceptual Perspective on the Demand for Telecommuting*, Thesis (PhD)-Claremont Graduate School.

Wright, P. and Oldford, A. (1993). Telecommuting and employee effectiveness: Career and managerial issues. *International Journal of Career Management*, 5(1), 4-9.

York, T. (1999). Telecommuting trials. *InfoWorld*, (21-22), 87-88.

SECTION III: DEVELOPMENT OF INTERNET AND SYSTEM POLICIES

Chapter XI

Classifying Web Usage Behavior in the Workplace: An Artificial Neural Network Approach[1]

Murugan Anandarajan
Drexel University, USA

INTRODUCTION

The ubiquitous nature of the World Wide Web (commonly known as the Web) is dramatically revolutionizing the manner in which organizations and individuals alike acquire and distribute information. Recent reports from the International Data Group indicate that the number of people on the Internet will reach 320 million by the year 2002 (Needle, 1999). Studies also indicate that in the United States alone, Web commerce will account for approximately $325 billion by the year 2002.

In addition to being a channel for commercial exchange, the Web also provides employees access to the world's biggest playground. This fact was highlighted in a recent *Newsweek* article whose headline read, "The Internet has brought distractions into cubicles, and now corporate America is fighting back" (Nelson & Cheney, 1987). Workplace Web users, however, may not view this as a potential problem. The sentiments of users on this issue were reflected in a succinct comment made by an employee in a recent interview with the author:

Looking up a work-related news story easily leads to checking the baseball standings or a movie review. It will only take a couple of seconds, right? A couple of seconds is no big deal in the greater scheme of things.

The problem, however, is that seconds turn to minutes, then add up to hours. A study conducted in a manufacturing firm found that in a typical 8-hour working day, over 250,000 Web sites were accessed by a workforce of 386 employees. Of particular concern to the organization was the discovery that approximately 90% of the accessed sites were non-work-related (LaPlante, 1997). Recent research by the Aberdeen Research Group (Wu, Massart, & Jong, 1997) indicates that employees can squander anywhere from 30 minutes to 3 hours a day on non-work Web-related activity.

The cost of ignoring this phenomenon can be enormous. According to the Gartner group, such activities cost US companies approximately $50 billion in productivity alone each year. In addition, such usage leads to increased security costs, network overload, as well as the risk of civil and criminal liability. These issues have prompted organizations to show a growing interest in understanding and managing Web usage behavior in the workplace (Cronin, 1996; McWilliams & Stepanek, 1998).

So, how do organizations deal with this emergent behavior? Monitoring can vary from a laissez-faire attitude to the blocking of Web sites. However Web surfing is a gray area, and an overzealous policy can be just as harmful as a nonexistent one. For instance, stringent blocking can hamper an employee's use of a vital tool for business purposes. Thus, it's not surprising that a recent survey found that approximately 73% of organizations have only acceptable usage policies or no restrictions at all (Yasin, 1999).

Recent literature on Internet security recommends that an organization's Internet security program should focus on modifying user behavior (McBride, 2000) as well as user education (Yasin, 1999) to reduce the problem. However, a fundamental decision problem facing Internet security managers is how to identify the Web usage behavior of employees in the various functional and operational levels within an organization a priori. A review of the information systems literature indicates that there are no established guidelines, which implies that managers have to rely on their judgment to make such decisions. This can be precarious since such multi-cue judgments are inherently difficult for unaided human judges (Kleinmuntz, 1990).

This study proposes the use of an artificial intelligence based model (in terms of artificial neural networks and genetic algorithms) to assess and classify employees by their Web usage behavior. Based on an operational definition of Web usage behavior (Anandarajan, Simmers, & Igbaria, 2000,) individuals are classified as a *high non-work users* if they scored highly on accessing non-work-related Web pages such as arts and entertainment, travel and leisure, living/consumer, and sports/news. Individuals were classified as *low non-work users* if they scored low on accessing these pages.

The output of this intelligent system can be extremely beneficial to managers in the development of cognitive training and socialization programs which are vital in the modification of employees behavior as well as attitudes towards Web usage (McBride, 2000). Thus, this decision tool will aid managers in designing effective Internet security strategies.

The rest of this paper is organized as follows. The next section reviews the concepts of behavior-based artificial intelligence. This is followed by the development methodology and evaluation of the classifier models. The paper concludes with implications of the study for managers and directions for future research.

BEHAVIOR-BASED ARTIFICIAL INTELLIGENCE

In the last few decades the field of artificial intelligence (AI) has focused almost exclusively on problems of identifying, formalizing and representing knowledge. This classical, or traditional, AI approach (also known as knowledge-based AI) defines intelligence in terms of knowledge, which is based upon Newell's principle of rationality.

In recent years, however, the AI community has begun to stress the importance of embodied intelligence within these systems. This movement has been referred to as the *behavior-based AI approach* (Steels, 1990). This approach defines intelligence in terms of observed behavior, i.e., understanding common behavior through the construction of artificial systems, which account for the environmental pressures on the self-preservation of the system (Smithers, 1992). Researchers have used artificial neural networks to design behavioral-based systems, in order to stay close to plausible biological structures (Arbib & House, 1987; Pfeifer & Verschure, 1992).

Artificial Neural Networks

An artificial neural network (ANN) is a parallel, dynamic system of highly interconnected and interacting parts based on the principles of neurobiological models. ANNs have at least two potential strengths over the more traditional model-fitting techniques such as regression (Bishop, 1995). First ANNs are capable of detecting and extracting nonlinear relationships and interactions among predictor variables. Second the inferred patterns and associated estimates of precision of the ANN do not depend on various assumptions about the distribution of variables.

As in the brain, the fundamental building block of an ANN is the neuron. As illustrated in Figure 1, this artificial neuron receives a multitude of inputs, which represent the attributes or stimuli in a data set. Through the use of a learning algorithm, the optimal connection weights, which represent both the strength and nature of the connection between neurons, are determined. These weights are then applied to each input and the weights and the inputs are aggregated. An activation function (F) is then applied to the aggregated value to produce an output for a single neuron as follows:

$$Y = F * \left(\sum_{i=1}^{n} x_i w_i \right)$$

Activation functions are needed to introduce nonlinearity into the network. The selection of the activation function depends on the nature of the input data and objective of the network (Fausett, 1994). Since one of the objectives of this study is to interpret the final outputs of the neural network as posterior probabilities for a categorical target variable, the softmax function (Bishop, 1995; Finke & Muller, 1994; McCullagh & Nelder, 1989) was used and is defined as:

$$y_k = \frac{\exp(net_k)}{\sum_j \exp(net_j)}.$$

Figure 1: The Functioning of an Artificial Neuron

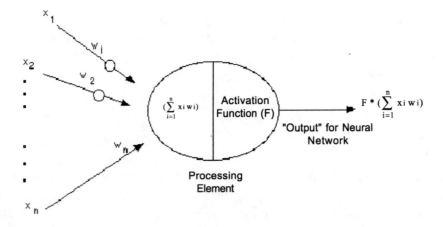

This study compares the predictive ability of two ANN topologies to profile Web usage behavior. The first topology, multilayer perceptron, is based solely on feed-forward connections; while the second topology, simple recurrent network is based on both feedback and feed-forward connections. These network topologies are described briefly below:

Multilayer Perceptrons (MLP) topology is one of the most widely implemented neural network architectures. This network has a three-layer, feed-forward, hierarchical structure. The complexity of the network determines the accuracy of the network model. A typical MLP is shown in Figure 2.

One of the traditional weaknesses of the MLP network is its inability to fill in patterns, because of their complete reliance on feed-forward connections. For instance, if part of the input pattern applied in the network is missing or corrupt, larger errors will be propagated through the network to the output. For a behavior-based system to be more effective, an ANN with feedback loops and additional sensors would be necessary. One such ANN topology is called the simple recurrent network (SRN).

Figure 2: General Structure of the Multilayer Perceptron Network Topology

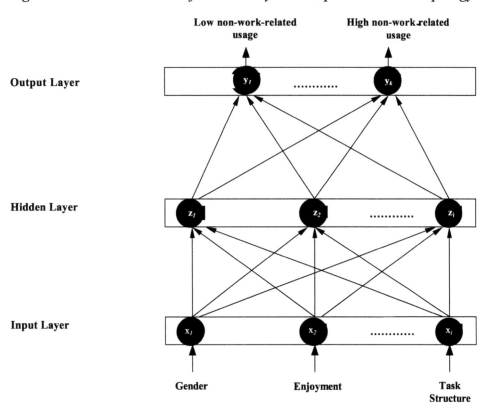

The SRN topology has a small number of neurons in the input layer which receive feedback signals from the hidden layer. These self-excitatory units, which act as sensors, are commonly referred to as context units and are very common in the brain. A context unit is defined as "an input layer unit in a simple recurrent net that receives information from hidden units" (Elman, 1990). These units remember past activity and are useful when the past value of the network influences present information processing.

As illustrated in Figure 3, in the SRN topology, the output of the hidden layers from the previous time step are copied to the context units $(C_1..C_n)$ in the input layer. In addition, the context units are locally recurrent (i.e., they feedback to themselves). The network combines the past values of the context units with the present inputs to obtain the present net output. The use of feedback connections in the simple recurrent model makes it less sensitive to noise and lack of synchronization. In addition, it also permits the network to learn at a faster rate than the feed-forward network (Simard, Ottaway, & Ballard, 1989).

Figure 3: General Structure of the Simple Recurrent Network Topology

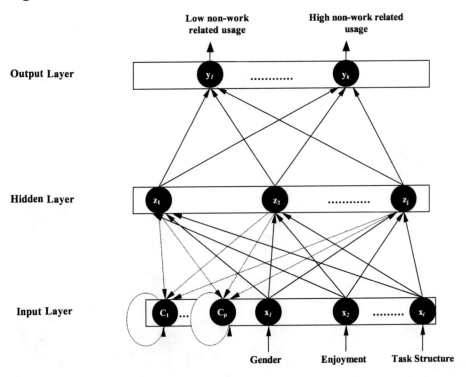

ANN Learning Algorithms

As discussed earlier, each connection in the ANN has a weight, which are initially generated from random numbers ranging from (-1 to 1). The output value of a neuron is a function of the weighted sum of its inputs. A large positive value will influence the next neuron to activate, while a large negative value will inhibit activation of the next neuron. The determination of these weights is a critical component of the learning process and is generated by an iterative training process where case examples with known decision outputs are repeatedly presented to the network. A commonly used learning method in ANN is the back propagation algorithm, which relies on gradient techniques for network training (Wong, Bodnovich, & Selvi, 1995). However, research has shown that BP may not necessarily provide the best ands fastest way to train neural networks (Archer & Wang, 1993; Curry & Morgan, 1997; Lenard, Alam, & Madey, 1995).

This study uses an alternate approach to learning, i.e., selectionism, where a complete behavior system is generated by an evolutionary process. Evolutionary development has been shown to be an extremely important source for generating more complexity in systems (Ray, 1992). It has also been proposed by neurobiologists to be the major mechanism underlying new functionality in the brain (Changeux, 1986). One such selectionist technique is called genetic algorithms (GA).

GA is a stochastic, heuristic optimization search technique that is designed after the natural selection process followed in biological evolution, i.e., it follows the nature of sexual reproduction in which the genes of two parents combine to form those of their offspring. This method has shown to perform well in obtaining global solutions for difficult nonlinear functions (Arbib & House, 1987; Archer & Wang, 1993). This generate-and-test strategy identifies and exploits regularities in the environment and converges on solutions that are globally optimal or nearly so.

When GA is applied to determine the weights of an ANN, an initial population of chromosomes (which in this study are the weights) representing possible solutions to a problem is created. Each set of chromosomes is represented by a sequence of genes. The potential of a chromosome as a possible solution is determined by its fitness function, which evaluates a chromosome with respect to an objective function. Each of these individuals has certain characteristics that make them more or less fit as members of the population. The fittest chromosomes will have a higher probability of mating than lesser-fit members, to produce progeny that have a significant chance of retaining the desirable attributes of their parents. For a more detailed description of genetic algorithms, please refer to Arbib and House (1987), Archer and Wang (1993), Baeck and Schwefel (1993), and Berardi and Zhang (1999).

METHODOLOGY

Data Collection

The data used in this study was collected using a survey instrument, which was mailed to a random sample of 1,500 alumni of a university in the northeastern United States. Participation in the study was voluntary and people were assured that their individual responses would be treated as confidential. Three-hundred and twenty-five surveys were returned within two weeks and another 170 were received within a month after a follow-up postcard was mailed. After discarding 50 surveys because of incompleteness, there were 445 useable surveys. The participation rate is consistent with other studies where potential respondents are not screened for their willingness to take part in the survey (Miller & Dodge, 1979; Scandura & Lankau, 1997). Of the 445 individual responses, 334 had Internet access at work. Of this sample, however, only 154 reported using the Web at work. Table 1 summarizes the characteristics of the samples used in this study.

Variable Selection

The choice of input variables used in the classification models is an important consideration in the design of the neural networks. Based on previous IS literature, predictors of Web usage behavior—low non-work-related usage and high non-work-related usage—were classified using *1-of-C coding*. i.e., each dummy variable was given the value 0 except for the one corresponding to the correct category, which was given the value 1. Web usage behavior was analyzed with regard to nine characteristics (i.e., nine input neurons). The variables include motivational factors—perceived enjoyment (Davis, 1992; Malone, 1981; Webster, 1989) perceived usefulness (Adams, Nelson, & Todd, 1992; Davis, 1989, 1992); skill—experience (Daly, Lancee, & Polivy, 1983; DeLone, 1988; Igbaria, Pavri, & Huff, 1989) and formal/self-training (Adams et al., 1992; Amoroso & Cheney, 1991; Igbaria, 1995; Nelson & Cheney, 1987; Raymond, 1988); task structure (Tushman & Nadler, 1978; Umanath & Kim, 1992); and demographic factors—gender (Gefen & Straub, 1997; Harrison, Rainer, & Houcwarter,

Table 1: Respondent Profiles

Demographics	Sample 1 n = 154		Sample 2 [1] n = 162	
Gender				
Male	97	63.5%	99	61.1%
Female	57	36.5%	63	39.0%
Age				
20-30 years	32	20.7%	99	61.3%
31-40	49	31.7%	49	30.0%
41-50	41	26.8%	10	6.5%
51-60	24	15.5%	3	2.4%
over 60	9	5.3%	0	0.0%
Size of Business				
1-999 Employees	76	48.8%	99	61.1%
1,000-9,999	40	25.9%	37	23.0%
over 10,000	39	25.3%	26	16.0%
Current Position				
Top-Level Manager	27	17.1%	13	8.3%
Middle-Level Manager	30	19.8%	24	14.7%
Lower-Level Manager	14	9.0%	25	15.7%
Professional	60	39.0%	48	29.9%
Administrative Support	10	6.3%	29	18.2%
Other	13	8.8%	22	13.3%

[1] Out-of-population sample

1997), education, and income. Table 2 provides a summary of these input variables and its corresponding measurement instrument. Univariate analysis was performed to determine whether the data consisted of the two different groups of Web users. As can be observed from *t-values* in Table 3, all variables, except education, were statistically significantly different for both groups. Table 4 provides the correlation matrix of the variables as well as the reliabilities of the measures, which were greater than the threshold criteria suggested by Nunnally (Nunnally, 1978).

Table 2: Summary of Variables Used in this Study

Variables	Definition	Previous Studies	Items and Scale
Demographic Factors			
Income level		Gefen & Straub, 1997;	Single item
Gender		(Harrison et al., 1997;	Single item
Education		Williams, Ogletree, Wodburne, & Rafeld, 1994	Single item
Motivational Factors			
Perceived Usefulness	The degree to which a person believes that using a particular system would enhance his or her job (Davis, Bagozzi, & Warshaw, 1989).	Adams et al., 1992; Davis, 1989; Davis, 1992; Igbaria, 1993; Robey, 1979;Thompson, Higgins, & Howell, 1994.	*Six-item scale [1=strongly disagree to 5 =strongly agree]* The Internet provides the precise information I need The Internet provides up-to-date information The Internet is user friendly The Internet is accurate The information content on the Internet meets my needs Using the Internet would increase my productivity on the job
Perceived Enjoyment	An individual's tendency to interact spontaneously, inventively, and imaginatively with the computer(Webster, 1989).	Davis, 1992; Malone, 1981 Webster, 1989)	*Four-item scale [1= strongly disagree to 5= strongly agree]* Spontaneous Imaginative Flexible Creative
Computer Skills			
Experience	User's knowledge or expertise in and performing tasks on the Internet (Ajzen & Fishbein, 1980)	DeLone, 1988;Igbaria et al., 1989	*Four-item scale [1 =none to 5= very extensive]* Using Internet search engines, such as Yahoo, Infoseek Downloading files from the Internet Creating Web pages Accessing the Internet

Table 2: (continued)

Formal Training / Self Training	Instruction on the use of the Internet focusing on efforts to transfer knowledge(Nelson &	Amoroso & Cheney, 1991; Igbaria, 1995; Lee, 1986; Nelson & Cheney, 1987; Raymond, 1988	*Four-item scale [1 = very little to 5 = very extensive]* Vendors or outside consultants In-house company courses By a fellow worker Self-study; self-taught
Task Structure	The extent to which there are known procedures that specify the sequence of steps to be followed(Tushman & Nadler, 1978; Umanath & Kim, 1992)	Tushman & Nadler, 1978; Umanath & Kim, 1992	*Four-item scale [1= very little extent to 5 = very large extent]* To what extent is there a defined body of knowledge that can guide you in doing your work? To what extent is there a understandable sequence of steps that can be followed in doing your work? To what extent can you actually rely on established procedures and practices to do your work? To what extent are your tasks the same from day-to-day?
Web Usage	System usage has been the indicator of technology acceptance. Cronin (1996) among others suggests the Websites used in this study.	Adams et al., 1992, Cronin, 1995; Davis, 1989; Davis, 1992; Straub, Limayem, & Karahanna, 1995)	*Seven-item scale [1= very unlikely to 5 = very likely]* Work-related web sites Competitors, Suppliers, Customers Non-work related Web sites Arts and entertainment , Travel and Leisure, Living/Consumer, Sports/news

Table 3: Comparison of the Two Groups

	Work-related Web Usage		Non-work-related Web Usage		
	Mean	*SD*	*Mean*	*SD*	*t-test*
Income	3.932	1.503	4.713	1.780	-2.917 ***
Gender	1.411	0.495	1.238	0.428	2.322 **
Education	4.151	1.036	4.150	0.969	0.004
Perceived Usefulness	3.088	0.833	3.408	0.891	-2.287 ***
Perceived Enjoyment	1.764	1.256	2.572	0.479	-5.348 ***
Web Experience	2.203	1.696	3.538	0.976	-6.029 ***
Web Formal Training	1.208	0.987	1.683	0.739	-3.394 ***
Web Self Training	2.562	2.028	3.825	1.100	-4.847 ***
Task Structure	2.610	1.059	2.006	0.884	3.837 *

* $p<0.01$
** $p<0.05$
***$p<0.001$

Designing and Implementing the Artificial Neural Networks

The ANNs for this study were developed on NeuroSolutions, a Windows-based neural software application. The optimum weights that were loaded into the networks were obtained using Genehunter, a Windows-based GA software application. Since the sample size used in this study was relatively small, the k-fold-cross validation method was used to evaluate the performance of the classification models. This technique has been described in detail and used extensively in numerous studies (Baker, Kornguth, Lo, Williford, & Floyd, 1995; Wu et al., 1997). By using this method all data sets are eventually used to both train and test the network.

The 154 data sets were randomly divided into k = 5 groups. The first group was set aside and the remaining (k-1) = 4 groups were used to train the classification models. These training samples were used to determine the best set of weights for the network, which allows the ANN to classify the input vectors with a satisfactory level of accuracy. The kth group was then used to test the ANN's classification ability. This process was repeated for all 5 groups. The steps followed in designing the networks are described below:

Step 1: Designing the Training ANN Model
(a) The networks were designed by inputting the characteristics of the Web usage behavior with respect to factors such as income (x_1), gender (x_2), etc., together with the output variable characterizing the Web usage behavior. The input data was standardized between the range (−1 to 1), so that large measure variables would not provide a greater influence on the network. The standardized data set was calculated as follows:

Table 4: Variable Correlation (n=154)

Variables	Reliability	1	2	3	4	5	6	7	8	9	10	11
						Correlations						
Income[a]	1.00	1.000										
Education[a]	1.00	0.292	1.000									
Web Experience	0.90	0.230	0.096	1.000								
Web Formal Training	0.61	0.162	0.090	0.553	1.000							
Web Self Training[a]	1.00	0.186	0.175	0.844	0.522	1.000						
Perceived Enjoyment	0.78	0.198	0.086	0.649	0.603	0.641	1.000					
Task Structure		-0.355	-0.107	-0.297	-0.136	-0.206	-0.204	1.000				
Perceived Usefulness	0.83	-0.023	0.073	0.359	0.268	0.270	0.212	-0.001	1.000			
Gender[a]	1.00	-0.312	-0.244	-0.170	-0.045	-0.121	-0.158	0.098	-0.197	1.000		
Work-related Web Sites	0.79	0.231	0.000	0.440	0.266	0.367	0.399	-0.298	0.183	-0.186	1.000	
Personal-related Web Sites	0.67	-0.231	0.000	-0.440	-0.266	-0.367	-0.399	0.298	-0.183	0.186	-1.000	1.000

[a] These variables were measured with a single item

The absolute values of correlation > .10 are significant at .05 or lower

$$S_n^m = \frac{2(X_n^m + X^{m\,min})}{(X^{m\,max} - X^{m\,min}) - 1}, \, m = 1,2,....9, n = 1,2,.....154$$

where,

X_n^m = Each data point in the corresponding row and column

$X^{m\,min}$ = minimum along the input columns

$X^{m\,max}$ = maximum along the input columns

(b)   In creating the hidden layer^2 the standardized inputs were multiplied by weights (which are created in step 2) leading to each hidden neuron. At each hidden neuron, the input weight products were summed and a sigmoid function was applied to adjust the sum back to the range {0 to 1}. Thus, for each hidden neuron column we have the following:

$$z_j = \text{sigmoid} \left(\sum_{i=1}^{m} x_i \, w_{ij}^{(1)} + w_{bias}^{(1)} \right)$$

where,

x_i = Standardized input data

$w_{ij}^{(1)}$ = Weights between input and hidden neurons

$w_{bias}^{(1)}$ = Bias term for the weights between input and hidden neurons

The neurons in the hidden layer are then multiplied by the weights leading to the output, where the softmax activation function was applied to produce the posterior probabilities. Thus the output neurons (y_k) were determined as follows:

$$y_k = \frac{1}{1 - \exp(-(\sum_{j=1}^{2} z_j \, w_{jk}^{(2)} + w_{bias}^{(2)}))}$$

where,

$w_{jk}^{(2)}$ = Weights between hidden neurons and output

$w_{bias}^{(2)}$ = Bias term for the weights between hidden neurons

Step 2: Determining the Optimum Weights Using GA
(a).   This study uses genetic algorithms to determine the optimum weights that would be used to test the ANNs. An initial population of 26

chromosomes representing possible solutions to a problem was randomly generated. As mentioned previously, a chromosome is equivalent to a set of weights. The chromosomes' potential as the optimum solution is determined by the mean squared error which was used as the fitness function.

(b) Based on these relative fitness values, individuals in the current population were selected for reproduction. Although the chromosomes are selected at random, the probability of selection is proportional to the chromosome fitness, i.e., the higher the fitness function value of the individual, the higher its chances of being chosen for the reproduction process. The selection strategy used in this study is called the *roulette wheel* selection, where a roulette wheel with slots (S) is sized according to the total fitness function and represented as,

$$S = \sum_{i=1}^{popsize} fitness(F_i)$$

where,

F$_i$ indicates the fitness of the value of the chromosome according to MSE.

Popsize =Number of individuals in the population

This selection process is based on spinning the wheel and with each spin a single chromosome is selected for a new population. In accordance with the theory of inheritance, the fittest chromosomes will be selected more than once, while the least fit will die.

(c) The selected parent individuals from the current generation were then recombined using a crossover operator to produce two new offspring, one of which moved into the next generation. The mates for the crossover were chosen randomly from the initial population with the restriction that no individual can crossover with itself. The crossover rate was set at P$_{CROS}$=0.9, i.e., there is a 90% probability that crossover will occur. Since the crossover process may sometimes lose some potentially useful information, mutation was introduced with a very small probability (P$_{MUT}$= 0.005). Following the crossover and mutation, the new population was ready for its next generation.

(d) The remainder of the evolution was basically cyclic repetitions of the steps given above until the system converged to the lowest average MSE (i.e., no improvement in the overall fitness of the population). This was reached before the 500th iteration of the genetic algorithm. This set of weights was then loaded into the ANN for the testing stage.

Step 3: Testing the ANN

To test the robustness of the predictive ANN models, the training and holdout data sets were applied to the networks. The confusion matrix shown in Table 5 presents the correct and incorrect classifications of the training and holdout samples. As can be observed in Panel (a), the ANNs classified the training sample with a true positive ratio of over 96%. This is not surprising, since the networks were built with the same data sets and thus an optimistic bias would be present. Of greater interest were the true positive ratios of the holdout sample (i.e., data sets that the network had not seen before). As can be observed in Panel (b), both neural network models had a classification accuracy of over 85%. To further compare the effectiveness of neural networks, its results were compared with those of a multiple discriminant Analysis (MDA) model, which had a true positive ratio of only 48%. Thus, both neural network models outperformed the statistical technique.

EVALUATING THE NETWORK'S PERFORMANCE

In the Web usage problem, the percentage of correctly classified observations may not necessarily be the most useful measure. An important goal of the classification models was to minimize the probability of misclassification, where misclassification was calculated in terms of type I and type II errors. A type I error is where *a high non-work-related Web user is incorrectly classified as a low non-work user*, and type II is where *a low non-work-related Web user is incorrectly classified as a high non-work user*. Based on the assumption that both types of errors were equally serious, an error rate was calculated, where the error rate is the ratio of the number of errors to the number of cases examined. As can be observed in Table 5, the ANN (SRN) had the lowest error rate of 0.08, indicating that it was a superior classifier in terms of misclassification than ANN (MLP) and MDA.

Since the classification of Web users is fraught with uncertainty, it is important to account for the risk inherent in such problems. Most previous studies in ANN classification have examined the issue of uncertainty in terms of symmetric or zero-one loss function, i.e., zero losses are assumed for taking the correct decisions, and misclassifications are given a unit loss. Although this symmetric function may be valid for some applications, in the current context it would result in a classifier with very little practical use. Since misclassifications may carry different penalties, and the goal is to minimize the overall loss or risk, this study used the asymmetric loss function to calculate the cost of the misclassification, i.e., zero cost is assigned when a

Table 5: Classification Accuracy of Classification Models

Panel (a): Training Sample

Classification Method	ANN (MLP)		ANN (SRN)		MDA	
	Actual Group Membership		Actual Group Membership		Actual Group Membership	
Predicted group	Group 1	Group 2	Group 1	Group 2	Group 1	Group 2
Group 1	309	6	314	2	155	35
Group 2	11	290	6	294	165	261
True-pos. ratio	96.56%	97.97%	98.13%	99.32%	48.44%	88.18%
Type 1 error	0.03		0.01		0.52	
Type 2 error	0.02		0.01		0.12	
Error rate	0.03		0.01		0.32	

k-1 fold cross validation method was used in this study, where k=5
n=616
Group 1= Low non-work usage (320)
Group 2 = High non-work usage (296)

Panel (b): Cross Validation (In Sample)

Classification Method	ANN (MLP)		ANN (SRN)		MDA	
	Actual Group Membership		Actual Group Membership		Actual Group Membership	
Predicted group	Group 1	Group 2	Group 1	Group 2	Group 1	Group 2
Group 1	70	11	73	6	49	38
Group 2	10	63	7	68	31	36
True-pos. ratio	87.50%	85.14%	91.25%	91.89%	61.25%	48.65%
Type 1 error	0.13		0.09		0.39	
Type 2 error	0.15		0.08		0.51	
Error rate	0.14		0.08		0.45	

n=154
Group 1= Low non-work usage (80)
Group 2 = High non-work usage (74)

Panel (c): Cross Validation (Out-of-Sample

Classification Method	ANN (MLP)		ANN (SRN)		MDA	
	Actual Group Membership		Actual Group Membership		Actual Group Membership	
Predicted group	Group 1	Group 2	Group 1	Group 2	Group 1	Group 2
Group 1	85	9	90	6	63	30
Group 2	16	53	11	56	38	32
True-pos. ratio	84.16%	85.48%	89.11%	90.32%	62.38%	51.61%
Type 1 error	0.16		0.11		0.38	
Type 2 error	0.15		0.10		0.48	
Error rate	0.15		0.10		0.42	

n=163
Group 1= Low non-work usage (101)
Group 2 = High non-work usage (62)

correct decision is made and different levels of costs are assigned for type 1 or type 2 misclassification errors. Since type 1 errors are considered the more serious error type, it is assumed that the cost of a type 1 error is 10, 20, 30, 40, 50 times as large as that of a type 2 error, which is assigned a value of 1.0. In reality the selection of the cost ratio depends upon the specific scenarios facing organizations. These cost ratios were combined with the posterior probability outputs of the ANN models to produce a loss matrix (Berardi & Zhang, 1999), which provide threshold values, which can help managers make minimum risk decisions. The expected loss of misclassification was calculated as follows:

$$\text{Expected Loss} = \pi_0 \cdot c_0 + \pi_1 \cdot c_1,$$

where,

π_0, π_1 = Posterior probability of high and low non-work users respectively

c_0, c_1 = Cost of misclassifying of high and low non-work users respectively

Table 6 reports the findings of the expected costs for the various misclassification cost ratios. As can be observed the ANN (SRN) classifier model dominates the other classification models with the lowest expected loss for the cost ratios. This implies that the ANN (SRN) model is the most cost-sensitive classifier.

Next, using these threshold values the cross-validation samples were reclassified. Reclassification is done by simply combining the posterior probabilities from the networks with a suitable matrix of loss coefficients, thus not requiring any network training (Bishop, 1995). As expected Table 7 reveals a decrease in type 1 errors as the relative cost of type 1 errors increases. Further, from the results presented in Tables 5 and 7, it can be observed that the misclassification rate of type 1 errors is lower for asymmetric cost function than it is for the symmetric cost function. This is to be expected since the goal under the symmetric cost function is to maximize the correct classification (Berardi & Zhang, 1999), while the goal of the asymmetric function is reduce the most costly error. Thus, by using the output of the ANNs and asymmetric cost functions, managers can make minimum risk decisions.

To further validate the results of this study, data was collected from four organizations in the United States, using the original survey instrument. The demographics are given in Table 1. The results of the out-of-population samples are shown in Table 5, Panel (c), and as can be observed the true positive ratio for the ANN (SRN) network was 89.11% and 90.32% for group 1 and group 2, respectively. In addition, the overall error rate of this classifier model was lower than the ANN (MLP) as well as MDA classifier. The out-

Table 6: Loss Matrix for the Classification Models

Misclassification Error	Cost Ratios				
Type 1: Type 2	*10:1*	*20:1*	*30:1*	*40:1*	*50:1*
Classifier Model					
ANN (MLP)	0.01	0.03	0.04	0.05	0.06
ANN (SRN)	0.01	0.02	0.03	0.03	0.04
MDA	0.22	0.43	0.65	0.87	1.08

Table 7: Reclassification of Holdout Samples Utilizing the Asymetric Loss Ratios—SRN Network

	In-Sample Misclassification			Out of Sample Misclassification		
Cost Ratios	Type 1 Error	Type 2 Error	Cost Ratios	Type 1 Error	Type 2 Error
10:1	53.85%	46.15%	10:1	64.71%	35.29%
	7	6		11	6
20:1	53.85%	46.15%	20:1	58.82%	41.18%
	7	6		10	7
30:1	38.46%	61.54%	30:1	35.29%	64.71%
	5	8		6	11
40:1	30.77%	69.23%	40:1	23.53%	76.47%
	4	9		4	13
50:1	23.08%	92.31%	50:1	11.76%	88.24%
	3	12		2	15

of-population data was reclassified using the asymmetric cost ratios. As with the in-sample cross-validation data set, the ANN (SRN) classifier decreased type 1 errors as the relative cost of the type 2 errors increased (see Table 7). Based on these observations, the external validity of the ANN classifier could be considered strong.

CONCLUSIONS

Anecdotal evidence indicates that as Web usage in organizations grows, the level of employee non-work usage is rising as well. Such usage has serious repercussions, which include loss of productivity, clogged networks and potential civil and criminal liability, all which could amount to an enormous cost to the organization. To date, most organizations have attempted to combat the problem by incorporating an acceptable usage policy, which research has shown to be largely ineffective. Research also indicates that the modification of user behavior through cognitive training and socialization is necessary in developing an effective Internet security strategy.

This study proposes the use of AI-based behavior models, in terms of which can profile employees' Web usage behavior a priori. Such classification models can prove to be immensely useful to managers in the development of Internet security strategies. The data used to develop the classifiers were collected through a survey instrument. The classification performance of two neural network topologies, namely, ANN (MLP) and ANN (SRN), and traditional statistical technique MDA was compared using symmetric and asymmetric loss functions. The overall results show that the classification performance of the neural network models was far superior to the MDA model. Specifically, however, the results show that the ANN (SRN) model outperformed the ANN (MLP) model for all data sets. ANN (SRN)'s superior classification performance could be attributed to the features of context nodes and feedback loop, which make it more suitable for behavior-based AI systems. In addition a loss matrix was created to consider uncertainty, which is typically inherent in such problems. The results indicate that the ANN (SRN) classifier produced lower threshold values than the ANN (MLP) and MDA models, which implies that the ANN(SRN) model is the more risk-averse classifier amongst the models examined in this study. The results reveal that by using these threshold values, the more costly misclassification error (type 1) can be reduced. Further, the external validity of the models was checked with an out-of-population data set. The results indicate that the models were generalizable to various organizations.

A major limitation of this study is the use of a dichotomous classification of Web users. Future studies may reveal that Web users can be categorized by other classifications. Also not all possible variables were considered in developing the classification models. For instance variables such as management and organizational support could be considered. Future research will have to examine what these variables are and formally incorporate them into the models. Moreover, this study only compared the ANN topologies, while holding all other parameters constant, for instance, the sample sizes of the data sets were limited, and the various proportions between low and high non-work usage were not considered.

From an IS research perspective this study introduces ANN as an alternate tool to the more traditional statistical techniques. The methodology presented in this study can be applied to wide-ranging problems such as end-user classification and prediction of information system utilization, amongst others. It could also be utilized as an analysis tool for contingency models, such as the information-processing framework.

Users of these classification models may be cautious of such aids, since it appears to take decision making out of their hands. However, by having the ability to profile the various types of Web users, managers can specifically design their Internet security strategies more effectively. The implementation of such strategies, for example, through socialization and cognitive training may reduce the occurrence of non-work usage behavior. These classifier models can also complement organizations' current strategies by providing managers with insights into the characteristics of the Web users. This would aid the manager in approaching employees about the subject of Web usage in a more informed manner.

ENDNOTE

[1] A later version of this chapter will appear in *Journal of Management Information Systems*.

[2] After extensive experimentation a two hidden neuron were found to be the most suitable network structure.

REFERENCES

Adams, D. A., Nelson, R. R. and Todd, P. A. (1992). Perceived usefulness, ease of use and usage of information technology: A replication. *MIS Quarterly*, 16, 227-247.

Ajzen, I. and Fishbein, M. (1980). *Understanding Attitudes and Predicting Behavior*. Englewood Cliffs, NJ: Prentice-Hall.

Amoroso, D. L. and Cheney, P. H. (1991). Testing a causal model of end-user application effectiveness. *Journal of Management Information Systems*, 8(1), 63-89.

Anandarajan, M., Simmers, C. and Igbaria, M. (2000). An exploratory investigation of the antecedents and impact of Internet usage: An individual perspective. *Behaviour & Information Technology*, 19(1), 69-85.

Arbib, M. A. and House, D. H. (1987). Depth and detours: an essay on visually guided behavior. In Arbib, M. A. and Hanson, A. R. (Eds.), *Vision, Brain and Cooperative Computation*, 129-163. Cambridge, MA: The MIT Press/Bradford Books.

Archer, N. and Wang, S. (1993). Application of the back propagation neural network algorithm with monotonicity constraints for two-group classification problems. *Decision Sciences*, 24(1), 60-75.

Baeck, T. and Schwefel, H. P. (1993). An overview of evolutionary algorithms for parameter optimization. *Evolutionary Computation*, 1(1), 1-23.

Baker, J. A., Kornguth, P. J., Lo, J. Y., Willliford, M. E. and Floyd, C. E. (1995). Breast cancer: Prediction with artificial neural network based on BI-RADS standardized lexicon. *Journal of Radiology*, 196, 817-822.

Berardi, V. L. and Zhang, G. P. (1999). The effect of misclassification cost on neural network classifiers. *Decision Sciences*, 30(3), 659-682.

Bishop, C. M. (1995). *Neural Networks for Pattern Recognition*. New York: Oxford University Press Inc.

Changeux, J. P. (1986). *Neuonal Man: The Biology of Mind*. Oxford, UK: Oxford University Press.

Cronin, M. (1995). *Doing More Business on the Internet*. Van Nostrand Reinhold: ITP Inc.

Cronin, M. J. (1996). *The Internet as a Competitive Business Resource*. Boston: Harvard Business School Press.

Curry, B. and Morgan, P. (1997). Neural networks: A need for caution. *Omega*, 25, 123-33.

Daly, E. M., Lancee, W. J. and Polivy, J. (1983). A conical model for the taxonomy of emotional experience. *Journal of Personality and Social Psychology*, 45(2), 443-457.

Davis, F. D. (1989). Perceived usefulness, perceived ease of use and user acceptance of information technology. *MIS Quarterly*, 13, 983-1003.

Davis, F. D. (1992). Extrinsic and intrinsic motivation to use computers in the workplace. *Journal of Applied Social Psychology*, 22, 1111-1132.

Davis, F. D., Bagozzi, R. P. and Warshaw, P. R. (1989). User acceptance of computer technology: A comparison of two theoretical models. *Management Science*, 35, 982-1003.

DeLone, W. H. (1988). Determinants of success for computer usage in small business. *MIS Quarterly*, 12(1), 51-61.

Elman, J. L. (1990). Finding structure in time. *Cognitive Science*, 14, 179-211.

Fausett, L. (1994). *Fundamentals of Neural Networks*. Englewood Cliffs, NJ: Prentice Hall.

Finke, M. and Muller, K. R. (1994). *Estimating A-Posteriori Probabilities Using Stochastic Network Models*. Hillsdale, NJ: Lawrence Erlbaum Associates.

Gefen, D. and Straub, D. W. (1997). Gender differences in the perception and use of e-mail: An extension to the technology acceptance model. *MIS Quarterly*, 21(4), 389-400.

Harrison, A. W., Rainer, R. K. and Houcwarter, G. (1997). Gender differences in computing activities. *Journal of Social Behavior and Personality*, 12(4), 849-868.

Igbaria, M. (1993). User acceptance of microcomputer technology: An empirical test. *International Journal of Management Science*, 21(1), 73-90.

Igbaria, M. (1995). Testing the determinants of microcomputer usage via a structural equation model. *Journal of Management Information Systems*, 11(4), 87-105.

Igbaria, M., Pavri, F. and Huff, S. (1989). Microcomputer application: An empirical look at usage. *Information and Management*, 16(4), 187-196.

Kleinmuntz, B. (1990). Why we still use our heads instead of formulas: Towards an integrated approach. *Psychological Bulletin*, 107, 296-310.

LaPlante, A. (1997). Start small, think infinite. *Computerworld*, 24-30.

Lee, D. S. (1986). Usage pattern and sources of assistance to personal computer users. *MIS Quarterly*, 10(4), 313-325.

Lenard, M., Alam, P. and Madey, G. (1995). The applications of neural networks and a qualitative response model to the auditors going concern uncertainty decision. *Decision Sciences*, 26(2), 209-227.

Malone, T. W. (1981). Toward a theory of intrinsically motivating instruction. *Cognitive Science*, 4, 333-369.

McBride, P. (2000). Develop secure Internet practices. *Internet Security Advisor*, 18-25.

McCullagh, P. and Nelder, J. A. (1989). *Generalized Linear Models* (2nd ed.). London: Chapman & Hall.

McWilliams, G. and Stepanek, M. (1998). Taming the info monster. *Business Week*, June 22, 170-172.

Miller, T. R. and Dodge, H. R. (1979). Ratings of professional journals by teachers of management. *Improving College and University Teaching*, 27(3), 102-103.

Needle, D. (1999). Surprise! e-Commerce will drive net growth. *PC World*.

Nelson, R. and Cheney, P. (1987). Training end-users: An exploratory study. *MIS Quarterly*, 11(4), 547-559.

Nunnally, J. C. (1978). *Psychometric Theory* (2nd ed.). New York, NY: McGraw-Hill.

Pfeifer, R. and Verschure, P. (1992). Distributed adaptive control: A paradigm for designing autonomous agents. Paper presented at the *Proceedings of the First European Conference on Artificial Life*, Cambridge, MA.

Ray, T. (1992). *An Approach to the Synthesis of Life*.

Raymond, L. (1988). The impact of computer training on the attitudes and usage behavior of small business managers. *Journal of Small Business Management*, 26(3), 8-13.

Robey, D. (1979). User attitudes and management information systems use. *Academy of Management Journal*, 22, 527-538.

Scandura, T. A. and Lankau, M. J. (1997). Relationships of gender, family responsibility and flexible work hours to organizational commitment and job satisfaction. *Journal of Organizational Behavior*, 18(4), 377-391.

Simard, P. Y., Ottaway, M. B. and Ballard, D. H. (1989). *Fixed Point Analysis for Recurrent Networks*. San Mateo, CA: Morgan Kaufmann.

Smithers, T. (1992). *Taking Eliminative Materialism Seriously: A Methodology for Autonomous Systems Research*. Cambridge, MA: MIT Press/ Bradford Books.

Steels, L. (1990). *Exploring Analogical Representations*. Cambridge, MA: The MIT Press/Bradford Books.

Straub, D., Limayem, M. and Karahanna, E. E. (1995). Measuring system usage: Implications for IS theory testing. *Management Science*, 41(8), 1328-1342.

Thompson, R. L., Higgins, C. A. and Howell, J. M. (1994). Influence of experience on personal computer utilization: Testing a conceptual model. *JMIS*, 11(1), 167-187.

Tushman, M. L. and Nadler, D. A. (1978). Information processing as an integrating concept in organizational design. *Academy of Management Review*, 3(4), 613-624.

Umanath, N. S. and Kim, K. K. (1992). Task-structure relationship of information systems development subunit: A congruence perspective. *Decision Sciences*, 23(4), 819-838.

Webster, J. (1989). *Playfulness and Computers at Work*. Unpublished doctoral dissertation, New York University, New York.

Williams, S. W., Ogletree, S. M., Wodburne, W. and Rafeld, P. (1994). Gender roles, computer attitudes and dyadic computer interaction: Performance in college students. *Sex Roles: A Journal of Research*, 29(7-8), 515-526.

Wong, B. K., Bodnovich, T. A. E. and Selvi, Y. (1995). A bibliography of neural networks application research: 1988-1994. *Expert Systems*, 12, 253-61.

Wu, W., Massart, D. L. and Jong, S. D. (1997). Kernel-PCA algorithms for wide data Part II: Fast cross-validation and application in classification of NIR data. *Chemometrics and Intelligent Laboratory Systems*, 37(2), 271-280.

Yasin, R. (1999). Web slackers put on notice. *Internet Week*.

Chapter XII

Managing Large Modules— E-mail or Web Sites?

Elayne Coakes
University of Westminster, UK

Dianne Willis
Leeds Metropolitan University, UK

INTRODUCTION

This paper address issues concerning the suitability of particular media as mass communication tools in an UK higher education setting. It looks firstly at the use of e-mail as a communication method whilst managing two large modules. The paper then goes on to examine the use of a Web site to provide a mass communication method more suited to the needs of both the staff and the students.

A variety of issues are examined:
* the applicability of e-mail as a communication medium,
* the applicability of Web pages as a communication medium,
* the types of information which are normally communicated,
* the certainty with which staff can utilize the technology to update students on recent developments,
* the ease of accessibility of the communication medium, and
* the student's responses to the communication experience.

An in-depth case study will look at how two large modules are managed through the use of Web Sites on the Internet, discussing the reasons why such a tactic was embarked upon, the pros and cons of using such technology and tips for others wishing to adopt a similar approach. For the purposes of this paper, distance learning will not be considered as the university in question has no plans to follow or adopt such an approach for these modules.

BACKGROUND TO THE STUDY

The University of Westminster is a large modern university operating on four sites across the centre of London and West London. It was Britain's first polytechnic, established in 1838 in Regent Street, and it still uses these original buildings for lectures and seminars. It became a university in 1992 and is now recognized in the *Financial Times* annual survey as the top English "new" university.

The university has a population of both full-time and part-time students drawn from the local surrounding areas but also has a large population of international students. Many of these students (over 33%) are studying post-graduate or post-experience/professional updating courses

The Westminster Business School operates out of the Marylebone campus, which is situated close to Regents Park and is thus a very popular location for students to attend courses, as not only is it in the centre of London but is also easily accessible by public transport.

COMMUNICATION MEDIA

This section discusses the theoretical background to communication studies looking at "fitness for purpose" for each of the media.

To begin with, a brief overview of the communication process and its constituents would be useful. A basic theoretical model of the communication process states that messages are "sent" and "received," confirmation of receipt and interpretation of the message indicates that it is a two-way communication process (Warner, 1996). The efficiency of this process is subject to a variety of issues such as:

- Effectiveness–How do we measure this when using e-mail or a Web site?
- Simultaneous reception of information by recipients–The information is available simultaneously, but how do we measure if students have accessed it?
- Acknowledgement of receipt–With e-mail a receipt can be provided, but how is this addressed using a Web site?

- Speed–How quickly does the information reach the recipients?
- Cost of the process–Is it cost effective?

All of these factors will be considered in the case study section of the paper.

It can be said that one of the major benefits of the growth in the use of the Internet has been the ability to communicate using e-mail as a medium. E-mail is still the most regularly used aspect of the Internet and the level of usage is growing. E-mail has become a common mode of communication for many people, though exceptions must be made for those who do not have easy and regular access to the technology required. Adequate access to the technology is assumed in this paper. However, communications theorists argue there are problems with the use of e-mail as the sole communication medium. Culnan and Markus (1987) suggested that a lack of face-to-face communication changes the intra- and interpersonal variables because of a lack of social context. Sproull and Kiesler (1986) argued that e-mail was devoid of social cues and this would seriously affect communication patterns. E-mail provides neither audible nor visible cues to the communication process and as such can be seen as a relatively impoverished communication style. Recent developments, (Bavelas et al., 1999) in the form of "emoticons," typewritten symbols that imitate facial expressions, are helping to bring a visual dimension to e-mail which was not previously there, for example: J, [type : followed by)], L, [type : followed by ( ]; however, the effectiveness of these "emoticons" is difficult to measure. Hirscheim (1985) argued that one of the major benefits of using e-mail is to support communication between people who are geographically distant, though in this instance, the geographical distance is not great. The lack of richness of the communication process leads us to the initial premise that although widely utilized, there are significant problems with the use of e-mail as the sole communication medium.

There are further problems with an e-mail system in that it is not always possible to ensure that the recipient has received and read the message in an appropriate time frame. This may be caused by a variety of problems, both technical and human. These issues are discussed in more detail and possible solutions posited in Willis and Coakes (2000).

Further analysis of the current situation indicates that e-mail lacks the collaborative dimension that is needed in today's world. In an academic setting, the ability to discuss matters in "real tim" rather than waiting for a reply from a tutor via an e-mail system may be of great importance. There are some e-mail systems which allow simultaneous transmission on split screens but these do not allow full collaboration as there is still a gap between reading the message and composing the reply (Marvin, 1999).

IS E-MAIL A SUITABLE MASS COMMUNICATION MEDIUM?

A traditional view of the mass communication process would have the university providing content and it passing to the students via the e-mail medium as shown in Figure 1.

This model allows no interaction. We posit that what is required in the modern communication environment is a more interactive model which allows students to influence the content, as well as be recipients of information. In our paper, the aim of mass communication is to provide information simultaneously to a large number of students. We have to seriously question whether e-mail is the correct option given the problems outlined above.

Further analysis leads us to the model outlined as Figure 2 which, offering limited interaction, we feel is likely to be more effective and more satisfactory than the traditional model outlined above.

This model gives students the option of simply gaining information via the medium, or engaging and interacting with it by influencing the content. From the preceding arguments, it is doubtful that e-mail can fulfil the role of the appropriate medium in the new model so an alternative has to be found.

The ability to interact is an aspect that has acquired great importance in the communication process and a method must be found which does not have the weaknesses of e-mail. What is required is a medium that can have input from both staff and students and which can change rapidly to respond to these needs. As the staff and students are already familiar with e-mail and the Internet, a move to a more directly Web-based approach using a specially designed Web site is likely to provide a viable solution. This is supported by the fact that students have better access to Web Sites and are more used to

Figure 1: A Traditional Mass Communication Model

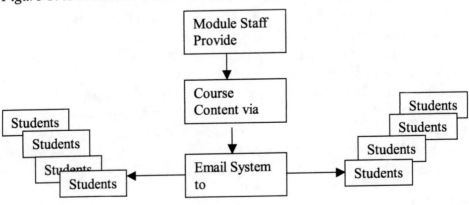

Figure 2: An Interactive Mass Communications Model

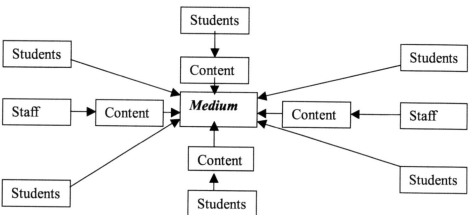

using this medium now than in the past. Many organizations limit the size of e-mails which can be sent across the network, which can cause real problems when disseminating large amounts of information. The authors feel the use of a Web site accessible from any location and requiring only a browser offers a realistic alternative.

PROPOSED MODEL—WEB SITE DESIGN AND DEVELOPMENT ISSUES

Much of the work on Web site design has been done with businesses as the main focus. However, this does not mean to say that these principles are not useful when designing and creating a Web site for an education module. As the case study shows, the availability and accessibility of the information on the Web site can be a valuable tool in promoting the module with other students.

Kalakota and Whinston (1997) point out that global hypertext publishing promotes simplicity in the way in which online information is accessed and received by individuals. Everything is in the same format and this means that navigation between sites brings up information which is readily understandable and easy to interpret. This deals with the requirement that students will get the same information wherever they access the site, an important consideration from the point of view of the usability of the site and the efficiency of the communication process.

Avgerou and Cornford (1998) consider a socio-technical approach to information systems development. The basic principle of this approach is to improve the way people communicate with each other and do their jobs.

Applied to our current scenario, it is perhaps not so easy to define the 'job' of a student, but the principle of an information system revolving around the stakeholders and relying on technology to facilitate the process is pertinent to our analysis. The main concern for the staff developing the Web site is to ensure that the anticipated benefits of the new communication method come to fruition.

Good site design is also an important feature and one of the earliest examples of a Web design methodology was developed by John December (www.december.com). If a Web site is to be used as the medium, it needs to adhere to a series of principles. It is important not to merely duplicate practices intended for paper and other media-there is the potential for a Web site to do more and this potential should be realized. December's methodology has implications for communicators that can be applied to an individual site as well as the Web as a whole:

1. *Planning is the process of defining and gathering information about the Web site's audience, purpose, objectives and policies for information and development of use.* In our case this means looking at what information is needed on the site-can all the information be supplied via the Web site, or will developments be to some extent student-driven, meaning that the site is continuously changing? Consideration of what was happening with the module Web Sites would indicate evolution from use.

2. *Analysis involves evaluating information consistency and correctness as well as checking the technical makeup of the site.* Again, from the case study it can be seen that technical problems regarding the format of the information needed to be solved early on in the process to enable access problems to be solved.

3. *Design is the process of creating a map of relationships among pages of the site and the look and feel of individual pages.* Figures 4 and 5 give the basic navigational layout of the two Web pages-In the case where there is more engagement by students, the site is more complex.

4. *Implementation*-The process of creating files. The information contained on the Web pages is likely to be redeveloped using the DreamWeaver software to try to minimize problems of access.

5. *Promotion*-The site can be used as a promotional vehicle to the extent that students who are interested in the module can look at its shape and feel without actually studying the module.

6. *Innovation*-This is a process of continually evolving the site to meet user needs. There is no "final state." Requirements will change on a frequent basis and these requirements must be met. Value can be added to the site by links to other Web Sites of interest to the students.

In this case, the staff developing the Web site had little formal training on Web site design and development. The use of the FrontPage software was found to be very helpful as the package allows the development of good design features such as buttons and frames without in depth knowledge of the background programming involved. However, the drawback of this approach is that the developers do not fully understand the process involved in designing a good site and need to rely on feedback from the stakeholders as to whether or not the design conforms to requirements. This iterative approach using prototyping is a well documented method and has proved to be very useful where time is short and there is good user participation in the process.

This is borne out by the fact that the students involved in the Strategies for Information Management module have had more influence on the design of their module Web site than those involved in the Business Information Systems module, where user participation has not been so high. Feedback was sought in the following areas:

* Was all relevant information available?
* Was site navigation easy?
* Was access to any part of the site problematic?
* Was the information always up-to-date?
* How easy was it to influence development of the Web site?

Questions relating to the fact that the site was produced in English, which was not the first language of all of the students, were not explored in depth. This is an area which can usefully be explored in a future study. No feedback was received relating to cultural concerns, and English (or perhaps more accurately, American English) is recognized as the principal language of the Internet and students studying a course at a UK university, delivered in English, could reasonably expect to be able to communicate in this language. The development of better and more efficient translation packages would give scope for accessing information in a variety of languages, but this is something for the future rather than the present.

In terms of the ability to interact, asking students to access a Web site is not necessarily more effective than the simple use of e-mail–it is the add-ons of lecture notes, seminar notes and feedback which will make the medium more successful.

This is discussed in more detail in the pros and cons section of the case study. Bringing what we have learned from the methodology of Web site design to our earlier model, it becomes obvious that the final communication model that needs to be adopted is one which uses a combination of a Web site and e-mail systems to allow maximum access as detailed in Figure 3.

Figure 3: Final Mass Communication Model for Staff and Students

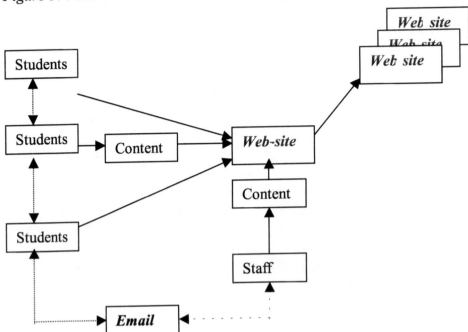

Kling (1996) looked at the benefits of electronic newsgroups, bulletin boards, conferences and distribution lists and the ways in which these change the communication model. What kind of social relations develop via computer networks? Will the resulting communication help or hinder the dissemination of information needed by the students in the case study? There is some evidence to suggest that electronic communities help to foster a sense of community amongst geographically isolated people, and this would be of obvious benefit to the groups being studied as they are unable to meet physically, but may wish to feel part of a group (Kling, 1996). Therefore, it can be seen that in order to provide a sense of community for the large numbers involved in the case study, some communication medium other than the Web site needs to be added to foster a sense of group identity. The more involved group in the case study is working towards this conclusion from their own experience.

THE CASE STUDY

Module 1-Business Information Systems

The first module is actually not just large, but is officially classified by the university as "mega." It takes in over 700 students across the two semesters. Students are not evenly spread across the two semesters as more than 400 attend the module in the first semester. This module—An Introduction to Business Information Systems 1—is compulsory for all business school students to take in their first year; this involves students from eight full-time courses. In addition, it is compulsory for students taking a number of other degree courses across the other London campuses, plus students taking a degree course at another central London university attend this and other business modules. To complicate the module further, in the first semester, a number of study abroad students also undertake the module; these students come from a number of countries including a large cohort from Japan, a number from the US, and others from Europe under various exchange schemes. There is also a cohort of evening part-time students taking the module. Each year a number of additional courses outside the business school also choose to take up the module, so the size is still growing (two additional courses come onstream in the academic year 2000/2001).

All this provides a very diverse student population, many of whom are not located on the Marylebone campus for their degrees or are in full-time work. The major issue in running this module thus becomes "How do you communicate with students?" bearing in mind the issues over "home" location for many students and also country of origin, as many of the full-time "normal" students are international in origin as are the study abroad students.

Communication of the same message, simultaneously, clearly, unambiguously, to all students and staff is a major issue for this module. Due to the size of the module it has proved impossible to gather all students together in one lecture theatre at the same time, so repeat lectures are held and students never meet as one complete cohort. In addition, the module is taught by a large team, comprising a mixture of full-time staff and part-time visiting lecturers, who attend the university often only when they are teaching.

Management of the module was taken on board by one of the authors some 3 years ago before it became the size it now is. It was still very large but at that time the Westminster Business School had not completed its revalidation of the undergraduate program that made the module compulsory for all undergraduates attending the school to take the module. On completion of the revalidation, the complexity of the situation became immediately apparent and discussions were held on how to communicate effectively with the students. First ideas included a module notice board, but there was no obvious physical site for this considering the split sites over which the module operated. The lectures were held on one campus (which had the largest lecture theatre) but the students were largely not located on that campus; in addition, seminars and computer laboratory workshops were held on another site. (The

Regent Street campus has two locations for seminar rooms.) Staff teaching on the module were not necessarily located at the same campus site as the lecture theatre or seminar rooms.

Failing a physical notice board it became apparent that a virtual notice board was required and this has now developed into a full module management site.

Module Web Site

In Figure 4 we show a navigation map of the module—each year this is modified according to student comments as to what they find they need and was missing, or what they found hard to locate, etc. This is how it currently stands but it may be different next year! As this module is for first-year undergraduates, the navigation is kept fairly simple and the site is not complex but is intended to give the necessary basic information without the need for paper copies being provided by staff of anything other than the most initial module details, especially including the Web site address! In the first lecture, an abbreviated module description is handed out with a copy of workshop materials; all other materials from then on, including assessments, are provided through the module Web site. Using the Web site successfully becomes part of the teaching and learning aims of the module which has "being able to use the Internet and Internet databases" as one of its learning outcomes.

The module therefore holds the virtual equivalent of a module handbook with all the necessary details for students and staff of how the module runs. It holds:

- The module topics that will be covered in the lectures, seminars and computer workshops.
- The module learning outcomes.
- The lecture schedule, including who will be taking the lecture and what the background reading from each of the recommended module text books is for each lecture, plus the different times and locations of lectures. This enables students (exceptionally) who have missed their scheduled lecture to attend at another time.
- The lecture outlines, usually provided in the form of PowerPoint slides (translated into FrontPage), are supplied after the lecture has taken place.
- A schedule of seminars and workshops for students, including a list of which tutors will be taking what classes, when. Students are provided, in the business school, with a personalized timetable of their activities so class lists on the Web are not now provided normally, although they have been in the past.

Figure 4: Site Navigation Map for Business Information Systems

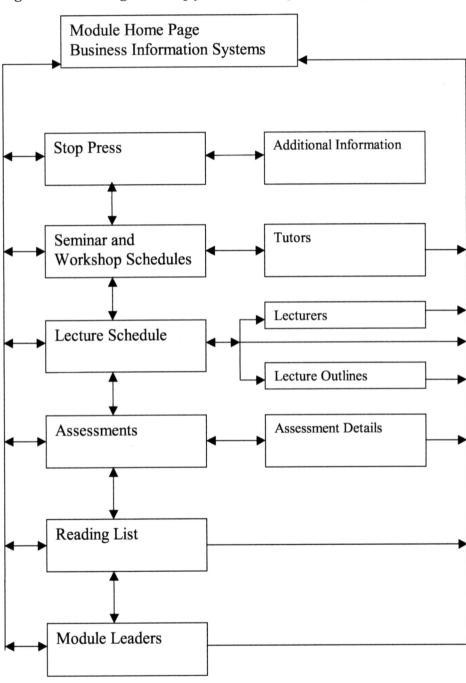

- A schedule and outline of what assessments are to be undertaken and when, what the pass criteria are and what has to be completed in order to pass the module.
- Assessment details as required, e.g., essay titles and instructions, examples of multiple-choice questions, etc.
- A full reading list, which includes links to other university Web Sites which have subject matter of interest, such as links to software training programs on the Web, and also links to commercial Web Sites of interest to the students undertaking this module.
- Details of the module leaders' and tutors' location and preferred method of communication, also when they are available in their office for personal visits, as well as hotlinks to their e-mail addresses.
- Finally, the Web site contains a "Stop Press" page—this is used to communicate urgent matters to students, such as changes in office hours, when and where they can collect their assessment results, lecture cancellations or changes, etc.

Module 2-Strategies for Information Management module

This is a large postgraduate module that is compulsory for students on two master's programs and available for students on other masters programs as an option. Typically only a small number of students take it as an option, but they can come from any of the university's four campuses. It runs for both full-time and part-time students. Numbers are normally around 80 plus and increasing each year. Again many students are international.

This Web site has again been used as a method of ensuring that communication is kept consistent and constantly available, but in addition it has been used to provide additional teaching materials around and between formal lectures and seminars. Thus articles and Web site links have been added on a regular basis, items of interest from lecturers' reading have been added, and seminar materials have been collated on particular discussion topics and posted. The site has also been used to make available to students generic comments (after the event!) on how they performed in formative assessments and on how the end of module exam will be marked—again generically, with comments such as: ...70+ would expect mention of all points or equivalent and deals with all tasks and questions, etc.

Students on this module are more assertive about what they want from a Web site and have been instrumental in suggesting changes and additions to content and layout. A navigation map is shown in Figure 5. As can be seen the site is more complex and has more layers and information available, whilst still supplying all the basic information as in the undergraduate module. Students would prefer that

Figure 5: Site Navigation Map

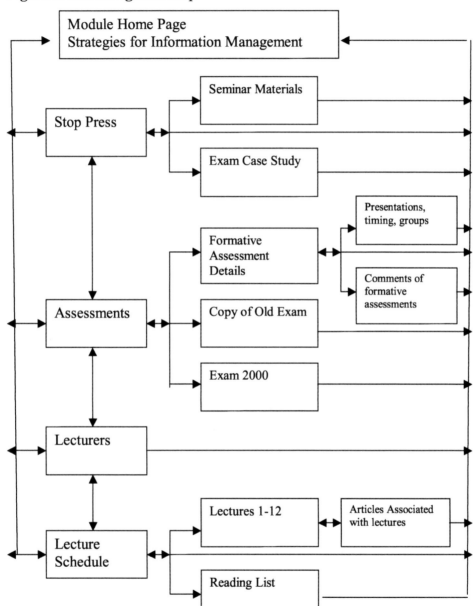

lecture notes are posted in advance of lectures, but so far this has not been done but is still under consideration as a possible enhancement of service.

PROS AND CONS OF USING A WEB SITE FOR DISSEMINATING INFORMATION

During the course of the study, one problem that became apparent was that e-mail was not always being accessed quickly enough and therefore the communication process was breaking down. This was a strong driver in the move towards providing a Web site alternative. If the modules were to be adequately managed, providing the same educational experience for all students reliance could not be placed in a communication medium which was patently not working effectively.

The Web Sites have been made available on the Internet rather than the university intranet as the diverse population of students means that access to the intranet is more involved. This is perhaps a cultural issue in that using the Internet enables students to access the information whatever their location, and we have already seen that the course has a multicultural aspect. Intranet access is freely available on university premises but requires a password from outside the university due to the use of firewalls and security measures. It is staff's perception on these modules that some students will not have easy access to the sites, which is essential for them to fulfil their purpose.

The major pro in the use of this type of communication is the secure knowledge that you have done your best to make all the necessary information available to all the stakeholders—staff and students—in one place that can be accessed by all. It makes it much harder for students to claim "but x told me something else" as all students are automatically referred to the Web site when querying something. In addition, having the information provided in written form, rather than verbal, attempts to provide some security, in that, for those students for whom English is not their first language, consistency of interpretation of instructions is provided. The issue of closure and understanding that what has been achieved is complete and unambiguous is discussed in Coakes and Willis (2000) and also the potentialities for misinterpretation, misunderstanding and misinformation through the written word in Willis and Coakes (2000), where we also discuss the often slapdash and haphazard way that e-mails are written. Spell-checking is not always performed; proof-reading is less critical; text is not "polished"; part-sentences are utilized; etc. It is often treated as an extension of speech and thus less "formal" than paper-based memos etc. Responses to communications are "dashed off" without due care, or at least the care required of a written, paper-based reply, which a Web site environment can provide. A particular issue with using only e-mail as a means of communication is the lack of guarantee of delivery. Not just physical delivery through the technology, but also a guarantee that the e-mail has been accessed and actioned by the recipient. As an experiment a number of e-mails with read receipts were sent over a period of months to a selected population of IT-oriented students. The read receipts were often returned up to 6 weeks after the e-mail was sent!

Other pros involved in using a Web site are the way the Web site actually develops interactively with the student comments; it is enhanced with new references, updates to materials, and answers to questions raised in seminars and through student e-mails. This interactive aspect is considered by students to be an important point in the Web sites' favour, in particular as it shows that lecturers are listening to them and are involved in the teaching of the modules. All staff also access this material and thus can ensure that they all talk with "one voice" in relation to queries and also ensures that they have all the vital module information readily available in good time for preparation of seminars and are kept informed of what has been covered in lectures, etc. The Web Sites are also available to potential and forthcoming students as a "taster" of what will be coming and are often accessed in advance of taking the module, as students choose their options or want to know what they can expect for the next semester or academic year.

Putting answers to student queries on the Web sites saves, in the end, lecturer time. It can also be shown that using such Web sites 'save staff time' in other ways. For instance, by ensuring that all essential information, such as assessment details are on the site, duplicate copies do not have to be provided in office hours to students who have lost their originals; this also reduces student stress as they know they always have access to vital details even should they lose the originals.

Another saving in staff time has been provided through posting a set of generic comments as feedback on formative assessments on the postgraduate module. Students can compare their work against the comments and see where they may have fallen short without talking to lecturers. Students have valued this feedback and have successfully used it to enhance their exam performance.

The use of a Web site also provides a learning experience for students in Web navigation and the utilization of essential 21st century skills such as file downloading.

It was originally suggested that provision of Web Sites for modules would save the university money on printing costs. It is doubtful whether a Web site can be justified by this. Certainly, for students using the Marylebone

Road campus, all printing in the computer labs is free of charge, and all students taking this module will use these labs or have access to them during the course of these modules. Typically, students will provide themselves with hard copies of all materials rather than relying on virtual copies for reference. It does save staff time, however, as shown above, during office hours, but this may be balanced out by the cons shown below.

The cons are threefold: firstly the time involved in developing and managing the site can be considerable, especially at the beginning of a semester, and is a constant drain, as the site has to be updated regularly; secondly, students cannot be forced to use to the Web site, although we can make it very difficult for them if they don't; and thirdly, the technology! The technology used at present is FrontPage 2000 on standard PCs, that, as users of this software package will be aware, has a number of idiosyncrasies which can make life frustrating at times. In order to make life as easy as possible, ftp is used to transfer files from the PC on which they are created to the host file server rather than the software "publish" routine.

Lessons for organizations who wish to use Web Sites for communication with staff can also be learnt from this experience with students. Firstly, use of a Web site is always optional and cannot always been relied upon to replace hard-copy output. Many staff members will be reluctant to use the new technology and may take some time to adjust. Secondly, if used for such communications as newsletters, the take-up and reading is likely to be lower, at least initially, than with traditional output. Lastly, the time cost of maintaining such communication methods must not be underestimated. There is an expectation that Web Sites will be updated frequently—far more often than papercopy—and this can lead to a considerable burden on the person who is responsible for such updates. Many of the other comments on accessibility, etc. made above can also be generalized to other organizations, as can the hints and tips below.

HINTS AND TIPS

- Plan what you need to put on and ensure that you always have it available in word-processed form on a floppy disk or similar medium, as well on the Web site. You are often required to provide this type of information to various parts of the university at short notice, and printing from Web Sites can be problematical.
- Test the printing—you will never be sure that it will print correctly from all users' machines, but if you can get it printing correctly in the student labs you have solved half the problem.

- Don't attach Word or PowerPoint files as a norm—this does save formatting but many PCs cannot access PowerPoint slides in particular, and many net browsers do not permit users to access Word files, especially in commercial premises, due to issues over viruses.
- Experiment with the easiest way for you to update Web Sites. If you work at home on these types of updates, you will probably find that using simple ftp transfer methods is best.
- Liaise with your university technicians to ensure that your Web site has all the correct access codes for what you want to do with it.
- If you provide links to external Web Sites ensure that you obtain their permission to do so, as otherwise you could be in breach of copyright laws.

PLANS FOR FUTURE DEVELOPMENT

As discussed earlier, these Web Sites are not static. We have talked about the need for interactivity and this is a factor for future development. Issues such as speed of response and download time are important considerations if moving towards a multimedia approach, and this may negate some of the positives of the change to a Web-based solution.

Students have been, generally, enthusiastic about using the Web Sites and suggested to other members of staff running modules in the business school that they might provide a useful model. In fact, given the positive experience of the students at Westminster University, it is intended to apply the Web site approach to the E-Commerce modules at Leeds Metropolitan University for the coming year. Although these modules do not involve such large numbers, (approximately 120 students per module), the principles of more efficient communication are applicable whatever the numbers involved. At Westminster University, these are not the only Web Sites in existence in the business school (some course sites, for instance, predate them); however, they are probably seen by more students than others. There are always issues and enhancements however, now that the basics are working, that could be provided.

Firstly, it is intended that the Web Sites be translated into another software format—DreamWeaver has been suggested as suitable—as soon as the author can learn the new software. However, no software is "foolproof" and this may simply change one set of problems for another.

In line with the findings from the theory discussed above, it is intended that interactive discussion groups be started on the postgraduate site for both seminar and assessment topics. These groups would be moderated but should be available for module-related discussion. It is important that the students perceive these as leading to the development of a community for them to be effective. Hit counters have proved not to work successfully in FrontPage and it is hoped that under new software they would, so that usage of particular facilities could be monitored; however, these are not a good measure of the extent to which participation is leading to learning. This is better monitored by feedback from the students on the effectiveness of the sites and the future development needs.

A suggested enhancement, which is not directly related to the Web site, is the use of a CD-ROM to provide students with all "static" material and additional learning opportunities. This could take the place of the final pieces of paper for these modules and make them truly "virtual" in material delivery. As discussed earlier, the Web site should not just be used as a means of transmitting paper materials; it is the links to other sites and sources of information that add value. In this respect, a CD-ROM would reduce "clutter" on the site and enable a more proactive learning approach to be adopted.

Other enhancements will no doubt be provided as time and software capabilities permit and as the students suggest. The obvious development is to move towards a multimedia-based Web site with enhanced capabilities; however, the real issue of importance is student ease of access. If more complex presentation leads to poor access, this has to be abandoned in the light of the sites' main aim of supporting students.

In conclusion, it has to be said that the use of a Web site has been very successful to date and has the potential to allow delivery of such large modules on other courses with the ability to manage the process–a truly enabling technology.

REFERENCES

Avgerou, C. and Cornford, T. (1998). *Developing Information Systems: Concepts, Issues and Practice*. 2nd edition, Macmillan Press.

Bavelas, J.B., Hutchinson, S., Kenwood, C. and Hunt, D. (1999). Using face-to-face dialogue as a standard for other communication systems. *Canadian Journal of Information Systems*, 22(1).

Coakes, E. and Willis, D. (2000). Computer mediated communication in universities and further education establishments–A comparison of use and utility. In Khosrowpour, M. (Ed.), *IRMA Conference Proceedings Challenges of Information Technology Management in the 21st Century*, 202-206. Hershey, PA: Idea Group Publishing.

Culnan, M. J. and Markus, M. L. (1987). Information technologies. In Janlin, F. M. (Ed.), *Handbook of Organizational Communication: An Interdisciplinary Perspective*. Sage.

December Communications, Inc. (2000). *Developing Information Content for the World Wide Web*. Available on the World Wide Web at: http://www.december.com. Accessed March 8, 2000.

Hirscheim R. A. (1985). *Office Automation: Concepts, Technologies and Issues*. Wokingham: Addison-Wesley.

Hoffman, D. L. and Novak, T. P. (2000). Commercial scenarios for the Web: Opportunities and challenges. In Chatterjee, P. (Ed.), *Journal of Computer Mediated Communication*. Available on the World Wide Web at: http://www.ascu.org/jcmc/vol11/issue3/hoffman.html.

Kalakota, R. and Whinston, A. B. (1997). *Electronic Commerce: A Managers Guide*. Addison-Wesley.

Kling, R. (1996). *Computerization and Controversy: Value Conflicts and Social Choices*. Academic Press.

Marvin, L. E. (1999) Spoof, spam, lurk and lag: The aesthetics of text-based virtual realities. *Journal of Computer Mediated Communication*. Available on the World Wide Web at: http://www.ascu.org/jcmc/vol1/issue2/marvin.html.

Sproull, L. and Kiesler, S. (1986). Reducing social context cues: Electronic mail in organisational communication. *Management Science*, 32(11).

Warner, T. (1996). *Communication Skills for Information Systems*. Pitman.

Willis, D. and Coakes, E. (2000). Enabling technology for collaborative working–A socio-technical experience. In Clarke, S. and Lehaney, B. (Eds.), *Human Centered Methods in Information Systems: Current Research and Practice*. Hershey, PA: Idea Group Publishing.

Chapter XIII

Managing E-business: Security Issues and Solutions

Keng Siau
University of Nebraska-Lincoln, USA

Shane Meakim
J. D. Edwards, USA

INTRODUCTION

What would you do if I told you that I could read your mind? Given that I am not a psychic, but a Web site administrator, you would probably not believe me. There are organizations that maintain databases of almost every consumer in the United States and even the world. One organization claims to have a database that encompasses 90% of all US consumers. Once an organization was given the name of a man and was told he lived in the US. In less than 48 hours they found where he worked, where he lived, who he was married to, how many times he was married, the contents of his financial portfolio, what credit cards he had, and what he bought at grocery stores. Amazingly, this information was obtained legally from various Web sites. The fact that you use a computer at home does not ensure your anonymity. You are being tracked in more ways than you could possibly think. As you surf the Net, facts are compiled about you. These pieces of information can range from the places or sites you visit and how long you stayed there to where you come from. These issues concerning trust, security, and privacy in cyberspace must be addressed in the near future and are critical to the growth of electronic business (Siau & Whitacre, 2001; Keen et al., 2000; Turban et al., 2000; Fingar et al., 2000; Kaufman et al., 1995; Ford & Baum, 1997).

THE WILD, WILD WORLD OF THE INTERNET

The Internet originated with the creation of ARPANET in the late 1960s by the US Department of Defense (Comer, 1999). Originally, governments, scientists, and educators used this network to exchange information and data (Comer, 2000). The original Internet started in 1969 as a network of a few remote computers and has grown to over 40 million computers today. The reasons for the rapid expansion of the Internet are the various technological advances in personal computers, telecommunications, and economies of scale in the computer world.

Where We Have Come From and Where We Are Going

In the last five years, business has taken the Net from a research-orientated tool, where professors and scientists shared information, to a tool used by vast numbers of people with different interests all staking a piece of the (Net) action for their own. The Internet is a unique entity because no organization or person has total control or ownership of the it (Siau, 1999; Siau & Whitacre, 2001). The no-ownership structure, coupled with the open architecture of the Internet, has resulted in the emergence of privacy and security issues. Many organizations and people, each expressing concerns and seeing a need for a safe and reliable Internet as a platform for commerce, have initiated a movement to develop information security to protect their interests. This presents an apparent conflict since companies are just as interested in sharing data, information and knowledge as they are concerned with protecting what they possess. This situation has resulted in ad-hoc security schemes addressing the issues of privacy, security, trust, integrity, authentication, access control, and non-repudiation. As the number of new users connecting to the Internet increases at an almost exponential pace, it is natural that organizations implement user tracking systems. This has in turn exposed security holes, weaknesses, and privacy issues and has turned the focus from Internet content to issues of privacy and anonymity.

As the Internet continues to grow and expand, the telecommunications infrastructure "legacy system," consisting of a morass of cable, fiber optics, DSL (digital subscriber line), ADSL (analog digital subscriber line), HDSL (High-bit-rate digital subscriber line), switches, modems, hubs, and routers, fades to the background while new technologies such as wireless digital networks and other technologies emerge as the Internet of the future. The Internet has become more a way of life than any other technology as a result of the developing infrastructure and expanding connectivity. Businesses, organizations and individuals are conducting all facets of business in a cyberspace with no direct human involvement. This has increased the need for organizations and people to develop protection against being taken advantage of by unscrupulous individuals. This has culminated in a general movement toward develop security policies, hardware, and software. Businesses, however, have recognized that solving the Internet's (and their own internal) security and privacy problems could necessitate the expenditure of a great deal of time, money, and effort.

E-business and the Need for Security

As mainstream society embraces the Internet at an ever-increasing pace, and as people begin to make more online purchases, precautions to assure and ensure consumer privacy move to the forefront of organizational concerns. Forrester Research projects $144 billion in Internet purchases by individual consumers in 2003 and $1.3 trillion in Internet purchases by businesses in that same year. This is a huge market! No business is willing to give up any market or potential market simply because they have failed to take the necessary steps to ensure that e-consumers feel just as safe as when they purchase goods from a brick-and-mortar store. Two main types of transactions need to be considered when devising security policies: business-to-business Transactions and business-to-consumer transactions. Both transaction types appear to be quite similar but the situations are different. For example, a B2B transaction averages $75,000, but a B2C transaction averages $75-$100. In addition, the mechanics of a B2B transaction are different from a B2C transaction. When a B2B transaction takes place there may be bargaining, negotiation and various steps that need to be followed, such as appropriating money for the purchase from a bank, before the transaction is completed. A B2C transaction, in contrast, is normally more of a one-time event that may even be done as a result of an impulse. Also the information disseminated during the transaction and the way the transaction takes place are much different for the two types. In a B2B transaction, one company is working with another, such as a supplier working with a manufacturer. In these types of situations the supplier might have access to the manufacturer's inventory and be able to see how often they use a part and other related information. However, during a B2C transaction the process needs to be simple and the consumer must be able to complete the transaction with relative ease. So, depending on the type of situation, different security measures and precautions need to be considered.

SECURE E-BUSINESS

In 1999, Corporate America spent $4.4 billion on sales of Internet security software, including firewalls, intrusion-detection programs, digital certificates, and authentication and authorization software. By 2003, those expenditures could hit $8.3 billion (BusinessWeek, 2000). Security is becoming more expensive as those who want to wreak havoc on businesses become smarter and the use of technology by legitimate customers and miscreants alike increases. But it is an expensive necessity, since e-business transactions are estimated to be $450 billion in 2000 (BusinessWeek 2000). House Hold International, a leading provider of consumer loans and credit cards in the United States, Canada and the United Kingdom, had a security budget over $3.5 million for the year 2000 alone. Thus, the situation companies find themselves in is this: are they willing to spend $3.5 million on security so that they have a chance to penetrate the potential $144 billion B2C and $1 trillion B2B markets? Of course, if the business idea is sound, the amount to be spent on security is minuscule compared to the potential payoff.

What Is Security?

Security is more than just managing risk. Security encompasses guarding against espionage, sabotage, crime, attack, and danger, as well as providing freedom from unwanted attacks. Intellectual property, such as marketing information, product information, and pricing is now seen as an asset and viewed as keys to a company's success. Protecting information is not only necessary for a company to survive, but it has gained importance as a contributing factor to the company's success from a customer perspective. Security is prerequisite for e-business (Fingar et al., 2000). Security policies are necessary to determine what behavior is and isn't allowed by establishing the necessary procedures needed for the organization. These policies help establish cohesiveness throughout the organization because the policies will typically be administered by a governing body such as a network administrator, CIO, or a combination of both. As a result of the increased use of e-business as a vital strategic component for most companies, computer security is now a global issue that affects more than just a corporation; it affects consumers and suppliers too. As a result, companies spend many hours trying to devise a plan that will accomplish the task of keeping their competitive edge, while simultaneously assuring consumers shopping on the company site that their personal information is secure.

Trust Models

In order to implement a successful security infrastructure, the organization must decide who to trust and how much to trust them. Two equally detrimental scenarios become apparent: trusting people too much or trusting people too little. Trusting someone too much may be inviting a security breach. Alternatively, trusting people too little may result in poor customer, supplier, and user relationships due to the extremely stringent security procedures they encounter as they interact with the system. For example, Ford opens its system to suppliers so they can check Ford's inventory levels, and the suppliers can supply the necessary parts without Ford's having to manually submit an order. The supplier assumes responsibility for ensuring that its actions do not breach security. In addition, Ford must consider the fact that suppliers should not have to navigate an unnecessarily complicated security system in order to obtain the information they need. On the other hand, a consumer who might be buying a car online from Ford doesn't need the same type of information as a supplier, so s/he should not have access to the same information as the suppliers. Thus, when deciding what information should be given to different people (customers or suppliers), an organization has three options in deciding whom to trust: trust everyone all the time, trust no one at any time, or trust some people some of the time. The first option may be the easiest to implement because it requires very little effort, but if one person takes advantage of the situation for his or her own benefit, it could ruin everything for everyone. If an organization employs the second option, it will maintain the most control because it is the most restrictive. However, productivity in this situation is impaired because of the many obstacles and hurdles between the user and the information needed to do her/his job. This can also lead to high employee turnover because employees don't want to deal with the restrictive nature of the security placed on the system. Thus, the third option is probably the best to pursue because the organization can grant control as needed, placing trust and responsibility with those given access while simultaneously maintaining system security.

After deciding who should be trusted and how much trust they should be given, an organization must implement a security framework including such items as firewalls, passwords, encrypted tunneling, and public key infrastructure. Just a few years ago a pharmaceutical company's Web site was hacked and a notice was posted on the site. The notice content indicated that the company was engaged in merger negotiations with another company. The notice was not a devastating attack on the company, but was intended to raise the stock price, allowing the hackers to profit from the system security breach. Thus, in the case above as well as other security attacks (such as denial of service), a company must be concerned with how security issues, concerns, and solutions will affect their business and must formulate a security policy based on the concerns. Implementing a successful security policy has many requirements, which we will discuss in the next few sections.

SECURITY POLICY

Most people think of information security as hardware or software that keeps a system safe, arguably one of the biggest misconceptions about security. Security encompasses many different aspects that must be identified and addressed before implementing the hardware and software tasked with keeping information secure. To implement a successful security policy, the policy must be enforceable—a rule without enforcement is not a rule at all. Many users lack the in-depth understanding and knowledge of any security infrastructure, so the rules must be understandable by the layperson. Balancing security with users' needs is a necessity because, as mentioned previously, if people can't get what they need to perform their jobs, productivity decreases as a consequence. The last aspect of a security policy is probably the most difficult because the policy must continuously evolve as the organization grows and changes and as technology becomes more sophisticated. The security policies should also discuss why there is a need for a particular policy, how a violation will be handled, and to whom the policy pertains. In addition, the policy must be designed specifically to fit each organization because a generic policy structure that fits all organizations does not exist.

Determining the Policy Structure

Regarding how to devise a policy structure, the development team or person must account for the size of the organization and determine whether there should be one encompassing policy that pertains to everyone or a few small documents that may cover different issues such as acceptable use, user accounts, remote access, and information protection. There is much more than what appears on the surface in regards to the issues mentioned above. For example, acceptable use generally includes a description of what should and what should not be done by persons using the system. This can encompass everything from installing personal software on the system to which Web sites can be viewed by an individual. In fact, acceptable use is often an entirely separate issue, and companies sometimes have hundreds of pages devoted specifically to the topic. The next section is devoted to a more detailed examination of acceptable use.

Acceptable Use Policies

These policies outline users' rights, responsibilities, and proper use of the computer system. For example, should users be allowed to copy files that are not their own, but to which they have access? Two of the responsibilities of a user might be to keep their passwords private and not to access the system for their personal use. In regards to proper use, the following should be considered: Who are the users sending e-mail to? Which Web sites are they visiting? How are they portraying themselves as a person and representative of the company in cyberspace? These are all key pieces to a secure information system. Another issue regarding user accounts might be individual passwords, which is probably the point at which information security is at its weakest. People have passwords and share them with others because they think a password is not important. Password information can also be obtained by manipulating employees over the phone or just watching over their shoulder. The above examples clearly highlight the importance of establishing a policy to govern the system on-site; however, a different policy should be devised and established when considering users accessing the same information from home or off-site.

Remote Access Policy

This policy is very important to a company because allowing remote access may expose an entire intranet to outside attacks if people are allowed access to the network from an external and insecure environment. This might be done through a dial-up connection, ISDN/frame relay, or Telnet access from an Internet connection, a cable modem, or an encrypted tunnel. An issue specific to this topic is who should have this type of access: everyone, only important executives, or salespeople. The policy should discuss and lay out in great detail how the network can be accessed. After developing an information security policy, attention must be given to one of the most important security measures, the information protection policy.

Securing the Company's Information

This policy details the processing, storage, and transmission of sensitive information not only to people within the company, but also to those external to the company. This measure is necessary to make sure confidential information is not modified or disclosed about the company. This policy defines user system privileges. It discusses how information is disposed of when thrown away; whether it needs to be shredded if it is on paper, or a hard drive needs to be low-level formatted to erase the sensitive information. The policy also discusses what can be printed and how information can be stored.

There is much more to a network than the technology that protects an information system. As a result, the information security policy on paper that is developed by a CIO, committee, or network administrator is just as important as the technology that protects the system.

The above discusses the steps necessary to implement a security policy behind the scenes. However, that begs the question: What kind of technology is there that supports those procedures developed to protect the company? In the next section we will discuss the public key infrastructure (PKI), one of the foundations that ensures system integrity and security. But before we can understand how all these different components integrate to create a PKI infrastructure we must examine the backbone behind PKI—encryption.

ENCRYPTION

Encryption works by using two keys—a public key and a private key. These two keys are related mathematically so that one key cannot be decrypted without the other.

Encryption has the following property:

$M = decrypt$ (private-key-user1, encrypt (public-key-user1, M))

and

$M = decrypt$ (public-key-user1, encrypt (private-key-user1, M))

The public key is typically used as the key that performs the encryption. When a message is being sent, the sender uses the receiver's public key to execute the encryption of the information. The encrypted message is sent to the receiver:

Encrypted-message = encrypt (public-key-receiver, M)

To retrieve the original message M, the intended receiver will use his/her private key to decrypt the message:

$M = decrypt$ (private-key-receiver, encrypted-message)

In this case, public and private keys ensure confidentiality and privacy.

Another feature that helps to ensure confidentiality and privacy is known as digital signature. To sign a message, the sender encrypts the message using his/her private key:

Encrypted-message = encrypt (sender's-private-key, M)

The recipient uses the sender's public key to decrypt the message. The recipient knows the sender is the one who actually sent the message because only the sender has the private key needed to perform the encryption:

$M = decrypt$ (sender's-public-key, encrypted-message)

Interestingly, more than one level of encryption is possible to provide for both privacy and authentication. For example, in the following case:

Encrypted-message = encrypt (public-key-receiver, encrypt (private-key-sender, M))

The message M is first encrypted with the sender's private key and then encrypted again with the recipient's public key. Then the decryption is performed in the reverse order:

M = decrypt (public-key-sender, decrypt (private-key-receiver, encrypted-message))

The encrypted-message is decrypted first with the recipient's private key and then decrypted with the sender's public key. The result is M, the original message. So, if a meaningful message results after the decoding, one will know that the message is authentic and reputable.

There are many different standards and methodologies to perform this encryption. One of the popular methods is RSA, named after its founders Ronald Rivest, Adi Shamir, and Leonard Adelman, who first published the algorithm in April 1977. The RSA algorithm can use a short key or a long key for added privacy, and in most cases the RSA standard uses 512 bits.

PUBLIC KEY INFRASTRUCTURE (PKI)

With communications on open networks, public key infrastructure (PKI) is a solution to the basic security issues associated with sending information over a company's Internet, intranet, extranet, virtual private networks (VPNs) or secure VPNs (SVPNs). PKI is a comprehensive set of functionalities for encryption and digital services that consists of several components, including a directory, certification authority (CA), and certification revocation lists. PKIs integrate digital certificates, public-key cryptography, and certificate authorities into a total, enterprise-wide network security architecture. A typical enterprise's PKI encompasses the issuance of digital certificates to individual users and servers; end-user enrollment software; integration with corporate certificate directories; tools for managing, renewing, and revoking certificates; and related services and support.

A PKI can unify the different security measures into a single infrastructure umbrella. The PKI eliminates any need for incompatible, ad hoc security techniques that were designed when information security was in its infancy. PKI simultaneously addresses the following issues (Fingar et al., 2000):
- Authentication (a user is who s/he says s/he is),
- Authorization (the user is authorized to be where s/he is on the network),

- Non-repudiation (the user is the one who really sent the message), and
- Privacy (no one has read or tampered with a user's message).

Virtual Private Networks

Encryption and the use of the PKI enable the formation of virtual private networks (VPNs); however, a VPN can exist without implementing a PKI on the system. A VPN is one or more WAN links over a shared public network, typically over the Internet or an IP backbone from a network service provider (NSP), which simulates the behavior of dedicated WAN links over leased lines. In cyberspace, members of VPNs will be identified by their digital certificates.

VPNs have no geographical boundaries and are commonplace today. Think about AOL, Compuserve, and MSN. They all provide the backbone so companies can incorporate VPNs into their organization. In the case of a member using the backbone of AOL, the client computer calls its local ISP and connects to the Internet. Then the user would launch special client software that recognizes a specified destination and negotiates an encrypted VPN session. The encrypted packets are wrapped in IP packets to tunnel their way through the Internet using the connection to AOL. The VPN server then negotiates the VPN session and decrypts the packets. Local ISP connections can be provisioned using many technologies, from dial-up and ISDN for small sites to leased lines or frame relay for larger sites. With emerging technologies such as DSL, cable, and wireless connections, users now have options that provide both low-cost and high-speed access.

Public Key Certificate—A Foundation for VPN

In cyberspace, a public key certificate (PKC), also known as a digital certificate, is a special electronic document that signifies that one has the correct authorization to the VPN.

The certificate is created by an independent authority called a certificate authority (CA). A CA is a service run by or on behalf of a VPN that decides who should have the membership privileges in the VPN. A few of the better-known authorities are Verisign, Thawte, and Entrust. The PKC identifies the individual as a member of the VPN. The PKC can be used by an individual as part of the process to sign digital documents in a legally binding manner. It is also used to encrypt information and guarantee that the communication is sent to only the desired party. The PKC grants the bearer access to the VPN.

As one can imagine, not all certificates are the same. Some certificates have more "privileges" than others. For example, a certificate issued by teachers going to the Economics 101 Web site may have real meaning to those members that visit the site, but the same certificate will not be of any use to those needing access to sensitive material on NASA's VPN.

GLOBAL PUBLIC KEY INFRASTRUCTURE (GPKI)

Now that we have a basic understanding of encryption, PKI, and VPNs, we can start to understand how we can incorporate the three components to create a global public key infrastructure (GPKI). VPNs cannot simply offer their services and information to those who find it interesting, even though the Internet was originally created for that purpose. The original open-use concept, the way the Internet was first used and developed, has evolved over time into the medium it is today. Because the Internet has evolved from the original open, research-based medium where there was no need for security, many of the protocols used on the Internet today are insecure.

In addition, it is not enough to simply restrict system access to only those that should have access to information by using a firewall. With the current emphasis on protecting corporate intellectual property, the implementation of firewall technologies certainly enhances overall security, but at the same time, certain disadvantages are inherent in the implementation. Firewalls might impose redundant identification and authentication measures on a user. Not only can this become cumbersome, but it can also appear to be arbitrarily strict and impede productivity. The implementation of these types of security architectures has arisen as a result of the corporate enterprise being made available to many segments of the outside non-trusted world, such as customers, potential customers, suppliers, shippers, third-party sales brokers, business partners, and potential business partners. In order to make the required variety of information available to this heterogeneous society, it has become necessary to define and refine exactly what data each group needs to see in order to effectively and efficiently become a part of the enterprise. The controls implemented should be out of necessity and follow certain rules of business conduct. These business rules should take into consideration the sensitivity of the data being made available to each group, such as business partners or customers, as well as the role each business partner has within the organization. This is where and how GPKI comes in useful.

Cross-Certification

One VPN can make ad hoc security decisions about how it interacts with other VPNs. This is very similar to how businesses interact with one another and conduct transactions to complete a business process. VPNs work similarly in that they can decide which PKCs they are going to accept and which they are going to reject. The VPN can honor the PKC from another CA as equivalent to its own certificates, or it can restrict access and limit what the holder of the PKC is allowed to do. It is similar to allowing a few users privilege to read, write, and execute, and limiting most to only reading. Even if the VPN has never seen a particular user before, it can decide to honor the certificate based on the reputation of the CA. This is similar to the use of VISA or MasterCard. It does not matter which banks, organizations, societies or clubs issued the VISA or MasterCard. As long as the credit card bears the VISA or Master logo, it is accepted at any store that accepts VISA or MasterCard.

When an unknown user approaches a VPN with an unknown certificate, the VPN has a number of different options. The first option is denial. This is logical, considering that some information can be very sensitive to certain organizations. The second option is for the VPN to try and authenticate the user. The CA will normally perform this authentication process by trying to reconcile where the request came from and decide whether to permit access. The VPN performs this task by searching the GPKI for this particular CA and establishing its relationship to other CAs known to the VPN. If it is similar then the VPN may decide to trust the certificate and grant access. Because there are so many different certificates, a system has to be put in place that works as a directory service, similar to a phone book or 411. The third option is implementing a hierarchy of CAs that occurs when multiple signatures appear on a certificate. The VPN will continue to check the layers of signatures until it finds one it recognizes through a process called cross-certification. This allows a VPN to make sure those needing access can gain access and keep others who don't need access away.

Figure 1:

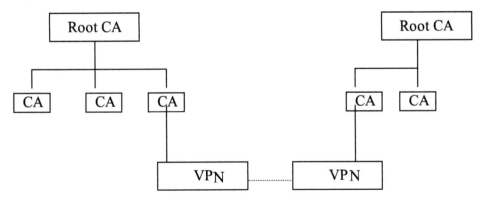

Certificate Revocation List

Having access to a VPN is like belonging to a club. Just as a club has rules so does a VPN. So when a rule is broken, membership can be revoked in a VPN just as membership can be revoked in the real world. When a rule is broken, the VPN keeps track of the rule violations and places the certificate on a certificate revocation list (CRL). This list keeps track of the revoked certificates and is checked whenever someone tries to use a certificate issued by that CA. The VPN, when going through the validation process, not only tries to authenticate the certificate but also checks to make sure the certificate is not on the CA's CRL. This can be a long process but CAs cache each other's CRLs to minimize the processing time it takes during the validation.

GPKI Hierarchy

The underlying idea of security is based on trust. There are two prominent models, the Big Brother model and the Little Sister Model. In the Big Brother model, there is a central authority. It is a hierarchical model where the root CA is the authority and is the trusted third-party that all other CAs defer to and where all trust is derived. The idea of a central CA has recently gained more support in view of new advances in PKI technology and the advancement of the Internet. Some organizations support the idea that every computer connected to the Internet should have its unique certificate ID. Nevertheless, the central authority model has a number of flaws; one is the fact that if your CA isn't part of the hierarchy, your VPN is out. Also, everyone wants to be the central authority and no one can agree on who should be the central authority. This is why there is motivation in the business world for many organizations to become VPNs under their own choice. In credit card transactions the hierarchy is impersonal and is suited for the one-to-many transactions that take place; however, this would not be a good solution for business-to-business transactions.

In the Little Sister Model, trust is outside the GPKI and it is up to the institutions, their VPNs, and their CAs. When two VPNs decide to do business, they trust each other and give access to their respective VPNs.

GPKI—A Foundation for E-business

E-business using GPKI comes from an enterprise network management perspective because it eliminates hard-to-manage modem banks. But VPNs are also an important part of e-business strategy. Some companies are using VPNs to network remote employees, driving down response times and improving access to business information. Other companies are using VPNs to tie their customers, partners, and suppliers into their network as part of an overall e-business strategy. Either way, VPNs require PKI to authenticate the connection points in the VPN, and organizations that are using VPNs are starting to evaluate their overall PKI architectures as a result. As technology continues to develop, companies must realize the need to implement a security system using PKI because of the encompassing nature of this standard. E-security systems must provide flexibility, functionality, and scalability. In order to replace paper processes, such systems also need to provide accountability and trust in electronic processes. To accomplish this goal, a growing number of companies are deploying PKI. PKI will continue to evolve to meet the high standards established by the security community. PKI will continue to become more and more integrated into a business's e-business strategy because of the threat from hackers. A study in 1991 found that over 80% of attacks were from an internal source such as disgruntled employees. That number, however, dropped to 75% in 1997 and to the 50% mark in the year 2000. A recent example involves a security breach at Microsoft. The hackers downloaded source code for the Microsoft Windows operating system. Thus, security does not simply involve preventing employees from accessing sensitive information (such as salaries). Rather, because information is so precious and valuable, organizations must protect themselves from external as well as internal attacks. That is also why, even before the organization buys all the necessary security-related hardware and software, they must develop a security policy as a basis for all further security development. State-of-the-art technology alone cannot prevent security breaches in the absence of well-written and thought-out policies governing external and internal systems uses and users.

CONCLUSION

The need for information security and privacy in today's world is especially important if a business offers e-commerce to its customers and desires to make those customers feel comfortable and safe in their transaction decisions. This can be accomplished using many different security measures such as PKI and passwords. Each security measure has both advantages and disadvantages, and by employing different techniques, a network can have the right mixture of security for certain parts and pieces of the network. This is all accomplished by performing a risk analysis and ranking data assets in a hierarchy of importance. One of the most common ways to ensure security is using cryptology algorithms to encrypt the information. The most common encryption technique is the RSA standard in 56-bit or 128-bit encryption. All of these techniques must be used and tailored on a worldwide basis through the understanding of the public key infrastructure.

The world has embraced globalization, and whatever telecommunications network is utilized, it must be able to handle all different types of requests and accesses. By employing the concept of a global public key infrastructure, we may be able to go from a series of ad hoc security techniques to a seamless network where people can feel assured of both privacy and security.

However, even with the most sophisticated technologies protecting an organization's information system, the necessary thoughts and precautions must be implemented to have a system that balances the need between users, suppliers, customers, and sensitivity of information on the network. Operating without sound security policies, including the necessary technologies, is analogous to locking the car doors but leaving the windows down. If someone can call and get a password to log in to the network remotely because users do not follow security policies, the most sophisticated security technology in the world is not going to prevent them from wreaking havoc on your system. The combination of a sound security policy along with the global PKI infrastructure will create a strong global cyberspace that is necessary in today's e-business.

REFERENCES

Adam, N., Dogramaci, O., Gangopadhyay, A. and Yesha, Y. (1999). *Electronic Commerce—Technical, Business, and Legal Issues*. Prentice Hall.

Amor, D. (2000). *The E-Business (R) Evolution*. Prentice Hall.

Comer, D. (1999). *Computer Networks and Internets*, Second Edition. Prentice Hall.

Comer, D. (2000). *The Internet Book*, Third Edition. Prentice Hall.

Csinger, A., Siau, K. (1998). The global public key infrastructure: Terms and concepts. *IEEE Computer*, September, 30-31.

CyberCrime. (2000). *Business Week*, February 21, 36-42.

Drew, G. (1999). *Using SET for Secure Electronic Commerce*. Prentice Hall.

Fingar, P., Kumar, H. and Sharma, T. (2000). *Enterprise E-Commerce*. Meghan-Kiffer Press.

Ford, W. and Baum, M. (1997). *Secure Electronic Commerce*. Prentice Hall.

Kaufman, C., Perlman, R. and Speciner, M. (1995). *Network Security—Private Communication in a Public World*. Prentice Hall.

Keen, P., Balance, C., Chan, S. and Schrump, S. (2000). *Electronic Commerce Relationships—Trust By Design*. Prentice Hall.

Pfleeger, C. (1997). *Security in Computing*. Prentice Hall.

Schneider, G. and Perry, J. (2000). *Electronic Commerce*. Course Technology.

Siau, K. (1999). Internet, World Wide Web, and creativity. *Journal of Creative Behavior*, 33(3), 191-201.

Siau, K. and Whitacre, K. (2001). Internet and e-business security. In Dhillon, G. (Ed.), *Information Security Management: Global Challenges in the Next Millennium*, 125-134. Hershey, PA: Idea Group Publishing.

Stallings, W. (1999). *Cryptography and Network Security—Principles and Practice*, Second Edition. Prentice Hall.

Stallings, W. (2000). *Network Security Essentials—Applications and Standards*. Prentice Hall.

Turban, E., Lee, J., King, D. and Chung, H. (2000). *Electronic Commerce— A Managerial Perspective*. Prentice Hall.

Turner, C. Reid (1999). Create a private network across the Internet. *Smart Computing*, October, 10(10).

Chapter XIV

Reducing Legal, Financial and Operational Risks: A Comparative Discussion of Aligning Internet Usage With Business Priorities Through Internet Policy Management

Claire A. Simmers
St. Joseph's University, USA

Adam Bosnian
Elron Software Inc., USA

The increased reliance on the Internet exposes organizations to a number of legal, financial, and operational risks through inappropriate workplace information technology (IT) behaviors. This article explores these IT workplace behaviors and how Web and e-mail usage can be effectively aligned with business priorities while allowing for some personal use. The development of alignment is explored through the discussion of eight organizations, six small/mid-sized and two large. The organizational responses converged in policies and processes for controlling actual or potentially detrimental IT workplace behaviors, thus reducing the risks. Alignment is achieved through Internet policy management (IPM), which integrates an enterprise-wide written Internet usage policy (IUP), effective communication of the IUP and enforcement through Web and e-mail content monitoring/filtering software.

INTRODUCTION: THE NATURE OF INTERNET MANAGEMENT

Once primarily used for e-mail and retrieving information, the Internet is now embraced as a critical component of staying competitive in the 21st century. The Internet is a tool that lowers the cost of communication and is restructuring the way work is done. The Net is becoming the backbone for everything from linking supply chains to storing knowledge, and most benefits are in business practices and integration. It is estimated that the Internet could add approximately 0.4 percentage points to annual productivity growth over the next five years (Mandel & Hof, 2001). The Internet is used in the workplace as a tool for both external and internal communication. External information sharing is in the areas of e-commerce, marketing, supply chain management, remote site connectivity, and customer support. Internal information sharing is found in employee and benefit information, inter- and intra-department coordination, and knowledge storage and management.

Not only has the Internet altered the competitive environment, but also the nature of work has changed. The Internet has played a pivotal role in obliterating the once clear-cut lines between work and personal life. Employees are working more than ever and many people bring their work home. In many jobs, work expectations are 24 hours a day, 7 days a week (24-7), without regard to place or time; intertwining of work and personal clocks is now commonplace. Since employees have less personal time, the Internet has become a valuable tool for their personal life, allowing them to book appointments, research trips, manage personal finances and keep in touch with family. In some ways, the Internet allows employees to have a more flexible work schedule because they are able to conduct some of their personal business during traditional work hours and to work at home or on the road.

While the Internet can create many desirable organizational outcomes, it can also generate undesirable outcomes such as the loss of intellectual property, sexual harassment lawsuits, productivity losses due to surfing abuse, and network bandwidth overload. It is becoming increasingly clear that employers have an obligation to proactively manage the Internet-connected workplace. Companies need to set up a middle ground between no or limited access and unrestricted access by managing Internet usage to the benefit of both employers and employees. The first step to aligning individual Internet usage with business priorities is having an Internet usage policy (IUP). An IUP defines appropriate behaviors when using company Internet resources. An effective IUP can allow for some personal surfing and e-mail but prevents excessive surfing, pornography, confidential data leaks, viruses, or violent content, thus reducing legal, financial, and operational risks. Active promotion of and training in the IUP are integral to successful alignment. Coupling monitoring/filtering software with actual usage reports and timely feedback to individual users can ensure compliance to the IUP.

We will call this process of alignment between individuals and the organization—Internet policy management (IPM). IPM is the regulation of Internet activities so that targeted outcomes remain within acceptable limits. Many people assume that Internet policy management must be avoided because it connotes "Big Brother" or an invasion of privacy. Others take the position that the Internet exposes organizations to too much risk, so Internet usage is nonexistent or strictly limited. However, either too much or too little Internet management can be dysfunctional for an organization. An optimal level of Internet management that sparks motivation, creativity, innovation, and initiative can result in more desirable outcomes. Figure 1 depicts the general relationship between Internet policy management and outcomes. It shows that optimal outcomes will be achieved when businesses restrict usage by policy and check the policy by monitoring/filtering software. If there is no access or if access is severely limited, organizational outcomes may suffer. Blocking Internet sites is also problematic. Blocking does not lead to optimal outcomes because blocking is difficult to keep updated, easy to get around and does not provide feedback mechanisms. At the other end of the spectrum, vague, not enforced, or no policies will expose the organization to a number of legal, financial, and operational risks. Losses of confidential information, network congestion, threats to network integrity, diversion of employee attention, and most importantly, increased legal liability are the most common examples.

This paper explores the place of Internet policy management in aligning individual Internet usage with organizational priorities by focusing on one basic but fundamental issue–how to reduce legal, financial, and operational risks. In conventional accounts of Internet usage the emphasis is on how the Internet becomes useful and usable from either a technical perspective or an end user's perspective. This work focuses on how increasingly the reductions of legal, financial, and operational risks are treated as fundamentally a business practice issue that integrates technologically based solutions with people-based solutions, thus bringing organizational and individual priorities into alignment.

Figure 1: The Nature of Internet Management

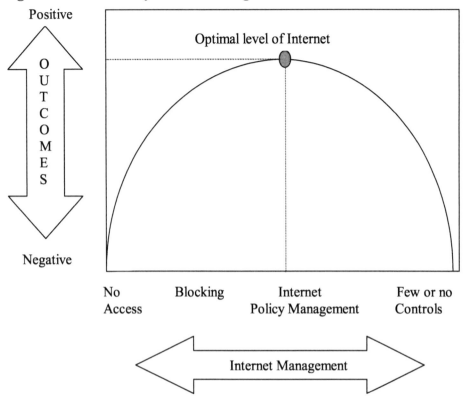

Despite the need for Internet management, most companies don't couple their policies on work-related Internet usage with monitoring/filtering software. A majority of companies ask their employees for little more than compliance to a formal usage policy. However for a growing number of businesses this just isn't enough. There's increasing sentiment among executives that a more hands-on approach to Internet management is needed. In a recent survey of 200 US business executives by Dataquest, 82% said Internet usage should be monitored at their companies, but only 34% said they have already instituted such a program. However, Web monitoring is expected to jump from the 34% in 1999 to 66% by 2001 (D'Antoni, 2000). Analysts and human resource experts recommend that organizations should deal with inappropriate workplace information technology (IT) behaviors such as surfing before they create a legal mess. Employees could be offended by coworkers' surfing habits or e-mails and bring a sexual harassment or civil rights suits against employers. Internet policy management is an effective way to limit legal liability (Roberts, 1999).

The essential components of Internet policy management are:

(1)   An explicit and clearly communicated Internet usage policy,
(2)   Means for securing sensitive data and applications,
(3)   Tools for monitoring and recording Internet and e-mail usage,
(4)   Plans for training end users in the proper use of all available access and security technology (search engines, encryption tools, and the use of browsers, for example),
(5)   Policies on reporting and communication of the results back to the appropriate users, and
(6)   Application of discipline measures as prescribed in the policy document for violations of the IUP.

The first step in IPM is to create a clear Internet usage policy. The policy should state that the Internet is a privilege, not a right and that inappropriate use will result in penalties. It is important to define what inappropriate Internet usage is. Managers should consider how much personal Internet usage is appropriate for a given situation, how convenience is balanced against security, and how much corporate computing resources (machine time, network bandwidth, data storage space) should be devoted to Internet browsing compared to other IT needs. In addition, managers should outline the ramifications for violating the IUP. Elron Software, on their Web site (http://www.elron.com), has available a template for creating an IUP. The template includes a summary, overview with definitions of and philosophy, and then detailed policy provisions. The employee is asked to acknowledge receipt of the policy. The policy should parallel the organization's culture and should emphasize that the Internet is a business resource. Other examples of such policies can be found by searching for "Internet policies" on any search engine (Wonnacott, 1999). Once a draft IUP is written, an organization's management and legal staff should review it. An important component of Internet Policy Management is promotion and enforcement. The IUP should be widely publicized through seminars, performance reviews, and informal rap sessions. Equally important to compliance is monitoring and reporting software. Employers must be honest about the monitoring, when the monitoring will happen, and why and how it will be done. Monitoring should not be put in place to "catch" people but to reinforce the business usage of the Internet and the responsibilities that employees have to use this resource properly. Enforcement of the IUP can be done by:

•   On a periodic basis (weekly, monthly, bimonthly) generate Internet usage reports to get feedback on policy compliance.

- Per action steps established in the IUP, take action against those who violate policy. Some steps might include visiting chronic offenders or their managers and issuing a written reprimand.
- Web sites you identify in usage reports as inappropriate can be added to the filtering feature of your monitoring tool.
- Periodically review and update the IUP to reflect current employee and organizational needs.

The technical aspects of monitoring are not a major hindrance in IPM. There are many monitoring and blocking solutions available. For example, many routers allow ports to be disabled to deny specific Internet traffic. Blocking servers are popular alternatives, but many of these products are combined with firewalls and proxy servers. There are also several NT-based proxy alternatives; proxy servers can be configured to permit specific traffic through to the network (Wonnacott, 1999). There are also full-service providers of Internet management solutions such as SurfWatch Software, a Los Gatos, California-based division of Spyglass, Inc., and Elron Software Inc., a Burlington, Massachusetts-based division of Elron Electronic Industries, Ltd.

If Internet policy management is not being used in an organization, action can still be taken against offending employees for abusing their Internet privileges. As a company resource, Internet access along with company computers are subject to general company policy and discretionary usage. However, if managers are aware that employees are visiting sexually explicit Web sites or involved in other inappropriate activity, but do not take action, the organization could be at risk for a hostile-workplace complaint. Even if there is a legal victory in court, the unfavorable publicity and legal expenses are detrimental to your organization. Thus it is increasingly incumbent upon businesses to set and enforce Internet usage policies and to protect business interests. The federal government is becoming more active in Internet usage management with the passage of the Children's Internet Protection Act. Public school and library districts are now required to implement filtering technology to maintain federal funding (Ohlhorst, 2001). Increasingly, IPM is a necessity that mitigates management headaches, reduces the risk of harassment suits, and allows the business potential of the Internet to be unlocked.

THE CASE STUDIES

The following discussion is based on eight case studies and considers how and why an Internet policy management program reduces risk and optimizes the potential for positive organizational outcomes. Each organization thoughtfully determined their policy in accordance with their overall mission. They carefully communicated this policy and then installed a monitoring solution. Elron Software, Inc. collected data for an ongoing research project involving the study of the adoption and implementation of Internet policy management. Two companies are in the enterprise category (corporation with more than 1,500 users) and six are in the small- to mid-size category (companies with less than 1,500 users). Interviews were conducted with information systems professionals who were responsible for establishing an Internet protection and security presence at their organizations. While securing the Internet and e-mail was and is a primary concern, they all envisioned their role as more encompassing. Thus not only was protection of network and servers a high priority, but protection against employee abuse, protection of the confidential company data, and minimization of lawsuits due to inappropriate Web surfing and e-mail usage were also concerns. Table 1 presents summary information on each of the companies. The two of the companies are publicly traded, three have nonprofit status, two are private corporations, and one is a school. The largest company in terms of employees is 20th Century Fox with 35,000. Surfing abuse by employees was an issue identified by seven of the eight organizations. Half of the eight said limiting legal liability was a critical issue in Internet usage.

The first organization, 20th Century Fox, is part of Fox Entertainment Group, Inc., 83% owned by The News Corporation Limited (NYSE: NWS). Fox Entertainment is principally engaged in the development, production and worldwide distribution of feature films and television programs, television broadcasting and cable network programming. Fox has total assets, as of September 30, 2000, of approximately US $17.2 billion and total annual revenues of approximately US $9 billion. The company's studios, production facilities, and film and television library provide high-quality creative content, and the company's broadcasting and cable networks provide extensive distribution platforms for the company's programs. The company is headquartered in Los Angeles, California.

The second organization is the JFK Medical Center. As one of the largest hospitals in the central New Jersey area with renowned specialty care centers and a reputation for excellence, JFK Medical Center strives to fulfill a mission of "providing progressive medical care with a compassionate touch."

The third organization is Irvington High School, which is located about 40 miles southeast of San Francisco. It is a typical high school with 1,600 students and enjoys a distinguished reputation for its scholastic achievement. In fact, Irvington High has been named a National Blue Ribbon School, as one of California's most distinguished schools.

Table 1: Companies at a Glance

Company	Industry	Type of Company	Number of Employees	Title of Contact Person	Issues
20th Century Fox	Entertainment (television, film, books, newspapers, magazines, etc.)	For-profit, publicly traded	35,000	Director of Information Protection	-Protect confidential company data in e-mail, FTP and newsgroup postings -Prevent offensive Web surfing
JFK Medical Center	Health (patient care, surgery, rehabilitation, research.)	Nonprofit	5,000	System Analyst	-Prevent offensive Web surfing by employees -Limit legal liability -Prevent network congestion -Boost employee productivity
Bard	Manufacturing (Heating, ventilation, air conditioning.)	For-profit	400	IS Director	Surfing abuse by employees
Bricker & Eckler, LLP	Legal	Private		Chief Information Officer	Leverage the Internet to increase firm billings without increasing staff
Davis & Kuelthau, S.C.	Legal	Private		Manager of Information Systems	-Prevent offensive Web surfing by employees -Limit legal liability -Prevent network congestion -Boost employee productivity
Lake Charles Memorial Hospital	Health (patient care, surgery, rehabilitation, research	Nonprofit	1,000	Chief Information Officer and Network Administrator	Needed a way to reduce potential legal liability resulting from employee misuse of e-mail
New Mexico Mortgage Finance Authority	Finance	Nonprofit		Systems Manager	-Prevent offensive Web surfing by employees -Limit legal liability -Prevent network congestion -Boost employee productivity
Irvington High School	Education (secondary)	School	1,800 users	Technology Coordinator	Limit surfing abuse by students and faculty

The fourth organization is Lake Charles Memorial Hospital. Lake Charles is one of the largest facilities serving southwest Louisiana and the southeast Texas communities. A continued commitment to innovative treatments, procedures and technology has established Memorial as the region's leading family-centered medical complex. In addition, Lake Charles Memorial is a not-for-profit medical center, owned and operated by the Southwest Louisiana Healthcare System and governed by a local board of trustees. The hospital is one of the only tertiary care centers in the region.

The fifth organization is the New Mexico Mortgage Finance Authority (MFA). Using federal, state, and private capital, the MFA is a housing agency for the state. The organization works through third parties such as realtors, bankers and nonprofits to help people finance a home. In addition, to this primary goal, the MFA also manages other federal- and state-funded housing and related programs, some of which provide housing assistance to HIV-positive and homeless people. The MFA is not interested in making money; whatever money the MFA saves goes towards low-income housing. Therefore, the MFA is interested in being efficient.

The sixth organization is Bard Manufacturing. Bard Manufacturing is a third-generation family-owned business that specializes in air conditioners and heat pumps, primarily for commercial sites. For the past 80 years, Bard, which carries the slogan, "Keeping the World Comfortable Since 1914," has been an industry leader. With corporate headquarters in Bryan, Ohio and a manufacturing facility located in Madison, Georgia, the company relies on its modern facilities, state-of-the-art equipment, and roughly 400 employees to help deliver consistent, quality products for its globally expanding market.

The seventh organization is Bricker and Eckler LLP (B&E). Access to resources is the theme at the Columbus, Ohio-based law firm of B&E. The firm has become one of Ohio's leading law firms during the past half century of its practice. Established in 1945, B&E represents businesses, numerous nonprofit organizations, government agencies, school districts, and municipalities.

The final organization is Davis & Kuelthau, S.C. Since 1967, their clients have allowed them to play a significant role in building their businesses, as well as assisting them in ensuring their personal financial security and that of their families. However, at Davis & Kuelthau, they believe their role extends beyond that of legal and business counsel. They strive to educate their clients about the law to ensure that they have the tools necessary to identify legal problems, needs and opportunities, as well as to minimize the risk of legal consequences. They have offices throughout Wisconsin and successfully serve a diverse group of public- and private-sector clients nationwide.

LEGAL, FINANCIAL, AND OPERATIONAL RISKS

20th Century Fox

Jeff Uslan joined 20th Century Fox at the company's Los Angeles, California, headquarters in 1999 as the manager of information protection. "I was hired to establish an Information Protection and Security presence at Fox," said Uslan. "Although securing the Internet and e-mail was and still is a primary concern, the protection of our network and servers remains a high priority as well. We needed to make sure the Internet connection wasn't abused by employees and the hundreds of contract workers who are granted desktop Web and e-mail access." While 20th Century Fox is faced with the same host of issues presented to any company or organization that provides employees with desktop-level Web and e-mail access, the issue of protecting company data is most critical. 20th Century supplies Web and e-mail access to thousands of people affiliated with the company. As Uslan points out, protecting 20th Century's intellectual properties is not a small task–especially considering one keystroke could result in the loss of a confidential movie/TV script or contract detail. "We have firewalls to protect from external hackers," explains Uslan. Uslan illustrates 20th Century's need using a real-world example of an upcoming movie release. A competing studio could prematurely receive details–possible via the Internet–on the theme and time frame of an upcoming 20th Century movie. The result could be million dollar losses at the box office if that competing studio were to beat 20th Century to the market with a similarly focused movie theme. In addition to scripts for movies and TV shows, 20th Century must also be careful to make sure people affiliated with the company do not leak details about ongoing contract negotiations.

JFK Medical Center

At JFK Medical Center, thousands of employees, from doctors and nurses to executives and staff members, have access to the Internet. "There is a ton of valuable information that our employees can access via the Internet that is critical to the efficiency and effectiveness of this institution," said Bill Thorpe, system analyst for the medical center. "However, there is a lot of garbage out there. Our concern is focused primarily on protecting JFK from legal liabilities; however, saving our bandwidth and improving employee productivity are also important goals." Thorpe explains that the Internet opens any organization up to legal and other liabilities if it is used inappropriately. With thousands of employees at JFK, Thorpe does not have the time or the manpower to manually monitor where people are going on the Internet. "We were looking for a tool that had the ability to monitor thousands of workstations and users and block any kind of suspicious activity. We have a primary goal here of providing excellent patient care. Surf abuse can only harm that prime objective."

Irvington High School

Bill Stanley, the technology coordinator at Irvington High School, said, "However, once we got past the physical layer, I realized we had an operational layer or moral factor involved. ... In a school setting, Internet access is fraught with many hazards." By "hazards," Stanley is referring in particular to surfing abuse by students and faculty. "We want to encourage students to perform online research and gain a larger world view, but teenagers often have a tendency to move outside of the educational constraints," he said. Although he may not have anticipated that janitors would be using the school's Internet connection to visit pornographic sites, Stanley was concerned that students were left completely unprotected from these sites—not to mention the host of other sites that aren't appropriate for the classroom.

Lake Charles Memorial Hospital

After a recent industry seminar, the president of Louisiana-based Lake Charles Memorial Hospital, Elton L. Williams, Jr., had reason for concern. A hot topic at the seminar was the issue of employee e-mail usage. "We have about 1,000 employees across the hospital's six locations," said Mr. Westmoreland, the system administrator. Employees at the remote offices are connected to the headquarters via an ISDN line. Did Lake Charles have any means to protect the hospital against liability stemming from potentially offensive e-mail distributed by employees? "I knew we needed an e-mail policy and a way to enforce it; otherwise, we could be held liable if an employee was exposed to inappropriate Internet content," said Mr. Williams.

New Mexico Mortgage Finance Authority (MFA)

So where does an Information systems manager fit into an organization like the MFA? "People are depending on us for their livelihood, and having an inefficient, slow, insecure network is not a good excuse for failing to provide these services. Also, we are watched very closely by the state legislature to make sure we are doing our job well," remarked Mr Flint, the systems administrator. Like many financial institutions, the MFA is interested in the management of its assets—producing one-quarter billion dollars annually. "On every level of this organization we need to be organized and in control." Mr. Flint continued, "The MFA has an integrated system that links all of its systems together. All employees have Internet and intranet access. Although we have employees with all different kinds of jobs, it is important for them to know what is going on in each department," said Flint.

Bard Manufacturing

About a year ago, Bard first began providing Internet access to its employees through a direct 56 Kbps connection to a local ISP. Almost immediately, the Internet proved to be a tremendous resource for the company's overall business. The operations staff was using the Internet for tracking parts through UPS and FedEx. Bard's engineers were using it for troubleshooting and to relay information back and forth from Bryan to the manufacturing plant in Madison. Administrative assistants were using it for scheduling flights and arranging other travel information. However, Roy Crooks, the IS professional, was not surprised to learn that despite all of the positive examples of Internet usage, there were management concerns of surfing abuse by employees. For example, some employees were reportedly spending excessive work hours accessing Internet sites that were not job-related. If Bard didn't take action against surfing abuse there could be several negative consequences. The most obvious, of course, was a decrease in employee productivity. In addition, Crooks was already considering an investment in more network bandwidth to compensate for increased Internet traffic. Finally, there was the legal aspect. Without an Internet acceptable usage policy in place, Bard could be liable for sexual harassment charges if an employee was subjected to pornographic material on another employee's computer terminal.

Bricker & Eckler, LLP

At Bricker & Eckler, LLP (B&E), revenue has been stimulated by the use of technology. Eric Schmidt joined the firm as IS director, and he was promoted to the position of chief information officer. According to Schmidt, during his tenure, B&E has "held the line–we've increased revenues without increasing the number of employees. We want people to have more efficient access to all of our resources," explains Schmidt. "We have lots of attorneys that work from home, including those working from Cincinnati, Athens (Ohio), and across the country in Colorado and Montana. We want them to each have efficient access to all of our resources because the firm reaps the benefits." Utilizing an authentication program provided by the company firewall and a high-speed Internet connection, the attorneys are able to securely conduct client research and transmit confidential data over the Internet. Prior to rolling out the Internet resource throughout the firm, however, Schmidt and the firm's managing partner developed and clearly communicated a policy for Internet usage.

"The legal liability is the biggest driver for our Internet policy," said Schmidt. "You really don't know how much a sexual harassment lawsuit may cost until you get burned." According to Schmidt, B&E hasn't seen a problem with inappropriate Internet usage by employees. "We told every employee that they are being monitored because I really think it is important to let them know up front," he said. "I think it was something they understood and expected. We explained the Internet was a resource that was used to better serve our clients."

Davis & Kuelthau, S.C.

Ask the law firm of Davis & Kuelthau why they first became interested in Internet content filtering solutions, and "To practice what we preach" will be in the answer. As a full-service law firm dedicated to "educating its clients about the law to ensure that they have the tools necessary to identify legal problems and minimize the risk of legal consequences," Davis & Kuelthau recognized the value of taking the same precautions within its own organization. Brian Drier, manager of information systems, the firm was concerned about the liabilities associated with inappropriate Internet usage–primarily legal liabilities, employee productivity and maintaining a safe work environment. "Organizations look to us as experts in advising how to protect themselves from these kinds of Internet problems, so we lead by example and take the same precautions within our own company."

For Davis & Kuelthau, the Internet is an invaluable tool for doing business. "Our position is that the Internet is a fantastic resource," said Drier. "Many of our lawyers need to do research and stay current on the latest legal issues and rulings, while our administrative staff needs to get information and communicate with the outside world. We wanted to open up this resource to all employees for personal and professional use–but we knew that it needed to be managed properly. Our biggest concerns were legal liabilities and productivity."

Because their largest practice area is labor and employment law, Davis & Kuelthau completely understands the issues surrounding sexual harassment and employee privacy concerns. By preventing Internet users from disseminating offensive content, the firm is complying with the Supreme Court's recent revision of the Communications Decency Act (CDAII), which mandates that "employers take any and all necessary precautions to ensure a safe and hostile-free work environment." Another legal precedent, the Hooper Doctrine, also mandates that employers use all tools available to ensure the safety of workers.

Another major concern of Davis & Kuelthau was the issue of productivity. "We want to make sure that work is getting done," said Drier, "and we also want to make sure that our PCs are being used efficiently and for business purposes. We want to preserve our investment in those critical company resources and be able to make intelligent planning and forecasting decisions."

Aligning Internet Usage Through Internet Policy Management

While the eight organizations represent a cross-section of United States companies, there are parallel themes among them. The goal of the firms was to use the communication and productive enhancing power of the Internet while minimizing the legal, financial, and operational risks of the Web. They wanted to allow employees the greatest amount of freedom and latitude to use the Internet as a tool in their work, while recognizing the cost/benefit trade-offs. They were sensitive to user needs for personal use of the Internet and for privacy. The organizations wanted to manage the Internet so that all parties were in a win-win situation. It was recognized that the technical and social systems within the organization had to be integrated.

All organizations expressed a need for a solution that was based in a systems approach. They needed flexibility and customizability, low maintenance, a high degree of accuracy, multiple features, ease of use, and integration with current technologies. They wanted to deploy the latest Internet technologies to streamline business processes, trim costs, and offer customers and suppliers the ease of electronic communication while protecting organizational information and resources and respecting employee rights. In short, the eight organizations wanted to leverage the power of the Internet, while responsibly and proactively managing its use.

All of the eight organizations represent a growing number of corporations that monitor employee Internet usage. International Data Corporation (IDC), a leading market research firm, estimates 3.9 million businesses will implement Web-filtering software by 2003–and the software is most popular among larger organizations. IDC predicts that 80% of large companies will purchase Web-filtering software in the next 12-24 months. The growing trend is to deploy Internet filtering software primarily to reduce legal exposure. Organizations are trying to avoid potential costs, not to mention public embarrassment, by utilizing filtering software to develop and enforce Internet usage policies. As the above cases demonstrate, it is not only large companies that can benefit enormously from Internet policy management.

The eight organizations chose to adopt the six-step Internet policy management model outlined in the beginning of the chapter. They developed an explicit and clearly communicated Internet usage policy, adopted the means and tools for monitoring Internet and e-mail usage, trained end users, had policies in place on reporting and communicating the results, and finally applied discipline measures as prescribed when necessary. The New Mexico Mortgage Finance Authority has an Internet usage policy that makes employees aware of the company's expectations and also serves as a guideline for what is acceptable Internet usage. MFA employees are able to surf after hours, but they are aware that their surfing is being monitored. At Lake Charles, "We had a couple of people that thought we were going to block access to fishing sites," explains Westmoreland. "We let them know that pornographic sites were the only ones that were going to be blocked." At 20th Century Fox, employees understand the benefits of content-filtering technology–employees don't receive junk e-mail, malicious code or viruses. 20th Century Fox, like the other cases in this paper, but unlike many others, provides unlimited Internet access to employees. However, site accesses and Internet communications are carefully monitored.

After extensive evaluation of the leading corporate Internet access control packages, Elron Software's Web Inspector,™ ranked #1 by International Data Corporation (IDC) research, was chosen by the eight organizations. Web Inspector™ allows organizations to monitor, report, and block access to Web content. This product offers a wide variety of surfing reports and statistics on organization, group, and individual Internet usage. Rated #1 in reporting by *Network World Magazine*, Web Inspector™ offers powerful standard and custom reports with proactive alerts. Organizations can generate data by sites visited, most active users, and time of day. A customizable SurfTime™ meter can calculate exactly how much an organization is spending due to recreational surfing.

Using Elron Software's SmartList,™ Web Inspector™ is content-sensitive. Rather than blocking by URL alone, Web Inspector™ is able to inspect and verify suspect sites based on the actual text on the Web page, in the meta tags, as well as the URL name. Where some list-based products may block a site because of the terms "Middlesex county" or "sex education," Web Inspector's sophisticated technology is able to determine these sites are appropriate based on content.

DISCUSSION

These eight organizations are examples of how to reduce legal, financial, and operational risks by aligning Internet usage with business priorities through Internet policy management. They have a socio-technical approach where the needs of employers and employees are balanced. Products offered by Elron Software, Inc. and other similar companies, provide the enabling technology. If integrated with the cultural and social structure of the organization, it is possible to help maximize the productive use of the Internet and e-mail access while effectively and efficiently managing the risks. Many companies still don't understand the nature of the Internet, or have not been able to leverage it effectively. Some companies refuse to provide desktop Internet access because they aren't sure how to manage employee access and protect the organization. On the basis of the case discussions presented in this paper, we believe that Internet policy management is a model that greatly extends the ability of organizations to reduce the legal, financial, and operational risks associated with the Internet. Internet policy management is flexible enough to be successfully incorporated into a variety of organizations.

REFERENCES

D'Antoni, H. (2000). Web surfers beware: Someone's watching. *Informationweek,* 772, 167-168.

Mandel, M. J. and Hof, R. D. (2001). Rethinking the Internet. *Business Week* March 26, 117-141.

Ohlhorst, F. J. (2001). Filtering software blocks headaches, litigation. *Computer Reseller News*, 926, 53-54.

Roberts, B. (1999). Filtering software blocks employees' Web abuses. *HRMagazine*, 44(9), 114-120.

Wonnacott, L. (1999). Policing the Internet: If your users can't surf responsibly, you may have to monitor them. *InfoWorld*, 21(13), 13-14.

Chapter XV

Universal Site Accessibility: Barrier Free For All

Beth Archibald Tang
University of Virginia, USA

INTRODUCTION

At least 15% of the American population has a disability (Kaye, 1998); some estimate it is as high as one in five. For research studies, the United States government usually defines the term *disability* as a limitation in a person's major life activities during daily living, working, and attending school (Job Accommodation Network, 1992).[1] Assistive technologies—the tools that help individuals complete their daily tasks—serve as adjuncts that help to bridge the gap between dependence and self-reliance.

Webmasters[2] have their tools, too. They use software that enhance the sites and make them interesting. While Web usability specialists place emphasis on completing tasks, the purpose of some Web sites may be more about evoking a "wow" response, and less about imparting information that visitors can use. On occasion, being able to access these Web pages requires that users go to a third-party Web site and download plug-ins to listen to an audio file, watch a video clip, or read downloaded documents. For people with disabilities, however, many of the Web sites inadvertently establish barriers that could be prevented.

The ethical implications of these barriers can be profound and, in some cases, require legal remedies. Government legislation and international technical standards may provide a compelling force for an organization to design accessible Web sites, but as Paciello (2001) writes, if the "driving force of the Web is to get your content and Web services to the public, … [w]hy wouldn't you design and create that information for the widest population, including people with disabilities?"

No Quick Fixes

Organizations unfamiliar to accessibility face a challenging task. Adequate time should be planned to review sites and to phase in improvements. While there are no quick fixes or all-purpose tools to "make" sites accessible, there are checklists,[3] software programs (both free and commercial),[4] and training[5] to provide the background and assistance necessary. Judicious use of the resources will inform the long-term plan for accessibility.

This chapter does not provide technical coding workarounds or programming scripts—other Web sites already do this[6]—but will discuss what accessibility is and why it is an important issue in both the legal and ethical sense. This chapter is especially for organizations facing Web accessibility mandates for the first time; at the end, organizations will have not only an understanding of the issues, but also an overview of how to improve their Web sites for people with disabilities.

BACKGROUND

Access to the Internet offers both freedom and frustration. When Tim Berners-Lee envisioned what the software program he originally called Enquire would be able to do, he imagined that the World Wide Web would be able to provide a new kind of mechanism that would bring "the workings of society closer to the workings of our minds" (Berners-Lee, 1999, p. 2). With this freedom, however, arises a responsibility on the part of the organization as an owner of a Web site. Organizations open themselves to enhanced contact and should approach this with the concept of universal design in mind.

In universal design, the needs of individuals are considered with regard to products, environments, and services. More specifically, there are no barriers when someone visits a Web site. Some people already encounter difficulties with an unreliable Internet connection, older equipment, early version browsers, and limited computer memory. Coupled with less than the latest software and hardware, Web-based barriers for people with disabilities are compounded by movies without captioning or descriptions, audio files without text transcripts, poor contrast in image colors, poor readability of font types, flashing images, and documents in inaccessible formats.

Basic Testing

How can an organization determine if its Web site is accessible? To answer that question, the following are some quick and easy tests to sample how Web sites may appear to some people with disabilities. It is a good idea to have several individuals, in various departments and with various levels of Internet skills, document their results, so a record of progress can be maintained. These basic tests can form a baseline by which to measure progress.

- View the organization's site (or any site) in the "other" browser, i.e., one that is not the default or frequently used browser. How well does it hold up in comparison to the "favored" browser?
- If the Web pages are optimized for 800 by 600 pixels, view the pages in another screen size, such as 640 by 480 pixels. Does it require excessive horizontal scrolling?

For optimum accessibility and in support of the concept of "best viewed in any browser," webmasters should refrain from requiring a certain browser or version. Screen size is another issue. It is better to scale down, rather than scale up, and assume everyone has 17-inch monitors.

- Next, select a different font type and a larger font size from the default set-up. Does the site still retain a quality appearance?

The Web site should be able to degrade gracefully; that is, a site's layout—independent from the content—should hold up well regardless if one person chose 10 point Times New Roman font and another one chose 14 point Arial. Header tags, in addition, should be used as they were intended, to note the start of a new section. Screen reading programs use these tags to allow users to jump to major sections; using a header tag for the effect rather than for its purpose takes away from the site's utility.

The next few items refer to visual and audio elements that may not be available on some organizations' sites; plenty of examples are available at CNN.com and Yahoo.com for the purpose of these tests.

- Turn off all images and scripts, refresh the site and clear the cache. Is it possible to explore the site as easily and as well as when the images and scripts were on?
- Download a video, such as a movie trailer. With eyes closed, listen to the movie. Is it possible to envision what is happening in the video?
- Next, turn off the speakers and watch the movie trailer again. Is it possible to tell what the actors and the narrator are saying?

The purpose of these three exercises was to demonstrate the importance of alt tags (text descriptions of images), closed captioning, and descriptive audio. People with disabilities rely on these elements to provide them with information they need; if they cannot access information on an organization's site, they will go away, removing any chance for business transactions or good word of mouth about the site's services. To simulate mobility issues, try this last test:

*   Disconnect the mouse or set it aside. Navigate using only the Tab key. How efficient is it?

A simple way to prevent extraordinary amounts of tabbing is to insert a "skip navigation" link that jumps from the start of the navigation bar, if it is at the top of the page to the main body of the Web page. One last accessibility test is to look at the file sizes of the various Web pages. If they are more than 50 kilobytes each, then it is very likely that users with older modems will experience lag times between selecting a link and getting the page.

These examples are designed to simulate how people with disabilities experience a site. Universal design shows consideration of the end users, regardless of disability or hardware and software. If people with access issues cannot successfully use a Web site, they will go elsewhere.

Communication

While accessibility facilitates communication, it is independent from content since it is focused on the format of the information. Since the World Wide Web is all about communication, the importance of accessibility is readily apparent. Levine, Locke, Searls, and Weinberger (1999) elegantly state that "Markets are conversations" (p. xii). Moreover, organizations "that don't realize their markets are now networked person-to-person, getting smarter as a result and deeply joined in conversation, are missing their best opportunity" (p. xiii). By going beyond the so-called brochureware, organizations realize that there is more to static Hypertext Markup Language (HTML) pages. Moving toward dynamic, targeted content in formats such as Extensible Markup Language (XML) that can be read as easily with a personal computer (PC) browser as with a wireless device not only facilitates communication, but also allows for ease of use in personalized and customized settings.

Without careful consideration, not only of the content, but also of the message to be conveyed through the medium of the Web site, it is likely that sites may confuse, mislead, or enrage their users. Political correctness aside, savvy Web writers know that messages must be written appropriately and carefully for the target audience in the language that they will understand. Trustworthiness and reliability must also be readily apparent; for without these elements, word will spread quickly that a site cannot be deemed worthwhile. Fickle browsers and shoppers will vote with the mouse (or keyboard) and go elsewhere.

It is important to understand who may arrive at a Web site. The exercises above gave an indication that nothing can be assumed and it is important to test for as many variations as possible.

At this point, we should step back and understand why universal design is also a legal concern. This context will help organizations to better understand the impact that accessibility will have on a Web site in the short- and long-term. Universal design helps not only people with disabilities, but also their nondisabled peers, since such design is both good programming and good practice.

LEGAL ISSUES OF ACCESSIBILITY

This section covers the main federal accessability legislation that impacts organizations with Web sites.

ADA

The major purpose of the Americans with Disabilities Act (ADA) of 1990 is to improve the employment of people with disabilities by making it against the law to discriminate against them. Employers are required by the ADA to provide reasonable accommodations for the known limitations of qualified individuals who are employees or who may be employees. (Companies can, however, claim undue burden if they meet certain conditions.) Employers are also prohibited from discriminating against an otherwise qualified employee based on the simple need of an accommodation.

In the Fall of 1996, the US Department of Justice said that the ADA was applicable to Web sites. As of this writing, no lawsuit has set a precedent for this position.

Section 508

On December 21, 2000, the US government published the final rule for Section 508 of the Rehabilitation Act. These standards require that:

When Federal agencies develop, procure, maintain, or use electronic and information technology, they shall ensure that the electronic and information technology allows Federal employees with disabilities to have access to and use of information and data that is comparable to the access and use of information and data by Federal employees who are not individuals with disabilities, unless an undue burden would be imposed on the agency. (Electronic and Information Technology Accessibility Standards, 2000)

The rule also stipulates that people in the public with disabilities will have the same rights to access, and that lawsuits may be filed six months after implementation of the final rule if sites do not meet the accessability requirements.

The Architectural and Transportation Barriers Compliance Board (also known as the Access Board) released these accessibility standards for public comment in late March 2000. The Access Board modeled 11 of the 16 standards (see Table 1) after the Priority 1 checkpoints—there are an additional two levels of voluntary compliance—of the Web Content Accessibility Guidelines (version 1.0) written by the World Wide Web Consortium Web Accessibility Initiative (W3C/WAI). This means that the accessibility standards meet the *basic* requirements of accessibility, according to the W3C/WAI. A recent report (McClure, Sprehe, & Eschenfelder, 2000) further identifies accessibility as one element in a three-dimensional performance measures policy. While accessibility in this report refers more to the general sense, Appendix A of that report provides well-thought-out criteria to evaluate federal Web sites.

With the release of the Section 508 standards and the ADA, the US government has acknowledged the importance of accessibility, and that people with disabilities comprise a significant portion of the digital divide. Reports such as the one by Wellner (2000) estimate that more than 40% of people with disabilities are online; they spend more time than their nondisabled peers online; and, about half the online disabled community say that the Internet has significantly improved their quality of life.

Fortunately, the private sector is not far behind accessibility awareness. Businesses and organizations, for example, are beginning to realize the impact of a well-designed Web site. Good, clean design attracts visitors and keeps them longer (Nielsen, 1999). While the purchasing power of people with disabilities can only grow, the potential economic power of a new customer base and target audience is worth the effort to design an accessible site.

There has also been discussion in the information technology (IT) industry about the long-term impact of Section 508 (New, 2001). Section 508 only applies to certain types of government Web sites, but it will very likely impact the private sector with subsequent releases of new software packages, new devices, and so forth. The private sector maintains that producing one line of products for the government and another for commercial sales is not economically feasible. So, it is very likely that the accessibility standards will find their way into products and Web sites.

Table 1: Standards Pertaining to Web-Based Intranet and Internet Information and Applications

Section 508 referring paragraph	Web content accessibility guideline (version 1.0) equivalent	Section 508 accessibility standard
a	1.1	A text equivalent for every non-text element shall be provided (e.g., via alt, longdesc, or in element content).
b	1.4	Equivalent alternatives for any multimedia presentation shall be synchronized with the presentation.
c	2.1	Web pages shall be designed so that all information conveyed with color is also available without color, for example, from context or markup.
d	6.1	Documents shall be organized so they are readable without requiring an associated style sheet.
e	1.2	Redundant text links shall be provided for each active region of a server-side image map.
f	9.1	Client-side image maps shall be provided instead of server-side image maps except where the regions cannot be defined with an available geometric shape.
g	5.1	Row and column headers shall be identified for data tables.
h	5.2	Markup shall be used to associate data cells and header cells for data tables that have two or more logical levels of row or column headers.
i	12.1	Frames shall be titled with text that facilitates frame identification and navigation.
j	7.1	Pages shall be designed to avoid causing the screen to flicker with a frequency greater than 2 Hz and lower than 55 Hz.
k	11.4	A text-only page, with equivalent information or functionality, shall be provided to make a Web site comply with the provisions of this part, when compliance cannot be accomplished in any other way. The content of the text-only page shall be updated whenever the primary page changes.
l	n/a	When pages utilize scripting languages to display content or to create interface elements, the information provided by the script shall be identified with functional text that can be read by assistive technology.
m	n/a	When a Web page requires that an applet, plug-in or other application be present on the client system to interpret page content, the page must provide a link to a plug-in or applet that complies with Sec. 1194.21(a) through (l).
n	n/a	When electronic forms are designed to be completed online, the form shall allow people using assistive technology to access the information, field elements, and functionality required for completion and submission of the form, including all directions and cues.
o	n/a	A method shall be provided that permits users to skip repetitive navigation links.
p	n/a	When a timed response is required, the user shall be alerted and given sufficient time to indicate more time is required.

Note: Adapted from Electronic and Information Technology Accessibility Standards; Final Rule, 36 C.F.R. § 1194 (2000)

Table 2: Selected Accessibility HTML Coding Examples

Section 508 referring paragraph	Section 508 accessibility standard (abbreviated)	HTML example

a	Text equivalent	Alt tag: `<img src="map.gif" alt="County map of West Virginia">` OR `<img src="spacer.gif" alt="">`
		`<img src="spyglass.gif" alt="Search">`
		`<img src="abclogo.gif" alt="ABC red bicycle logo - Link to home">`
		Note: Usually alt tags are limited to five or six words; if a more detailed description is needed, it is better to use longdesc.
		Longdesc: `<img src="abclogo.gif" alt="Link to home" longdesc="abclogo.htm">`
		On abclogo.htm page: The logo for ABC company is represented by a figure on an old-fashioned red bicycle...
		Note: Longdesc may not be supported by all browsers, so d links are a compromise.
		D link: `<a href="abclogo.htm" title="Description of image">d</a>`
		(see above for abclogo.htm description)

e, f	Image maps	See alt tags (above) for the image map as a whole; for each element in the image map: `<area shape="rect" coords="0,0,30,30" href="search.htm" alt="Search">`

g, h	Tables	Provide a title (caption):
		`<caption>Preferred Colors by Type of Bicycle</caption>`
		Associate cells with headers:
		`<th id="t1">Type of Bicycle</th>`
		`<td id="header1">Tricycle</td>`

i	Frames	Name each frame logically: `<frame src="search.htm" title="Search">`
		Use noframes in the frameset:
		`<noframes>`
		`<a href="search.htm" title="Search">Search the site</a>`
		`</noframes>`

m	Applets, plug-ins, applications	Test for presence of applets, plug-ins, applications and allow for alternatives:
		`<script>...script goes here ...</script>`
		`<noscript>`
		`<p>To search, <a href="search.htm">go to the text-only Search page</a>`
		`</noscript>`

Know the Users

As stated above, more and more people, including people with disabilities, are online. These individuals provide unique challenges in Web design that may have been overlooked, such as the readability of font type and size, or image contrast; however, consideration of accessibility benefits the broader target audience. For example, with "clean" coding (or HTML programming), suddenly downloading times improve, meaningful alt tags replace useless image file names and sizes, and "stickiness" of a site increases to a measurable degree as evidenced by fewer calls and e-mails to the Webmaster for help.

With increasing Internet connectivity and heightened access to information, it is a challenge to design for accessibility, but it is not impossible. The W3C/WAI sketched several scenarios[7] that provide real-world examples of different people with different types of disabilities and how they use the Web. Throughout all of the sketches, the goal to communicate information clearly and accessibly remain paramount. Organizations that have well researched the target audience will attain the most success at reaching and retaining them.

Log Analysis

One way to better understand visitors to a Web site without actually interviewing them is to study the Web site's history. Mena (1999) describes how log files provide insight about a Web site's users: When a user selects a link or types in a Web address, the information is recorded on the computer that provides the Web site services (known as a server). When the server presents the Web page in the user's browser, that information is stored in a log file. Sprehe (2000) emphasizes that recording just Web site hits is not a meaningful measure of anything; measures of documents downloaded or numbers of user sessions per time period are more relevant. The following defines some of the important elements in a log file.

- Address or domain name of site visitor
- Web address of referring site, if any
- Browser/platform (user's Web browser and operating platform)
- Visit date and time
- Actions the user completed (or did not complete)
- Pages and files viewed
- Results of viewing files
- Files downloaded and file size

In short, log files list all Web activities, including who visited, when they visited, and in what activities they engaged while at the site. Use of a log analysis tool, such as WebTrends (WebTrends, 1999), to find out where users are going and if they are encountering any errors, can also help organizations determine how well the site is working. Log files tell organizations if users are encountering problems (e.g., 404 error/file not found codes), how long they remained on the site, and whether they went more than one click deep, i.e., past the home page. By understanding the target audience, it is possible to understand the importance of what accessibility means and what accessibility can do.

TIPS TO ENCHANCE ACCESSIBILITY

There are simple checks that can be done almost immediately to ascertain whether a Web site meets minimal accessibility requirements. One of the easiest is to use an accessibility checklist. "Section 508 Web Accessibility Checklist for HTML," was developed by Paul Bohman for Web Accessibility In Mind (WebAIM)[8] and provides one of the best examples of a checklist-based approach to assessing accessibility. Checklists are but one part, though. Convention suggests that organizations:

- Chart the long-term trends in the log files to ascertain what errors are commonly encountered, what links are broken, and if it is apparent that users are finding the site's "important" sections.
- Run the basic tests listed above.
- Check HTML coding.
- Use several screen readers to scan the site, e.g., JAWS, Window-Eyes, IBM Home Page Reader (it would be best to ask screen reader users to test the sites for you).

Many Web sites targeted to people with disabilities provide information on adaptive equipment and can provide information upon request as to which vendors sell which screen readers and other assistive technology. Organizations should also:

- View the site in a variety of browsers, including Netscape Navigator, Internet Explorer, and others.[9]
- Test for accessibility for colorblindness (www.visibone.com/colorblind).
- Use alt tags, d links, and longdesc for images/graphics and write tags with meaningful information.
- Provide documents in alternate and accessible formats, e.g., text, HTML, or some other word processing format, in addition to Adobe Acrobat (PDF).
- Check for Priority 1 accessibility by running Bobby and other tools.

Bobby is a well-known tool that still requires a human to make final judgements; it is "a free [Java] service provided by [the Center for Applied Special Technology] to help Web page authors identify and repair significant barriers to access by individuals with disabilities" (Center for Applied Special

Technology, 2000). Simply running a Bobby check and making the recommended edits is no guarantee that a site is accessible. Once a site is deemed Bobby acceptable, webmasters can post the Bobby image on their site. Displaying the logo is no guarantee of a site's accessibility; therefore, web sites should pass several accessibility tests. More complex activities to make sites accessible include:

- Reviewing the necessity of using plug-ins to access pages, and drafting a plan to provide the pages in alternate formats.
- Developing and using style sheets to control font and presentation, and allowing user flexibility in setting preferences.
- Reducing use of unnecessary tables for formatting.

Tables 1 and 2 show the relationship of selected points listed above with regard to Section 508, along with sample coding to meet accessibility requirements.

Lessons Learned

Lessons learned are valuable, as well, at both the individual and organizational levels. In fact some organizational lessons learned are available for study from the Accessible Web Authoring Resources and Education (AWARE) Center (aware.hwg.org/studies) and at Usability.gov.

Recording wisdom at the individual level is also important; for example, one webmaster learned that a splash page (a series of animated, or moving, images designed to develop interest in the content of the Web site) did not achieve its intended goal. After analyzing the log files, the webmaster discovered that users were actually leaving the site rather than exploring any further. The Webmaster and the organization concluded that since splash pages are a drain on bandwidth and can trigger seizures in some people with photosensitive disorders, the introductory splash page should be removed from the site. In addition to the above resources, webmasters should investigate print resources such as Nielsen (2000) and Constantine and Lockwood (1999) for lessons learned.

Aside from Section 508, Webmasters should also be aware of other accessibility standards. On the W3C/WAI Web site, there is a list of international accessibility policies; as of the date of this writing, Australia, Canada, Denmark, the European Union, France, Ireland, Italy, Japan, Portugal, and the United Kingdom maintain such policies. In the United States, only California, New York, and Texas have accessibility policies.

Action Plan

In light of a possible lawsuit from someone who cannot access a Web site, some entities may posit that retrofitting their organizations' Web sites poses too large an expense; in actuality, updating "from this point on," not retrofitting, is the goal. Organizations should conduct a thorough assessment of the effort required and then outline a plan of action for current and future Web efforts. This will provide a good faith demonstration that the organization is in the process of making the site accessible. Simply adding contact information on Web pages to request documents in an alternate format will not meet accessibility requirements, but it is another good faith effort to show that the organization is attempting to address user needs. This undue burden analysis (Tang, 2000) provides documentation of the existing accessibility issues and also outlines the plan of action. Of course, this plan is not a static document. As technology enables change, so should the document be updated, as well as the Web site.

Teaming for Accessibility

Within an organization, the technology group may find itself at odds with the content group. In the expanding discussion of usability over accessibility, the two camps will realize that the goal is to improve the user experience. The Section 508 standards are necessarily vague because they must address technological issues that are yet to exist; in the meantime, designers and information architects must face the nebulous, qualitative aspect of accessibility. Coders, on the other hand, work against specifications that are measurable. If the programming tool identifies coding errors, then those can be fixed and success is measured if all of the browsers can display the page appropriately.

It is important for technologists and content specialists to work together, for this is a team effort. It is the responsibility of the Web development team to specify the roles of each of the players. The medium requires development of a new set of skills in crafting metadata. The Section 508.gov web site provides links to training resources that webmasters can access to help keep their skills up to date. As of this writing, in late June 2001, the Section 508 web site will post a self-paced training module for Webmasters.

FUTURE TRENDS

The Web in the workplace necessarily carries with it certain responsibilities and requirements, one of which is accessibility, or universal site design. It is also likely that the remaining priority levels will eventually be phased in as requirements, so familiarity with both Section 508 and the W3C/WAI levels will be invaluable. Web designers can begin to start coding in Extensible Hypertext Markup Language (XHTML) markup, which is a reformulation of HTML 4.0; XHTML can be considered "HTML 5.0." This format is compatible with HTML but has strict requirements, like XML, such as consistency with coding in lowercase due to case sensitivity; some examples are listed in Table 3.

Since more of the older generation is online, sites that are easy to use and uncluttered are in high demand. Given that the number of senior citizens is expected to grow significantly when the "baby boomer" generation reaches retirement age soon, accessibility plays an even more important role. This virtual flood of newly minted senior citizens will also need the flexibility that well-designed electronic and information technology devices can offer.

Finally, selecting a piece adaptive equipment or setting preferences for Web site appearance and functionality will be as ubiquitous as choosing a brand and type of toothpaste. It is already possible in many large superstores and office supply centers to choose from a number of mouses or trackballs. Keyboards come in many "flavors," also, from traditional to wireless to ergonomic ones. Browsers and screen readers, too, will soon catch up with accessibility standards to allow for the consistent use of cascading style sheets and longdesc, to name a few.

CONCLUSION

Accessibility allows choice, and not just the choice of a lesser of two evils. Because one person prefers to just read a transcript and another wants to experience the Web-based presentation in full, designer-based selections should not prevail. Users should be able to decide what they want in the format

Table 3: HTML and XHTML Comparisons

Coding element	HTML	Preferred XHTML
Horizontal rule	`<HR> OR <hr>`	`<hr />`
Attributes	`<table rows=4>`	`<table rows="4">`
Elements	`<b><i>example</b></i>`	`<b><i>example</i></b>`

that they want it. Since it is impossible to replicate exactly the experience and personal configurations of every user, Web designers must build in flexibility.

Principles of accessibility ensure that individuals, regardless of disability, browser version, or modem speed, are able obtain access to Web sites as well as their nondisabled peers. Accessibility helps not only people with disabilities, but also those who choose to turn off certain features to reduce drain on bandwidth or who surf the Web on a personal digital assistant (PDA) or Web-enabled cellular phone. Universal design ensures that barriers are removed, so that individuals can interface with the Web site in order to obtain the information they need to complete the tasks they wish to achieve. In December of 2000, the US federal government released accessibility standards that provide for individuals who encounter inaccessible Web sites to file lawsuits.

While the threat of a lawsuit is a concern, the fact that accessibility is a civil right should not be discounted. The impact of an accessible site is a benefit to businesses and organizations that choose to implement Section 508 as a voluntary standard. No doubt these standards will become de facto guidelines for the private sector as vendors that sell electronic and information technology to the federal government choose to incorporate the accessibility standards into one line of products, rather than maintaining two discrete lines.

ENDNOTES

[1] The severity of a disability is different for everyone, even among those who have the "same" disability.

[2] The terms *Webmaster* and *Web designer* will be used interchangeably in this chapter.

[3] The W3C/WAI list of checkpoints (www.w3.org/TR/WAI-WEBCONTENT/full-checklist.html) ("plain English" versions are also available as Quick Tips [www.w3.org/WAI/References/QuickTips]) and the unofficial Section 508 checklists (access.idyllmtn.com/section508) compiled by Idyll Mountain Internet are two good resources; more can be found by searching on "accessibility checklist" in any search engine.

[4] The Accessible Web Author's Toolkit [www.awarecenter.org/tools] provides a listing of the most commonly used tools; a more extensive list is available at the W3C/WAI's site (www.w3.org/WAI/ER/existingtools.html). It should be noted that many Web design programs, such as those published by Macromedia and Allaire (recently purchased by Macromedia), offer built-in tools that validate tags, check for deprecated tags, and even run spell-checking utilities.

[5] In addition to resources provided by the World Wide Web Consortium Web Accessibility Initiative (W3C/WAI), training for accessibility is also available from the US federal government via the Access Board (www.section508.gov/classes.html) and online organizations such as the HTML Writer's Guild (www.hwg.org/services/classes).

[6] See the Trace Center (trace.wisc.edu), the W3C/WAI (www.w3.org/WAI), and the Center for Information Technology Accommodation [www.itpolicy.gsa.gov/cita] for technical assistance.

[7] See the W3C/WAI's "How People With Disabilities Use the Web" document (www.w3.org/WAI/EO/Drafts/PWD-Use-Web/Overview.htm).

[8] Prior to delving into accessibility in-depth, readers may also wish to browse the resources at WebAIM (www.webaim.org), especially the tutorials.

[9] Other popular browsers include Opera (www.operasoftware.com), WebTV (developer.webtv.net/design/tools/viewer), and Lynx (lynx.browser.org), in addition to the AOL browser (webmaster.info.aol.com).

REFERENCES

Berners-Lee, T. and Fischetti, M. (1999). *Weaving the Web: The Original Design and Ultimate Destiny of the World Wide Web by its Inventor*. San Francisco, CA: HarperCollins.

Center for Applied Special Technology. (2000). *What is Bobby?* Available on the World Wide Web at: http://www.cast.org/Bobby/WhatisBobby907.cfm. Accessed June 2001.

Constantine, L. L. and Lockwood, L. A. D. (1999). *Software for Use: A Practical Guide to the Models and Methods of Usage-Centered Design*. New York: ACM Press.

Electronic and Information Technology Accessibility Standards. (2000). *Final Rule*, 36 C.F.R. § 1194.

Job Accommodation Network. (1992). *The Americans with Disabilities Act: Questions and Answers*. Available on the World Wide Web at: http://www.jan.wvu.edu/links/ADAq&a.html. Accessed June 2001.

Kaye, H. S. (1998). *Disability Watch: The Status of People with Disabilities in the United States*. Available on the World Wide Web at: http://dsc.ucsf.edu/UCSF/pub.taf?grow=3. Accessed June 2001.

Levine, R., Locke, C., Searls, D. and Weinberger, D. (1999). *The Cluetrain Manifesto: The End of Business As Usual*. Cambridge, MA: Perseus Books.

McClure, C., Sprehe, J. T. and Eschenfelder, K. (2000). *Final Report: Performance Measures for Agency Websites*. Available on the World

Wide Web at: http://fedbbs.access.gpo.gov/library/download/MEA-SURES/measures.pdf. Accessed June 2001.

Mena, J. (1999). *Data Mining Your Website*. Boston: Digital Press.

New, W. (2001). IT accessibility standards stir industry opposition. *Government Executive*. Available on the World Wide Web at: http://www.govexec.com/dailyfed/0101/010901td.htm. Accessed June 2001.

Nielsen, J. (1999). Usability as barrier to entry. *Alertbox*. Available on the World Wide Web at: http://www.useit.com/alertbox/991128.html. Accessed November 28, 1999.

Nielsen, J. (2000). *Designing Web Usability: The Practice of Simplicity*. Indianapolis, IN: New Riders Press.

Paciello, M. G. (2001). Web Accessibility: Applying the golden rule. *Web Techniques*. Available on the World Wide Web at: http://www.webreview.com/2001/03_23/webauthors/index04.shtml. Accessed June 2001.

Sprehe, J. T. (2000). Hits don't measure up. *Federal Computer Week*. Avaiable on the World Wide Web at: http://www.fcw.com/articles/2000/11b/pot-sprehe-11-13-10.asp, Accessed June 2001.

Tang, B. A. (2000). The Web, accessibility and undue burden. *Federal Computer Week*. Available on the World Wide Web at: http://www.fcw.com/fcw/articles/2000/0612/web-dotgov-06-15-00.asp. Accessed June 2001.

WebTrends Corporation. (1999). *WebTrends Log Analyzer*. Portland, OR.

Wellner, A.S. and Gardyn, R. (2000). The internet's next niche. *American Demographics*. Available on the World Wide Web at: http://www.demographics.com, Accessed June 2001.

Chapter XVI

An Accounting Framework for Identifying Internet Abuse

Asokan Anandarajan
New Jersey Institute of Technology, USA

C. A. Srinivasan
Drexel University, USA

Current accounting methods used by companies do not charge departments appropriately for Internet usage. The problem is compounded because information technology (IT) departments have lacked the ability and process to track Internet usage. Currently time and costs for Internet usage by departments are often allocated based on head count or perceived usage. This crude allocation method could result in disproportionate allocation and charges, some departments being attributed more than their share while other departments get "free rides." This paper recommends the use of an activity-based costing system for budgeting the costs associated with Internet usage. The costs thus budgeted can then be compared to actual costs to arrive at a variance. If such variance is unfavorable, and it is significant, then managers should be penalized as this could reflect abuse with respect to Web usage. Penalization could take the form of reducing departmental incomes by the variance. If managers are evaluated on departmental earnings, then there will be an incentive to investigate the problem and take remedial action.

INTRODUCTION

In the past few years Internet access for office workers has become almost commonplace. Corporations are increasingly using the Internet as a tool for meeting their business needs. In particular, for many departments within companies, the use of the Internet has become a "mission-critical" tool. This is because the Internet facilitates communication, enables close collaboration on projects without the need for travel or expensive telephone bills, and improves productivity of knowledge workers. A pervasive problem associated with Internet use by employees is the potential for abuse. If workers utilize part of their office time for "surfing" the Internet for personal pleasure or any other reason not related to the business, this represents a drainage of company resources. One obvious strategy for most companies would be to monitor employees during office hours.

However, it has to be noted that there may be legal implications of monitoring about which the company should be aware. The employee may have the right to take legal recourse if they feel that such monitoring infringes on their rights of privacy. Privacy has long been a legal and social issue in the United States and many other countries (Mizell, 1998). A special organization called the Electronic Privacy Information Center (www.epic.org) is now trying to establish means of recourse for individuals who feel that their privacy has been infringed on the Internet. A survey conducted and discussed by Mizell appears to indicate that, overall, about one third of employers engage in electronic surveillance of their employees in some form or other. This has been a concern addressed by the American Civil Liberties Union (ACLU). Eight years ago, Pinsonneault and Kraemer (1993) warned management of the consequences of attempting to implement control in this new nebulous area. This warning has been more recently echoed by Varney (1996). The purpose of this paper is to generate an accounting framework that could provide a mechanism for employers to identify potential Internet abuse without encroaching on issues relating to employees' privacy.

The Web's technology is pervasive throughout most organizations today. This presents management with various problems involving infrastructure, support, and control. Currently, three basic types of Web computing exist. They are:

1. Net access–this enables various forms of information to be accessed.
2. Net-enabled applications–whose actual code is tied to the Internet.
3. Net administration–is the process of managing and controlling the Internet infrastructure.

The migration to Net-based computing has been quite rapid. The Net has become a mission-critical component of most organizations' computing infrastructures. Advantages of Web-based computing to an organization are many, including rapid access to information and easier customer access. However, there are distinct disadvantages as well. The disadvantages include inability to monitor employee usage and devising a method to distribute the internal costs of this new form of computing. The latter, in particular, results in potential for abuse. In particular, lost productivity due to employees using the Internet for private use is a potentially significant cost to companies. A survey recently published by IDC research, stated that an average of 30 to 40% of Internet access from within the corporate workplace was not business related. Thus, if a company spends $100,000 on supporting an Internet computing structure it may be safe to assume that $30,000 to $40,000 are "unnecessary costs."

Currently, the US Department of Labor estimates that surfing on the Internet by employees for personal use may cost corporations up to $3 million a year for every one thousand employees (*The Industry Standard*, January 2000). While these estimated costs are only approximations, and no one can completely be certain, *The Sacramento Bee* (July 1999) reported that organizations lose an estimated $50 billion a year in productivity due to employees Web surfing for personal interest in the workplace. In particular, the proliferation of Web sites has exploded, making it very tempting for workers to "visit" while they are ostensibly working for the company. In general, while no one can be certain as to the extent of the abuse and the actual dollar cost to a company as a result of this abuse, there is a general consensus that abuse does exist.

While such abuses are unproductive for the company, the problem is exacerbated because many current accounting methods used by companies do not charge departments appropriately for Internet usage. The problem is compounded because (a) information technology (IT) departments have lacked the ability to track Internet usage and/or (b) the accounting department has lacked the appropriate process and not implemented the techniques for doing so. Currently time and costs for Internet usage by departments are often allocated based on head count or perceived usage. This crude allocation method inevitably may result in disproportionate allocation and charges, some departments being attributed more than their share while other departments get "free rides." Perhaps as a result of an inappropriate or inefficient allocation method, the perception by users and department managers is that the corporate Internet connection is without cost. This results in irresponsible usage, with users deploying heavy bandwidth application with a complete disregard for the associated cost.

In many corporations all departments contend equally for access to the corporate Internet connection. This means that business-critical applications and departments get totally submerged in the vast sea of traffic along with noncritical and even non-work-related usages. (This is equivalent to a busy city where emergency vehicles such as ambulances, police cars and fire trucks have no preference over ordinary traffic.)

The need to assure access for business-critical departments and users translates into the need to allocate bandwidth by department and individual. The bandwidth allocation needs to be dynamic so that if a particular department is not using their allocated bandwidth, others should be able to use it so that their applications run faster rather than letting the bandwidth sit idle. This should be complemented by a proper accounting system that can identify inefficient or improper usage and communicate appropriate information to managers.

The purpose of this paper is twofold. Firstly, to recommend steps to develop and implement an effective corporate Internet access policy (hereafter referred to as IAP). Secondly, using currently applied concepts and techniques, to recommend a broad accounting framework that has the potential to identify and report disproportionate and inefficient Internet use.

CONTRIBUTION OF THIS STUDY

An argument can be made that developing an accounting framework may not be essential since problems of Internet abuse can be resolved using appropriate hardware and software. For example, a company could purchase a firewall that could potentially prevent access to unauthorized Web sites by employees. The Firewall could be set up so that only company-authorized Web sites are accessible to employees. Abuse could be prevented since sites that are not business-related are automatically blocked out. It could hence be argued that the Firewall would automatically eliminate many instances of abuse. However, the inclusion of a Firewall does have disadvantages. The most important are cost considerations. These costs can be dichotomized into two categories, direct and indirect. Direct costs relate to costs associated with purchasing and implementing the Firewall. Indirect costs relate to the time of managers designated to monitor the system. Direct costs could, in effect, be considered as a "one-time" expenditure and, hence, an investment. Indirect costs, on the other hand, would be recurrent since constant monitoring by managers would be required. There is a distinct opportunity cost here since the time could be spent more productively on other areas of company work.

An accounting framework, as recommended in this paper, would only involve a "one-time" cost, namely, time costs associated with devising and setting up a system for identifying the probability of Internet abuse. Once the system is operational, it can be programmed such that the computer only reports Internet usage time "abnormalities." It has to be emphasized that the recommended accounting framework be used to complement any software solutions that the company may have and is not intended as a substitute for them. For example, if the accounting system indicates excessive or disproportionate costs of Internet usage, software (discussed in detail in the next section) can be used to identify exact monitoring and the length of time used by different individuals. This should facilitate investigation by management.

OVERALL FRAMEWORK FOR IMPLEMENTATION

The Internet can be a powerful and versatile business asset. It can be used to improve communications with customers and partners, reduce internal cycle times, disseminate information internally and externally, and build new client relationships. It provides, at little cost per user, a vast and highly customizable information resource. Internet access and bandwidth are important corporate resources and should be treated as such. As mentioned above, this paper recommends a two-stage approach to developing a framework for attempting to prevent, identify, and report potential Internet abuse. These steps will now be considered.

Stage 1: Developing an Effective Corporate Internet Access Policy

Developing an effective corporate Internet access policy should be a team effort. The goal should be not only to clarify the company's policy regarding use of the Internet to shield the enterprise against potential liability, but also to encourage effective use of resources and to provide positive direction for their appropriate use.

The purpose of an IAP should be threefold.
1. To increase employee productivity.
2. To enhance network bandwidth.
3. To reduce legal liability.

An IAP should possess the following characteristics.
1. Be explicit about the level of personal surfing that is acceptable.
2. Depending on the type and cost of the physical connection, specify some degree of flexibility to allow appropriate personal use of the Internet during non-work hours.
3. Establish a clear understanding of the legal issues involved, namely, sexual harassment, copyright infringement, misrepresentation, among others.
4. Ensure network security is part of the job description.

Stage 2: Developing an Accounting Framework for Estimating, Identifying, and Reporting Costs Associated with Possible Internet Abuse

We break this down into a four-step process as discussed below.

Step 1: Determine demand

Determine the exact demand for Internet time based on the anticipated workload and needs of the employees. Internet usage needs to be understood at the department and application level to ensure that bandwidth capacity corresponds with the company's demand. By tracking and planning by department, not only will the IT departments be able to plan for future bandwidth needs, but the accounting department will be better able to plan for the associated costs.

Step 2: Adopt a total quality management (TQM) perspective

Step 1, i.e., determining the exact demand for Internet time based on anticipated workload and needs is the first step in developing a budget. Step 2 complements the first step by making managers responsible for budgeted times allocated to them and for explaining unfavorable variances in Internet usage.

Once budgeted times are determined, individual work teams should be made in charge of their own budgets. This is referred to as the TQM approach. Adopting the TQM approach may provide control over improper usage. (However, a limitation is that a significant proportion of these times, and hence computed costs too, may be valid in a firm and therefore this would not provide management with a clear perspective as to what activities these costs were related.)

Step 3: Determine available tools to monitor Internet usage

The first two steps deal with estimating anticipated times for Internet usage, and the marketplace provides firms with a choice of tools that provide monitoring and charge-back capabilities. One example is Vera Web from Veramark. This is an Internet accounting solution that allocates network usage to users and budget centers while assisting managers in controlling personnel productivity through monitoring (Veramark Online, 2001). It records Internet transactions by communicating directly with firewalls and proxy servers. Log files are translated into management reports with drill-down capabilities. The reports can be e-mailed to managers; these reports can also summarize the most active network users and Web sites. Another example is a product called RuleSpace Enterprise Suite. It utilizes an intelligent content recognition technology to dynamically analyze Internet content using pattern recognition (RuleSpace, 2000). It has been noted that employers need tools that aid in enforcing acceptable-use policies in an unobtrusive and efficient manner. The advantage of a tool such as RuleSpace is that it is unhindered by growth of a network, because it is not client-based software and it is not dependent on the maintenance of site lists.

However it is important to emphasize that the limitation of systems such as these is that the charge back methods are based on grouping usage into cost centers. This may encourage managers to view them as overhead charges to be lumped into a cost pool, rather than look at the costs from an activity perspective.

Veraweb and RuleSpace can be used to provide departmental managers with itemized charges. This will increase the accountability for Internet use within their departments. Once managers and users are made aware that Internet connections and usage are not free, the likelihood of using the resource responsibly will increase.

Step 4: Determine and activity-based costing (ABC) system to budget costs

While the steps discussed earlier relate to determining budgeted times (step 1), setting up accountability for the budgeted times (step 2), and monitoring actual usage (step 3), it is important to convert the budgeted times thus set up to dollars. In this step we recommend the use of an activity-based approach for determining the dollar amount associated with using the Internet. While it would be theoretically possible to convert the budgeted time into dollars using conventional costing systems, the numbers would only be very approximate at best. It is useful to have a system that breaks down the budget by activities. ABC is very different from conventional accounting systems. Conventional systems break down costs by *function* while ABC analyzes the same costs by *activity*. Being able to identify which activity drove up costs facilitates strategic decision-making. The use of an activity-based cost system is applicable in this instance because as Kaplan and Cooper (1999) note, "areas with large expenses in indirect and support resources, especially where such expenses have been growing over time, are high potential ABC applications." In order to achieve the major goals of, in this instance, identifying abnormal or excess costs associated with Internet use, managers need to fully understand the cost and time and quality of activities performed by employees or machines throughout an entire organization. ABC methods enable managers to cost these activities out. Activities are defined by Kaplan and Cooper (1999) as those processes that occur over time and have recognized results. Activities are, in effect, considered to be consumers of resources in production of materials, services, events or information. In order for employees to understand the costs of their activities, they must first understand the activities that they perform.

Historically, ABC has been used in manufacturing organizations. The reason for this is that manufacturing companies have been able to track activities and their costs as they related to particular products. This has not been the case for service organizations where there is no production. Service companies did not have statutory requirements to measure the costs of their products to customers. Most costs were considered fixed. In reality, the fixed costs are short run costs. The use of ABC is more important for service companies than it is for manufacturing companies. This is because service companies have no idea how much it costs them to provide any customer with a product or service.

In summary, this paper recommends the use of an activity-based costing system for budgeting the costs associated with Internet usage. The costs thus budgeted can then be compared to actual costs to arrive at a variance. If such variance is unfavorable, and it is significant, then managers should be penalized as this could reflect abuse with respect to Web usage. Penalization could take the form of reducing departmental incomes by the variance. If managers are evaluated on departmental earnings, then there will be an incentive to investigate the problem and take remedial action. It has to be emphasized that unfavorable variances may not necessarily be indicative of Internet abuse; it could be indicative of stringent budgeting. However, investigation will ensure that the budget for the following period more precisely reflects departmental demand for Internet time.

The next section discusses the key elements in the setting up of an ABC system. An example using a small hypothetical financial services institution is used to develop a theoretical model to show the following:

1. how an ABC model could be used to estimate the costs associated with Internet access by employees,
2. determining the costs for unproductive use of the Internet on company time, and
3. how to recognize and reward supervisors who are responsible for control of the resources.

As previously mentioned, the company that will be used in our hypothetical example will be a service organization. This type of organization is used because service industries tend to have an inability to monitor costs associated with their products and services. It has to be noted that currently only 37% of all jobs in the US have Internet access and these jobs tend to be in the service sector, rather than in traditional factory manufacturing jobs, where most employees are not office staff, but rather assembly line workers. The example presented below to show the implementation of ABC for the purpose of budgeting and identifying costs of Internet usage is strictly hypothetical.

HYPOTHETICAL EXAMPLE FOR MODEL DEVELOPMENT

Erich Jackson, the head of First State Bank, adopted the use of the Internet to enhance communication internally and improve communications with customers. The management felt that, through the use of the Internet, the productivity of employees had improved. However, the head of the bank recalled how 10 years earlier, the bank suffered due to employees spending too much time on the phone for personal business. Customer service and productivity suffered. The bank's solution was to closely monitor the length of the calls, the number of times particular numbers were dialed and the calling distance. This monitoring had proven effective because most of the bank's customers were local. It was relatively easy to weed out those who abused phone privileges. However, the Internet was different. Employees had to use the Internet for a number of work-related issues. These included examining financial information and Web sites of clients, reviewing competitors' sites, evaluating financing news, and keeping up with various industry trends to facilitate assisting in loan activity. However, Jackson realized that abuse must be occurring when customers complained about service and productivity decreases.

Jackson decided to implement ABC for all activities. The steps involved are:

1. Identify and analyze the activities. Activities that are non-value-added, but are needed should be classified as overhead.

2. Identify cost drivers for each of the activities and accumulate budgeted costs.
3. Trace the costs to activities. Outputs consume activities that in turn have consumed costs associated with resources. Multiply the percent of time expended by an organizational unit on each activity by the total input cost for that entity.
4. Analyze and attribute costs. The calculated activity costs can be used to identify candidates for improving the business process.

Solution

It was decided to estimate usage in the main office and the branch. Results of implementing the steps stated above are now discussed.

Identify activities

In this hypthetical case, the activities associated with Internet-related activities were determined to be administration, bandwidth utilization, hardware, software, licensing, support, monitoring tools and business process supported. The difference between a conventional and an ABC approach is that conventional accounting analyzes costs by function, while ABC analyzes the same costs by activity. Activity analysis provides a greater insight into the sources of cost generation than when such costs are accumulated by function. Please refer Figure 1 for a comparison of an activity-based approach and the conventional approach.

Identify cost drivers and accumulate costs

Refer to Table 1 for the cost drivers identified. As shown in the table, after due consideration it was decided that the cost driver for the administration,

Figure 1: Traditional versus ABC

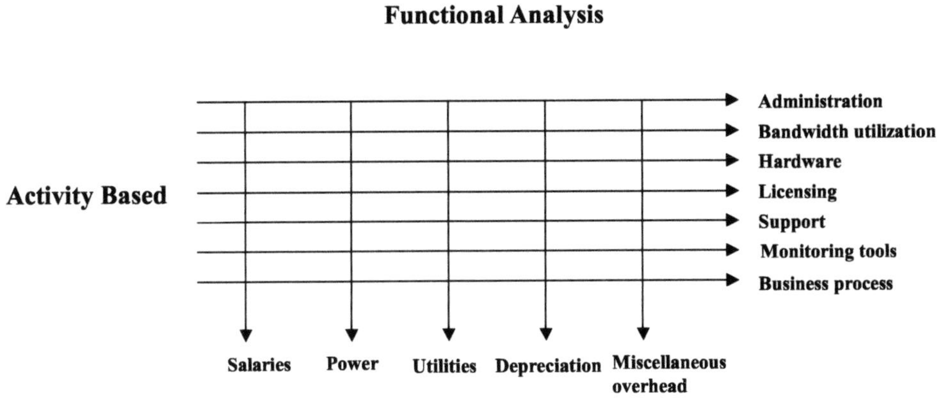

Functional Analysis

Activity Based

Administration
Bandwidth utilization
Hardware
Licensing
Support
Monitoring tools
Business process

Salaries   Power   Utilities   Depreciation   Miscellaneous overhead

Table 1: Analysis of Activities and Cost Drivers

Internet-related activity	Cost drivers	Total cost	# of cost drivers branch	# of cost drivers main office
Administration	Number of users	$300,000	300 users	200 users
Bandwidth utilization	Amount of use per user	$1,370 per day	Budgeted 6 hours per day	Budgeted 6 hours per day
Hardware	Number of users	$100,000	300 users	200 users
Licensing	Number of users	$75,000	300 users	200 users
Support	Number of users	$50,000	300 users	200 users
Monitoring tools	Amount of use per user	$220 per day	Budgeted 6 hours per day	Budgeted 6 hours per day
Business process support	Sales per transaction	$2,575,000	3,000,000 transactions	500,000 transactions

hardware, licencing, and support activities would be number of users; for the designated activities of bandwidth utilization and monitoring tools, it was estimated to be the amount of usage per user; finally for the designated activity of providing business process support, it was sales per transaction. For each, the total cost was obtained from the accounting system. The number of cost drivers can be obtained from company records (for example, in the case of administration, the number of users are available from personnel files).

Trace the costs to activities

Table 2 (column 6) shows the budgeted costs for each of the activities determined earlier. These costs can be derived from conventional accounting records.

Analyze and attribute costs

Table 2 shows the allocation of the costs to the respective activities based on the amount of resources consumed by each activity. (Detailed computations of how these costs were arrived at are shown in the appendix.)

As shown in Table 2 the branch will be charged $632, 739 for Internet usage. The main office will be charged $590,609. The ABC system is used to determine the budgeted amount of use.

Subsequently monitoring tools can be used to track the bandwidth use and actual costs of usage determined. Supervisors can be held responsible for variation in costs exceeding 5% of the budget. As punishment for abuses, a potential strategy could be to charge these additional costs against net income, thus affecting the office's profitability. Rewards would include a bonus. The monitoring tools enable each office (main and branch) to be a cost center. If it is found that employees do use disproportionate amounts

Table 2: Computation of Cost Allocation Using ABC

Activity	Branch office	Main office	Branch office	Main office	Total cost
Administration	300	200	$180,000	$120,000	$300,000
Bandwidth utilization	6 hrs worked per day	6 hrs worked per day	$828	$525	$1,370 per day
Hardware	300	200	$60,000	$40,000	$100,000
Licensing	300	200	$60,000	$40,000	$100,000
Support	300	200	$30,000	$20,000	$50,000
Monitoring tools	6 hrs worked per day	6 hrs worked per day	$126	$84	$220 per day
Business process support	3,000,000 transactions	500,000 transactions	$2,200,000	$370,000	$2.575 m
			$2,530,954	$590,609	
TOTAL			**$2,530,954**	**$590,609**	

of time relative to the budget, the implications are that the bank will need additional bandwidth, which is costly. However, after investigation, especially with the monitoring tools, the bank can identify where employees surfed and block access to sites that are considered inappropriate. An advantage of using the software thus recommended is that the number of "hits" for particular sites can also be monitored. However, this type of investigation will only be enforced if a comparison of actual costs versus budget based on ABC reveals excessive and significant variances.

DISCUSSION

In this paper we discuss how ABC can be used as a budgeting tool. ABC is particularly useful in service industries that generate a large amount of costs that are considered indivisible by conventional accounting standards. We illustrate how ABC can be used to identify activities and cost associated with each activity. However, it must be emphasized that because different departments and individuals within the department have a varying level of priority for access to the Internet, the level of access needs to be adjusted accordingly. (This is akin to letting the fire truck pass on a busy street.) Departments that need preferred access should be charged accordingly. Charging department managers with the responsibility for determining the priority of the Internet applications used by employees in the department may free up bandwidth across the corporation. Higher-level managers may be tasked with determining which department gets priority compared to others based on the business needs that each department serves. For example, in the bank case study we used, the customer service department may be given priority over the corporate accounting department because the need for real-time customer service is a critical component of the overall business strategy. Systems must be developed that provide the company with the ability to prioritize by group and by individual to maximize bandwidth usage within the organization.

Based on the company's Internet access policy and the findings from the ABC analysis, the company may choose to select different options for controlling Internet abuse, if it is felt that such abuses exist. An outline showing guidelines for managers is shown in Figure 2.

Figure 2: Guidelines for Managers

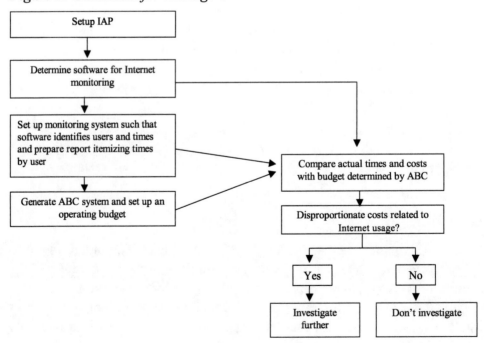

In general, potential actions managers could take are:

1. The department heads identify positions and job functions that require Internet access. Only those specific IP addresses should then be given access to the World Wide Web (WWW).

2. Set specific department targets and penalties if the deadlines are not met. This will put the responsibility to control unwanted use on the department head.

3. Access to the WWW can be granted during specific hours only, for example, between 1 pm to 3 pm, the time that encompasses the general lunch hour. Alternatively, companies could place stand-alone terminals with WWW access in the cafeteria. Web browsing from these terminals ensures that no opportunity costs are being lost, as this time is being used during the employee's lunch hour.

In conclusion, this paper only seeks to provide guidelines on how accounting concepts can be used as a tool to identify Internet abuse. However, this is a very complex area and cannot be dealt with by providing a simple framework. In addition, the case study was "simplified" by using a small bank with one branch. The problems are compounded as the size of the corporation and the numbers of people using the Internet, ostensibly for business purposes, increases. Thus, the solution provided in this chapter is not intended to be a panacea for all companies facing a variety of divergent problems. However, it seeks to provide a very general framework that can be used as an initial step in order to solve this growing problem.

A key component of the recommendations made in this paper involves monitoring the use of the Internet by employees. While the legal ramifications are not yet clear, I document some recent legislation that attempts to monitor issues of privacy of individuals on the Internet (please refer Table 3). The table attempts to highlight the key features of legislation enacted in the last 10 years that deals with electronic surveillance and privacy issues on the Internet (for more details, refer to Cavoukian and Tapscott 1997; Diffie & Landau, 1998).

When reviewing the legislation in Table 3, it is clear that the legislation most pertinent to the model advocated in this paper relates to the Communications Privacy and Consumer Empowerment Act of 1997 and to a lesser degree the Data Privacy Act of 1997. The purpose of these acts, and the Communications Privacy and Consumer Empowerment Act in particular is to protect individuals' privacy rights in online commerce. While the methodology advocated in this article may alleviate the concerns raised by organizations such as the ACLU, it is imperative that employers seek legal advice and examine the precise wording of this legislation before implementing any form of monitoring of Internet use.

Table 3: Brief Review of Pertinent Legislation Involving Electronic Surveillance and Privacy Issues

Legislation	Issues covered
Legislation dealing with federal agencies	
Computer Matching and Privacy Act of 1988	Attempts to control state and federal agencies' ability to disclose information and match files containing personal information of individuals
Federal Internet Privacy Protection Act of 1997	Prohibits federal agencies from providing personal information about individuals over the Internet
Social Security Online Privacy Protection Act of 1997	While not prohibiting, provides very strict guidelines to limit disclosure of social security related information about individuals since this information could be used by a hacker for illegal purposes including "masquerading"
Legislation dealing with consumers' rights	
Consumer Internet Privacy Protection Act of 1997	Requires a written consent from subscribers before an agency can disclose their subscribers' information to outside parties
Communications Privacy and Consumer Empowerment Act of 1997	Provides a broad range of recommendations, the purpose being to protect privacy rights of all individuals using the Internet
Data Privacy Act of 1997	The purpose is to restrict the use of information that is considered to be delicate in that it could enable an outsider to identify a person's identity

REFERENCES

Cavoukian, A. and Tapscott, D. (1997). *Who Knows: Safeguarding Your Privacy in a Networked World.* New York: McGraw-Hill.

Craig S. Mullens & Associates, Inc. (1996) *Managing Data Systems in the Age of the Web*, 2-3. Available on the World Wide Web at: http://www.craigsmullins.com/edge3396htm.

Diffie, W. and Landau, S. (1998). *Privacy on the Line: The Politics of Wiretapping and Encryption.* Boston: MIT Press.

Draycott, D. (2000). *Net Losses (Industry Trent or Event)*, 1. Available on the World Wide Web at: http://www.find articles.com/cf_0/m0COW/2000_April_6/62001827/p1/article.jhtml.

Kaplan, R. S. and Cooper, R. (1999). *The Design of Cost Management Systems.* Second Edition. Saddle River, NJ: Prentice Hall.

Mizell, L. R. (1998). *Invasion of Privacy.* Berkley: Berkley Publications Group.

Pinsonneault, A. and Kraemer, K. (1993). The impact of information technology on middle managers. *MIS Quarterly*, September.

RuleSpace, Inc. (2000). *News and Events*, 1. Available on the World Wide Web at: http://www.rulespace.com/press/releases/0022299.html.

Varney, C. A. (1996). Privacy in the electronic age. *Credit World*, January/February.

Veramark Online. (2001). *Enterprise Comunications Management*, 2. Available on the World Wide Web at: http://www.yearmark.com/wysiwyg/75.htm.

APPENDIX

Calculations for the allocations entered in columns 4 and 5 of Table 2.

Administration

$300,000 / 500 = $600 per user

(branch) $600 * 300 = $180,000

(office) $600 * 200 = $120,000

Bandwidth Utilization

Assume 6 hours per day of production per employee

(branch) 6hrs * 300 employees = 1,800

(office) 6hrs * 200 employees = 1,200

Thus giving a total of 3,000 hours

$1,370/3,000 = $0.46 per hour

1,800 * 0.46 = $828

1,200 * 0.46 = $525

Hardware

$100,000/500 = $200

300 branch * 200 = $60,000

200 main * 200 = $40,000

Licensing

$100,000/500 = $200

300 branch * $200 = $60,000

200 main * $200 = $40,000

Support

$50,000/500 = $100

300 branch * $100 = $30,000

200 main * $100 = $20,000

Monitoring Tools

$220/3,000 = $0.07 per hour

1,800 * $0.07 = $126

1,200 * $0.07 = $84

Business Process Support

$2,575,000/3,500 = $0.74

3,000,000 * $0.74 = $2,200,000

500,000 * $0.74 = $370,000

Chapter XVII

Web Management and Usage: A Critical Social Perspective

Steve Clarke
Luton Business School, UK

INTRODUCTION

This chapter seeks to apply learning from the fields of social theory and information systems to the specific context of the Internet. Key to this understanding is the extent to which the *scope* of information systems (IS) analysis is often seen to be problematic: IS "problems" are frequently "solved" by redefining organizational and human issues in technical terms, and developing the necessary technical solution. Studies on which this chapter are based have raised significant questions regarding such approaches, exposing many IS developments as not susceptible to a technical solution, but exhibiting complexities stemming from high levels of human activity. Arguably, such findings are of particular importance in Web development and management, depending as it does on the understanding and commitment of users who are often remote from and external to the organization. A clue to how such complex, human-centered issues may be dealt with is to be found in the scoping of these studies which, in systems terms, implies a need to assess the *system boundary*. Within this chapter an approach to such boundary setting is described, together with the way in which this may be used to inform choice of intervention strategy.

These approaches are then applied to the specific problem of Web management. The scope of the problem context is discussed, and an approach to determining how to progress Web development, having full regard for issues informed from our knowledge of social interaction, is outlined. An intervention framework is recommended which takes account of these social issues.

Finally, conclusions are drawn, and recommendations as to possible future directions are discussed.

Specifically, the objectives of this chapter are:

- To critically review both technology-based and human-centered approaches to information systems, and from this to situate IS and, by inference, Web design, implementation and management, as a domain best informed by social theory.
- From this background, to "scope" Web intervention and propose potential intervention strategies.
- Having regard to these findings, propose future directions for Web management, and potential implementation and management guidelines.

BACKGROUND: TECHNOLOGY-BASED AND HUMAN-CENTERED APPROACHES TO INFORMATION SYSTEMS

The Technology-Based Approach

It has been argued that the design and development of information systems (IS) has been traditionally dominated by technical, problem-solving approaches, leading to tensions when the system to be developed is more user-based. The need for discovering the requirements of users seems not to be disputed by information systems developers, but is typically achieved by including a user analysis stage within an existing problem-solving approach. This approach, inherited from computer systems development, relies primarily on the systems development life cycle (Figure 1).

The systems development life cycle is a stagewise or waterfall method, whereby each stage is undertaken in a linear sequence, and in principle requires the completion of one stage before the next is commenced. So, for example, work on system design would not be authorized until the system specification was written and approved. User requirements specification fits uncomfortably into this process, since such requirements are seldom fixed, but change over the life of a project.

Figure 1: The Systems Development Life Cycle

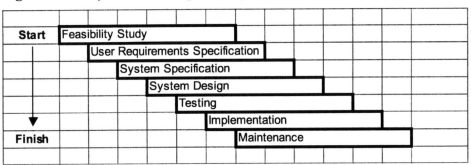

A number of methodologies adhere to these principles, through which information systems development is perceived largely as a technology-based, problem-solving, engineering task, geared to engineering the best solution to meet a given requirement specification within the known or anticipated constraints.

Technology-Based Approaches: The Problem

The argument for an alternative to these technology-based approaches is supported by the findings from a number of studies of systems failure. Examples range from simple failure to meet performance goals, to catastrophic failure of the type evidenced in the London Ambulance Service and Taurus, the London Stock Exchange System. The British Computer Society has a special interest group which looks at organizational aspects of information technology (OASIG). A study by this group (OASIG, 1996) concluded that up to 90% of information technology (IT) investments do not meet the performance goals set for them, and listed the technology-led nature of the process and the lack of attention to human and organizational factors as key issues in this lack of success.

Beath and Orlikowski (1994) support this view and mount a convincing critique of the interaction between users and systems professionals in IS, concluding that the concentration on and commitment to user participation is revealed as ideological rather than actual, with users frequently shown to be passive rather than active participants in the process. They see the various systems development methodologies as containing "incompatible assumptions about the role of users and IS personnel during systems development."

Human-Centered Methods

The limitations of technological approaches to IS gave rise, from the 1960s on, to the so-called "soft" or human-centered methods. It is argued that traditional "engineering" approaches are "hard" or technology-based, being premised on a view of the world which sees it as composed of determinable, rule-based systems. "Soft" methods, by contrast, take a human-centered stance: issues are seen as determinable only from the viewpoints of human participants. Many examples are available for the use of human-centered approaches to IS, including, for example, soft systems methodology (Checkland & Haynes, 1994) and interactive planning (Ackoff, 1981), which rely on a more holistic view: to understand an information system, the technology, organization, and human activity need to be addressed interdependently, not as separate, independent issues.

This recognition of the merits of both "hard" and "soft" approaches to IS has further given rise to a number of methods of IS development which may be categorized as mixed; for example: ETHICS (Mumford & Henshall, 1978; Mumford, 1994), multiview (Wood-Harper et al., 1985; Watson & Wood-Harper 1995), and client led design (Stowell, 1991; Stowell & West, 1994).

A clear trend can be discerned here, toward approaches which have the potential to address both technical and human-centered issues within a single intervention. In the next section, a theoretically and practically informed grounding for such an approach is developed and discussed.

Information Systems as Social Systems

The conclusion to be drawn is that a view of information systems as a purely technological domain is an inadequate one. Such a perspective reduces the complexity of the system of study and attempts to define it in terms of rules and procedures by which given inputs can be turned into predictable outputs: a so-called deterministic system. A human-centered approach is quite different. Human activity systems are "complex" and "adaptive," and cannot be fully described in terms of rules and procedures: to understand such systems requires recourse to social theory.

Furthermore, such a conclusion demonstrates the relevance of this debate to the World Wide Web. In the last 20 years or so, information systems have become more fragmented and distributed; "user" issues have grown in importance. Arguably, the World Wide Web represents currently the most distributed form of technology-enabled information, in which a disparate user-base needs to be catered for. In effect, the social system to be "served" is gaining ascendancy over the technical system: this latter has the task of facilitating or enabling–technology has finally ceased to be an end in itself!

The question to be answered, then, is how this system of concern might best be perceived from a social theoretical perspective.

Many information systems theorists have found the classification presented in Figure 2 to be the most applicable categorization of social theory within the IS domain. This is drawn from original work by Burrell and Morgan (1979), according to whom all social theories can be categorized into one of four paradigms: functionalist, interpretivist, radical humanist and radical structuralist. A functionalist approach sees social action as the application of labour to advance humankind through instrumental means. The world is seen as a set of problems to be solved: objective problems which can be determined independently of any human viewpoint. In Web design (Figure 3), for example, this describes well a technological, expert-informed approach, where the views of users are seen to be secondary. Through interpretivism, the world becomes socially constructed through communicative action. Here, the Web (Figure 3) would be understood as a social, communicative, subjective phenomenon, in which the views and opinions of participants become fundamental to its understanding.

Figure 2: A Classification of Social Theory

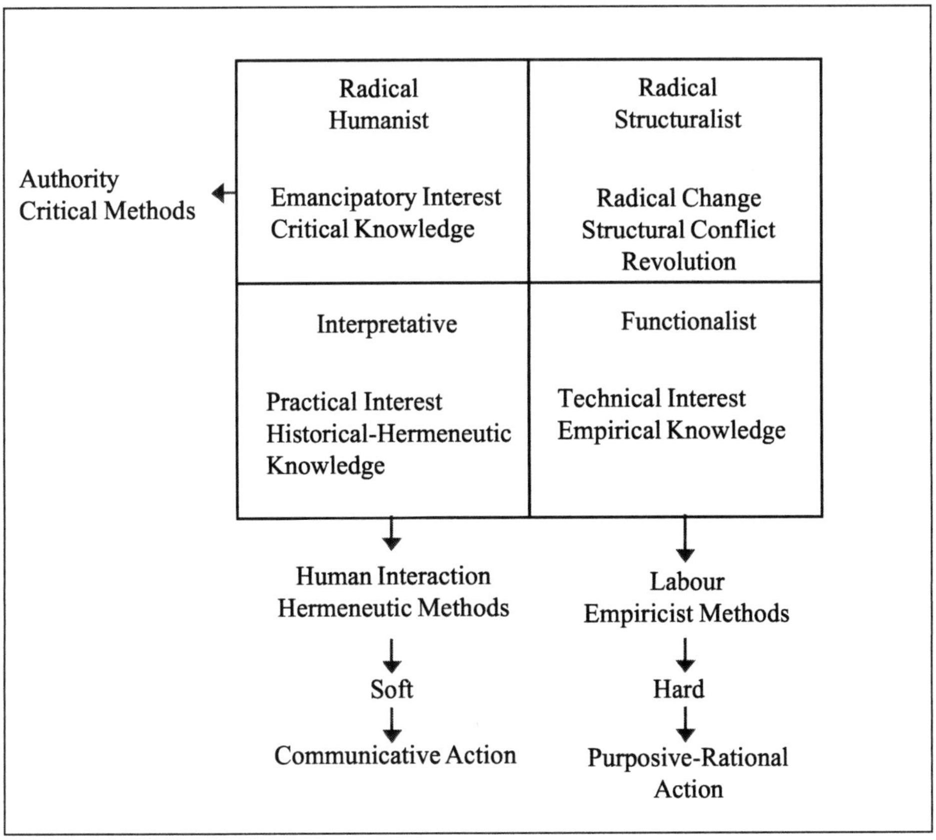

From a radical humanist, or critical perspective, the early, technological, view of IS as functionalist, "hard," problem-solving is seen to be an impoverished one, over-focused on the use of computer technology. "Soft" or human-centered methodologies have been pursued as a solution to this problem and have been to some extent successful. But recent thinking questions the ability of "hard" and "soft" approaches to achieve the agenda they apparently set out for themselves and points to a need to combine approaches under the umbrella of social theory. Radical humanism offers the potential to achieve this and is therefore pursued in the next section, with focus on two issues of particular relevance in Web management:

1. Determination of the scope, or boundaries, of the system.
2. Given the boundaries, choice of development, implementation, and management methodologies.

To complete the picture from the perspective of social theory, radical structuralism looks to ways of changing the world in which we live by altering the material conditions that surround us. In terms of Web management and usage, this might be relevant where direct political action were required – for example, if a particular political regime banned the use of Web technologies. My own view is that this perspective has limited relevance in Western industrialized economies, but I would be interested to hear from others with alternative viewpoints.

Figure 3: Social Theory and the World Wide Web

Radical Humanist	**Radical Structuralist**
The Web as a social construction, but now introducing a need to ensure inclusion of those involved and affected to challenge authoritative views.	The Web as a social form. Change society to match the Web!
Interpretative	**Functionalist**
Web management and usage seen to be a social construction. Technical (functionalist) issues serve only to enable the social interaction.	Web management and usage as a technical problem, to be solved by experts. References to underlying user issues.

SCOPING WEB MANAGEMENT: THE CRITICAL ASSESSMENT OF SYSTEM BOUNDARIES

In Web management, making a decision on the system boundary is therefore an issue to be settled before further progress can be made. Whilst the problem of system boundaries has exercised the minds of both academics and practitioners for many years (for a summary of early work, see Jones, 1982), it is from Ulrich (1983; 1988; 1996) and Midgley (1992) that the recommendation to critically challenge what should or should not be considered part of any system is drawn. Midgley's approach is to begin with a boundary definition which is accepted as arbitrary, and progress by " ... looking for grey areas in which marginal elements lie that are neither fully included in, nor excluded from, the system definition." The critical choices made at the boundary are of truth and rightness: truth being represented by questions of what is, and rightness by questions of what ought to be. In respect of the World Wide Web, it is interesting to reflect that, whilst most involved in its use and management would accept it to be an open system, the manner in which Web sites are implemented and managed frequently fails to take full account of this. Taking such a stance gives a starting point for the critique of boundary judgements in a Web-based intervention as represented by Figure 4.

Here, a typical approach to Web design, implementation and management is represented by the primary boundary. The information to be included is often corporate, but at best might be requested from an expert group (marketing, for example). Most of the activity takes place between designers and managers, with system users cast in a passive role.

By contrast, it is recommended that critical assessment of the system boundary be undertaken by a representative sample of participants in the system. The approach might work as detailed below.

1. An arbitrary system definition is presented (Figure 4). The primary boundary represents the main area of concern, whilst the secondary boundary encompasses that which is seen to be marginal to that area. Beyond this, all other issues are represented by the "wider system."

2. A brainstorming session (de Bono, 1977) is set up, attended by representatives of all the key participant areas. The purpose of the session is to enable participants in the system (those "involved and affected") to conduct the critique on their own behalf.

3. The system is critiqued within the brainstorming session by a combination of Midgley's and Ulrich's approaches to boundary critique:

Figure 4: Critique of the System Boundary (Midgley, 1992)

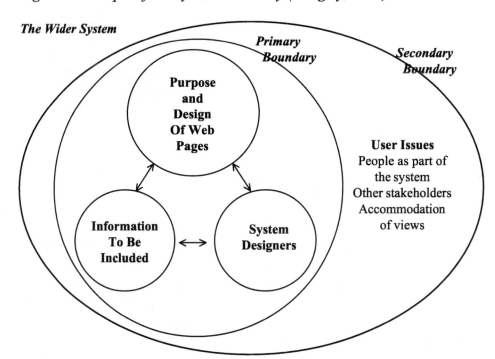

a) Midgley's (1992) approach to examining what is in the margin for elements which support the secondary boundary or the primary boundary.

b) Ulrich's (1996) approach to challenging system boundaries through 12 "critically heuristic boundary questions" which address issues of motivation, power, knowledge and legitimization (see Table 1).

This reconceptualization of the system is an important part of the intervention, focusing discussion not on a clearly defined technical or organizational problem to which a solution is to be found, but on the complex interaction of all the issues involved in maintaining a Web presence. The effect will be to change the focus from technology or organizational functions to the views and ideals of the stakeholder groups involved in the system. The task becomes not one of how to engineer a solution to a known and agreed problem, but how to study and improve a problem situation made up of complex interacting issues. People are not only part of the system, they are the primary focus of study.

From the issues raised by boundary critique, it becomes possible to consider intervention strategies.

Table 1: Critically Heuristic Boundary Questions

Question	"Is" Mode	"Ought" Mode
1	Who is the client? Whose purposes are served by the system? *The Web site manager.*	Who ought to be the client? *All who are involved in and affected by the system of concern.*
2	What is the purpose? *To present a corporate presence via the Internet.*	What ought to be the purpose? *To meet the changing requirements of all involved and affected.*
3	What is the measure of success? *Up-to-date Web presence.*	What ought to be the measure? *"User satisfaction."*
4	Who is the decision taker? *Senior management.*	Who ought to be the decision taker? *Decision rests with management, but should be informed by participant involvement.*
5	What conditions are actually controlled by the decision taker? *Resources, final approvals.*	What components of the systems ought to be controlled by the decision taker? *Should manage, not control.*
6	What conditions are not controlled by the decision taker? *External factors.*	What resources and conditions ought to be part of the system's environment? *All on which it potentially impacts.*
7	Who is the system's designer? *Web designers under the Web site manager.*	Who ought to be the system's designer? *Web design should be professionally carried out, but informed by the changing requirements of participants.*
8	Who is involved as an expert, what is the nature of the expertise, and what role does the expert play? *Designers: control the whole development within guidelines laid down by management.*	What kind of expertise ought to be involved, who should exercise it, and what should his/her role be? *Mixture of technical and social issues to be considered.*
9	Where is the guarantee of success? With experts, political support, etc.? *Experts.*	Where ought the guarantee of success to be? *Full participation.*
10	Who represents the concerns of the affected (but not involved)? *Not represented.*	Who ought to represent these concerns? Who among the affected ought to become involved? *The views of all involved and affected should be taken into account.*
11	Are the affected given the opportunity to emancipate themselves? *Not involved.*	To what extent ought the affected to be given such an opportunity? *Participation only works where users are free and able to participate.*
12	What worldview underlies the system of concern? *Command and control system.*	On what worldview ought the design of the system to be based? *Inclusive, participative, informed.*

MANAGING AND IMPLEMENTING THE WEB: POTENTIAL INTERVENTION STRATEGIES

Recasting the system of concern through boundary critique leads quite naturally to a refocusing of the methodological approaches seen to be relevant.

By way of example, three general possibilities are considered here in relation to Web management. Firstly, a methodological approach which addresses both functionalist and interpretivist issues could be chosen; secondly, different methodologies could be chosen pragmatically to address the problem context encountered, and mixed within the intervention; thirdly, a "critical complementarist" approach could be taken to the intervention, informed by critical management science, and aimed at using a variety of methodologies within a critical framework. The first two possibilities are discussed below under the heading of mixing methods.

Mixing Methods

A methodological approach to address both functionalist and interpretivist issues presents two main problems:

1. The lack of detailed knowledge of the problem context renders choice of methodology difficult if not impossible. Each potential methodology will have strengths and weaknesses vis-a-vis the others, making a choice of the most applicable methodology at this stage seem at best premature.

2. In a similar vein, it seems probable that no one methodology would address all of the issues within the problem context. As Jackson and Keys (1984) have observed: "No single methodology has been or will ever be developed that is sufficient to deal with the wide variety of issues that we are confronted with in contemporary society."

Similarly, the pragmatic mixing of methodologies raises unresolved issues. The lack of detailed knowledge of the problem context surfaces again here: even if methodologies are to be mixed, which methodologies should be chosen? In addition there are theoretical objections to a contingency-based approach to methodological mixing. For example, the realist ontological stance of hard methodologies is seen by many to be incompatible with the nominalist ontology of soft methodologies, giving rise to practical difficulties in moving between a highly participative problem-structuring approach to a more objective problem-solving one.

Methodologies from Critical Management Science: A "Critical Complementarist" Approach

It has been argued that the relativist stance of interpretivistic approaches render them "*completely uncritical* of the potential dysfunctional side effects of using particular tools and techniques for information systems development. Different products of systems development are simply viewed as the result of different socially constructed realities" (Hirschheim & Klein, 1989). This lack of critique is a key issue in Web interventions. Widening system boundaries requires participants to consider issues beyond those visualized within the accepted scope of an intervention: participants need to "examine and re-examine taken-for-granted assumptions, together with the conditions which gave rise to them" (Midgley, 1995), in order to reach a richer understanding of a given problem context, undistorted by preconceptions.

The approach taken to Web management therefore has to make a critically informed methodological choice, and for this, mixing the chosen methodologies within a "critical complementarist" framework offers the most favourable solution.

Critical systems thinking (CST) and its practical counterpart, total systems intervention (TSI), offer a "critical complementarist" approach which is seen to be capable of resolving both the theoretical and practical difficulties. CST is founded on the critical theory of Habermas. Habermas' (1971) "theory of knowledge constitutive interests" proposes all human activity to be conducted in satisfying three cognitive or knowledge constitutive interests: technical, practical and emancipatory. This Habermasian perspective sees the functionalist approach to information systems development as an insufficient basis, serving only the technical interest. What is needed in addition is social science, to service the practical (hermeneutic) interest in achieving communication and consensus, together with critical science to deal with issues of power and domination, serving the emancipatory interest. Critique is applied in a Kantian (Kant, 1724-1804) sense, aiming to: (i) free participants from purely instrumental (technical) reason; (ii) enable practical reason, to examine and reexamine assumptions made; and (iii) inform the choice and mix of methodologies in relation to the changing nature of the problem contexts and the strengths and weaknesses of the available methodologies.

The process of TSI operationalizes a critical complementarist approach based explicitly on CST. This is shown in Figure 5 and described in summary in the following text.

TSI is iterative and recursive. Iteration implies that the process is continuous, rather than a start-end method, which stands in contrast to the project management nature of traditional approaches to IS. The TSI ideology explicitly recognizes the part played by both technical and human activities in organizations, and the extent to which human interpretation may in some instances so distort the so-called "real World" that study of the latter may become meaningless.

TSI provides a critical framework within which choice and implementation of methodologies in an intervention can be managed pluralistically. The problem context is viewed as a "mess" within which creativity (e.g., brainstorming, metaphor) is used to surface the issues to be managed (Figure 5);

Figure 5: The Process of Total Systems Intervention (TSI) (Flood, 1995)

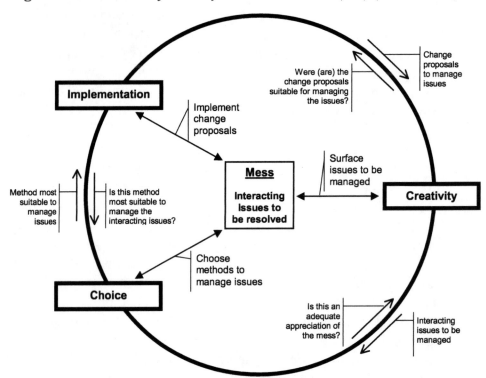

reflection on creativity then seeks to critically determine whether an adequate appreciation of the "mess" has been gained. Methodologies are then chosen to address the issues surfaced, using the complementarist framework (Table 2) to determine, by use of metaphor, whether the key concern is one of design (technical), debate (practical) or disimprisonment (emancipation). A methodology or mix of methodologies may then be chosen to address the problem context, with critical reflection on whether these methodologies are indeed the most suitable being carried out prior to implementation.

In the next section, an example is given of this approach in action.

Boundary Critique and TSI in Operation: A Web Example

The following is a summary of an actual implementation, detailing changes made as a result of the approach recommended in this chapter. Space considerations prevent a detailed analysis of the case, but full details are available from the author.

The Problem as Stated

A new research centre in a major UK university requires a Web presence. The research centre manager should inform the Web designer of her require-

Table 2: The Complementarist Framework (Flood, 1995, p. 183)

Designing	Debating	Disimprisoning
Machine Organic Neuro-Cybernetic	Socio-Cultural	Socio-Political

ments, at which stage the work will be programmed and an estimated time for completion given.

Boundary Critique

Whilst boundary critique, continues throughout the intervention, initial analysis gave a quite different perception of the problem context to that which was stated in the original problem. The effect was to focus the development not simply on a "Web presence," but to widen this to all communicative research activity. This proved of immense value since, rather than proceed immediately to designing a system, focus was switched to a finding-out exercise which ultimately significantly enhanced research activity within the centre.

Intervention Methodology

Participative forums were set up to determine the way forward. These were facilitated using recognized methodologies, key among which were brainstorming and lateral thinking (de Bono, 1977), idealized design (Ackoff, 1981) and metaphor (Morgan, 1986).

Outcomes

One of the criticisms levelled at this type of analysis is that it delays action. In the case of this intervention, it is important to note that the initial stages of setting up participative groups took less than two weeks. One of the early outcomes of the group discussions was that "Web design" should not be held up whilst discussions continued, but could be adjusted later to take account of any required changes. In a sense, therefore, this approach achieved the best of both worlds: it refocused the development to best serve those for whom it was intended, whilst not prejudicing the need for a Web presence early in the life of the research centre.

The final outcome has yet to be seen, but the development is progressing and improving all the time under this "critical complementarist" approach. Of course, it will never be finished, since such a concept is at odds with the

Table 3: Boundary Critique

Initial boundary (From the above)	Drawn around the Web designer and research centre manager.
Marginal area	Other involved participants. Activities complementary to Web design (e.g., intranets, e-mail, other communication forms, communicative activity ...).
Reconceptualized boundary	Primary boundary to include all marginal elements.

continuing nature of this type of intervention. The objective, if you like, is continuous improvement, and this is something that all participants feel they are achieving.

This concludes the chapter as far as the methods used and their outcomes and derivations are concerned. However, a number issues have been raised by both the theoretical and practical work undertaken, and the discussion below reflects these.

DISCUSSION: FUTURE TRENDS

The impetus for undertaking this study has been the failure of hard and soft systems development methodologies to address the needs of all participants in the system. Theoretically it has been demonstrated that this failure, at least in part, can be traced to the uncritical nature of both hard and soft methodologies, and a need, from a social systems viewpoint, to combine hard and soft approaches within a critical framework.

Critical boundary setting, focusing on the normative system definition, has further enhanced this study. Just as a structured approach tends to focus on technical issues, so a concentration on "what is" tends to lead to a belief that there is only one accurate perception of the system of concern. A critical approach to boundary judgements has opened up a wider consideration of "what ought to be" in Web management, including those involved and affected as participants with whom expertise is seen to reside. The richness this has brought to "user analysis" within the Web systems domain contrasts with the simplicity with which this part of a Web-based intervention is normally undertaken.

Since the early stages of this study, theoretical and empirical work in this domain has progressed significantly, and this chapter would be incomplete without a consideration of these issues.

A useful general summary of thinking concerning mixing of methodologies, methods or techniques can be found in Mingers and Gill (1997). In outline, the thrust of both theoretical and empirical analysis has focused on the perceived shortcomings of approaches which concentrate on a single methodology or paradigm, and alternative conceptions of how methodologies, methods or techniques drawn from different paradigms might contribute within a single intervention. So, for example, Mingers and Brocklesby (1997) see the main approaches to mixing "methods, methodologies and techniques within the broad field of management science" as the system of systems methodologies (Jackson & Keys, 1984) and TSI. They criticize these approaches for effectively promoting the use of whole methodologies—a view which it could be contended is supported by the strong suggestion within TSI that there should be dominant and dependent methodologies within an intervention. A better approach, they suggest, would be to mix methodologies, or parts of methodologies, from different paradigms, promoting this approach as "multimethodology." They argue, for example, that TSI: "provides no structure for the ongoing process of the intervention—leaving that entirely up to the selected methodology," and offering in its place an: "appreciate, analyze, assess, act" framework.

Midgley (1997) argues that it is more helpful to think in terms of methodology design than just the choice of whole methodologies or even, by implication, simple choice of parts of methodologies, and promotes the idea of the "creative design of methods" as an application of their oblique use (Flood & Romm, 1995), and as a way of enhancing TSI in practice.

Another stream that has informed intervention practice in recent years is action research (AR). AR explicitly relies on critical reflection as a means of validating the outcomes of a given investigation and in this sense may be seen to have much in common with the critically informed intervention approach recommended in this chapter. Further information on the position of AR in relation to organizational intervention may be found initially in Flood and Romm (1996) and Clarke and Lehaney (1997).

My position in relation to the approach taken is embryonic, and it offers many challenges which have not as yet been addressed by me or other practitioners. To progress this, I feel concentration now needs to be on a Kantian view of critique as promoted and developed, for example, by Ulrich (1983), and on creatively designing methods, having regard to the issues raised from the critiques of TSI and the system of systems methodologies, always within a critical framework. Finally, action research practice needs to be embedded into the intervention framework.

CONCLUSIONS

Arguments about whether to use a hard or soft methodology and which hard or soft methodology to use in Web development, implementation and management seem to offer only a limited perception of most problem situations. A "critical complementarist" view gives a richer image. The argument should not be about whether to use this or that methodology, but rather what critically, theoretically, and practically informed mix of methodologies best deals with the problem contexts encountered in a given intervention. From this perspective, the hard-soft debate seems to offer only a partial view of the world of the Internet. Web-based systems are not per se computer systems, but are systems of human activity or micro-social systems; consequently, functionalist science or interpretative sociology appears an inadequate basis on which to study them, a wider critical social context seeming more relevant.

The approach currently most widely tested in this respect is total systems intervention, underpinned by the theoretical endeavour of critical systems thinking, but emerging evidence suggests developing this into a richer critical systems practice, focusing on a Kantian view of critique within a broader action research framework.

From all of this can be drawn general findings, together with guidelines for future development, implementation and management of the Web, which are presented in summary form below.

Findings
From the discussions of this chapter, the following general findings can be distilled:
1. The domain of information systems is dominated by technology-based methods, weakly mediated by human-centered ones.
2. Human activity is more fundamental to the domain than such an approach acknowledges, and consequently the investigation of methods underpinned by theories of social interaction are indicated.
3. From research in the social domain, a foundation in critical social theory emerges as a promising direction.
4. Within such an approach, the first issue to be addressed is that of *understanding* the problem context. For this, critical social theory points to the use of critical systems heuristics and critical boundary judgements to critique and determine the system boundary.
5. Boundary critique further informs intervention strategy. The methods required must embrace functionalist (technological), interpretivist (human-centered), and radical humanist (emancipatory, participatory, "social inclusion") issues.
6. The most widely tested approach in this respect is total systems intervention (TSI). A brief example of the application of TSI within a university research centre is included.

7. In any future work, the ongoing research in the application of critical theory to management issues must be considered, and a brief outline of this is provided.

Given these findings, how might a manager seek to put them in action?

Guidelines: The Implications for Managers

- Determine the initial scope of the system of concern.
- Identify the social group(s) involved in and affected by that system.
- Form representative samples from these groups.

In terms of management action, the challenge here is *not* to see Web development and management as a problem to be solved by an expert group of developers. A framework (for example, of user groups) needs to be established, from which the contribution from those participating in Web usage can be drawn. But a word of caution: the groups and membership of them should not be fixed and, of course, should not be limited to managers or those in authority.

Actions

- Conduct boundary critique to initially determine the system of concern. Continue this throughout the project.
- Use participative forums to discuss all issues of Web design, development and implementation.
- Choose and implement the relevant methodological approaches in a critical complementarist framework.

Initially, formal boundary setting sessions will be needed to set the scene. Quite quickly, groups will form their own clear views about the scope of Web developments within a particular organizational context (it will become "culturally" ingrained), and less time will be necessary in formal sessions to discuss this. The particular forums can then be used to surface Web issues; the only primary requirement in terms of expertise will be a facilitator who can assist with guidance on the TSI process, in respect of which the earlier university case provides a brief example.

Web management is a task to be conducted within a social framework. A purely technical approach or even a technical approach informed from participative analysis is insufficient to address the complexity of the problem contexts encountered. It is essential to recognize that what is being dealt with is a social system, albeit enabled by technology, and, this being so, it is difficult to envisage how such an undertaking could be informed from anywhere other than social theory.

What has been presented in this chapter is argued to be a thoroughly theoretically and pragmatically informed approach based on these principles. Try it–it works!

REFERENCES

Ackoff, R. L. (1981). *Creating the Corporate Future*. New York: Wiley.

Beath, C. M. and Orlikowski, W. J. (1994). The contradictory structure of systems development methodologies: Deconstructing the IS-user relationship in information engineering. *Information Systems Research*, 5(4), 350-377.

Burrell, G. and Morgan, G. (1979). *Sociological Paradigms and Organizational Analysis*. London: Heinemann.

Checkland, P. B. and Haynes, M. G. (1994). Varieties of systems thinking: The case of soft systems methodology. *System Dynamics*, 10(2-3), 189-197.

Clarke, S. A. (2000). From socio-technical to critical complementarist: A new direction for information systems development. In Coakes, E., Lloyd-Jones, R. and Willis, D (Eds.), *The New SocioTech: Graffiti on the Long Wall*, 61-72. London, Springer.

Clarke, S. A. and Lehaney, B. (1997). Total systems intervention and human inquiry: The search for a common ground. *Systems Practice*, 10(5), 611-634.

De Bono, E. (1977). *Lateral Thinking*. Aylesbury, UK: Pelican Books, Hazell Watson & Viney Ltd.

Flood, R. L. (1995). Total systems intervention (TSI): A reconstitution. *Journal of the Operational Research Society*, 46, 174-191.

Flood, R. L. and Romm, N. R. A. (1995). Enhancing the process of methodology choice in total systems intervention (TSI) and improving the chances of tackling coercion. *Systems Practice*, 8(4), 377-408.

Flood, R. L. and Romm, N. R. A. (Eds.). (1996). *Systems Practice*, 9/2. London: Plenum.

Habermas, J. (1971). *Knowledge and Human Interests*. Boston: Beacon Press.

Hirschheim, R. and Klein, H. K. (1989). Four paradigms of information systems development. *Communications of the ACM*, 32(10), 1199-1216.

Jackson, M. C. and Keys, P. (1984). Towards a system of systems methodologies. *Journal of the Operational Research Society*, 35(6), 473-486.

Jones, L. M. (1982). *Defining Systems Boundaries in Practice: Some Proposals and Guidelines*. *Journal of Applied Systems Analysis*, 9, 41-55.

Midgley, G. (1992). The sacred and profane in critical systems thinking. *Systems Practice*, 5(1), 5-16.

Midgley, G. (1995). What is this thing called critical systems thinking. *Critical Issues in Systems Theory and Practice*, 61-71. Hull, UK: Plenum.

Midgley, G. (1997). Developing the methodology of TSI: From the oblique use of methods to their creative design. *Systems Practice*, 10(3), 305-319.

Mingers, J. and Brocklesby, J. (1997). Multimethodology: Towards a framework for mixing methodologies. *Omega*, 25(5), 489-534.

Mingers, J. and Gill, A. (Eds.). (1997). *Multi Methodology*. Chichester: Wiley.

Morgan, G. (1986). *Images of Organization*. Beverly Hills, CA: Sage.

Mumford, E. (1994). Technology, communication and freedom: Is there a relationship? *Transforming Organizations with Information Technology*, A-49, 303-322.

Mumford, E. and Henshall, D. (1978). *A Participative Approach to Computer Systems Design*. London: Associated Business Press.

OASIG. (1996). Why do IT projects so often fail? *OR Newsletter*, 309, 12-16.

Oliga, J. C. (1991). Methodological foundations of systems methodologies. In Flood, R. L. and Jackson, M. C. (Eds.), *Critical Systems Thinking: Directed Readings*, 159-184. Chichester: Wiley.

Stowell, F. A. (1991). Client participation in information systems design. *Systems Thinking in Europe (Conference Proceedings)*, Huddersfield, Plenum.

Stowell, F. A. and West, D. (1994). Soft systems thinking and information systems: A framework for client-led design. *Information Systems Journal*, 4(2), 117-127.

Ulrich, W. (1983). *Critical Heuristics of Social Planning: A New Approach to Practical Philosophy*. Berne, Haupt.

Ulrich, W. (1983). *The Itinerary of a Critical Approach*. Berne, Haupt.

Ulrich, W. (1988). Systems thinking, systems practice and practical philosophy: A program of research. *Systems Practice*, 1(2), 137-163.

Ulrich, W. (1996). A primer to critical systems heuristics for action researchers. *Forum One: Action Research and Critical Systems Thinking*. Hull, UK, University of Hull, Centre for Systems Studies.

Watson, H. and Wood-Harper, T. (1995). Methodology as metaphor: The practical basis for multiview methodology. *Information Systems*, 5, 225-231.

Wood-Harper, A. T., Antill, L. et al. (1985). *Information Systems Definition: The Multiview Approach*. London: Blackwell.

Chapter XVIII

Fuzzy Boundaries, Strange Negotiations: Problems of Space, Place and Identity in Cyberspace

Andrew Wenn
Victoria University of Technology, Australia

INTRODUCTION

In cyberspace, hundreds of thousands, perhaps already millions, of users create online personae who live in a diverse group of virtual communities where the routine formation of multiple identities undermines any notion of a real and unitary self. Yet the notion of the real fights back. People who live parallel lives on the screen are nevertheless bound by desires, pain and the mortality of their physical selves.

S. Turkle
Life on the Screen: Identity in the Age of the Internet, (1996, p. 267)

In all this talk of the virtual world it is easy to forget that someone has to do the wiring.

R. X. Cringley
Nerds 2.0.1–A Brief History of the Internet, 1999

In 1997, attempting to focus attention on the imploding boundaries between organism and machine Mizuko Ito wrote about multi-user dungeons (MUDs). These are communities where people who have created online personae come together as a virtual community and act out roles in ways that they imagine this person would. Whilst others have extolled the virtualness of these online worlds (Benedikt, 1991; Heim, 1991; Rheingold, 1995), Ito showed us that there are other ways of seeing that reveal these worlds as a "complex interaction between a network of various 'real world' material technologies as well as the cultural capital of its users and designers" (Ito 1997, p. 91). Whilst much of Turkle's (1996) book focuses on life beyond the screen and people's behavior in what many see as the virtuality of cyberspace, towards the end of the book, she hints that there is a physical world that these "cyberplayers" are bound to and will ultimately die in (1996). In a rather more pragmatic vein, Cringley reminds us that some one has to do the wiring, that there is a complex material technology beneath all this. It is this interplay between the virtual and material technologies that I wish to explore here.

When writing about the multiplicity of identity and the virtuality of cyberspace many authors examine MUDs (Benedikt, 1991; Rheingold, 1995; Bromberg, 1996; Turkle, 1996; Ito, 1997). The ways in which people construct characters and roles within these worlds that are often overseen and controlled by a hierarchy of wizards who, as they gain more experience and move further away from the players' world, become gods and attain "near absolute power to implement decisions on their MUDs" (Ito, 1997, p. 90). In my attempt to display the way the boundaries between the physical and non-physical are collapsing I wish to take something a little more prosaic than an online community and far more ubiquitous. It is something that an estimated 50 million people have, it is used for business, for pleasure, for profit, to maintain contact with friends and loved ones, for intimacy and slander–that is the e-mail address.[1]

In what follows, I show that the e-mail address is often the result of negotiations between humans and nonhumans, that it points to spaces where texts are held, that it can be used to deliberately conceal identity or it can result in an owners identity being altered with their grudging acceptance. Much of the evidence I use to support my argument is the result of far more extensive work being undertaken into the role of the Internet in libraries, in particular at the State Library of Victoria (SLV) which has a number of public access Internet (PAI) computers (Wenn, 1999; 2000). I have also drawn on my own experiences as an e-mail user and onetime systems administrator as well as those of friends and colleagues who were kind enough to share their experiences with me. My method of presentation is multi-vocal in that it makes use of interviews with a number of people who use e-mail on a day-to-day basis or who are responsible for providing e-mail facilities.

What this chapter attempts to do is to raise the awareness of how technology and humans interact and the richness and complexity of these interactions. These relationships don't just occur when the Internet is used as a plaything. In fact one of the reasons for selecting e-mail as the underlying vehicle to examine these issues is that its use is all pervasive within business environments as well.

The organization of this chapter is as follows. In the next two sections I will consider some theoretical and analytical tools that will enable us to firstly deconstruct the e-mail address as a signifier of place, boundaries and human identities–either real or virtual–and secondly to show how these entities create and/or move across these boundaries doing what we could call boundary work (Star & Griesmer 1989). In the next section we consider the origins of the e-mail address, in particular the ubiquitous "@," and the work an e-mail address does. E-mail messages must be stored somewhere before they can be read; they will sit in this place waiting for the recipient to retrieve them and read, print or discard them. The e-mail address signifies where the messages are held, or does it? Electronic messages must originate from somewhere, but even where they come from can be problematic as we shall see in Section 5, which considers such places of origin and spaces for storage. Even a cursory perusal of Table 1 reveals that a single person can have a multitude of e-mail addresses or even share one with others, but the careful reader will note that there are different levels of negotiation that take place between the actants involved (the actual person in real life, the technology, organizational policies and other humans). Section 6 discusses many of the machinations that are necessary for a e-mail address to be mapped onto something the actual user may feel comfortable with or even one that is seemingly not connected with a person in real life. Throughout, the thoughtful reader will see how the actors in the vast hybrid that comprises an e-mail network play various roles in "creating the environments that then impose on them" (Weick, 1979, p. 130). The reader will also see how in some instances standards are created by machines and at other times by humans and then how these standards are imposed on others. She will also read of how these others may usurp or weaken the hold these standards have on them. It is precisely due to the fact that e-mail addresses are often assigned through negotiations with machines, that we need to consider some theory about boundaries, boundary work and cyborgs.

BOUNDARIES AND BOUNDARY WORK(ERS)

Table 1: Some Variety of Ways an Actual Person Can Be Mapped Into the Internet; Often the Actual Person Gains a New Identity as the Result of Negotiations With Technologies and/or Humans

Actual person	Net identity	Negotiated with	Reason
Andrew Smithson	Andrew.Smithson@vu.edu.au	organisation	Uniform address system as adopted by organization.
	asmithson@westgate.vu.edu.au	system administrator	Naming scheme adopted by human administrator.
	beebop@excite.com	self	Self-defined alias to show area of interest.
	ASmithso@slv.vic.gov.au	technology/ system administrator	8 characters are all that is allowed by storage technology.
	ASmithso@newvenus.slv.vic.gov.au	technology	The old version of the above address. Newvenus is gradually being removed from domain.
	valued-excite-customer@excite.com	technology	Means of replying to newly registered freemail users.
	AndrewSmithson@hotmail.com	self	Choose hotmail.com domain as area for being the real-world identity.
	AndrewSmithson99@hotmail.com	self/ technology	Net identity negotiated between technology and self because someone was already registered as AndrewSmithson.
	root@yarranet.net.au	technology	Mail is directed to this address when problems occur with the UNIX server of which he is administrator. It refers to the fact that a person who can log in as this has control of the whole system.
	sysadmin@yarranet.net.au	technology	Similar to root
	webinfo@slv.vic.gov.au	technology/ system administrator	Also known as Web administrator, this is the name included at the bottom of many of the SLV's Web pages. Also named as the contact point if errors are found in the Web site.
	an299908@annon.penet.fi	technology	An anonymous remailer strips off any identifying information and forwards the message to the destination. The origin of the message is unknown except to the owner of the remailer.
Susan	helpdesk@vu.edu.au	department	This is used by a number of people who work in the IT help area. So it actually refers to whoever is on duty at the time.
Farries book suppliers	123456.9876@compuserve.com	Compuserve	An organisation that uses Compuserve, a quite different network from the Internet.
X	????@????	technology	A hacker or some other person who wishes to remain anonymous.

In her delightful study of the work of high-energy physicists, Sharon Traweek identifies a number of social worlds and describes how work is done either to maintain the boundaries between these worlds or to try and break them down. It is useful to engage with her work here because the examples are much more down-to-earth than the more abstract concepts that arise in the world of e-mail addresses and storage spaces. The world of the high-energy physicists at SLAC is one world with a very distinct culture and purpose. It exists as a community within the larger San Francisco community, a larger social world that sometimes has disagreements with the SLAC community. To overcome the concerns of those outside SLAC, a Public Information Office was established to make the work of the high-energy physicists more visible and understandable. As Traweek, says:

> *All of the employees of the Public Information Office are Caucasian, like almost all of the audiences they address. The activities of this office indicate that SLAC sees its role in community-laboratory interactions as didactic. That is, disagreement with the lab's policies is seen as the result of lack of information, which SLAC will supply* (1988, p. 22).

This office and its employees cross the boundaries, performing boundary work, between the two worlds. They perform the task of translating the acts of the SLAC world into terms the public, the world outside SLAC, can understand and the hope is that the two worlds will coexist in a more harmonious fashion.

Traweek shows how organizations and people perform boundary work moving knowledge between the world of science and the citizen, but machines and/or combinations of humans and machines can perform at problematic boundaries also. We will see later that an e-mail address is actually more than just a string of symbols with meaning to a few. On another level it is also the result of policies, standards and technological configurations. It can also be seen as a human-machine hybrid, a cyborg in fact (Haraway, 1991, 1997).

CYBORG MATTERS

In what follows, it will be helpful to appeal to what has been termed "cyborgology" at times (Gray et al., 1995). This appeal enables us to move beyond the idea that there are very distinct boundaries between human and animal or, as in this case, between humans and machines. At its simplest to understand, a cyborg is my aunt with a pacemaker (a machine embedded in her body, monitoring and determining the rhythm of her heartbeat) or it is my body that has been reprogrammed via an immunization to resist tuberculosis or it is the diabetic who uses a machine to monitor blood-sugar levels (Mol & Law, 1998). As Gray et al. say, "[c]yborg society ... refers to the full range of intimate organic-machinic relations" (p. 3). Cyborgs appear in a myriad of forms. In fact there has been more than one attempt to classify them (Gray et al., 1995). For the purpose of this chapter I will employ the cyborg as a tool to assist us in understanding the human-computer hybrid that comprises an e-mail system.

Whenever a user sends an e-mail, they interact with a machine. Superficially these interactions can be seen as simply sitting in front of a screen and typing at a keyboard. But upon deeper observation and analysis of what actually constitutes a user's practices when utilizing an e-mail system, we find that there are a wide variety of actants involved–technology in form of the local client machine for sure, but there are also machines that act as mail hosts sending and receiving e-mail over the network; disk drives and operating systems; organization policies on naming conventions and usage; and other users. Now this technology may not be embedded in the user, as in the more popular cyborgian image, but humans and technology are certainly intermeshed in a symbiotic relationship; a heterogeneous association of actors[2] performing in ways that will breach boundaries. "A cyborg is the figure born of the interface of automaton [self-controlled, self-governing machines] and autonomy [humans]" (Haraway quoted in Gray et al., 1995 p. 1).

Why do I consider this call to cyborgology useful? Well, at the risk of pre-empting what follows, let's take one example. Our mythical user Andrew Smithson had a problem printing from his computer. On occasions like this he knows to e-mail the Help Desk where he works. He duly composes an e-mail message, addressing it to helpdesk@vu.edu.au (see Table 1). Shortly after sending it off, he receives a reply from "helpdesk" stating that his message has been received and will be given due attention. He is even given a job number.

Now, this reply has been automatically generated by the computer system that receives the Help Desk's mail. This is one example of a cyborg relationship. The reply e-mail simultaneously assures Andrew that his problem will receive attention, thus providing some relief for his frustration at not being able to print, and it also registers the problem in the Help Desk database so that the staff who attend the desk (note that it is possibly more than one) are aware of his problem. But on with our fiction.

Sometime later Andrew receives a phone call from a person identifying herself as Susan from the Help Desk. She tells him that she received his e-mail and fault report and could she make an appointment to come over to his office and fix the problem.

Notice how the Help Desk has assumed a more human form, even if it is still only a voice on the phone. The e-mail address has now become a boundary worker between the computer user and the technician. Thus the address does boundary work; helpdesk@vu.edu.au is both a machine and the people employed in that position.

At the appointed time, Susan arrives, examines the situation, sits at the computer and makes a few changes to a configuration file, and "hey presto" the problem is solved–helpdesk@vu.edu.au as flesh has performed what Andrew thinks is a miracle. The symbiosis of human-network-e-mail-computer-software-telephone-human, a cyborg, has worked across boundaries brought different social worlds together. It has translated Andrew's problem into the technical solution of an altered configuration file and a working printer. There is a sequel to this story though.

When Susan arrives back at her desk she calls up the fault report database and registers Andrew's job as having been fixed. The fault management software flags the record as complete and initiates an e-mail to andrew.smithson@vu.edu.au reporting that job number such and such is complete and closed and gives the time of completion. The cyborg in a slightly different configuration performs again.

AT THE BOUNDARY

A typical e-mail address such as awenn@westgate.vu.edu.au consists of a number of parts. We have the addressee name (awenn) the domain name (westgate.vu.edu.au), which may also include a computer name (westgate), and the two being separated by an @. However before we examine the semiotics of the e-mail address let's consider two origin stories. They attempt to answer the questions: What is this @? and Where did it originate?

Origins 1

The @ symbol–*commercial at, at, klammeraffe* (German "spider monkey"), *strudel* (Hebrew "after the sweet"), *grishale* (Danish "pig's tail"), *apestaartje* (Dutch "(little) monkeys tail"), *escargot* (French "snail"), *arobase* (French), *a commercial* (French), *snabel* (Danish "snail"), *heliko* (Esperanto), *dalphaengi* (Korean)–has numerous names, many of them alluding to its shape[3] "is a contraction of the Latin word *ad* meaning "to, toward, at" and was used in accounts or invoices" to indicate the price of an item (Quinion, 1997, p. 1), for example 3lbs of butter @ 2d a pound. According to Quinion, "[i]n cursive writing, the upright stroke of the "d" curved over to the left and extended round the "a"; eventually the lower part fused with the 'a' to form one symbol" (Quinion, 1997, p. 1). I can certainly remember it being used in this way in arithmetic textbooks in Victorian primary schools at least into the 1960s.

Nowadays many information-technology-based transactions would be impossible without it, even though its use in that arena was almost accidental.

Although the *commercial at* is part of the standard ACSII and EBCDIC computer character sets, it was not always on the keyboards of typewriters. An examination of the many keyboards pictured in Beeching's *Century of the Typewriter* reveals that it was on many from about 1880 onwards. Others such as the Sholes keyboard of 1873 and the early Caligraph models give preference to the ampersand instead (Beeching, 1990, pp. 42-44). Nowadays many information-technology-based transactions would be impossible without it.[4]

Origins 2

He had no idea he was creating an icon for the wired world.

Hafner and Lyon

Where Wizards Stay Up Late: The Origins of The Internet, 1998, p. 192

However the "@,"was not always universally accepted. In fact, in the early days of e-mail, all users were only located on the one computer and there was no need to designate the machine to which the message should flow, just the user name would suffice. However, once the network came to consist of more than one machine, things became complicated. Whilst care could be taken that no two users had the same login name[5] on a single machine, with the expansion of the network it was quite feasible that Anne Barker could have an account on more than one machine (host) but used only one to read her e-mail. Similarly, there could possibly be more than one Tom Jones with access to the network via different machines. Hence the host name would also have to be included in the e-mail address, thus ensuring that the message was directed to the appropriate person. To enable the user name to be distinguished from the name of the computer by the mail software, some form of separator was required. A symbol that could be used to designate the split between user and machine. Ray Tomlinson, the developer of the first multi-machine e-mail program, just surveyed his keyboard for the least commonly used nonalphabetic character that wasn't a special symbol that would be interpreted by the operating system of the computer he was using and struck upon the at sign (@; Hafner & Lyon, 1998).

The general form of address on the Internet is:

addressee_name@domain_name

where, in the majority of cases, the addressee is the name of a particular person. This may have been assigned by the organization for which they work and may or may not directly include their name. For example, my addressee name at my place of work is Andrew. Wenn, made by concatenating my firstname and my surname with a dot in between and the domain name is vu.edu.au. On the other hand e-mail addresses at the State Library are limited to 8 or fewer characters and although they are derived from the person's name, are far more cryptic and certainly less accessible unless one happens to know the rule by which they are formed. (The reasons for this and other limitations that are necessary we will discuss later–at this point I wish to discuss the various ways physical and net identity are co-constituted.) If I was an employee at the SLV my addressee name would be A Wenn–probably not so cryptic–but if my name was Christine Andropolous or even something like Andrew Smithson the addressee name would be C Andropo, and A Smithso, respectively all in the slv.vic.gov.au domain (See Table 1).

Of course we are also assigned names in real life. For instance, my legal registered name is Andrew Wenn, yet in face-to-face conversation with friends I am referred to as "Blue" or "Andy" or "Andrew." The names we are referred to by have a particular status, be it for legal, ontological or identification reasons or a sign of familiarity. So it would be wrong to assume that the assigning of names and/or creation of new identities is a phenomenon that has arisen purely from the advent of the Internet. Certainly it now occurs more frequently and has more widespread consequences, and it is only at the closing of the second Christian millennium that these names have been negotiated with machines. Throughout the remainder of this chapter, I will be making extensive use of the mapping of actual person's identity to Net identity as signified by the e-mail address. Many of these possible mappings are shown in Table 1, that also attempts to identify the parties involved in the negotiations for the creation of this net identity.[6]

Separating Human from Machine?

At the first glance then it would appear that the @ sign acts as a boundary between the human and the machine but, in fact, the situation is far more complex. On one level, it would be true to consider it as a boundary object, that is, something that inhabits different social worlds and satisfies the requirements of those worlds. As Star and Griesmer say, "They [boundary objects] have different meanings in different social worlds but their structure is common enough to more than one world to make them recognizable, a means of translation" (1989, p. 393). In one social world the "@" signifies purely and simply that this string of characters is an e-mail address. In the world of the computer programmer, particularly one who is writing an e-mail-reading program, it becomes a delimiter. Thus although an e-mail user may not be a computer programmer and the programmer may not be an e-mail user (highly unlikely!) we have a recognizable symbol that allows a flow of meaning from one world to another. And it is the programmer that gives the technology, the computer network that the e-mail travels through, the means to recognize the "@" sign and perform the necessary translation, the mapping of user to domain to mailbox.

It is just this problem of place of origin and space for storage that I wish to discuss in the next section.

SPACES & PLACES

Storage

Your own address is not pinned to a place; it is simply an access code, with some associated storage space, to some computer located somewhere on the Net. It does not matter much what sort of computer it is or where you find it.

William J. Mitchell
City of Bits: Space, Place and the Infobahn, 1995, p. 9

The storage space that Mitchell refers to is the equivalent of the mailbox that might be stuck on your front fence or in your door or at the local post office. The point I wish to make here is that pace Mitchell it does matter where you find your e-mail. Email addresses point to spaces, spaces where messages are stored.

Veronica is a librarian who is responsible for purchasing books and during the course of her work uses e-mail daily. I asked her if it was important where her e-mail was stored.

Veronica: I don't know exactly. It's not machine-specific. I
assume that it is the F: drive, as that is a drive on the
network with areas where people store files but only the
person owning those files can read them. It's not G:, C:
or A:.
I can read my mail from anywhere as long as I log in under
my sign-in. But this is only deductive thinking.

Andrew: Is it important to you to know where you e-mail is stored?

Veronica: No. It's not important to me at all as long as I can
access my e-mail. And to me that means access it from any
machine on the LAN.

No matter what the e-mail address, the electronic text has to be stored somewhere. We can see that, on one level, Veronica really doesn't care where her e-mail is stored, just that it must be on a network drive so that she can access it from any computer on the LAN (local area network); this is because she may move from computer to computer during her working week. Note also that it matters that the space where this mail is stored is a private space.

Some months after my initial interview with Veronica the network to which her computer was connected crashed and she was unable to use it. Consequently she was not able to carry out her work as efficiently. But worse was to come. When her network login was restored she was unable to access her mailbox, the space on the mail server that was reserved for her. She told me "The IT staff can see where my mail is but they just cannot connect my sign-in to the file on the server. It's frustrating." So although things appeared correct on one level, there was a lack of cooperation on the part of the technology; the e-mail address and login (sign-in) may have been valid, but the link between the space and the login had been destroyed.

Before moving on to consider another meaning of the e-mail address I will leave you with these questions. Where does your e-mail go when you delete it? What happens if your mail server goes down and the disk where the mail is stored is corrupted and has to be replaced? Is the e-mail lost forever? Maybe the fact that an e-mail address points to a space on a piece of hardware is more important than Mitchell would have us believe.

Spaces & Places One–Responsibility/Ownership

Arising out of the use of e-mail is the question of responsibility–who do you go to in the first instance if you consider an e-mail message harmful, defamatory wrong, offensive, etc. The first port of call would be the organization referred to in the domain name, as this signifies where the e-mail originated from. It is connected to a physical person or organization by virtue of the fact it has been registered with the appropriate authority. Hence we have domains such as: hotmail.com, for the free e-mail service now owned by Microsoft; slv.vic.gov.au, the domain name for the State Library of Victoria; or irma-international.org, the domain that belongs to IRMA.[7]

I had been talking to a patron who was bemoaning the fact that the mail facility associated with the Netscape browser was not available for use within the SLV. He had an e-mail address that everyone knew and he was unable to use it from the SLV because the particular mail protocol known as POP,[8] which would have allowed him to log in to his computer in his home country and read his mail, was unavailable.

User A: It's a real pity because now I cannot e-mail anyone. I'd have to open a Hotmail account but everyone knows my other e-mail address.

Do you know where a cyber cafe is?

The fact the SLV didn't offer the facility to use e-mail is problematic for this user in two ways. Firstly he couldn't use the space, the facilities at the SLV, which were free. He would have to seek out a cyber cafe that offered

POP mail access and pay for the service. Secondly, if he did wish to use the SLV space, then he would have to obtain a new e-mail address, to change his online identity. This question of identity and ownership is something I will explore in a later section. For now I wish to explore the concept of space designated by an e-mail address.

Robert was until recently head of the IT department at the SLV, where there are public access e-mail facilities available.

Andrew: One of the people that I was interviewing downstairs, one of the patrons, was complaining about the fact that you had cut off the POP mail.

Robert: The Netscape mail?

Andrew: Yeah.

Robert: One of the reasons, or there are a number of reasons, for doing that at the time was that we didn't go out to make mail available generally. So the only thing that they could use was Hotmail, not using Netscape mail. The other reason we didn't do it was that we cannot control what people say and if it had have gone out it would have effectively gone out under the State Library banner head. Which left us open to possible legal, um, um, ramifications. ...
If any libellous material had been printed or sent across the network, and certainly we don't want to become one of the sources, or accused of being one, for people to spam or flame other people's works.

Andrew: Yeah.

Robert: So we, I mean we continue to do that–they can use mail on the basis that they link to a system that they use their own mail from.

Andrew: Basically so that it bypasses the State Library?

Robert: Yep, yeah. As the, as the um, the originator of the mail, the message.

So there are two reasons for not allowing patrons to use a mail service hosted by the State Library. One is that they didn't really want to encourage people to use mail (something which I discuss elsewhere), but the second reason which is relevant to my argument is that messages would go out under the SLV banner, that is, the slv domain name, which appears explicitly in the header of the message for all to see (Figure 1) and in other places in the message that are normally not seen by the average user. The SLV would be acting as an ISP if it allowed PAI computers to access POP mail, and as Edwards says, "... the ISP runs the risk of being regarded as the publisher of libellous remarks, originated by another person, but published by them. ..." (1997, p. 191). It is this notification of the domain, this identification of the organization where the mail originated from, that has legal ramifications. The message has been linked back to a physical entity. The patrons are allowed to use e-mail as long as it is a system that is accessible through the Web browser and does not use the slv domain. So we can say that e-mail originates from spaces, spaces where letters are composed.

By now, I hope you are beginning to see that cyberspace is not all that virtual, that it in fact has ties back to the real world and not just because that is where our mortality eventually lies but because there are legal, implementation and other system issues to consider. Turning to the question of identity, here I will show that creation of an online persona is often a matter of negotiation between a number of actors that may include organizations, system administrators, individuals and technologies.

IDENTITIES

User C: The reason behind my e-mail address was I wanted to use my surname but somebody had already taken it so I bolted the year of birth beside so I could easily remember who I am. The surname has some historical significance to it–XXXXX[9] was a revolutionary.

Negotiating and Assigning

Recall that an e-mail address in its most common usage points to an area on a disk, a file name where the messages are stored. Many older e-mail systems that have their origins in the DOS operating system would only allow users to have login or user names up to 8 characters long. This was due to the fact that the underlying file system was designed to accept file names of this length and with a possible 3-character extension. Thus the technology imposes limitations on the user's login.

At the SLV, the policy on usernames is to take the first letter of the person's first name and append the surname on to it to make up the 8-character login. I was

Figure 1: The Header Of an E-mail Message. This is the Text That Can be Seen by Anyone Receiving Email. Notice That the Domain Name and the Organization Where It Originates From Are Easily Identified.

```
Subject: Re: Hi
Date: Wed, 17 Mar 1999 15:29:18 +1000
From: "Veronica Robertson" <vroberts@newvenus.slv.vic.gov.au>
Reply-To: vroberts@newvenus.slv.vic.gov.au
Organization: State Library of Victoria
To: Andrew Wenn <Andrew.Wenn@vu.edu.au>
```

discussing this with Veronica, whose surname is Robertson which as you can see is longer than the allowed 8 characters.

Andrew: Does it worry people with longer names that the system only allows 8 character names?

Veronica: ... We have no choice about the sign-in. It's set for us. The people who do have their names shortened wish they could have more say in it.

I would have liked either Veronica or Robertson. Either would have been better than Roberts. I don't like Roberts. For one thing there are other people with that surname. It's confusing and it's not me.

Andrew: Do you ever get e-mail addressed to Roberts?

Veronica: No, but most people would read the name in the signature. We have the option of including a signature or not. I do.

Now, I too wish to create a fictional identity. This time with the express purpose of extending the boundaries of this text a little further. Although there are people of Scandinavian origin working at the SLV, there is no one of Icelandic origin. Icelandic nomenclature for the surnames of offspring is created by taking the name of the father and appending to that name, sdottir or sson, depending on whether the child is a female or a male, thus creating a new surname. This means siblings of differing genders will have different surnames. Take for example, children born to Ragnar Thorsson; a female will have the surname of Ragnarsdottir whilst a male will have the surname Ragnarsson. If we use technology that only allows 8-character names then both Bjarn (male) and Gudrun (female) are rendered genderless, as their surnames are truncated to Ragnars.

For a free mail system, such as Hotmail, the user may choose their own name, subject to the very important limitation that it does not duplicate a name that has already been registered and matched to a user and a mailbox. But more on this in a minute. Addressee names can be purely related to the user's name, for example, BillSmith@hotmail.com, but often some form of nickname is chosen. This may be to conceal the identity, gender and race of the owner or might be selected so as to enhance or even create a virtual identity for the person registering the name. In fact, it would perhaps be better to regard the addressee name as reflecting a particular persona rather than a person in the same way IRC nicknames, MUD names and others designate a person's alternative persona (Rheingold, 1995; Stone, 1995; Turkle, 1996). So, for example, I might choose to use an addressee name of FoxyLady or silversparrow, depending on how I see myself and want others to see me.

As stated previously, duplicate names are not allowed, and to prevent this, when registering an addressee name at free mail service, it will inform you that that name has already been taken and to select another one. The service may even make a suggestion for a name. Normally this is formed by adding some digits on the end. Thus because Bill Smith is already registered it may suggest that BillSmith99 be used instead.

Now, this only covers part of the e-mail address–the human side. We also need to cover the machine side, which relates in many ways to the domain where the e-mail is stored. Several years ago, before the introduction of what is known as a common address system (CAS), I used to tell people my e-mail address was awenn@westgate.vut.edu.au.[10] Now, the westgate.vut.edu.au forms what is know as a domain name. More correctly, it is the name of a machine, westgate, located in a particular domain, that is, vut.edu.au. That is, westgate is the name of a computer located somewhere within the set of buildings connected by a network of cables that forms the Internet subdomain designated to belong to Victoria University of Technology. This is designated by the string vut.edu.au. The significance of this is that at one stage, and for many people still, the machine is explicitly named. If we were to examine the contents of the storage device on that machine we would be able to locate an area of the disk that stores the e-mail belonging to user awenn, that is, the mailbox. Now, however, I have an e-mail address that conforms to CAS, which is of the form Andrew.Wenn@vut.edu.au. The computer where the mailbox resides has been rendered invisible–it is located somewhere in the vut domain. Email addresses have been ordered by the organization so that they have a particular style.

Can you see how the online identity established via the rules governing the e-mail address, rules imposed both by the organisation and the technology, is problematic?

Identities Two–Reclaiming

The last line of the interview fragment in the previous section mentions a signature. This is a text file, generally containing information about the sender, that can be automatically appended to an e-mail. Veronica uses this facility to wrest back some of her lost identity because she includes her full name in the signature (Figure 2). People receiving the e-mail can see that she is not vroberts as her e-mail address may imply but Veronica Robertson. As Veronica says, "People can read that to find out who I am."

Identities Three–Ownership

Recall the user I interviewed in relation to the use of POP mail. During the interview, he implied he would resist changing his e-mail address if possible. He wanted to keep the same e-mail address, the same identity, because that was how he was known. Unfortunately the place where he wanted to e-mail from would not let him do that. He would have to open another account, create a new identity and send e-mail from another domain. He was hoping that a cyber cafe would offer the facilities that the SLV didn't so that this change would not be necessary.

Identities Four–Dual

Whilst one user was resistant to change, an e-mail address can be altered by other means. The domain name may be changed. Or, as in the following case, where changes in the technology meant that it was possible to establish an alias so that the name newvenus (the name of the e-mail gateway) could be removed, the section after the @ so the domain newvenus.slv.vic.gov.au becomes the same as slv.vic.gov.au. In effect, as Veronica says below, you may have dual e-mail addresses that point to the same mailbox.

Andrew: At one stage your e-mail address had @newvenus in it ...

Veronica: That is, newvenus is the main server–but they are moving away from server names as part of your e-mail address.

Andrew: Do you know why they are doing that?

Veronica: I guess it makes the system more flexible. We have had dual mail addresses for a while.

Andrew: When you say you had dual mail addresses, what do you mean?

Veronica: Well it didn't matter whether you had newvenus or not in the address. So, for instance, it could be vroberts@newvenus.slv.vic.gov.au or vroberts@slv.vic.gov.au–the mail was routed to your mailbox. The push is to take newvenus out of the address.

This change in effect means that the computer named newvenus could

Figure 2: Veronica Robertson's Signature File as Automatically Appended to Each E-mail She Sends; Note the Difference Between her Actual Name and the Addressee Name in the E-mail Field

Veronica Robertson	ph: + 61 03 9669 9888 Ext 4141
Serial Barcoding Project	Fax: + 61 03 9663 1480
State Library of Victoria	E-mail: vroberts@slv.vic.gov.au
328 Swanston Street	
Melbourne, Victoria 3000 Australia	

disappear from the slv domain altogether–it has been rendered invisible. Removing the machine name allows the system administrator more flexibility in that the e-mail system can be upgraded, another computer installed, for instance and the e-mail addresses can remain the same–there is no system-wide disruption when e-mail addresses have to be changed.

Identities Five–Multiple

So far we have seen that e-mail address can be things that people resist changing and can give people new and not-so-popular identities, people within an organization can have two e-mail addresses, different e-mail addresses can point to the same storage space, and the technology can be utilized to reassert the sender's original identity. Table 1 attempts to summarize many more ways that e-mail addresses are the result of negotiations between the individual, the organisation, and the technology.

Whilst a person may have two e-mail addresses it is also possible for one e-mail address to point to a group of people. For instance, the address helpdesk@vu.edu.au is a generic e-mail address that sends e-mail to whoever is on duty at the Help Desk at that particular time–the e-mail address is shared between several staff members, all who have permission to read and respond to e-mail and hopefully the problem being referred to in the original message. There is also another instance where an address is shared by a number of people. Consider this:

Andrew: So did you get an e-mail address before you left?

James: No. I got one when I came out here. But the funny thing is that my family uses that address at home. So I am always writing to myself.

Andrew: I suppose you write to people back home telling them your e-mail address.

James: Yes.

James did not have an e-mail address before he came to Australia; he acquired one then sent details back to his family via the post. Once he had done that, they also use the same account to read the mail he sends to them and they reply using the same address–"I am always writing to myself." Unlike the Help Desk example, where the staff are within the same physical building, this time the users are separated by thousands of miles. The boundary between the physical and the virtual identity has become blurred: who actually is helpdesk; who does James' address refer to?

Another example and one that begins to return us back to the development of online virtual identities is AndrewSmithson99@hotmail.com. Andrew originally wanted an address as AndrewSmithson@hotmail.com but that name had already been registered. The technology handling the registrations suggested he use AndrewSmithson99@hotmail.com. He agreed and this became his new online identity. On the other hand, beebop@excite.com really reveals very little about the real-life identity behind the user other than the possibility that they may have an interest in that particular style of jazz.

Identities Six–Anonymous[11]

Andrew: Who is "deepspace?" Is there any difference between the online person and you in real life? If so can you explain what that is?

User B: Deepspace is simply a made-up name. There is no meaning behind it nor is it a nickname or a user-name for games, etc. There is absolutely no difference between Deepspace and me in real life. The sole purpose for using an alias for the same e-mail account is because my other e-mail name, "TomCarr," relates to my real name. Therefore, when e-mailing other people that I do not know or if I want to remain anonymous in every possible way, I then use my other [Deepspace] e-mail address.

Later when in conversation with him, he elaborated.

User B: Sometimes I don't want people to know who I am; I want to remain secret. For example, I e-mailed Bayside Trains the other day. I was really cross; they had cancelled another train. So I got stuck into them about cancelled trains they had cancelled the train four times in the last week. They would have got this long, angry e-mail from Deepspace.

Another example and one that harks back to the legal implications mentioned previously, but with truly cross-boundary applications, is the address concocted by a computer configured to act as an anonymous remailer. This is a technology that can receive e-mail from people who wish their identity to remain hidden from receivers; it removes all of the identifying information from the original message, creates a new e-mail address such as an299908@anon.penet.fi and forwards the message on to its final destination. Only the administrator of the anonymous remailer has the information available to connect the new address with the source address. The machine anon.penet.fi, which is located in Finland, is particularly famous as its administrator was subject to a request from the US courts, which the Finish police felt obliged to comply with, to reveal the identity of a particular person who was distributing copyright materials belonging to the Church of Scientology. The identity created by the technology was matched to the real-world sender and recorded in a database, and that particular record was retrieved and handed over to the authorities rather than having to hand over the whole database of 600,000 other users (Dyson, 1997, pp. 235-239; Grossman, 1997).

CONCLUSION

"E-mail stung by love bug." "How a backhoe and a bug stopped a nation" (Barker, 2000). On two consecutive days *The Age* carried articles on its front page detailing how the damaging of physical cables and spread of malicious software "brought Australia's communications system to its knees." These two events are useful in that they enable us ground in the physical world things that might seemingly be based in that rather nebulous concept "cyberspace." There is nothing more physical, more real than a backhoe, and it actually did damage to some other real entities–a communications cable which is part of the network between Australia's two largest cities Melbourne and Sydney. The "Love Bug" virus, which was unleashed from some, at that time, unknown location by an unknown Internet user, served to compound the problem. According to the article, "[t]hey shut down the Australian Stock Exchange, infected banks and finance houses, blacked out mobile phone networks and jammed automatic teller machines across the country" (Barker, 2000, p. 1).

Along with Cringley's quote at the start, reporting these events here nicely brackets the chapter, bringing into focus the interplay between the technology, the human, organizations and the "cybernetic construct" of a virus that feeds off people's e-mail address books and propagates throughout the network. Opinion is that if the cable hadn't have been severed then the virus would have wreaked more havoc than it did.

One of the roles of this chapter was to assist people to make sense of the complexities of technology. I have argued that an e-mail address is not simply just a string of characters but has associated with it some storage space, which may or may not be under the user's direct control. The address may act to change people's identities either through the desire of the person using it or because of technical constraints or organizational policies. Being the owner of a domain name has legal consequences, especially if you are an organisation like a library or an ISP that allows users to send messages out with your domain clear for all to see in the address. I have used the concept of the cyborg and boundary work to show how socio-technical systems are reconfigured in fluid ways depending on the tasks to be performed. Some of these configurations will be more permanent than others, but what it is important to realize is that the systems addressed here are heterogeneous associations, and only by taking a holistic view and seeing them as such can we begin to make sense of them.

Whilst acknowledging that there are regions of the Internet where the virtual may seem to exist, closer examination reveals a number of things not mentioned in the literature that analyses the socio-technics of the Internet. There is not a seeming dichotomy between the real and physical worlds but a complicated interplay at the boundaries between these worlds, the humans and the technologies that co-construct them. Identities are not always determined by the physical person but by the technology also. There is a complex interaction between the name we may know a person by and their actual identity on the Internet, which is often the result of multiple negotiations between the various actants involved. Whilst much emphasis is given to the virtual spaces that are created by being online, physical space and how it is identified plays an important part also.

ACKNOWLEDGEMENTS

I would like to thank Dr. Michael Arnold, Dr. Rosemary Robins and Dr. Julie Fisher for their constructive comments about an early version of this chapter. The editors also provided me with wonderful food for thought, and even if in the end I decided that the inclusion of all their suggestions would have required a radical rewrite, a number of their suggestions have found their way into it, for which they have my heartfelt thanks.

ENDNOTES

[1] In many ways, I feel there is a similarity in the function of an e-mail address to that of the "handle" used by many CB radio users who selected a handle to suit the persona they wished to project. Of course a CB handle is not associated with some form of digital storage.

[2] My rationale for regarding the entities involved as actors is outlined in Wenn (in press), in which I follow Akrich and Latour (1992).

[3] It may have many names, but when I asked people of various ages and backgrounds hardly anyone knew what it was called. When I mentioned the name *commercial at*, a few recognized what I was talking about and some of the older people remembered it appearing on invoices. Most thought it was a symbol of 19th-century origin. See also Quinion's remarks (1997) on this.

[4] One has only to look around any CBD, bookshop or newspaper to begin to realize that @ is being increasingly used as an icon signifying comfort with? acceptance of? that state of Western technoscience at the close of the second Christian millennium. As evidence I advance the @home network (http://www.@home.com/) and its appearance in various book titles, for example, Microsoft Corporation's CEO Bill Gates latest book, *Business @ the Speed of Thought*. Neither of these two are surprising

perhaps given their connection with the technology. *The Age* of February 2, advertises its new *Educ@tion liftout*; cafes and bistros appear with @s in their names. As I sit here writing this I reflect on my latest use of @. It was to write in the office diary my whereabouts for a Friday. I wrote Andrew W @ home. Looking back on my use of this, I originally started to do this because it was the "smart" thing to do; now it has become more of a shorthand way of signifying my intended whereabouts, even a habit.

[5] A login name, or account name, is just a word that a user types in to gain access to the computer system and their associated files and applications.

[6] The address 123456.9876@compuserve.com is actually the transformation of an e-mail address of someone using the Compuserve service. On the closed Compuserve network the address would be 123456,9876. So that e-mail can be sent via the Internet to a Compuserve client, it needs to be transformed either by human or machine. Essentially the "," has to be replaced with a full stop "." and compuserve.com appended after the "@" (Krol, 1994, p. 108). This "Internet friendly" address would then be transformed once it reached the gateway of the Compuserve network.

[7] I am reminded here of the stigma attached to having an address with the domain name of aol.com. See Grossman (1997) for details

[8] Describing the operation of the POP (Post Office Protocol) is beyond the scope of this paper, but basically it allows a user to access a remote computer to read their e-mail by providing an appropriate login/password combination. It also allows messages to be transferred and saved on the machine the user is currently using. Space again matters.

[9] XXXXX is used here because it is rather difficult to think up a pseudonym for a revolutionary and hide the identity of my informant.

[10] In fact this address is still active, but using a neat trick of the UNIX operating system I have any messages that come to this mailbox forwarded to my CAS address.

[11] For another view of anonymity on the Internet see Annette Markham's (1998) discussion with Lord Sheol in *Life Online: Researching Real-Life Experience in Virtual Space*, especially pp. 182-185.

REFERENCES

Akrich, M. and Latour, B. (1992). A summary of a convenient vocabulary for the semiotics of human and nonhuman assemblies. In Bijker, W. E. and Law, J. (Eds.). *Shaping Technology/Building Society: Studies in Sociotechnical Change*, The MIT Press, Cambridge, Mass, 259–264.

Barker, G. (2000). How a backhoe and a bug stopped the nation. *The Age*, May, 1 and 6. Melbourne.

Beeching, W. A. (1990). *Century of the Typewriter*, New edition, British Typewriter Museum Publishing, Bournemouth, England.

Benedikt, M. (Ed.). (1991a). *Cyberspace: First Steps*, Series Eds: Anon. Cambridge, MA: The MIT Press.

Benedikt, M. (1991b). Cyberspace: Some proposals. In Benedikt, M. (Ed.), *Cyberspace: First Steps*, 119-224. Cambridge, MA: The MIT Press.

Bromberg, H. (1996). Are MUDs communities? Identity, belonging and consciousness in virtual worlds. In Shields, R. (Ed.), *Cultures of Internet: Virtual Spaces, Real Histories, Living Bodies*, 143-152. London: Sage Publications Ltd.

Cringley, R. X. (1999). *Nerds 2.0.1–A Brief History of the Internet*. ABC TV, August 12.

Dyson, E. (1997). *Release 2.0: A Design for Living in the Digital Age*. New York, NY: Broadway Books.

Edwards, L. (1997). Defamation and the Internet. In Edwards, L and Waelde, C. (Eds.), *Law and the Internet: Regulating Cyberspace*, 183-198. Oxford, UK: Hart Publishing.

E-mail stung by love bug. (2000). *The Age*, May 1. Melbourne.

Gray, C. H. and Mentor, S. et al (Eds.), (1995). Cyborgology: Constructing the knowledge of cybernetic organisms. In *The Cyborg Handbook*, 1-14. New York, NY: Routledge.

Gray, C. H., Mentor, S, and Figueroa-Sarriera, H. J. (Eds.). (1995), *The Cyborg Handbook*: New York, NY: Routledge.

Grossman, W. (1997). *Net.Wars*. New York: New York University Press.

Hafner, K. and Lyon, M. (1998). *Where Wizards Stay Up Late: The origins of the Internet*. New York, NY: Touchstone.

Haraway, D. J. (1991). *Simians, Cyborgs and Women*. Routledge, New York.

Haraway, D.J. 1997, *Modest_Witness@Second_Millennium.FemaleMan© _Meets_OncoMouse.™* New York: Routledge.

Heim, M. (1991). The erotic ontology of cyberspace. In Benedikt, M. (Ed.), *Cyberspace: First Steps*, 59-80. Cambridge, MA: The MIT Press.

Ito, M. (1997). Virtually embodied: The reality of fantasy in a multi-user dungeon. In Porter, D. (Ed.). *Internet Culture*, 87-109. New York, NY: Routledge.

Krol, E. (1994). *The Whole Internet User's Guide and Catalog*, 2nd Edition. O'Reilly and Associates, Sebastopol.

Markham, A. N. (1998). *Life Online: Researching Real-Life Experience in Virtual Space*. Walnut Creek, CA: AltaMira.

Mitchell, W. J. (1995), *City of Bits: Space, Place and the Infobahn*. Cambridge, MA: The MIT Press.

Mol, A. and Law, J. (1998). *Situated Bodies and Distributed Selves: On Doing Hypoglycaemia*, Draft.

Quinion, M. B. (1997). Article–Where it's at: Names for a common symbol. *World Wide Words*. Available on the World Wide Web at: http://www.quinion.demon.co.uk/words/articles/whereat.htm Accessed March 17, 1999.

Rheingold, H. (1995). *The Virtual Community: Finding Connection in a Computerised World*. Melbourne: Minerva.

Star, S. L. and Griesmer, J. (1989). Institutional ecology, translations and boundary objects: Amateurs and professionals in Berkeley's museum of vertebrate zoology, 1907-1939. *Social Studies of Science*, 19, 387–420.

Stone, A. R. (1995). *The War of Desire and Technology at the Close of the Mechanical Age*. Cambridge, MA: The MIT Press.

Traweek, S. (1992). *Beamtimes and Lifetimes: The World of High Energy Physicists*. Cambridge, MA: Harvard University Press.

Turkle, S. (1996). *Life on the Screen: Identity in the Age of the Internet*. London: Weidenfeld and Nicolson.

Weick, K. E. (1979). *The Social Psychology of Organizing*. Reading, MA: Addison-Wesley.

Wenn, A. (1999). Libraries, users, librarians, information and the Internet: How do they interact to change a world? In Khosrowpour, M. (Ed.), *IRMA '99 Managing Information Technology Resources in Organizations in the Next Millennium*, May 16-19, 1045-1047. Hershey, PA: Idea-group Publishing.

Wenn, A. (2000). Topological transformations: The co-construction of an open system, In Clarke, S and Lehaney, B. (Eds.), *Human Centered Methods in Information Systems: Current Research and Practice*. Hershey, PA: Idea Group Publishing.

About the Authors

Murugan Anandarajan is an assistant professor of management information systems in the department of management at Drexel University. His current research interests include artificial intelligence-based classification, artificial life, and Internet addiction and abuse. His research has appeared in journals such as *Behavior and Information Technology, Computers and Operations Research, Decision Sciences, Industrial Data Management Systems, Information and Management, International Journal of Information Management, Journal of Management Information Systems, Journal of Global Information Systems, Journal of International Business Studies,* and the *Omega-International Journal of Management Science*, among others. He is the editor of a special section on "Internet Abuse in the Workplace" in the *Communications of the ACM* (December 2001). He is a coauthor of the book entitled *Artificial Neural Networks in Glaucoma Classification: A Concise Approach* (2002). Anandarajan was awarded the Lindback Award for outstanding research (1999) and the Pearson Horner Award for the best application paper (1999).

Claire A. Simmers received her PhD from Drexel University, Philadelphia, Pennsylvania in strategic management. She is currently an assistant professor in the management and information systems department at the Erivan K. Haub School of Business at Saint Joseph's University, Philadelphia, Pennsylvania. She teaches courses at the undergraduate, MBA and executive level in business policy, international management, and developing managerial skill sets. Her research interests are: strategic decision-making, work/life issues, and understanding the sociotechnical interface in using the Internet. Her work has been published in *Behaviour and Information Technology,* the *Journal of Business and Economics Studies,* and the *Journal of Organizational Behavior*. She is an active member of the Academy of Management, the Strategic Management Society, and the Information Resources Management Association.

***

Asokan Anandarajan is an accountant by profession and is a member of the Chartered Institute of Management Accountants (UK). He has a master's degree in business administration (MBA) and a master's degree in philosophy

(M.Phil) from Cranfield University in England. He obtained his PhD in accounting from Drexel University in 1994. He is currently an assistant professor of accounting and information systems at New Jersey Institute of Technology. His research interests include developing models for predicting bankruptcy of corporations and valuation of companies. Anandarajan has authored 20 publications in journals such as *Accounting Horizons*, *Auditing: A Journal of Theory and Practice*, *Research in Accounting Regulation*, *Advances in Management Accounting*, *Advances in Public Interest Accounting*, *Management Accounting*, and *Journal of Cost Management*, among others.

Uzoamaka P. Anakwe is an associate professor of management at the Lubin School of Business, Pace University, Pleasantville, New York. She received her PhD in organizational behavior from Drexel University, Philadelphia. She has published articles in the *Journal of International Business*, *Journal of Managerial Issues*, *Journal of Global Information Management*, *Information Technology and People*, *International Journal of Organizational Analysis*, *International Journal of Manpower*, *Performance Improvement Quarterly* and has forthcoming articles in the *Journal of Management Education*, *International Journal of Information Management*, and *Journal of Research on Computing in Education*. Her current research interests encompass information technology implementation, Internet usage in emerging economies, knowledge management, and conflict management within a multicultural context.

Bay Arinze is a professor of management information systems and MIS program coordinator in the Management Department at Drexel University. His current research interests include object-oriented computing, electronic commerce, enterprise solutions, and telecommunications. Dr. Arinze has published articles in *Journal of Management Information Systems*, *Decision Sciences*, *Decision Support Systems*, *IEEE Transactions in Engineering Management*, *International Journal of Man-Machine Studies*, *Computers and Industrial Engineering*, and *Computers and Operations Research*. He published a textbook with Wadsworth Publishers, entitled *Microcomputers for Managers*, in 1994. He has also served on various consulting projects and on the Philadelphia mayor's private sector task force on telecommunications.

Adam Bosnian joined Elron Software in May 2000. With more than 13 years of marketing and sales experience, he has been instrumental in new market development and rapid revenue growth for emerging technology companies. Bosnian brings a strong background in strategy development, corporate partnering, marketing communications, product life-cycle management and strategic partner relations. Bosnian holds a BS in electrical engineering from Worcester Polytechnic Institute, where he graduated with highest honors and as a member of the Tau Beta Pi National Engineering Honor Society.

Eunyoung Cheon received a master's degree in computer science from the University of Southern California and master's degree in management of information systems from Claremont Graduate University. Her research interests include e-business, virtual workplace, reengineering organizations, management of information systems, and synthetic wood material. She is a cofounder of TA WOOD and works as a researcher and consultant.

Steve Clarke received a BSc in economics from the University of Kingston Upon Hull, an MBA from the Putteridge Bury Management Centre, the University of Luton, and a PhD in human-centred approaches to information systems development from Brunel University–all in the United Kingdom. He is a reader in systems and information management at the Luton Business School, University of Luton. His research interests include: social theory and information systems practice; strategic planning for information systems; and the impact of user involvement in information systems development. Major current research is focused on approaches to information systems and strategy informed by critical social theory.

Elayne Coakes is a senior lecturer in business information management at the Westminster Business School, University of Westminster, teaching mainly in the strategies for information management field. Her research interests lie in the sociotechnical aspects of information systems. As a member of the BCS Sociotechnical Group she is active in promoting this view of information systems development and is currently principal editor of a book of international contributions to this field, *The New SocioTech: Graffiti on the Long Wall,* published by Springer-Verlag in April 2000. A follow-up book *Knowledge Management in the Sociotechnical World: The Graffiti Continues,* is due for publication late 2001 by Springer, and in addition she is a joint editor of a book due to be published in 2002 by Idea Group Publishing called *Socio-Technical and Human Cognition Elements of Information Systems*. She is also involved in a research group at Westminster looking at knowledge management. Coakes is an associate editor of *OR Insight* with special responsibility for knowledge management and is currently involved in editing a special edition of the journal *JORS* on knowledge management and intellectual capital. She has published a number of conference papers and articles in journals such as *Information and Management,*

Management Decision, *CAIS*, *Engineering Requirements*, as well as several chapters in books.

Patrick W. Devine is a graduate student pursuing his doctorate in management information systems at Drexel University. He received his BS and MBA from Saint Joseph's University. While at Saint Joseph's he received the 1998 Graduate Business award. His current research interests include: e-commerce, legal and ethical dimensions of Internet usage, and knowledge management systems.

Kristin Eschenfelder is an assistant professor at the University of Wisconsin-Madison School of Library and Information Studies. Her current research falls in the area of social informatics and focuses specifically on the social nature of large Web information systems and how we can improve the human and technical processes required to manage them. Eschenfelder also conducts research in the areas of information policy, looking at how our information and telecommunications laws and regulations shape our configuration and use of information and communications technologies.

Mark Griffiths is a chartered psychologist and reader in psychology at the Nottingham Trent University. After completing his PhD on fruit machine addiction (University of Exeter, 1987-1990), he secured his first lectureship at the University of Plymouth (1990-1995). Since then, he has established an international reputation for himself in the area of gambling and gaming addictions, which culminated in the award of the prestigious *John Rosecrance Research Prize* for "outstanding scholarly contributions to the field of gambling research" in June 1994 and the 1998 Celej Prize for best paper on gambling. He has published over 80 refereed research papers and has published over 250 other articles in a variety of outlets.

Magid Igbaria is a professor of information science at Claremont Graduate University and at the Leon Recanati Graduate School of Business Administration, Tel Aviv University. He holds a BA in statistics and an MA in information systems and operations research from Hebrew University and received a PhD in computers and information systems from Tel Aviv University. Igbaria has published articles on managing in a virtual environment, e-business, virtual workplace, computer technology acceptance, IS personnel, management of IS, economics of computers, compumetrical approaches in IS, and international IS in *Applied Statistics*, *Behaviour & Information Technology*, *Communications of the ACM*, *Computers & Operations Research*,

Decision Sciences, Decision Support Systems, Information & Management, The Information Society, Information Systems Research, Information Technology & People, International Journal of Information Management, International Journal of Operations & Production Management, Journal of End-User Computing, Journal of Engineering and Technology Management, Journal of Management Information Systems, Omega, Journal of Strategic Information Systems, MIS Quarterly, and others. He has served as a guest editor of *The Information Society, Communications of the ACM, Journal of Management Information Systems,* and *Journal of End-User Computing,* and coeditor of the book as *The Virtual Workplace.* He is the editor of *e-Service Journal.* He is/was also an associate editor of *ACM Transactions on Information Systems* (ACM TOIS), *Journal of Information Technology Cases & Applications* (JITCA), and *MIS Quarterly* (MISQ). He also serves/d on the editorial board of *Information Resources Management Journal* (IRMJ), *Journal of The Association for Information Systems* (JAIS), *Journal of Management Information Systems* (JMIS), *Journal of Engineering and Technology Management* (JET-M), *Journal of End-User Computing* (JEUC), *Information Technology & People* (IT&P), and *Computer Personnel.*

Shin-Ping Liu is a PhD candidate in interdisciplinary information science at the University of North Texas. Liu is the chief scientist at Transfinity Corporation, located in Las Colinas, Texas, and is responsible for the direction of research and development and project management. Prior to joining Transfinity, she was a multimedia Web designer specializing in streaming video, audio, and synchronized multimedia presentations for the Special Education Institute. Liu has patents and patents pending in compression and content delivery systems. Her degrees include an MS in Computer Science from the University of North Texas and a BBA from Tunghai University in Taiwan.

Shane Meakim received his BS in management information systems and economics from the University of Nebraska-Lincoln. He currently works for JD Edwards as a technical consultant. He is also an adjunct professor at the Arapahoe Community College in Colorado, where he teaches a variety of computer courses in the information systems program. His research interest is in information security as it pertains to consumers and companies in society today.

Guus G. M. Pijpers is chief information officer (CIO) at Philips Electronics in Eindhoven, the Netherlands. Previously he worked as information manager, IT auditor and management consultant at Akzo Nobel, KPMG and Philips Electronics. He received his PhD in management and computer science from Eindhoven University of Technology, the Netherlands, in 2001. He holds a master's degree in management science and a master's degree in computer science from the Open University, The Netherlands. His work, interests and research focuses on the use of information and information technology by higher management levels in an organization as well as the adoption, use, and effects of e-business on business processes and organizational entities. Personal homepage: www.guuspijpers.com. E-mail: ask@guuspijpers.com.

Ivan T. Robertson is deputy vice-chancellor at UMIST and director of the SHL/UMIST Research Centre in Work and Organizational Psychology. He is a chartered psychologist, fellow of the British Psychological Society and fellow of the British Academy of Management. His work experience includes several years in industry/national government as an occupational psychologist. Robertson has an international reputation for his work on psychological assessment in organizational settings. Since taking up an academic post in 1979 he has produced 25 books and over 150 scientific articles/conference papers. With Prof. Cary Cooper he founded the business psychology company Robertson Cooper Ltd. in 1999. His professional and consultancy activities focus on a range of issues including personnel selection assessment and development. He has advised many public and private sector organizations including the Cabinet Office, the Commission for Racial Equality, the Cooperative Bank, UBS and the UK Atomic Energy Authority.

Christopher Ruth is vice-president of supply chain management for Bass Hotels and Resorts. Prior to that, he spent several years in the information systems, systems integration and aerospace industries for General Electric and Lockheed Martin. Ruth has coauthored the book *Developing Expert Systems Using 1st Class*, (Random House, 1988). He has also served as an adjunct faculty member for George Mason University (Fairfax, Virginia) and has developed and instructed various courses in managerial applications for microcomputers for the Department of Defense. His research interests include technology adoption, structural equation modeling, business-to-consumer electronic commerce systems, and business-to-business e-procurement systems.

Keng Siau is a J. D. Edwards professor and an associate professor of management information systems (MIS) at the University of Nebraska, Lincoln (UNL). He received his PhD degree from the University of British Columbia (UBC), where he majored in management information systems and minored in cognitive psychology. Siau is currently the editor-in-chief of the

Journal of Database Management. He has published more than 35 journal articles that have appeared in *MIS Quarterly, Communications of the ACM, IEEE Computer, Information Systems, ACM's Data Base, Journal of Database Management, Journal of Information Technology, International Journal of Human-Computer Studies, Transactions on Information and Systems*, and others. In addition, he has published over 55 refereed conference papers in proceedings such as ICIS, ECIS, HICSS, CAiSE, WITS, IRMA, and HCI. He has edited two books, three journal special issues, and five proceedings–all of them related to systems analysis and design. He has served as the organizing and program chairs for the International Workshop on Evaluation of Modeling Methods in systems analysis and Design (EMMSAD) (1996–2001). Siau's primary research interests are in object-oriented systems development using unified modeling language (UML), mobile commerce, enterprise e-business, enterprise resource planning (ERP), and Web-based systems development.

C. A. Srinivasan is professor emeritus and retired head of the Department of Accounting at Drexel University. His research interests include management control systems, and accounting information systems with emphasis in security issues.

Lyndal Stiller-Hughes is a senior manager with Accenture (formerly Andersen Consulting). She is a graduate member of the British Psychological Society and associate member of the Australian Psychological Society. While on leave from Accenture, Stiller-Hughes completed her MSc in organizational psychology at the Manchester School of Management, UMIST, in 2000. She has worked extensively as a change management consultant with both public and private sector organizations in the UK, Australia, Malaysia and the US, covering a range of issues associated with the implementation of change, including technology integration, employee communications and involvement, change readiness and impact analyses, training and development.

Beth Archibald Tang, a Web designer, has expertise in information architecture, accessibility, and database design. With Internet experience that complements library studies, Tang has presented on searching Web sites effectively and designing accessible and usable sites. She is a contributing writer on these topics and others for both print and online industry magazines, such as *Federal Computer Week,* and *First Monday*. In addition, her interests converge at knowledge management, effective e-learning, learning styles, and accessible design. To that end, she is a contributing editor to *Learning Circuits* and an adjunct instructor for the University of Virginia. Tang obtained her MA in secondary education from West Virginia University. She can be reached via e-mail at bethtang@yahoo.com.

Dennis Tucker is the chief technical officer of Transfinity Corporation in Las Colinas, Texas. He is a computer science graduate from the University of North Texas. An expert in e-commerce, compression and content delivery systems, Tucker has previous experience as a senior software engineer and project manager and has patents and patents pending in compression and content delivery systems. Prior to coming to Transfinity, Tucker was owner and CEO of an ISP. As CTO, he is responsible for the design and direction of the Transfinity development effort.

Andrew Wenn is a lecturer in the School of Information Systems at Victoria University of Technology, Melbourne, and is currently undertaking his PhD in the History and Philosophy of Science Department at the University of Melbourne. His main field of research is the nexus between the social and the technical, particularly in the area of global information systems. This chapter is the result of an as yet incomplete study into the way the users, designers and technology are co-constituting one particular information service. Wenn has also published in the area of Internet-based education and e-commerce and small businesses in Australia.

Dianne Willis is a senior lecturer in information management at Leeds Metropolitan University. Her research interests include sociotechnical issues surrounding the implementation of new technology in business and social environments and gender issues in the field of ICT, particularly factors influencing participation levels in both academic and practical fields. Willis is a member of the BCS Sociotechnical Group and has recently coedited a book entitled *The New SocioTech: Graffiti on the Long Wall*, published by Springer-Verlag. A second book in the same series is currently under preparation. She is presently engaged in research into the effects of e-mail on communication patterns in educational establishments. She is also an associate editor of *OR Insight*.

Index